WOMEN & IRISH HISTORY

Margaret MacCurtain

WOMEN
&
IRISH HISTORY

Essays in honour of
Margaret MacCurtain

Edited by
Maryann Gialanella Valiulis
&
Mary O'Dowd

WOLFHOUND PRESS
& in the US and Canada
The Irish American Book Company

First published 1997 by
WOLFHOUND PRESS Ltd
68 Mountjoy Square
Dublin 1
Tel: (353-1) 8740354
Fax: (353-1) 8720207

Published in the US and Canada by
The Irish American Book Company
6309 Monarch Park Place
Niwot, Colorado 80503
USA
Tel: (303) 530-4400
Fax: (303) 530-4488

British Library Cataloguing in Publication Data
A catalogue record for this book is available from the British Library.

ISBN 0-86327-579-6

10 9 8 7 6 5 4 3 2 1

Typesetting: Wolfhound Press
Cover illustration: 'Hunter's Moon', a painting by Daniel O'Neill. Reproduced with kind permission of The Gorry Gallery.
Cover design: Slick Fish Design, Dublin
Printed by Redwood Books, Wiltshire, England

TABLE OF CONTENTS

Introduction

Writing in the preface to her pioneering collection of essays, *Women in Irish Society – the Historical Dimension*, Margaret MacCurtain described the then state of women's history and women's relationship to history:

> Many Irish women find it difficult to learn about their historical identity, or their role in the life of the country because they have neither the information readily available, nor the skills of evaluation at their disposal.[1]

That was written in 1978. It was Margaret MacCurtain herself who more than anyone else began to change women's relationship to history as well as their place in the historical narrative.

As a historian, Margaret MacCurtain pioneered women's history in Ireland. The essays in *Women in Irish Society* were the first collection by academic historians on women's role in Irish history. Its very presence urged others in the same direction, thus launching the current phase of women's history in Ireland. Margaret was justly proud of it. When asked in an interview in *History Ireland* which of her writings had been the most significant, the one she would like to be remembered for, she said:

> It would be a surprising choice, a small book – now out of print – from 1978 which I edited with Donncha Ó Corráin, *Women in Irish Society*. Its essays (there was one by Mary Robinson) are an expression of the vitality of the intellectual and creative energy of the 1970s.[2]

The energy surged throughout the field of women's history. Perhaps no one was better placed to launch this new history than Margaret MacCurtain. She was already a distinguished historian.[3] Her work has made a major contribution to Irish historiography. Thus her reputation helped to silence the critics and reassure the sceptics as to the academic legitimacy of women's history.

As a woman historian in Ireland, Margaret MacCurtain was, as Mary O'Dowd points out in her article 'From Morgan to MacCurtain', heir to a long if unacknowledged tradition of Irish women writing about the past. Women have been writing history in Ireland

since the late eighteenth century although this has not been reflected in the world of the professional historian. Margaret Mac-
Curtain was one of only a small number of women historians who
successfully pursued an academic career in mid-twentieth-century
Ireland. After receiving her B.A. from University College Cork,
Margaret went on to do an M.A. and Ph.D. in history at University
College Dublin, becoming the first woman to do so.[4] She took up a
lecturing post in the Department of Modern Irish History in University College Dublin in 1966 and remained a vital presence in that
institution until her retirement in 1994.

As a teacher, Margaret, or Sister Ben as she was known for years
in UCD, was much loved. Her history classes were renowned for
their challenging content, superb lecturing style and lively discussions. The corridor outside her office door was always filled with
students who came to talk to her about academic problems and
personal concerns. She gave them time and sympathy, advice and
understanding. Former students still remark on the personal attention which she gave them in an institution which often seemed
impersonal and uncaring. As Mary O'Dowd's study reveals, Margaret's interest in and enthusiasm for teaching links her to other
Irish women historians. There are, however, other links, as Margaret's career also reveals the difficulties which are frequently
encountered by women scholars even in the second half of the
twentieth century.[5]

Outside of academia, Margaret MacCurtain also played a leading role in changing Irish women's relationship to history. Time
after time, in venue after venue, she exhorted women to search
their houses, open the tea chests, scour the attic to find the letters,
diaries, committee books of their grandmothers and mothers. But
above all else, she was a guiding figure in making women's history
accessible to all who were interested. It would be difficult to find a
committee dealing with some aspect of women's history on which
Margaret has not served. From the Women's Commemoration and
Celebration Committee to the Irish Women's Archives and Resources Committee to the Irish Association for Research in
Women's History, Margaret MacCurtain has promoted women's
history.

Margaret's activism extended beyond the historical sphere. She
is not only a distinguished historian, she is also a maker of history.
Nowhere is this more evident than in her intervention in the 1995
Divorce Referendum when as an advocate of the Right to Remarry
Campaign she supported the view that an informed choice of
voting in favour of the Referendum was not incompatible with a

Catholic conscience. It was not a unique exercise. Margaret had long been involved in political activities – promoting reconciliation of the opposing traditions in Irish society, working for a more tolerant, more caring society.

As a member of a religious order, Margaret was involved in negotiating the changing relationship of her community to the Roman Catholic Church. As a Dominican, she sees herself as part of an order which has a 'great respect for intellectuality. They have a very positive approach to intellectual identity and I think this is terribly important for women to have a definite intellectual stamp.'[6] Certainly, her religious life seems to be integrated into her academic life – in her research and scholarly writing, and in her work as founder principal of the Senior College in Ballyfermot.

It is fitting that this collection reflects the growing sophistication of women's history. From Margaret's pioneering work through to the early work on women and families and the quest for the vote, we have now entered a different phase in women's history. As Joan Hoff points out, women's history has evolved from the emphasis on great women to the 'add women and stir' model where the broad historical outlines remain the same except that women's participation is noted. It is when we move beyond that stage that the true revolutionary potential of women's history is revealed – the potential to challenge what we think is historically important, what we consider the defining moments in history, and the time frame which we use in writing the historical narrative. It is the evolution of a new historical paradigm.

It is not a linear progression. The work of discovery – of digging women out of obscurity – goes on, as many of the articles in this volume indicate. Maureen Murphy's article on Asenath Nicholson provides an example of this process. Nicholson was an American reformer who came to Ireland in 1844 and 1846. She recorded her impressions of Irish society on the eve of, and during, the Famine. In particular, she highlighted the conditions of women's work, her impressions of women's lives. Her two accounts of her travels were consigned to obscurity. As Murphy points out, Nicholson 'shared the fate of other worthy women, she was ignored.'[7] Mary O'Dowd's article is also partly an exercise in recovering the writings and intellectual interests of forgotten or unacknowledged women scholars. The value of this type of recovery exercise is revealed in her study which tells not only the story of the women who have written about Ireland's past but also indirectly the story of the élite world of the male scholars which kept women historians on the periphery.

Other women historians in late twentieth-century Ireland continue the task of amassing more and more historical data about women's lives and women's roles. We are learning where to look for information about women and how to use traditional sources to have them yield information about women. Both Phil Kilroy in her new use of religious sources and Mary Daly in her analysis of the struggle to bring running water to rural Ireland demonstrate the ways in which knowledge about women can be gleaned from traditional sources.

Phil Kilroy's article on Madeleine Sophie Barat demonstrates the necessity of looking anew at traditional sources for the information which we can retrieve about women's spiritual and secular lives. Her article on the use of sources in women's religious history, focusing on the example of Madeleine Sophie Barat, illuminates some of the challenges of writing women's biography. With an abundance of source material and an official biography written for the purpose of canonisation, Kilroy asks for a reassessment of Madeleine Sophie's life 'removed from the previous constrictions enshrined in hagiography.'[8] Catherine Shannon also imaginatively demonstrates how literary texts can be used to reveal information about women's experiences which is not recorded in more traditional historical sources.

As Joan Hoff has indicated, borrowing from other disciplines is a characteristic of a more sophisticated phase of women's history, a phase which was strongly influenced by the new social history which emerged from the civil rights and women's movement of the late 1960s and early 1970s. Irish women's history has been influenced by intellectual developments within feminism in the United States and it is perhaps worth noting that four of the contributors to this volume are either American or based in American universities. But Irish women's history, largely due to the pioneering efforts of Margaret MacCurtain and others, has remained firmly rooted within the discipline of history and, as the essays in this volume testify, it is still strongly empirical in its approach. While acknowledging the value of gender history, Irish women historians have not become embroiled in the debate on post-structuralism which has received so much attention in American and British women's history journals and in which Joan Hoff has been a major contributor, as her essay for this volume indicates.

Despite the increasingly acrimonious nature of the debate elsewhere, there have as yet been few studies about Irish women published which could be clearly classified as gender history. Mary Daly's contribution to this volume is a model of how using gender as a category of analysis enables us to understand the workings of the State in ways which seem often inexplicable and far removed from concerns of gender. Her article, 'Turn on the Tap: the State, Irish Women and Running Water', demonstrates how the different policies pursued by the State in its dealings with electrification and running water were very much dependent on gender. Electrification was important for male farmers. Running water was important for farmer's wives – for rural women – and may have resulted in increased cost. The government powered ahead with electrification. Running water lagged behind. Women's work and women's tasks were simply not that important.

Daly's article highlights a consistent theme of many of the essays in this volume – women's relationship with the State. Many of the essays analyse the varied ways in which women negotiated their relationship to the State. Mary Cullen points to the need to analyse the wider political agenda of Irish suffragists. Her suggestion that the Irish suffrage movement reflected nineteenth-century liberal values has implications for its definition of the woman citizen. Cliona Murphy, on the other hand, looks at how the State is defined and argues that the nation and its ideology, nationalism, is a male construct which defines citizenship in a way which excludes women. As women tried to alter that relationship – primarily through claiming suffrage – male political leaders derided these claims as 'foreign imports', which posed a threat to national identity and/or the national struggle. Male nationalist leaders stressed women's maternal role in the nation's political life. Murphy analyses Irish nationalism within the broader European context and finds that, despite significant differences, nationalism throughout Europe was based on the same arguments and assumptions which denied women full participation as citizens of the State.

Maryann Gialanella Valiulis's article on jury service raises the same issue of women's relationship to the State. As women claim the right to full citizenship in the post-suffrage period, she finds the same resistance to admitting women as full participants in the nation. Using a comparative analysis of women's experience in Ireland and the U.S., Valiulis concludes that the same arguments and objections surface – revealing much about the common nature of the patriarchal nation state. Other contributions to the volume come to a similar conclusion. Hoff suggests that definitions of citizenship in the western world continue to be male-centred while, in an Irish context, Shannon argues that the nature of women's citizenship still poses a problem for late-twentieth-century republicanism.

The theme of women as citizens directly negotiating their relationship with the State moves Irish women's history beyond the confines of social and economic issues. It recognises that, in addition to their roles in the family and in the workplace, women have also played a significant role in politics, in the public sphere. Although they were denied formal recognition as full citizens, women played an active role in the body politic. Many of these essays force us to re-think our assumptions about women's place in society, to re-think the comfortable generalisations which conditioned our writing of history.

In particular, these essays call into question traditional historical assumptions about politics, about the separation of public and private spheres, about women as active agents – active players in the political narrative. What do we mean by political? By the public sphere? How real is the separation of the public and private spheres? Can voluntary organisations be political? Is politics only about war, rebellion and parliamentary debate or suffrage? Do women 'do' politics differently?

Maria Luddy's wide-ranging essay sets the tone for the discussion by arguing that it is necessary for us to examine the many ways in which women were active in politics – in agrarian unrest, in elections, in bread riots, in philanthropic organisations. She challenges us to re-think our standard definition of politics. Luddy suggests a new definition of politics:

> ... to include any action by an individual or group, in a formal or informal way, intended to affect or alter either the policy of government, or the behaviour or beliefs of individuals or groups within the local community, for the apparent benefit of a particular group or community.[9]

Within this broadened definition, many of women's activities traditionally dismissed as non-political, take on a political dimension. Luddy analyses the various philanthropic organisations in nineteenth-century Ireland and, within her definition, argues that they were, in reality, political organisations with a political agenda aimed at changing the society in which they lived.

Rosemary Raughter poses a similar question about the philanthropic activities of women in the eighteenth century and about the challenge which this work posed to the prevailing gender ideology of the period. She notes how women were often recruited into philanthropic activities because of a societal view of women's 'natural' qualities which made them more amenable to voluntary work and because of their 'natural' identification with concepts like service and sacrifice. However, Raughter points out that women's work in these organisations often challenged the very notions of womanhood which placed them in the domestic sphere and 'constituted, in effect, an assertion of women's right to self-expression as individuals and of ... [their] right ...to a place in public life.'[10] Within these organisations, women merged the public and private, the domestic and the political.

With the establishment of the Irish Free State in 1922, women's political activities continued. The Free State was full of contradictions for women. On one level, women were granted full and equal citizenship. However, various legislative measures were introduced which compromised that citizenship. Maryann Gialanella Valiulis analyses the struggle over jury service as one incident which typifies the Irish government's attitude toward women's participation in the public life of the state. She concludes that despite Irish women's organised and vigorous campaign to maintain the right of women to sit on juries, this issue demonstrates the resolve of the government to undermine women's claims to full citizenship.

Despite the government's policies and societal attitudes, women continued their political activities. Caitriona Beaumont points out that women's groups in the Free State – both feminist and non-feminist – formed a coalition and pursued a political agenda which aimed at improving the quality of life for women and children in the often harsh climate of the first thirty years of independence. Women's political activities were not simply reactive but rather directed towards change in areas they thought important. Thus they agitated for women in the Guards, fought to have the age of consent raised and protested against the double standard which penalised prostitutes but not their clients. In all their activities, Beaumont concludes, 'the women's movement of the 1930s and 1940s provided a vital link between the suffrage movement and the women's liberation movement of the 1970s.'[11]

The dominant ideology of the Irish Free State, as exemplified by the 1937 constitution, placed women in the home as mothers and housekeepers. Yet, as Caitriona Clear's article emphasises, the state provided no advice or guidance on how women should fulfil that role. Mary Daly's study of the lack of official interest in the provision of running water corroborates Clear's conclusions.

Not only was there a dearth of instruction about how women should fulfil their role in the home, the State remained indifferent to the plight of women in the home. Elizabeth Steiner Scott notes the lack of State involvement in domestic violence. The reality of the violent and harsh nature of many Irish women's lives was not allowed to upset the imagined ideal of Irish family life. As Joe Lee has pointed out, Irish people have a 'capacity for self-deception on a heroic scale.'[12]

Women's history also reveals the very real ways in which women and women's groups reflected the concerns of their society. Questions of war and peace, of violence and pacifism are themes which cut across a number of the essays in this volume. Rosemary Cullen Owens details the split within the Women's International League for Peace and Freedom as they divided on the question of the use of violence. Reflecting the split within the broader society about the legitimacy of the Free State and the continuing use of violence, the women involved in this group could not resolve their differences and, in the end, were forced to form two separate groups. Was freedom or peace to be their paramount concern?

Using the plays of Anne Devlin, Catherine Shannon examines how violence has disfigured women's lives through house raids, broken families and increasing use of tranquillisers. But Shannon also notes how the political situation in Northern Ireland inhibits women from confronting the violence directed against them by the men in their lives. Violence against women is doubly difficult to report and escape from when it becomes a life-threatening act of political disloyalty. Elizabeth Steiner Scott's examination of violence against women in nineteenth-century Ireland reaches conclusions that are similar to Shannon's analysis of contemporary Northern Ireland. Finally, Mary Cullen points to the lack of women's involvement in the current peace process and, through a survey of the Irish women's movement since the nineteenth century, suggests that feminism still faces a challenge to convince the general public that it is a movement that has a radical message to contribute to the debate about the future direction of Irish society.[13]

We began this volume by asking the participants to explore the ways in which women's history has challenged their understanding of traditional Irish history. The radical potential is evident in this collection. We are looking at Irish history in new ways, with different insights and perceptions. Concentrating on women challenges us to open up our definitions of State, nation, citizenship and power, a process which has been central to the Irish historiographical debate. Women's history thus moves us beyond the sterile debate on the national question and affords us a more nuanced and complex understanding of the past. *Women & Irish History* – a tribute to the founder of women's history in Ireland – demonstrates how our understanding of the Irish historical experience changes with the inclusion of women.

The Impact & Implications of Women's History
Joan Hoff

Even though I had been writing women's history since 1972, it was not until I became the Mary Ball Washington Chair in American History at University College Dublin twenty years later that I began to reflect upon the international implications of women's history as opposed to its important national impact in the United States. Partly this reflection arose because I found Dublin conducive to contemplation and good conversation, but mostly because there comes a time when writing women's history becomes more than an academic exercise if you are female. This truism was reinforced for me by a woman historian, Margaret MacCurtain, whom I did not meet in Dublin until the end of the academic year 1992-1993, because she was in the United States teaching as the John J. Burns Chair of Irish Studies at Boston College while I was at UCD.

Since this *festschrift* is to honour her, I want to begin my article with some personal observations about the importance of women's history and MacCurtain's impact on the field in Ireland. She has managed to keep a balance between theory and practice, between ideas and life, between belief and experience, between thought and action, no mean task given the changes in Ireland, the church, and religious orders in the last thirty years.

When we briefly met in Belfast at the XXIst Irish Conference of Historians, hosted by Queen's University, 27-30 May 1993, the setting was formal and not favourable to any personal exchange. Just before I left Ireland she had returned from the States and we finally found time to talk. At our first meal she explained to me the meaning of an Irish designated driver (we had taken her car): someone who drinks one drink for your two. With that remark, I became a grateful non-designated driver and strong admirer, thinking always of her with much fondness and respect. From then on I made it a point to see her when I returned to Dublin or when she came to the United States. Our last meeting in Washington, D.C. took us to the Vietnam Memorial on the weekend of the twentieth anniversary of the humiliating and chaotic evacuation of the U.S. embassy in Saigon in 1975, after she had just returned from an adventuresome auto and horseback trip in the American Southwest. Her reflections on these disparate experiences consisted of gems of wisdom and wit.

During my year in Ireland I had heard from everyone that I must meet Sister Benvenuta, as those who knew her longest still called her, and in the meantime I read a number of the books and articles she had written, or co-authored, or edited, noting with interest that she had gradually moved from mainstream Irish history (as I had from U.S. diplomatic and political history) to women's history. It is truly a significant career. Graduating from University College Cork in English and History, she conducted research at the Vatican Archives in Rome and at Spanish, Portuguese, and French Archives for a doctorate in Diplomatic Church History. She became and remained a lecturer in modern Irish History at University College Dublin until her retirement in 1994, where she also helped to found the Women's Studies Programme. Her absence from the classrooms and common room at UCD is still painfully evident. During those years she also lectured extensively in the United States and co-edited an eleven-volume *Gill History of Ireland*, writing the last volume on *Tudor and Stuart Ireland* in 1972. Before that, in 1969, she co-authored with Mark Tierney *The Birth of Modern Ireland*, which was translated into Irish in 1979. There followed other books and numerous articles, including an innovative form of history textbook for Irish schools.

But it was her work on women which fascinated me most for she personally captured the minds and voices of a most important group of women in Irish history: Roman Catholic sisters. Indeed, Margaret MacCurtain, like Gerda Lerner and Anne Firor Scott in the United States, pioneered the field of Irish women's history.

Her latest contribution published in 1995, *From Dublin to New Orleans: the Journey of Nora and Alice*, was co-authored and co-edited with Suellen Hoy. The sophisticated changes in the historical treatment of religious orders are evident in writing about other groups of Irish women, but no more so than in MacCurtain's and others' treatment of women religious in Ireland and those who left Ireland in the nineteenth century to establish convents and become teachers, nurses and administrators in the United States. These nuns continue to play unsung professional and feminist roles in modern Ireland. If voices of Irish women's history and women's solidarity begin anywhere, it is within religious sisterhoods.

As a member of the Irish Congregation of Dominican Sisters, MacCurtain's contributions to Irish history in general and women's history in particular place her at the top of a long line of Roman Catholic sisters who have contributed to the writing of history in their respective countries. Additionally, she has supported the efforts of the Association of Religious Archives of Ireland (now the Association of Church Archivists) to preserve and catalogue the records of religious orders, a source which was until recently not much appreciated by Irish historians.

And yet through her long and productive career, Margaret MacCurtain has retained a self-effacing, yet life-loving intensity about her person and her work – characteristics we might all try to emulate. My contact with her, however episodic, has led me to think more personally and professionally about the impact and implications of women's history, not simply in Ireland and the United States, but the entire world.

Citizenship and Nationalism

During the year in which I taught in Dublin I was forced to reconsider what citizenship meant for women outside the United States. But more importantly, the disintegration of Yugoslavia (and later the peace in Northern Ireland) also made me think about the meaning of nationalism for women and the connection between citizenship and nationalism. Neither subject had been given enough consideration by historians of women in the last thirty years.[1] Despite the dramatic developments in the field of women's history which I outline below, the topic of citizenship has remained only marginal in the literature. I had not been aware of this particular omission in the otherwise enormously productive field of women's history before living in Ireland.

I have argued for a number of years that women in the United States and most other western democracies remain second-class citizens, even after being granted the right to vote and accorded varying degrees of equality of opportunity in the work force and educational institutions. This is because they continue to lack three basic freedoms enjoyed by men under most constitutional and democratic governments: freedom from inferior legislative, constitutional or judicial status (usually meaning fewer individual, economic, educational, and legal opportunities and choices enjoyed by mainstream men); freedom from fertility and family discrimination (fewer reproductive rights, including access to abortion and an inferior position within traditional family hierarchies); and freedom from fear (fewer protections from the uncontrolled and often ignored violence against women throughout the world). In other words, a common inferior or second-class citizenship has been imposed on women throughout the world.

Why do women in most democratic western nations not have these three essential rights of citizenship in the twentieth century? The major reason stems from the male origins of definitions of democratic citizenship – definitions now employed in the new emerging democracies in Eastern Europe and Russia and most of the Third World. However, another reason lies in the fact that feminists and historians of women have not until recently focused on the general meaning of citizenship for women in their respective countries. Instead, they have championed certain aspects of male citizenship, such as equal political treatment under the law, rather than trying to transform traditional definitions of citizenship to meet the societal requirements of women. This is why we need a feminist approach to international law – to make sure that human rights include women's rights. We must rethink definitions of national and global citizenship based on equal rights so that they include those rights which correspond to women's experiences and needs, as they are reflected in different countries all over the world.

The history of citizenship for women in the United States and under United Nations covenants demonstrates that equal rights alone, while a necessary starting point for obtaining first-class citizenship for women, has not been enough. Such equality is typically based on male standards. Yet, women do not exist on an equal footing with men in either post-industrial or less developed nations.

In labour forces all over the world, for example, equal treatment (and its opposite, special or protective treatment) is still defined by men and does not offer women true equality. Equal treatment invites women to perform as 'ideal [male] workers' without the flow of domestic services historically provided male workers by women.[2] This inequality was quickly recognised by over-worked feminists in the 1970s when they said: 'I need a wife.' Special treatment of women workers has resulted in the past in protective legislation discriminating against average working women and in the present in the creation of special, usually inferior, 'mommy tracks' for professional women. Neither legal/cultural approach results in equality or full citizenship for women.

Unless women simply want to aspire to act as, and be treated as, men, despite the odds against achieving this status, equitable, not simply equal, treatment of women must be included in any definition of national or global citizenship in the future. As feminist attorneys have said: 'the rhetoric of human rights, on both the national and international levels, regards women as equal citizens [when they are not], as 'individuals' subject to the same level of treatment and the same protection as men. But the discourse of "traditional values" may prevent women from enjoying any human rights, however they may be described [because male standards are still the norm].'[3]

Likewise, nationalism, be it after the American Revolution or the Irish Rising – or in the former Yugoslavia and other recently liberated communist nations – was usually not favourably disposed toward the needs or rights of women.

Throughout the nineteenth and twentieth centuries, the emergence of nation states based on democratisation and industrial modernisation changed the socio-economic and legal relationship of women to men *without transforming* their over-all societal status. Instead, women remained as they had been since the beginning of recorded time – inferior to men. This historical continuity in subordinate female status has prevailed despite various improvements or declines in the working and legal experiences of women over several millennia.

It was naïve to think that history would not repeat itself with the alleged triumph of capitalism and democracy over communism and totalitarianism.[4] Current criticism of the failure of communism to provide equality for women through a combination of paid work and subsidised motherhood, should not blind us to how unequal women remain in the western industrialised countries. And for the same reasons: a sex-segregated labour market and dual work load for most married women who work outside their homes. Democracy and capitalism may be recognised as an inexorable trend (or end) of history, according to writers on both the left and right, but it is usually not pointed out that this 'relentless progress' has always been at either the expense or neglect of women, especially when accompanied by burgeoning nationalism.

Reviewing the evolution of the concept of democratic citizenship, the United States in the last two hundred years provides one example of the problematic connection between nationalism and citizenship and how American citizenship, as in so many other countries, disadvantages women. Likewise, MacCurtain and others have pointed out some of the problems facing Irish women after the Rising. In keeping with most post-liberation countries, the Irish Republic utilised female symbols and imagery for its own purposes without recognising women as full citizens. Mary Condren, for example, has interpreted the symbolic and mythopoeic ways in which Irish men used pagan and Christian sacrificial imagery and theology to destroy female images and genealogies during and after the Rising to subordinate the claims of feminism to that of nationalism and the state. Her work is a powerful indictment of all wars, whether imperialist or nationalist, and of liberation movements for betraying and destroying women's bodies as well as their minds and voices.[5]

After the American Revolution, citizenship was exclusively male-defined in terms of very specific rights and obligations for a small, privileged group of white men. The best analogy I can think of is that citizens were like members of a private male club, who agree or consent to join, in return for paying a membership fee – men accept certain obligations and duties in return for receiving certain benefits. The basic post-revolutionary benefit was the right to vote, along with other individual rights guaranteed but not yet implemented in the Bill of Rights. But early United States citizenship status also carried with it the obligation of civic duty or service. At the end of the eighteenth century these obligations or duties of citizenship were few, but very specific. First, there was the obligation of allegiance to the country, which at the very minimum meant to refrain from treason. Secondly, there was the obligation to pay taxes; third, the obligation to serve on juries. Fourthly, and perhaps most important in any post-revolutionary situation, there was the obligation of military service.

In fact, military service was probably the prime male-defining characteristic of citizenship when the United States came into existence. It has remained the most gendered aspect of any definition of citizenship down to the present because American women have, in the course of the last two hundred years, been grudgingly assigned (after years of protest and activism) the other three obligations of individual allegiance, payment of taxes, and service on juries. And while women have been admitted into the armed services of the United States in recent years, it is still being debated whether they should actually engage in combat.

It is from this first definition of citizenship based on the right to vote and other rights contained in the Bill of Rights and these four male-defined and hence gendered obligations that a second stage or definition of citizenship evolved in the United States. Accordingly, attempts were made to obtain more rights without an increase in reciprocal duties – again largely by white men demanding implementation of certain individual freedoms guaranteed by the Bill of Rights.[6] Women entered this process with the demand to vote in 1848 and since achieving that in 1920 went on to demand other rights possessed by white men for most of this century. The analogy now shifts to citizens as members of a private, exclusionary men's club being forced first by its male members to broaden benefits without increasing the dues or obligations of membership. And then being forced to admit other groups, such as women and minorities, to membership benefits – again without enlarging or even emphasising service or obligations owed to the club.

Finally, at the end of the twentieth century, citizenship in the United States has entered a third definitional stage. It remains gendered but also has become a commodity. This means that instead of being 'a status that in turn authorises civic participation, citizenship is increasingly likely to stand for a range of entitlements: [e.g.] to unemployment compensations, to welfare payments.'[7] In most European countries this last aspect of citizenship came into existence after the Second World War. It has been late in developing in the United States because of the lack of national health insurance and a penurious welfare system.

Now the analogy of the private men's club has disappeared altogether, because membership, far from exclusionary, includes everyone; and everyone is now dependent on the services provided by the club or, more precisely, the state. But as enticing as commodities in the form of entitlements are, they can always be taken away, especially in bad economic times. This was demonstrated in 1995-96 by the conservative Republican 104th Congress in the United States and by attempts to cut back on social services in western and eastern European countries.

What I find most interesting about this three-stage development in the concept of citizenship in the United States, and in so many other western nations established after the end of the eighteenth century, is that it began with the assumption that certain groups of people, such as women, slaves, Native Americans and even men without property, were dependent upon and therefore deserved to be ruled by an élite group of white men with property. In this third stage of development all citizens are dependent upon the state and what were once obligatory duties of citizenship (allegiance, taxes, jury and military service) have become irritants at best and duties to be dodged at all costs. In the case of military service in the United States, there is no longer any obligation to serve in the all-voluntary armed service. Does commodification make national citizenship obsolete in the United States and in other parts of the industrialised world? That is, has this type of open-admission citizenry, composed of indifferent and often hostile (if the private American militia movement is any example) members, made national citizenship meaningless? When the government no longer requires conscious consent or assent and duties in return for services, has the traditional concept of citizenship so changed as to represent a difference of kind, rather than simply degree? In other words, are we moving on to a type of global citizenship where individual equal rights and obligations will no longer apply? Has the social contract theory of nationhood, based on the concept of consenting, yet tax-paying, civic-minded citizens prepared to give as well as receive from the state, become *passé* at the end of the twentieth century? If so, what does this mean for women, who are still denied full citizenship rights under the old system of citizenship based on equal rights and obligations?

To begin to answer all these questions, but especially the last one about women, we must return to the traditional definition of citizenship in the United States and remember that it was based not only on individual rights in return for obligations, but also on freedom of choice – the choice to be a loyal, patriotic, civic-minded citizen or not. Because the traditional and contemporary definitions of citizenship are gendered, American women have never been accorded the same freedom or right of choice that American men have had. At the end of the eighteenth and early nineteenth centuries, women could not choose to vote, pay (or not pay) taxes in their own right, serve on juries, or join the military, as most white men could. Now they still do not have the right or freedom to choose all entitlements and services offered by the state to men. The current attacks on abortion and the welfare system in the United States and continued wage differentials between women and men are but three examples of how unequal rights remain for women and why women are still considered second-class citizens.[8]

If part of modern democratic citizenship is the idea of freedom of choice, I come back to the freedoms that women currently lack in most parts of the world – that is, the choices which are not available to them – which relegate them to second-class citizenship: inferior constitutional status, fertility and family discrimination, and the constant fear factor with which women live their daily lives in most societies because of the violence directed against them. Such violence appears based on the unstated but universal maxim that the right of women to control their physical, reproductive and psychic well-being is not currently a right of citizenship for most women as it is for most men.[9] Violence against women has never been given the same serious consideration that crimes of violence against men have received (especially in wartime) by the legal systems in most democratic countries, including the United States, the United Kingdom and the Republic of Ireland. Women simply do not have the same legal protections against violence, largely because laws are formulated to service men's fear of annihilation rather than women's fear of violation.[10]

As if the task of redefining citizenship while remaining wary of nationalism with its inherent co-option of, or violence towards, women is not enough for feminists all over the world, we must be on guard against the trendy concept of global citizenship. It portends a fourth definitional stage in the concept of citizenship (in addition to the three stages which I have already outlined) and it is apt to be more exclusionary than even the most traditional male definitions of national citizenship have been in the past. This is because the global economy is creating an even more élitist, male-dominated group of wealthy individuals who, if nothing is done to monitor and expose their intentions, will define global citizenship rooted in their own image – not that of women or other disadvantaged groups.

In other words, global citizenship based on a global economy may mark a return to my first citizenship analogy of the exclusionary all-male club made up of only the most wealthy property owners. This time, however, such citizenship will bypass nation states and require billions of multi-national corporation dollars to join. The entry fee will be prohibitively high because membership will carry with it the obligation and right to rule the world. As of 1996, there is every indication that such limited global citizenship will be heralded as a victory for international human rights, when in fact it is a euphemism for traditional male values on a global scale, with women's needs and rights and choices once again subordinated. Instead of commodified citizenship encompassing modest entitlements for the greatest number, global citizenship will mean enormous entitlements for a very few and sub-standard wages and benefits for everyone else.

While in Ireland, I could not help but notice that this kind of theorising about the national and global meaning of citizenship (or even nationalism except after peace came to the North) was not usually relevant to the everyday lives of the women whom I encountered outside academe. This was made even more evident to me at a panel of women from the Irish Republic and Northern Ireland in May 1995. With one of the lowest employment rates in Europe, especially among those who are married, Irish women in the South are still mainly concerned about obtaining children's allowance without incurring stigma and more respect for the unpaid work of married women. While in the North they feared being left out of the peace talks so that the defects of years of British rule based on unchallenged sectarianism with respect to women, would be ignored. They wanted women, regardless of religion, 'to be able to live lives of dignity.'[11]

As I listened to these women talk at cross purposes about their own views of citizenship and tried to relate them to mine as an American, I realised more than ever before the limitations of women's history – a subject which I had proudly taught and written. This, in turn, led me to review the impact and implications of women's history more seriously than ever before, paying particular attention to what I could learn from Irish examples – many of them from writings or edited works of Margaret MacCurtain.

Patriarchal History

The kind of history which many of us were taught from primary school through college is so familiar that we scarcely think of it as having a name. A shorthand term for that nameless though ubiquitous type of history is 'patriarchal', where the standards of power, prestige, and traditional periodisation abound. Such criteria have eliminated most women from historical consideration or have resulted in the peripheral inclusion of only the 'exceptional' among them.

Throughout the ages, the writers of patriarchal history have emphasised the exercise of public power as the most important aspect of human life. One of the recurrent activities in the public sphere has been abrupt or violent changes in relationships between individuals and nations and between humans and their environments. It is not only politics and wars which represent these values of power and prestige and which determine traditional textbook periodisation; the emphasis in patriarchal history on dramatic confrontations between powerful individuals rather than on the evolution of social relations does so also.

Consequently, one of the most common features of patriarchal history is the search for heroic or charismatic figures. This search has been reinforced in the United States by the rise of the cult of hero worship since the 1920s because of technological advancements in mass communication, but it is also not uncommon among historians of other countries. Thus, conservative historians of the present traditionally write about conservative leaders of the past. Radical historians look for radical models as subjects of their research. Labour historians focus on class differences, while gay historians search for examples of homosexuality. Minority or ethnic historians search for prominent representatives of their respective races or ethnic backgrounds. This attempt to find historical figures representing particular political, class, sexual, racial, or ethnic preferences became particularly evident in works published in the United States during the 1970s.

To the degree, therefore, that historians of women simply look for heroines from the past, they are continuing to write in a patriarchal mould. Even if they write about women who are less well known, they often resurrect them using traditional values of power and prestige. The same is true of historians who specialise in the study of minority or ethnic leaders. Since women and other subordinate groups have not produced many individuals who meet traditional patriarchal criteria, one soon runs out of these kinds of heroes. While some of these compensatory or remedial efforts are necessary to overcome the historical invisibility of these groups, such history contains serious limitations. For one, patriarchal history has placed far too much emphasis on atypical individuals whose public careers have little in common with the private lives of 'average' women. This emphasis on notable women, when continued by historians of women, also raises the political question of whether concentrating primarily on notable or exceptional women can contribute to the empowerment of all women.

Thus, much compensatory or remedial history perpetuates the patriarchal tradition of according more importance to the public than to the private sphere of human existence and usually consists of narratives about women's experiences that parallel those of men using standard political, socio-economic, and cultural terminology and periodisation. It is an attempt not so much to 'rewrite history', as Virginia Woolf advocated in 1929, by accumulating a 'mass of information' about women's daily lives, but to imitate conventional history.[12]

I believe that when women's history begins to be written in most countries, it passes through three discernible stages of development that diverge from traditional patriarchal history. They are: (1) the compensatory or remedial stage; (2) the pre-feminist stage; and (3) the feminist stage. A fourth, post-feminist stage under the influence of post-structuralism has emerged in a few western nations that is theoretically most sophisticated and intriguing, but carries with it some disturbing political overtones for modern women's movements which have fought both for women's rights and for the writing of women's history.[13]

Compensatory or remedial history constitutes a first step toward achieving historical visibility for powerless groups, who are traditionally relegated to the invisible confines of the private sphere. Nonetheless, early compensatory history is seriously flawed in practice because it usually only substitutes women for men. Even when prominent women emerge, as they inevitably do in most counties, the documentation of their lives and achievements, until the advent of women's history in the 1960s, was usually left to males who imposed their own values on them. First, they wrote about women prescriptively, assigning them status and societal value according to prevailing mainstream standards; that is, they took notable women, often female 'outsiders' for their times, and assigned them mainstream characteristics, and thus made 'acceptable' models out of the private and public lives of women ranging from those accused of being witches or committing heresy, such as Dame Alice Kytler of Kilkenny, Puritan Anne Hutchinson, and Quaker Mary Dyer, or Deborah Sampson Gannett and Constance Markievicz – both of whom assumed male dress and roles during revolutionary times – to Eleanor Roosevelt, Bernadette Devlin, and Mary Robinson. Second, in deciding that only certain records about these exceptional women should be preserved, patriarchal historians allowed much documentation to suffer from indifference at best, and deterioration or destruction at worst. Examples of Irish women playing significant roles in the past and present are still subject to this kind of treatment from the male-dominated profession of history.

The second stage of development in women's history can be considered pre-feminist. These histories usually contain some of the same remedial and contradictory features of the earlier conventional works, especially the concentration on 'notables'. Second-stage historians often begin to look at political events and movements other than wars and suffrage and to ask new questions of old data from a female – but not necessarily a feminist – point of view. (I am dating the emergence of modern feminism in the late 1960s to the formation of women's movements in many western democracies in the 1970s.) By and large, however, these historians continue to research the lives of 'exceptional' rather than ordinary women and to write political or institutional histories.

As they progress – at least in western nations over the past thirty years, these historians usually become more critical of their female subjects, especially those feminist reformers who first asked for voting or other rights for women. Thirty years ago the profession generally accepted a women's history which found fault with individual women and women's organisations because it dovetailed with the history being written in other fields which was also critical of mainstream politics and economics. This was in keeping with the student outbursts and general leftist criticism in the 1960s and early 1970s of the way in which the cold war was being fought.

Left-of-centre historians were quick to question the value and motives of middle- and upper-middle-class women reformers who emerged in England and the United States in the late nineteenth and early twentieth centuries.

The new social history of the late 1960s produced the third, or modern feminist phase in women's history which has been (and will be) emulated as historians in other countries also emerge from their pre-feminist mode of thinking. In keeping with their left-of-centre politics and often their involvement with campaigns for women's rights in the 1960s and 1970s, the women and men who wrote the new social history deliberately added a feminist agenda to their research programmes. While many of these historians initially used the conventional sources of their predecessors, they also freed themselves from these sources by employing new methodologies which questioned the older data. Two of the few second-stage female historians in the United States to make the shift to third-stage methodology and interpretations were Anne Firor Scott and Gerda Lerner. In Ireland, it was Margaret MacCurtain.[14]

Many of the questions which they ask came directly or indirectly from the political agendas of the feminist movements. In the United States, this meant that they arose out of the civil rights and anti-war movements. In Ireland, they emerged from the second women's movement in the 1970s. Most of these questions cannot be answered by traditional historical approaches to research. Conscious feminist historians all over the world have begun to use innovative methods involving oral history, ethnography, sociology, ethnology, semiotics, family reconstitution, collective biographical sketches (prosopography), and various forms of statistical and computerised demographic analysis, such as multiple regression analysis, and other micro-history techniques. Most recently, they have begun to answer such questions with post-structural perspectives borrowed from literature, philosophy, and film criticism. Once these innovations are adopted by third-stage historians in any country, they lead first to the reconstruction of the aggregate history of female and other sub-cultural groups from incomplete and hence largely ignored data, and second to the demystification of the concept of gender itself. Once believed inadequate for historical analysis, such sources as obscure legal, church, census, and other demographic records, as well as folklore, films, female literature, transcripts of interviews, music, and evidence of informal community and interest-group networks, have all yielded new and valuable historical information on women.

Third-stage historians almost always borrow from advanced methodology in a variety of disciplines from other countries. In the 1960s, and again in the 1980s, most borrowed from France and England. The 1986 International Conference on Women's History in Amsterdam demonstrated both the intellectual borrowing which had taken place since the 1960s, and the remaining differences in stages of writing the history of women in various countries.[15]

Since it was influenced by the new social history *and* feminist politics, the third stage of women's history was not initially taken seriously by the predominantly male historical establishment in any country – and still is not in many. Such men viewed such historical research as either marginal or too ideological and present-minded. In addition, they devalued the subject matter – female culture, female networks, sexuality, female socialisation, and women's life cycle within the family – and therefore often discounted feminist contributions to research as being unscientific or 'non-objective' and hence less deserving of recognition for promotion or tenure. Until this third stage in the writing of women's history emerged, even historians of the family largely ignored women because they did not employ gender analysis.[16]

Much third-stage women's history went beyond the male-defined interests and values of the early new social history by establishing gender as a fundamental category of analysis. Feminist historians all over the world began to demonstrate the importance of women struggling to reconcile their public and private roles. The relationship between the public and private spheres has profoundly affected how historians write about female sexuality, especially homo-social and/or homo-erotic bonding.[17] The conventional tendency has been to trivialise love relationships between women in comparison with the heterosexual home as a haven from the heartless world, or to stress how love relationships between women supported them in their public and private activities. Neither approach, however, has yet legitimised the single woman as a sexual being for whom no theoretical and historical heterosexual or homosexual apologia need be made.

Third-stage historians of women usually begin to restore women in positive ways to the sub-fields of economic, urban, religious, and family history, in which they had been ignored (or removed altogether) by traditional patriarchal historians and considered only negatively or marginally by the second-stage pre-feminist historians. Most important, some of these modern feminist historians took up the task of writing about class as well as racial, sexual and other significant differences among women.

Whenever it develops in a country, the most striking aspect of this third stage in women's history appears to be its ability to show the intersection of women's common experience over time with an improved understanding of the specific experiences of women in particular historical periods. Often centering on the life cycles of women, feminist historians try to reflect the totality of women's public and private lives. Three thematic areas of emphasis have emerged from such research. They can be summed up in the terms: family, functionalism, and feminism. Initially, third-stage historians successfully placed women as a gender category into family history. If anything, women's gender roles within the family have been analysed more extensively by third-stage historians than any other aspect of female life. Secondly, such historians expose the traditional way in which women were accorded 'functionalist treatment' – that is, the prescriptive view that female existence is largely circumscribed by roles within the patriarchal family structure.[18] They often conclude by redefining functionalism to mean the work of women inside and outside the home in relation to the predominant sexist and racist market and political economy. Thirdly, they attempt to trace the origins and development of several distinct types of historical feminism.

But despite the more sophisticated methodology, the new social history approach, and the left-of-centre backgrounds of many third-stage scholars, great emphasis continued, in the United States at least, to be placed on the private activities of women within the larger constructs of the family, religion, community, and female networks inside and outside the home. Because they concentrated on the similarities among women across class, race, and ethnic lines to a much greater degree than their liberal or radical colleagues in other parts of the world, the initial scholarship by third-stage historians in the United States suspiciously resembled the 1950s consensus scholarship, which the liberal and radical historians of women's history had originally repudiated. The bulk of the earliest historical writings of third-stage feminists painted a rather positive, homogeneous picture of U.S. women. To summarise, U.S. history looked more humane, more progressive, and more concerned about social justice when women were integrated into it. Yet at the same time, these writings also promoted the ideas of American exceptionalism, patriotism, and unending progress based on traditional middle-class, liberal notions about political and legal individualism. The same generalisations do not hold true with regard to the historical writings about women in other parts of the world where the influence of socialism in intellectual and political circles has been much greater since World War II than in the United States. This has meant that class, race, and comparative analysis appears consistently stronger in the writings of non-U.S. historians of women.

Despite the persistence of some aspects of patriarchal history, such as the continued destruction, indifference, or hostility to the papers of notable women, let alone the papers of average women, by family members and archivists, dramatic changes have taken place during the last thirty years in the writing of the history of women and, in some countries, in the profession of history itself. Many of those currently writing women's history have led the way in making curricular and textbook changes, as MacCurtain did, and in the training and placing of students and the hiring and promoting of faculty. This has been more true in the United States than in other countries, not only because of its affirmative action laws, but also because academe is less formally organised.

Other trends in this third stage of historiography about women have been revealed by surveys of articles and books written in the United States and abroad. For example, after reviewing U.S. and European periodical and monographic literature, in addition to Ph.D. dissertations from 1975 to 1980, Hilda L. Smith found a disturbing concentration on 'women's role in the family, the various stages in their life cycles (usually biologically determined), and their relationships among themselves rather than those with public institutions in general or men in particular (except in the family).' Smith saw the same trend continuing in periodic literature from 1982 to 1986 and concluded that women's history is in danger of becoming 'merely a branch of social history', to the neglect of women's intellectual, political, or other individual achievements.[19] However, the increased number of articles published in the 1980s on women and politics in the United States and other nations would seem to indicate that this particular trend is not continuing unabated. But a new problem arose in that same decade for those of us paying attention to trends in the writing of women's history.

Whenever historians enter this third stage of writing about women, they begin to apply more positive (and more complicated) interpretations and generalisations to women's private and public lives, compared to the standard views of women that prevailed under patriarchal history. Generally speaking, in the United States and in a few other western countries, the result by the first half of the 1970s was a historiography which stressed the commonality of subordinate and oppressive female experiences across class and race lines. The best examples of this type of women's history did this *without* minimising the differences between classes of women and women of colour. As the new history matures, it usually begins to stress how women were distinguished from men by socialised gender characteristics in almost every aspect of their private and public existence.[20] Gender analysis, in other words, became a major contribution of women's history to all other historical sub-fields including social, economic, political, and intellectual history *before* post-structuralist historians of women 'discovered' it in the last half of the 1980s. By that time, women's history was already explaining common gender experiences and identities among women without ignoring obvious class and race diversity. During that same decade, feminist activists all over the world had also succeeded in projecting some modicum of common female identity for political purposes, and in asserting themselves in various walks of public and private life.

At this crucial juncture, post-structural analysis and deconstructionist methodology entered the academic world in a select group of western nations and began to assert just the opposite, by denying commonalities among women of the past and present and by questioning whether there will be any distinctive female identity in the future. Some post-structural (gender) historians, for example, 'acknowledge, celebrate and support the instigation of all differences that divide and constitute both men and women' to the point that they no longer identify their work as being *about women* when they write gender history.

In this sense, deconstruction became a fourth stage in the development of women's history. Deconstruction represented a covert (but possibly unintentional) attack on political feminism in the United States, as well as on historians of women of the last twenty years who stressed the common personal and/or public experiences of women. For gender historians, material experiences became abstract representations drawn from textual analysis; personal identities and agency became subjects constructed exclusively by non-material discourses; and flesh-and-blood women became social constructs – with no 'natural' or physiological context except as a set of symbolic meanings constructing sexual differences.

Feminist politics, according to the post-structuralists, no longer could be used to alleviate conditions of oppression because 'identity is not an objectively determined sense of self defined by needs' any more than 'politics is ... the collective coming to consciousness of similarly situated individual subjects.'[21]

If experience cannot be based on relatively unchanging socio-economic categories or on the diversity and variability of common gender *identities*, then there cannot be a materially based history from which contemporary feminist activists could draw sustenance and advice for opposing and criticising the remaining areas of oppression experienced by women in the United States and other countries. Thus, instead of remaining simply another useful methodological innovation for studying women's history and making that history more relevant to radical political feminism, deconstruction became a potentially politically paralysing and intellectually irrelevant exercise for endlessly analysing myriad representations of incompatible cultural paradigms and discourses.

As gender came to be viewed more and more as a cultural representation of enormous importance for understanding all aspects of American life, including politics and economics, women's history found itself challenged by post-structural gender history. From the beginning, American post-structuralism threatened to sever the field of women's history from its political roots by insisting that there could be no experience outside of language. Valid as such an assertion may be in linguistic terms, it disturbed political activists, especially those representing women and racial minorities. It also was unintelligible to the vast majority of history teachers trying to integrate material on women into their classes, because it denied retrievable historical 'reality', substituting instead the 'linguistic turn', meaning historical analysis based on analysis of representation. Like all post-modern theories, post-structuralism casts into doubt stable meanings and sees language as so slippery that it compromises historians' ability to identify facts and chronological narratives. It also uses gender as a category of analysis to reduce the experiences of women, struggling to define themselves and control their lives in particular historical contexts, to mere subjective stories.

This line of argument is perplexing, because leading historians of women had been defining gender as the socially conditioned behaviour of both sexes, in their research since the late 1970s. Gender as a category of analysis did not need to be reinvented using a special linguistic jargon, except to eliminate the category of woman in the much-touted new field of gender history. Moreover, this original use of gender, in the hands of early practitioners, did not cut academic analysis off from the realities which women faced in their daily lives. Instead of promoting women's history into the mainstream, as predicted by some advocates of gender history, post-structuralism left political reformers without generalisations about the commonly shared experiences of women as a basis for activism. It also leaves most historians in the United States, and abroad, floundering as they try to convert facts into chronological narratives when faced with the 'linguistic turn'.

In this fourth stage of writing about women, gender history threatens to replace women's history in certain academic circles, even though it is beyond the understanding and does not serve the needs of the vast majority of women in the world. Ironically, American post-structuralism is either being ignored or subjected to rigorous questioning by many feminist activists and scholars abroad.[22] For example, Margaret MacCurtain and Mary O'Dowd said in 1991 that 'there are signs of a European reaction against' this distinction between women's and gender history, and 'a recognition' that its origins have more to do with the 'way in which women's history has developed in North America' than in any inherent supremacy of the post-structural gender history. They concluded that it 'may not necessarily be helpful in studying the history of women in other countries where, as in Ireland, much basic research still needs to be done.'[23]

Nonetheless, where post-structuralism is influential, historical writing about women has become more and more removed from the political and legal arena in which the battle for the rights of women and minorities was initially waged. In the process, gender history has inadvertently contributed to the rationalisation of the violent and abusive portrayals of women now so common in various forms of popular culture in the United States, because post-structural theories lead to a totally relativistic view of the world in which there are no centres of power, and no societal harms that cannot be deconstructed on paper. Reality, according to post-structuralists, consists only of decentered, genderless individuals whose very real and objective material problems and experiential contact with oppression can be reduced to linguistic exercises through deconstructing binary oppositions.

Yet difference and dominance go hand in hand, in the sense that both continue to be defined in America and other societies by male criteria. Simply because gender differences can be variously interpreted by researchers so that they are found to be 'historically and culturally specific', and because they are social rather than biological, does not mean that they are also benign, neutral, or non-categorical.[24] On the contrary, their very historical and cultural diversity often masks their oppressive commonality – namely, that gender is, in fact, about the power of men over women. Simone de Beauvoir captured the historical significance of this enduring patriarchal form of female oppression when she proclaimed in 1949:

'Throughout history [women] have always been subordinated to men, and hence their dependency is not the result of a historical event or a social change – it was not something that occurred.'[25]

I have analysed in other articles the misogynist origins, implicit racism, and politically paralysing aspects of post-structuralism as it is being touted in the United States.[26] Historians like myself who know, as Vicki L. Ruiz and Ellen Carol Du Bois have strongly asserted in their multi-cultural women's history reader, *Unequal Sisters*, that 'history is unavoidably political', also know that to pretend the 'linguistic turn' can be effectively political borders on nonsense. Linda Gordon has described this as tension between writing history with the 'mythic power' to inspire moral and political action and writing accurate history which, even if it cannot contain the absolute truth, in the way 'grand' patriarchal history purported to, will at least point out the 'objective lies' from the past about women's public and private lives. 'There may be no objective canon of historiography,' according to Gordon, 'but there are degrees of accuracy; there are better and worse pieces of history. The challenge is precisely to maintain this tension between accuracy and [the] mythic power [of history].' To the degree that historians of women exclusively emphasise one or the other, their writings will not serve the cause of political and legal reform on behalf of women in the United States and abroad. In particular, Gordon has noted that she fears that the current emphasis among historians of women on 'difference' is becoming a substitute, an accommodating, affable, and even lazy substitute, for opposition.[27]

Nonetheless, it is now common for post-structural and socialist feminists to deny both the categories of 'woman' and 'women', because they represent a false or fictive 'universalisation of sex class that does not focus on specificity and only recognises the homogeneity of women.' This criticism is almost as simplistic as were the early patriarchal views of women. While it is desirable to avoid imposing a 'false sense of commonality' on different groups of women in specific time periods, it is equally desirable to recognise that women are perceived in all societies as 'an always – already constituted group' because of the specific prevailing 'discourse of engendered sex "difference"', which presumes that sex and gender are the same thing. Rather than deny any 'specific unity' among women, therefore, we should try to identify it historically, along with a description of their relevant subjective and objective differences. In other words, as Zillah Eisenstein has noted, 'the tension between diversity and unity' must become the focus – not one extreme or the other.[28]

In summary, under the influence of feminist movements in far-flung parts of the world in the 1970s, historians of women first began challenging patriarchal stereotypes of women and then interpreting a set of common female experiences to explain how women sought to co-ordinate their private lives with their public ones. This synthesis is now being challenged by post-structural histories, some of which focus so much on the existence of multiple 'masculinities' that they are 'implicitly denying the existence of patriarchy' and espousing theories about the predominance of differences among women in which 'the voice of gender risks being lost entirely'. In other words, deconstructionist techniques that focus increasingly on 'male sensitivity and male persecution' downplay male privilege and, hence, not only depoliticise the use of the word *gender*, but also seem to deny that feminism can or should be a coherent philosophy or ideology in the writing of women's history.[29]

As a methodology for textual analysis, post-structuralism can be a useful tool for historians of women. In my own career, I have found such methodologies as structural functionalism, cliometrics, and corporatism also useful in writing women's history and economic, political, and diplomatic history over the last twenty-five years. But none of these post-1960s methodologies claimed the status of an ideology, even among its most enthusiastic adherents. The time which female post-structuralists have spent trying to include women as a gender into theories that basically ignored them, as a sex and as a post-modern category of analysis, reminds me of the same attempts several decades ago by so many socialist and Marxist feminists and by female psychoanalysts to put women into the theories of Marx and Freud, instead of developing a feminist version of materialism or psychology. After all, original feminist thinking is always harder than spending endless time adapting male thinking to fit women badly. Post-structuralism's claims to destroy history, or to resolve or remove all past contractions and dichotomies from history, are currently so exaggerated and misused in the United States, with potentially unfortunate results for women's history, that they need to be addressed frankly. We must demystify the demystifiers.

The methodological sophistication and growing number of practitioners and publications in women's history occurred long before the appearance of post-structuralism. Its explosion in the last quarter century has led some historians to suggest that women's history is on its way to becoming an *alternative*, rather than merely a sub-field, of the discipline, implicitly suggested in the somewhat presumptuous title of a 1995 *festschrift* collection of essays in honour of Gerda Lerner: *U.S. History as Women's History.* And there is no doubt that feminist historical scholarship has dramatically altered two sub-fields within the discipline of history – the new social history and the new legal history.[30]

Unfortunately, a less sophisticated and less constructive debate has been initiated by younger (and some older) post-structural historians for whom feminism and even the future of women's history has little relevance. They claim that women's history has lost its identity and go so far as to predict that women's history is about to 'dissolve'. Women's history will only 'dissolve' when it finally has nothing to offer contemporary feminism and not because of such predictions. If women's history appears to be 'dissolving', it is only because of the sea of relativity created on the head of a semiotic pin by deconstructionists, and not because it has lost its feminist moorings. These arguments by post-feminists are not unlike those by neo-conservatives who have tried to undermine all of post-World War II revisionist history with theories about post-history or the death of history now that the cold war is over.[31]

As the world enters a post-cold war era and the twenty-first century, women's history in the United States (and other countries) is alive and well, despite the extremes to which some want to carry post-feminist and post-structural arguments. Interestingly, commentators on the 1995 international women's conference in China wrote negatively about this same élitism of many western women from richer nations of 'the North' who were bickering over 'history as theory', and the question of whether it was demeaning even to talk about women's rights separate from human rights. In contrast, women of 'the South' or Third World were organising for pragmatic goals, such as access to capital, the right of inheritance, basic education for girls, and a voice in the political establishment and medical systems so that they could make practical choices about their reproductive health.[32]

Yet even in the United States, where women's history and women's studies are widespread, women continue to be studied and taught primarily as a separate group rather than integrated into general history classes or other fields. This makes the study and teaching of women within academic settings vulnerable to staffing and funding cutbacks, as well as attacks by neo-conservatives for being too 'politically correct'. Now post-structuralists maintain that feminist history has more to lose than gain in exempting itself from post-structuralism because contemporary intellectual culture has irretrievably lost faith in objective, knowable reality. They tell us to concentrate on *'how'* we know what we know, rather than *'what'* needs to be known and *'why'*, because that is in keeping with the demands of academic trendiness.

What feminist historians of women are offered instead is a return to invisibility and silence, but with the approval of our post-structural male colleagues. This price is too high to pay, at least in the United States, because thirty productive and successful years in the field of women's history do not deserve to be sacrificed on the unstable altar of post-structuralist relativism. The writing of women's history in any country almost always ends up threatening traditional patriarchal history with its criteria of power, prestige, and standard periodisation. Consequently, this attack on it by post-modern gender historians in the name of overturning false universal concepts of 'truth', has been unnecessary from the beginning.

This is not the first time that theories from Europe have disrupted certain American academic disciplines. In fact, this has happened so often, since World War II, that it is often said European theories come to the United States to die – meaning that they are not adopted across the Atlantic until they are on their way out abroad. Women's history will survive its predicted demise by post-modernism, despite the latter's current reign as the most destructive imported intellectual trend to hit the United States since the Second World War. The impact and implications of women's history have been too important and are too embedded in our hearts and minds to vanish when faced with the trendiness of yet another tired academic import.

From Morgan to MacCurtain:
Women Historians in Ireland from the 1790s to the 1990s
Mary O'Dowd[1]

A by-product of the expansion of research into the history of women over the past twenty-five years has been the development of a historiography of women historians. This literature has partly taken the form of a rediscovery exercise: who were the women historians of the past and what did they publish? But it has also been an exercise in intellectual history: identifying and categorising the interests of the women scholars and the genres in which they chose to write. For some, also, the investigation of women historians in the past has provided a base from which to launch a critique of the way in which history has been written without reference to women.[2]

The historiographical analysis which has emerged from these studies has given us a broad outline of the intellectual concerns of women historians in the western world, especially in England, France and the United States, from the medieval period to the twentieth century. The surprising point about this literature is the common themes and genres chosen by women when writing about the past. It is also clear that women historians' relations with the professional world of academic history writing have been problematic. The purpose of this study is to trace the history of women historians in Ireland and to assess if they shared the same interests as women historians elsewhere. A secondary aim of the article is to examine how the writings of the female scholars fitted into the wider story of the professionalisation of Irish historical studies which took place in the course of the nineteenth and twentieth centuries.

Publication of writing by women began in England and on the continent in the late seventeenth century and developed in Ireland in the eighteenth century. Poetry, novels and drama were the most popular genres used by women and writing about the past tended to be done through historical verse or novels. This was particularly the case in Ireland, where history was closely associated with politics and where it was rare for a woman to write explicitly on public affairs.[3] Women's awareness of the past, or at least their personal experience of it, might also be discerned in memoirs or journals which were occasionally published or written with publication in mind. The autobiography or memoir permitted its author to impose order and purpose on her personal past but, as the genre emerged in the eighteenth century, it was also influenced by other literary forms, particularly that of the novel. This is clearly evident in some of the most well-known memoirs by women in eighteenth-century Ireland, such as those by Laetitia Pilkington, Dorothea Herbert or Margaret Leeson.[4]

The political upheavals of the late eighteenth century led to an expansion in publications by women, and in Ireland this development coincided with the Gaelic literary revival which increased the popularity of research into the Irish past. Antiquarianism and archaeology became fashionable leisure occupations for men and women.[5] A small number of Irish women also undertook serious historical research. Charlotte Brooke, for example, learnt Irish and translated Gaelic poetry dating from the medieval period. Her *Reliques of Irish Poetry* included historical introductions to the poems as well as transcripts of some of them in Irish script.[6] Maria Edgeworth included antiquarian notes in the glossary to *Castle Rackrent* and demonstrated her awareness of the research being published by the *Transactions of the Royal Irish Academy* as well as an interest in Irish folklore.[7]

Another woman writer whose work was strongly influenced by the Gaelic revival was Sydney Owenson, Lady Morgan, whose historical novels drew on the research into the Irish past undertaken by antiquarians such as Charles O'Conor, Francis Walker and Sylvester O'Halloran. In many ways, indeed, Morgan's work served as an important popularising medium for communicating the work of the male scholars.[8] Morgan's novels also formed part of the propaganda war of the campaign for Catholic emancipation in the early nineteenth century, emphasising, as they did, the restrictions imposed on Irish Catholics by the penal legislation. Thus, indirectly, Morgan was not just commenting on history but was participating in the politics of her own time, although in several of the prefaces to her novels she was careful to deny that she was 'meddling in politics'.[9]

Edgeworth and Morgan were among the leading literary figures of their time and Brooke's scholarship was also recognised and praised, but all three, as women, were excluded from one of the most important intellectual developments of late eighteenth-century Ireland: the establishment of the Royal Irish Academy in 1782. In an event redolent of the relationship between women scholars and the male intellectual élite, Charlotte Brooke even failed to be considered as a suitable housekeeper in the Academy building. She ended her days in poverty.[10]

Apart from remaining on the periphery of the formal intellectual world, the writings of Brooke, Edgeworth and Morgan share a number of other characteristics which were to recur in the publications of Irish women writing about the past, and which they also had in common with women scholars in other countries. All three wrote in a number of different genres and approached history from a literary background. Their work was directed at a general rather than a specialised readership and, in the case of Morgan and to a certain extent Brooke, it presented in a popular form the less accessible research of male scholars. Brooke and Edgeworth also wrote a number of texts for children, a task which was to be increasingly considered a suitable literary pursuit for women.[11]

Towards the end of her life, Morgan added another theme to the history of women historians in Ireland. She initiated a major historical project on the history of women. She planned to write a multi-volume history of women from Biblical times to the early nineteenth century, but failing eyesight meant that only two volumes appeared. *Woman and her Master* is notable, however, as both the first history book and the first history of women to be published by an Irish woman.[12] It took the form of a collection of short biographies, which was a common format elsewhere for writing about the lives of women. Similar collections of 'women worthies' had appeared in England and on the continent and, as in Morgan's case, they were often written by women whose main literary output was in the form of novels.[13]

Woman and her Master focused on eminent women in the period before the end of the Roman empire and it was based on extensive reading in Biblical scholarship and ancient history. Although not directly concerned with contemporary issues, Morgan, as in her novels, made use of history to comment on women's status in early nineteenth-century Britain. The publication of *Woman and her Master* should be seen in the context of the public debate provoked by Mary Wollstonecraft's *Vindication of the Rights of Woman* which appeared in 1792. Morgan, like many of her contemporaries, disagreed with Wollstonecraft's emphasis on the equality of men and women, arguing instead that their characteristics were complementary rather than similar.[14] But Morgan supported Wollstone-craft's advocacy of better education for women and throughout *Woman and her Master* she emphasised places in ancient times where women had received a better education than was available to them in early nineteenth-century England.[15] A major theme in the book is the intellectual ability, and at times, the intellectual superiority of women. Morgan traced the cerebral strength of women back to Eve in the garden of Eden. Adam, according to Morgan, was the labourer in the garden while Eve was the thinker. Morgan defended Eve's succumbing to temptation as an intellectual decision arising out of Eve's sense of curiosity and desire for knowledge. Eve wanted, as Morgan put it, to 'be as are the Gods, knowing good from evil' and so, she chose to eat the apple while Adam, lacking intellectual curiosity, continued to labour in the garden in an unthinking fashion. Eve retained her mental alertness when she was thrust out of the garden and it became her principal legacy to womankind.[16] Apart from Eve, Morgan found other women in the Bible with similar mental energy and strength. The Queen of Sheba, she argued, was as wise as King Solomon and, while Jezebel's crimes were great, she was, according to Morgan, her husband's superior in deviousness and courage.[17]

Biographical studies by and about women continued to be popular throughout the nineteenth century. Among those who produced collections of lives on women in France and England were Anna Jameson and Julia Kavanagh, both of whom were born in Ireland although they spent most of their lives in England and on the continent.[18] The first collection of lives of Irish women appeared in 1877.[19] Its author, Elizabeth Owens Blackburne, like Sydney Morgan, Julia Kavanagh and other compilers of such collections, had established her literary reputation through the writing of novels but, she explained in her preface, the 'silent patriotism' of her life had been to 'preserve the names and achievements of some of the more gifted daughters of Erin'.[20] Despite its imitative style and the lack of formal historical training on the part of its author, the scholarly achievement of *Illustrious Irishwomen* should not be under-estimated. It was based on what Blackburne described as 'some years of reading' of manuscript sources in archives in Dublin and London. A valuable and remarkable aspect of Blackburne's biographies is her use of private papers from which she often quoted extensively, explaining in her note on sources that in 'every particular, where it has been at all practicable, original documents have been consulted'.[21] It is also worth nothing that, although Blackburne's purpose in researching and writing *Illustri-*

ous Irishwomen was patriotic, it was not narrowly nationalistic. She
included in her anthology women from very different political and
religious backgrounds and it is difficult to detect any strong political bias in any of her narratives.

Blackburne's volumes stimulated a series of similar publications
about Irish women. Many of these collections utilised Blackburne
as their principal source.[22] But in the early decades of the twentieth
century, biographies of Irish women had often a more narrowly
focused political or religious purpose and concentrated in particular on virtuous nationalist women. The supporting role offered by
wives, sisters and mothers of Irish rebel heroes was presented as a
role model which other Irish women were encouraged to imitate.[23]
Lives of Irish religious women, particularly founders of religious
orders, also began to be published for propaganda purposes.
Hagiographical in approach, biographies of women such as Mary
Aikenhead, Catherine Macaulay and Nano Nagle were intended
to document the actions of outstanding Irish Catholic women.[24]

Extolling the virtues of good nationalist and Catholic women
was combined in the writings of Helena Concannon who, in the
1920s and 1930s, published more books on the history of Irish
women than any previous (or indeed any subsequent) author.[25]
Although not based on archival research, Concannon searched a
wide range of printed sources for references to Irish women and
quoted extensively from them in her work. Her books are still a
useful starting point for research on women in early modern Ireland or women in religious orders in Ireland. The contemporary
significance of Concannon's work lay in its strong Catholic and
nationalist message. Maryann Valiulis has described the support
given by civil and ecclesiastical authorities in the Irish Free State to
the ideal of the republican mother. Concannon, in her writings,
provided historical and intellectual validity for this ideal. Eamon
de Valera recognised Concannon's contribution in the 1930s when
he nominated her for a seat in the Senate, and it is not unlikely that
Concannon's writings influenced de Valera's views on Irish
women and their role in society.[26] De Valera's support for Concannon thus integrated the biographical approach to Irish women's
history, initiated by Lady Morgan, into the national identity of the
Irish Free State.[27]

By the second half of the nineteenth century biography was,
therefore, not just established as a genre for writing about women
in the past but was especially popular among women writers. At
the same time the study of Irish history expanded, as archives were
opened to researchers; new sources were discovered and edited

and historical and archaeological societies were founded.[28] Women's participation in these developments was on the whole a peripheral one. They continued the popularising tradition established by Morgan and Brooke, but also took on auxiliary services, editing documents and acting as (often unacknowledged) assistants and researchers for their husbands. It was also frequently the women in a family who took responsibility for the preservation of the posthumous memory and documentary record of their male relatives, a task which combined the work of the biographer with that of document editor.

One of the first to attempt a synthesis of the new research into Irish history and antiquities was Mary Frances Cusack, who published *An Illustrated History of Ireland, 400-1800* in 1868. Like Morgan's work a generation earlier, Cusack's history was written to appeal to a wide audience. Based on secondary sources, it presented in a lucid and readable style the more scholarly but less accessible research of antiquarians, archaeologists and historians such as Eugene O'Curry, John O'Donovan, George Petrie, J. T. Gilbert and J. P. Prendergast. One of the most attractive features of the book was the illustrations of archaeological finds and objects which Cusack found in the museum of the Royal Irish Academy.[29] A strong supporter of Daniel O'Connell, Cusack's history conformed to the conservative nationalism of mid-nineteenth-century Ireland which O'Connell had popularised. While she emphasised the culture and civilisation of Gaelic society before the arrival of the Normans, she was reluctant to condone violent rebellion or to demonstrate any sympathy with Irish republicanism.[30] A member of a Catholic religious order when she wrote her history, Cusack was also concerned to trace the history of the church in Ireland and to praise the role of the Catholic clergy.[31]

Cusack also believed in the patriotic value of teaching Irish history in schools and was hopeful that her *Illustrated History* would be purchased for use in the new convent schools of mid-nineteenth-century Ireland. She produced an abbreviated version of her history for use as a textbook which seems to have been intended mainly for use in schools in England.[32] Thus through her popular form of writing and the publication of books for children, Cusack's history writing shared common characteristics with previous women writers, particularly Lady Morgan.

In the preface to the second edition of her *Illustrated History*, Cusack challenged 'those uneducated, or low-minded, even if educated persons, who consider that a woman cannot write history'. 'If women,' she asked, 'may excel as painters and sculptors, why may

not a woman attempt to excel as an historian?'[33] Yet Cusack was
unusual in mid-nineteenth-century Ireland for the high profile and
popularity of her historical writing. The public image of the historian was of a man of letters who combined scholarship with commentary on contemporary affairs, a role personified in Ireland by
the two most well-known historians of nineteenth-century Ireland,
J.A. Froude and W.E.H. Lecky. Women's role in this very public
form of scholarship was primarily a supportive one as editors of
documents for the male scholars or as unpaid research assistants.[34]

A significant editorial role was played by Mary Agnes Hickson
in one of the most well-known historical debates of late nineteenth-
century Ireland. The events in Ireland in the winter of 1641 had long
been a source of dispute, as historians and political commentators
analysed what actually happened in the events known as the
massacres of 1641. The historical arguments revolved around the
validity of the deposition evidence taken from Protestant settlers
in the aftermath of the rebellion. Selected extracts from the depositions were printed and reprinted many times in the course of the
seventeenth and eighteenth centuries, but the originals remained,
largely unexamined, in Trinity College, Dublin. In the 1880s Froude
and Lecky engaged in a well-publicised debate on the authenticity
of the depositions. But what is not always appreciated about the
debate is that neither Froude nor Lecky had looked at the original
depositions, nor had other historians who became involved in the
controversy.[35] In fact, the one person to systematically examine the
original manuscripts in the nineteeenth century was Mary Agnes
Hickson, who produced a two-volume edition of them in 1884. The
volume also included transcripts from and references to original
documents in the British Library, the Public Record Offices in
Dublin and London, the Bodleian Library, Oxford and non-depo-
sition records in Trinity College, as well as manuscript material
which Hickson found in her home region of County Kerry.[36] *Ireland
in the Seventeenth Century or the Massacres of 1641* also included a
lively introduction by Hickson, in which she took to task many of
the historians who had written about seventeenth-century Ireland
on the basis of secondary sources and had failed to consult the
original manuscripts.[37] J.A. Froude wrote a preface to the volume,
although Hickson went to some length publicly to distance herself
from identification with Froude's often polemical analysis of the
period and to indicate her admiration for Lecky's historical writing.[38] Despite Hickson's central role in the deposition controversy,
her contribution has often not been recognised in subsequent accounts of the debate.[39]

The historical research of other women also often remained unacknowledged or at least was subsumed under the names of their husbands. The publications of R.R. Madden on the United Irishmen were in fact the product of the joint research and collection of documentation by Madden and his wife, Harriet, who also 'corrected, revised, or transcribed' most of Madden's writing.[40] Rosa Mulholland, the wife of the prolific editor of documents, J. T. Gilbert, devoted fifteen years of her life to completing the *Calendars of Ancient Records of Dublin*, after her husband died. Although Mulholland's name appears as editor on ten of the seventeen calendars, the series is usually associated with Gilbert with no acknowledgment given to the contribution of Mulholland.[41]

Mulholland completed her husband's editorial work partly as a memorial to Gilbert. The cultivation and enhancement of the posthumous reputation of male relatives became, in the course of the nineteenth century, a significant aspect of women's contribution to historical research. These acts of family piety often involved the preservation of historical documentation and the editing of memoirs and other writings. They thus combined the older biographical tradition with the new nineteenth-century concern with documentary evidence. The widow of W.E.H. Lecky, Elisabeth, for example, wrote a memoir of her husband, edited a collection of his essays and left an endowment to Trinity College, Dublin to establish the Lecky Chair of History. She also presented her husband's books to the college library.[42] Rosa Mulholland and Mary Ferguson, the widow of James Ferguson, the first deputy keeper of the Irish Public Record Office, also wrote memoirs of their husbands which included, like that by Elisabeth Lecky, extensive extracts from their correspondence.[43]

Female relatives of other prominent historical and literary figures engaged in similar editorial work. Maria Edgeworth completed her father's autobiography, while Matilda Tone undertook, with her son, the editing of the correspondence and journal of her husband.[44] As Marianne Elliott has noted, the cult of Tone was in fact initially promoted by his widow.[45] Daniel O'Connell's daughter Ellen (Mrs Fitzsimons) began a memoir of her father; Mary O'Connell (Ellen's sister-in-law) compiled a history of the O'Connell family which included transcripts and extensive extracts from documents in the family archive, and the daughter of W. J. O'Neill Daunt, a friend and supporter of O'Connell, edited her father's journals posthumously.[46]

In a similar fashion, the wives, sisters and other women connected with the United Irishmen were interviewed by R.R. and

Harriet Madden in their research on the movement. Many of the women supplied the Maddens with family correspondence, personal memoirs and other reports and stories, much of which was subsequently published in *Lives of the United Irishmen*.[47] Madden's work remains a key source for information on the activities of the United Irishmen. In this sense, therefore, the women who responded to the Maddens' request for information have shaped the history of the United Irishmen as we know it today.

The contribution of women to the development of Irish history writing in the nineteenth century was, therefore, essentially an auxiliary one: synthesising and popularising historical research, editing texts, assisting male scholars and documenting the historical memoir of family members. A number of women such as Mary Frances Cusack and Rosa Mulholland also continued what seems to have been the increasingly lucrative market of writing books for children. It was not, however, until the beginning of the twentieth century that the writing and publishing of history books by women for a more adult audience became more common and consequently more central to the professionalisation of Irish history writing.

Two developments converged to account for the growth of women's interest in history. The Gaelic literary revival of the late nineteenth century created a new awareness of Irish literature and history, particularly of Irish society before the arrival of the English. Secondly, the improved facilities for the education of women meant that a significant number of women participated in the literary movement, writing fiction and verse but also taking an interest in antiquarianism, archaeology and history and in learning to write and speak Irish. They joined literary and historical societies and wrote and published on Irish history.[48] The admission of women into Irish universities from the 1880s onwards also led to women studying history at graduate level and acquiring positions within the academy.[49]

The writing of the women historians was central to the construction of the historical past on which the revival was based and of particular significance in this context was the work of Alice Stopford Green. In the first decades of the twentieth century, Stopford Green wrote a series of books which supported the literary movement's emphasis on the civilised and cultured nature of Irish society before it was debased by English influence. Stopford Green's interest in historical research was developed when she married J.R. Green, the author of *A Short History of the English People* (London, 1874). Like other wives of eminent historians, she assisted her husband with his research and after his death she revised and updated his publications.[50] Stopford Green also wrote two works on English medieval history before she began to research Irish history.[51] She thus brought to her Irish studies an approach and methodology developed in the context of English historiography. She shared her husband's concern to write about ordinary people rather than focusing on kings and statesmen and like him, she also believed in the social value of history as a means of creating a sense of pride in a people. She, accordingly, emphasised that history should be written in a popular and readable style. She made cheap copies of her Irish history books available in Ireland so that they could be read, as she put it, by the 'poor', and was gratified by the popularity of her books despite the critical appraisal which they received from a number of reviewers. Stopford Green believed that she was bringing 'about a new study of Irish history' by which she meant the history of people rather than of politicians and the utilisation of Gaelic literary material as historical sources.[52]

Reviewers accused Stopford Green of being too partisan, a view which has been echoed by many critics since.[53] Concentration on Stopford Green's nationalist bias overlooks, however, the new contribution which she made to the study of late medieval Irish society through her discovery of references to Irish merchants and trade in continental and English sources. It was not until the 1970s that her work in this area was extended and elaborated.[54] Stopford Green's willingness to defend and debate her work also drew attention to sources in the Irish language which had been ignored by political historians such as W.E.H. Lecky, Richard Bagwell and Robert Dunlop, who was one of the sternest critics of her work.[55]

Consistent with her belief in the social role of history, Stopford Green was, like Mary Frances Cusack, concerned with the educational role of history. She encouraged the development of history as a school subject in England and was, from its foundation in 1906, an active supporter of the Historical Association. She wrote for its journal, *History*, and served as its president from 1915-1918.[56] She also lectured and participated in discussions on the school history curriculum in England and wrote a series of booklets for use in Irish schools.[57]

In addition, Stopford Green's work continued the role of the woman historian as populariser of the work of the more scholarly but less readable research of male scholars. Eoin MacNeill, the early Irish historian, for example, recognised the value of her work in this regard and made his research available to her. She was also assisted in her writings by Celtic and Gaelic scholars such as Richard Best, Kuno Meyer and Douglas Hyde.[58]

Links and common themes can, therefore, be found between Alice Stopford Green's intellectual interests and activities and those of previous Irish women writers of the past. But Stopford Green also participated in the new developments in the Irish academic world of the late nineteenth and early twentieth centuries. She was an important patron and advocate of the introduction of rigorous scholarly standards to the study of early Irish history. She was involved in establishing a School of Irish Studies in Dublin, providing finance for visiting lecturers and funding travelling scholarships.[59] Stopford Green had a vision of the School as an international centre for Irish studies and wanted to 'attract and retain the interest of the world, and make Dublin the authoritative centre of all Irish studies'.[60] She also stressed that the School should employ 'first-rate men to direct that School in the best possible method', by which she meant the most up-to-date methodology in linguistic studies, then being developed by continental scholars.[61] Despite her friendship with Eoin MacNeill, Stopford Green disapproved of the suggestion that he be appointed to a Chair of Celtic Archaeology in University College, Dublin, arguing that 'for the present there should be no university professor who has not a European standing' in order to enhance the scholarly reputation of the college.[62] Nor did her support for Irish nationalism prevent her from defending the Royal Irish Academy against an attempt to replace it with a new National Academy for Ireland. Green argued that the Academy had an 'honourable tradition' in the 'study and investigation of Irish language, history and antiquities'.[63]

Another woman scholar who combined, like Stopford Green, a concern to popularise the historical and literary research of the Gaelic literary revival with an interest in fostering high scholarly standards, was Eleanor Hull. In 1926 Hull wrote a *History of Ireland and her People* (London and Dublin) which was intended for a general rather than a specialised readership. She also, like other women scholars, wrote a school textbook and a series of books for children.[64] But Hull, like Green, was also involved in the institutional development of the academic study of Irish history and literature. She was one of the founders of the Irish Texts Society which edited scholarly editions and translations of Irish historical and literary sources. She was secretary of the Society from its foundation to shortly before her death in 1935. During that time, the Society produced 29 volumes, the introductions to many of which acknowledge the editorial advice and assistance provided by Hull.[65] Partly through Hull's sponsorship, a number of other women Celtic scholars edited texts for the Irish Texts Society and served on its council.[66] Some later became involved in the institutional development of Celtic Studies and established a tradition of women scholars working in this field.[67] Thus indirectly, through Hull's efforts and the work of associations like the Irish Texts Society, the production of scholarly texts gained an academic status which it did not have in the nineteenth century, and women remained at the forefront of this activity into the twentieth century.

In England and other European countries, the improved educational facilities for women and the growth in awareness of women's status in society led to the development of research into the history of women. In England, for example, women scholars associated with the London School of Economics pioneered the development of economic and social history and this led some of them to focus on the history of women.[68] There was no equivalent development in Ireland, where the political situation to a large extent dictated the historical concerns of men and women. But it is noticeable that a number of Irish women historians with English (and particularly London) connections demonstrated an awareness of women's role in Gaelic society in their writings. Eleanor Hull, in particular, paid special attention to the role of women in Gaelic Ireland in her publications.[69] Another London-based Irish historian, Sophie Bryant, also highlighted the superior status of women in Gaelic society[70] and Alice Stopford Green, who, like Bryant, was associated with campaigns to improve educational facilities for women, also endorsed this view. Thus, English historiographical developments had a strong influence on interpretations of women's role in the Irish past. With the aid of women scholars such as Green, Hull and Bryant, the Gaelic literary revival created an image of a golden age for women in early medieval Ireland, which merged with the biographical approach of Helena Concannon to produce a powerful and enduring belief in the high status accorded to women in Irish society before it was destroyed by the establishment of English common law.[71]

Neither Stopford Green nor Hull attended university nor held academic positions, and in many ways their literary careers represent a transition period between the popularising and auxiliary role of women historians of the nineteenth century and the more scholarly and central position of women historians in the academy in the early years of the twentieth century. During their lifetimes, history was only slowly developed as a university subject in its own right. As indicated already, Elisabeth Lecky endowed the Lecky Chair of History in Trinity in 1907 and new chairs in history were also created in the constituent colleges of the newly formed Royal

University of Ireland established in 1908. A remarkable phenomenon of the development of history as an academic subject in Irish universities was the success of the first generation of Irish women graduates in acquiring academic posts in history. The first professor of modern Irish history at University College, Dublin was Mary Hayden, appointed in 1911;[72] the first professor of history in University College, Galway was Mary Donovan O'Sullivan, appointed in 1914;[73] and in Trinity College, Dublin, Constantia Maxwell was among the first generation of women graduates in history. She graduated with a first class degree and after a year spent in Bedford College, London, she was appointed assistant to the professor of history in Trinity in 1908 and became the first woman member of staff in Trinity. Maxwell was subsequently created a lecturer, then Professor of Economic History (becoming the first woman professor in the college) and in 1947 she was appointed to the Lecky Chair of History.[74] In Queen's University, Belfast, Maud Violet Clarke, a medievalist, held the chair of history temporarily from 1916 to 1919 when the holder of the chair, F.M. Powicke, was in the army.[75] In the 1920s and '30s, other women were appointed to academic posts in Irish history departments: in 1927 Síle Ní Chinnéide was appointed to a lectureship in history in University College, Galway with responsibility for lecturing in Irish;[76] and in the 1930s, Pauline Henley began to teach history in University College, Cork.

The low status of history in the academy and the small number of suitably qualified graduates in the new discipline may explain why women were academically so successful. History was not considered as prestigious a discipline as more well established subjects such as philosophy and the classics. The reluctance of the first Professor of Modern History in University College, Dublin, John Marcus O'Sullivan, to accept the chair in history instead of the chair in philosophy which he wanted is indicative of the low profile of history as an academic subject.[77]

The appointment of the women history professors, nonetheless, marked an important stage in the history of women historians in Ireland. No longer on the periphery, they were now not only at the centre of academic life but in a controlling position within it. The research activities and concerns of the women professors reflect their participation in the new university world of history, but also reveal their links and connections with previous generations of women historians.

The historical interests of Mary Donovan O'Sullivan and Constantia Maxwell were concentrated on economic and social history and had much in common with contemporary women academics in London and Cambridge with whom both had connections.[78] O'Sullivan wrote extensively on the history of Galway and published a history of the town in medieval and early modern times. In 1962 she completed a study of Italian merchant bankers in Ireland in the thirteenth century.[79] In addition, O'Sullivan, like some of her English contemporaries, was involved in the women's suffrage movement and this combined with her interest in social history led her to examine the role of women in Galway town.[80]

O'Sullivan also endeavoured to bridge the gap between history in the universities and history in the schools and the wider community. For much of her academic life, she was a committee member of the Galway Historical and Archaeological Society and served as secretary of the Society from 1932 to 1951. She was credited with inviting to the Society speakers of a 'high academic standing' whose lectures were open to the general public and appear to have been consciously presented in a popular style.[81] O'Sullivan also edited the journal of the Society for over twenty years and did much to establish the scholarly reputation which that journal still enjoys today.[82]

Constantia Maxwell's publications focused on the social history of eighteenth-century Ireland, although she also took an interest in eighteenth-century France. Her books were written in a popular and readable style and, as her obituary noted, she was 'probably the best known historian of her generation'.[83] Throughout her life Maxwell retained an interest in economic history. She taught a number of courses on it in Trinity and in 1939 she was given a personal chair in the subject. Maxwell spent much of her vacation time in London, where she established strong links with a number of women scholars; and in many ways Maxwell's historical writings are more clearly understood within an English historiographical context than an Irish one.[84]

Like other women historians, there was a strong pedagogic purpose to Maxwell's early publications. She was involved with the Historical Assocation and was clearly trying to provide for Irish history the kind of guides for students and teachers which the Association was producing for English history. She also wrote a school textbook which won approval from the Presbyterian Church as well as from the Department of Education in the Irish Free State in the 1920s.[85]

Mary Hayden, the first Professor of Modern Irish History at University College, Dublin, did not undertake any major research project. She spent a great deal of her academic life engaged in public campaigning for better conditions for women and in particular, for

improved facilities for women students and academics.[86] She wrote
a number of articles on women and childen in eighteenth-century
Ireland, but her most significant publication was a textbook of Irish
history which she co-authored with T.P. Noonan (Hayden in fact
wrote most of the book).[87] The merit of *A Short History of the Irish
People* was that it synthesised, in a more conservative nationalist
manner than the publications of Alice Stopford Green, the research
on Irish history which had been completed in the course of the
nineteenth and early twentieth centuries. Although based exclusively on secondary sources, the significance of Hayden's textbook
should not be under-estimated. It went through many editions and
was the mostly widely-used survey of Irish history in secondary
schools and universities from the time of its publication in the 1920s
until the late 1960s. It thus made a substantial contribution to the
shaping of several generations of Irish people's views and knowledge
of Irish history.

Despite their different interests and backgrounds, therefore, the
women history professors shared a common concern with teaching
and, in Maxwell's and Hayden's case, in writing texts for use by
students in schools and universities. All three were also concerned to
communicate the results of academic research to a wide audience.[88]

Thus, it might be suggested that, despite their positions in the
academy, the women history professors continued to fulfil the
traditional role of the women historian as synthesiser, populariser
and educator of the young. But the academic careers of all three
women history professors indicate that they also encouraged new
research and, in the case of Maxwell and O'Sullivan, were influenced by the work of contemporary women historians in England,
particularly in the field of economic and social history. All three
women professors appear to have also approved of the new developments in Irish history writing which took place in the 1930s.
O'Sullivan supervised a large number of research students in
Galway, while Hayden was very supportive of one of the leaders
of the new movement, R.W. Dudley Edwards. Maxwell, perhaps,
remained more aloof from developments in Irish historical research, but she nonetheless appreciated the work of her colleague,
T.W. Moody, in the institutional expansion of Irish history.[89]

Yet, although the women professors offered support for the new
developments in Irish history writing in the 1930s, their absence
from active involvement in the 'revolution in Irish history writing'
is also striking. In the new movement dedicated to 'the scientific
study of Irish history',[90] the historical writing of all three women
history professors was out of fashion and not in keeping with its

method or philosophy. Constantia Maxwell's history books were both readable and popular, but her failure to use primary source material and her self-proclaimed admiration for the Anglo-Irish landed gentry of the eighteenth century left her open to criticism from the reviewers in *Irish Historical Studies*, the flagship of the new form of history writing.[91] In her many book reviews in *Irish Historical Studies* and elsewhere, Mary Hayden refused to adhere to the new standards being set, and implicit in some of her reviews is her distaste for 'scientific' history.[92] Mary Donovan O'Sullivan's studies of the history of Galway were closer to the journal's methodology, but her book *Old Galway: the History of a Norman Colony in Ireland* (Cambridge, 1942) received a highly critical, and in many ways unfair, assessment from H. G. Richardson in *Irish Historical Studies*. In a review of almost six pages, Richardson criticised O'Sullivan's failure to consult medieval sources and made use of the review to demonstrate his superior knowledge of the history of medieval Galway. He paid scant attention to O'Sullivan's treatment of the Tudor period which he acknowledged formed the core of the book.[93]

In 1939 T.W. Moody was appointed to the Erasmus Smith Chair in History in Trinity College, Dublin, while in the same year Constantia Maxwell was awarded a personal Chair in Economic History in Trinity. Five years later, R. Dudley Edwards replaced Mary Hayden as Professor of Modern Irish History in University College, Dublin. With the academic appointments of Edwards and Moody, history in Ireland, with special emphasis on Irish history, became firmly centred in the academy. It is tempting, therefore, to view the succession of Hayden by Edwards and the appointment of Moody to the established chair in Trinity as the replacement of the history women by the history men. Edwards and Moody dominated the Irish history world for the next forty years. As history became a prestigious subject in Irish universities, women's involvement in the subject declined.

But if the methodology of the women history professors was found lacking by the criteria set by *Irish Historical Studies*, their pedagogic concerns conformed to the stated aim of the new journal, 'to be of service to the specialist, the teacher, and the general reader.' The editors hoped to combine in one journal 'what in England is distributed among several journals': *History*, the *Bulletin of the Institution of Historical Research* and *English Historical Review*.[94] Constantia Maxwell's work for the Historical Association would, therefore, have been within the remit of the new movement. A number of commentators have noted that the revolution in Irish history writing was slow to make an impact on public perceptions of Irish history or on its teaching in Irish schools,[95] but it might also be noted that, as a consequence, Hayden and Noonan's *A Short History of the Irish People* dominated the textbook market until the 1960s. It is intriguing to speculate if the book was in fact silently sanctioned by the two editors of *Irish Historical Studies* as a suitable textbook in Irish schools and universities, and particularly by Edwards, who had been a student of Hayden's. *A Short History* received the ultimate accolade from *Irish Historical Studies* when it was commended for its 'high degree of objectivity' in an obituary on Hayden in 1943, although regret was expressed that Hayden's treatment of the early 1920s in revised editions of the book revealed 'her strong personal feelings'.[96] As late as 1960, eighteen years after Hayden's death, *A Short History of the Irish People* was revised and edited by anonymous editors, although the substance of the volume was not changed. It remained recommended reading for history students in University College, Galway, University College, Dublin and Queen's University, Belfast until the 1960s.[97] Eleanor Hull's *A History of Ireland and her People* and Síle Ní Chinnéide's texbook in Irish, *Stair Euroip,* were also among the key texts recommended to Irish university students in the 1950s and 1960s, while Alice Stopford Green's work was listed as recommended reading by the Department of Education for schoolteachers during the same period.[98] Thus, it might be argued that the revolution in Irish history writing tacitly reinforced the tradition of women historians as textbook writers.[99]

Within the universities, the experiences of women historians in the middle decades of the twentieth century was a rather mixed one. The 1940s witnessed an increase in the enrolment of women graduate students in history, but the numbers declined sharply in the 1950s and '60s. In 1954 there were no women students enrolled for research in Irish history in Irish universities and in 1964 only five women graduates were registered.[100] At the same time a small number of women continued to be appointed to teaching posts in history departments including Maureen MacGeehin (later Wall), Miriam McDonnell (later Daly) and Margaret MacCurtain, all of whom worked in University College, Dublin.[101] In Trinity, Jocelyn Otway Ruthven replaced Margaret Griffith as lecturer in medieval history in 1939 and in 1951-2 Moody had as his assistant Clara Crawford, a doctoral student in medieval history. Dorothy Clarke was appointed to the history department in Queen's University, Belfast, in 1955.[102]

But with the exception of Otway Ruthven, who was appointed Lecky Professor in History in 1951, the academic status of women historians declined following the initial success of the first generation of women graduates.[103] As John A. Murphy has indicated in his history of University College, Cork, despite the formal admission of women students to Irish universities, academic life in the early and mid-twentieth century remained a male club, from many parts of which women were still excluded. The National University of Ireland had a marriage ban on non-statutory women staff which clearly had a detrimental effect on women's admission to the academy.[104] When Maureen MacGeehin married in the 1950s, she was asked by the college authorities in University College, Dublin to resign from her teaching position and, although she continued to lecture in history (through a redefinition of the official title of her post), she was not formally recognised as a member of the academic staff until the early 1960s and then at the lowest grade.[105] In over thirty years of distinguished service at U.C.D., Margaret MacCurtain never advanced beyond the grade of college lecturer.

The male control of the academy was mirrored in the historians' world in two other important ways. First, although a small number of women graduates continued to enrol for research, few were encouraged to continue their studies beyond master's level. Margaret MacCurtain was in fact the first woman graduate in University College, Dublin to complete a doctorate in history in 1963. The number of women doctoral students enrolled in other Irish universities from the late 1930s through to the late 1970s remained very low. The travelling studentship provided students from the National University of Ireland with the means to undertake doctoral research abroad, normally at an Oxbridge college and frequently at the University of Cambridge. The first woman to be awarded a travelling studentship in history was Katherine Walsh in 1968.[106] It is also worth noting that from the 1940s the history department at University College, Dublin established close ties with Peterhouse College in the University of Cambridge and sent some of its best graduate students to study there, a process which automatically excluded women because Peterhouse remained an all-male college until the late 1980s. In Trinity College, Dublin and Queen's University, Belfast, more students completed Ph.D.s in their home universities than in the National University system and this led to a slightly higher number of women registering in these universities for doctoral research in history. It may not be coincidental, however, that neither of the two most successful women historians to be employed in Trinity in the middle decades of the twentieth century completed doctoral degrees in the college.[107] In the 1950s and 1960s, it seems that women history graduates were not being trained for academic positions in the same way as their male counterparts.

The second means by which the general exclusion of women from public life was reflected in the world of Irish historians can be seen in the structural organisation of Irish history. *Irish Historical Studies* was officially published by two societies, the Irish Historical Society and the Ulster Society for Irish Historical Studies. Committee members of both societies formed the editorial board of the journal. The Irish Committee of Historical Sciences, affiliated to the International Committee of Historical Sciences, was also composed primarily from the committees of both societies, with additional members co-opted at the biannual meeting of the Committee. All three groups were slow to admit women to their ranks. It was not until 1973 that the Irish Committee of Historical Sciences had its first woman committee member, Miriam Daly, representing the Ulster Society for Irish Historical Studies, and it was to be another sixteen years before women committee members became a more regular phenomenon.[108] Other institutional developments in Irish history, such as the *Studies in Irish History* series and the Conference of Irish Historians, which were sponsored by the Irish Committee of Historical Sciences, were also slow to admit women.[109]

From the early 1970s the number of students enrolling in Irish universities dramatically increased and concurrently, there was a rise in the number of women students undertaking graduate research in history at doctoral and master's level. Since then, a succession of Irish women historians have completed Ph.D.s in English and Irish universities. Trained in the methodology of *Irish Historical Studies*, the approach of the women graduates is now virtually indistinguishable from that of their male peers. Less dramatic has been the growth in the numbers of full-time academic staff and consequently women historians still form a tiny minority of staff employed in history departments in Irish universities and, for most, promotion within their profession has remained elusive.

Thus despite the initial academic success of the first generation of women history graduates, women's contribution to the revolution in Irish history has been limited. In the middle decades of the twentieth century, Margaret MacCurtain was one of only a small number of women who were accepted into the academic world of Irish historians. Coincidentally or not, the advance of the scientific study of Irish history led to a decline in the status of women historians in the academy.

In conclusion, the research interests of women historians in Ireland since the eighteenth century not only had much in common with women historians elsewhere, but were often consciously developed in the context of intellectual developments which had their origins outside of Ireland. The biographical collections of Irish women's lives were imitative of similar collections published in England, France and the United States. Their authors, in Ireland and elsewhere, were primarily concerned with literature and often viewed their biographical narratives as another form of novel writing.

During the period of the professionalisation of Irish history writing in the second half of the nineteenth century, women in Ireland, as elsewhere, chose or were allocated an auxiliary if not a peripheral role. They edited documents, assisted their male relatives' research and popularised their research through the writing of general surveys or historical novels. The writing of Emily Lawless encapsulates the role of the woman writer of history in the nineteenth century. She wrote a number of historical novels, a general survey of Irish history and edited a text based largely on documents. She consulted Lecky on historical details, acknowledging her debt to his research but also pointing to her interest in dramatising history in a way of which she knew Lecky would not approve.[110] Bonnie Smith has argued that the familial nature of historical research in the nineteenth century allowed women access to historical writing, which the development of university departments was to destroy. This may be true, but public acknowledgement of women's contribution to historical research was often obscured by their male relatives' claims to sole authorship.[111]

In the late nineteenth century, women began to make a contribution to the writing of Irish history in their own right. They succeeded in having books published and in securing positions within the academy. The early progress of the women academics was not, however, continued in subsequent decades. Nor were the research interests of the women history professors in economic and social history developed, as the primacy of writing the political history of the new state dominated Irish historical studies. In the revolution in Irish history writing, the women were tacitly or otherwise allocated what Carolyn Steedman has called the 'mothering' role of writing school textbooks.[112]

Margaret MacCurtain retired from her academic post in the history department in University College, Dublin in 1994, just over a century and a half after Sydney Owenson, Lady Morgan, wrote the first history of women by an Irish woman and over two centuries after Charlotte Brooke became the first Irish woman to publish her historical research. MacCurtain's career reflects many of the problems which women historians in Ireland have encountered over that period, but it also demonstrates the positive contribution which women academics bring to academic life. MacCurtain's legendary popularity as a teacher and supporter of students links her to the previous generation of women academics. Her writings and publications on sixteenth- and seventeenth-century Ireland and her involvement in the development of settlement studies as well as women's history places her in a leading role within the Irish historical community of the last quarter of the twentieth century and demonstrates the progress which women historians have made. In addition, MacCurtain was responsible, jointly with Mary Cullen, for one of the most significant developments in the history of women historians in Ireland: the formation of the Irish Association for Research in Women's History in 1988. Although founded to foster research into women's history in Ireland, a valuable by-product of the activities of the I.A.R.W.H. is that it has established for the first time regular contact between women historians in Ireland. It has also, through its affiliation to the International Federation for Research in Women's History, encouraged much fruitful discussion of the history of women in Ireland within an international context. Thanks in particular to the efforts of Margaret MacCurtain, research in Irish women's history is now one of the most exciting fields of research in Irish history and is now making a substantial contribution to what is perceived as mainstream history – not an insignificant development after two hundred years!

The Use of Continental Sources of Women's Religious Congregations & the Writing of Religious Biography:
Madeleine Sophie Barat, 1779–1865
Phil Kilroy

The subject of this essay is Madeleine Sophie Barat (1779-1865), a Frenchwoman who founded the Society of the Sacred Heart in 1800, established schools in Europe and the Americas and soon after her death was canonised by the Roman Catholic Church.[1] Numerous biographies of Madeleine Sophie Barat have been written, either in preparation for the canonisation or in celebration of the event, and have carefully created the image of Barat which conformed to the expectations of the authorities examining her life, her writings and her work. The outcome was successful and Madeleine Sophie Barat was admitted to the honours list of the Church, awarded first the title of Venerable in 1879, then Blessed in 1908 and finally Saint in 1925.

The task of a new biographer of Madeleine Sophie Barat is one of deconstruction, of consciously stepping out of the context of Madeleine Sophie's beatification/canonisation process and retrieving, even rescuing, her from that constriction. This task is made easier due to the quality of the archival material available. Fortunately this is vast, accessible and well organised. Hopefully, the outcome of a new biographical study is a discovery of other aspects or dimensions of her life, within the personal domain as well as within the public sphere, which present this woman in new ways. So much of her life remained invisible or unknown because of the context and parameters of her time and culture. Thus, as well as retrieving Madeleine Sophie as a person in her own right, this essay may provide clues to the value which archives of an international religious congregation of women may have for the general reading public and why at this moment they can be of interest to historians, particularly as part of the process of retrieving women's history.

Within the Roman Catholic tradition, the process of canonisation is a structure created over several centuries which (if the process succeeds) confirms the saintliness of the person under examination.[2] Criteria have been established by Church authorities and holiness is defined according to patriarchal ground rules and perceptions. Within these confines the life of the prospective saint is written, employing a genre of hagiography whereby the person is presented as ready for sainthood either from birth or from a moment of deep personal conversion. The historical material concerning the person is all interpreted according to the purpose in hand: canonisation. Removed from the constrictions both of the canonisation process and the presentation of the person in hagiography, the historical material assumes a quite different value and purpose, and indeed it is placed in a much wider, broader context. This new exercise of biography becomes a genre of re-telling, or perhaps telling for the first time, the story of a life. In the nineteenth century, Madeleine Sophie Barat was evaluated by Roman Catholic Church authorities, by the Society of the Sacred Heart itself, and by her own contemporaries, within the perspectives of their day. In our time, in a different context and within a different consciousness, she can be studied anew and in a sense on her own terms, rather than as a subject for canonisation, which in turn was part of a political process designed to confirm the future of the congregation, the Society of the Sacred Heart, after her death in 1865.

There is no doubt in any case that Barat had made her mark as a woman religious, involved in the education of girls. Indeed her achievement was great by any standards. By the time of her death there were 3539 members of the congregation, with 89 houses in Europe, the Americas, Canada and north Africa. There were 5643 students in boarding schools, 6413 students in poor schools and 437 orphans.[3] Between 1800 and 1865 Barat had negotiated the foundation, development and expansion of communities of women dedicated to a common vocation within the Christian tradition of the Roman Catholic Church; schools for the wealthy and middle classes; schools for the poor, for orphans and for the deaf; and spiritual retreats for women. Inevitably these works brought Madeleine Sophie into close contact with ecclesiastical structures and Church figures in France, Rome and elsewhere, encountering particularly the tensions within and between Gallicanism and Ultramontanism. The ancient independence of the French Church had not been eroded by the French Revolution, and when the Roman Church intensified its claims to authority and jurisdiction in France, especially in the 1830s and 1840s, the Gallican tradition resisted such tendencies.[4]

Whether we evaluate her achievements as an educator, as a leader, as a woman of her time and within her time, as a negotiator with Church and State figures, or as a religious figure in nineteenth-century France the breadth of her legacy draws our attention. And all these levels need to be examined if we are to perceive her as fully as possible, without the slant and bias which come from beatification/canonisation processes and from hagiography. Up until recently very little critical work has been done on women such as Madeleine Sophie Barat and they remain shadowy figures, lost in the mists of sanctity as defined in the nineteenth century.

Such a many-sided study requires adequate documentation and fortunately this is available. The archive on Madeleine Sophie Barat is extensive and well preserved, both within the congregation and within several libraries in France and Italy. The largest holding of manuscript material on Madeleine Sophie Barat is preserved in the General Archives of the Society of the Sacred Heart in Rome.[5] These archives were completely re-catalogued fifteen years ago, according to a system devised by a French archivist, Charles Molette, which facilitated the collation of very disparate historical material held by 400 congregations of religious women in France.[6] The Roman archives of the Society of the Sacred Heart contains records not only of Madeleine Sophie Barat, but also of women from all over Europe (from 1760), and from the Americas (from 1818). As such they are of interest not just to researchers on Madeleine Sophie Barat but to those who wish to study the growth of education for women, as well as the wider social, cultural and political developments of the time. This archive contains at least 14,000 original letters of Madeleine Sophie Barat, well preserved and easily accessible. Some years ago printed transcripts were made of these letters and bound into 68 volumes. While these volumes do not pretend to be scholarly, critical editions, they are extremely useful to researchers, particularly since they can be easily checked with the originals. Jeanne de Charry is in the process of editing the letters between Madeleine Sophie Barat and Philippine Duchesne, 1805-1852, in four volumes. This is scholarly and critical work, and justly acclaimed so; the indexes and footnotes alone are a mine of information and provide many keys to the other letters in the major collection.[7]

The letters of Madeleine Sophie Barat are a mixture of personal correspondence and correspondence of a formal, administrative type. Most letters contain both elements and are a clue to her mode

of communication and government, as well as being an insight into
her own personality. To evaluate them, within the context of the
private and public life of the writer, demands detailed knowledge
of the political, social and economic developments in France and
Italy as well as within the Americas in the nineteenth century. It
also requires knowledge of the theological currents of the day, of
the spirituality of the period and how this was lived out in the lives
of religious women. In particular it is necessary to explore the
religious trends in France, before and after the French Revolution,
as well as the impact of the counter-revolutionary spirit in early
nineteenth-century France. A knowledge of the history of education in France, in Europe and in the Americas is essential for any
understanding of the contribution made by Madeleine Sophie
Barat in the field of education. In addition, it is important to
understand the social and cultural life of the day, and to situate
Madeleine Sophie Barat in this context, particularly since two
classes of religious were admitted into the Society: those who were
destined to teach, termed choir religious, and those who were
destined to do domestic and manual work in the schools and
communities, termed converse or co-adjutrix religious. Throughout her life, Madeleine Sophie tried to maintain a balance in numbers between the two types of religious within the congregation
and within each community. It is important to recognise that each
group exercised power, both in the public and private life of the
congregation, in different ways. Both experienced tensions, and
sometimes these erupted within communities or in the schools,
especially when Philippine Duchesne brought the congregation to
America in 1818. However, Madeleine Sophie maintained this
distinct system which mirrored French society in general at this
period and was part of the structure of religious life prior to the
French Revolution. In any case, she was no revolutionary, and she
did not see the need to change the social constructs of society. Like
so many of her contemporaries, she lamented the excesses of the
Revolution and the loss of old certainties.

Madeleine Sophie Barat was therefore a woman of tradition,
neither original or innovative in her thinking. Her instinct was to
preserve, conserve, restore. Yet within this context and within the
ecclesiastical and political constructions of the day (which she
readily accepted), Madeleine Sophie Barat established her own
leadership and created new possibilities for women which ultimately generated change within those ecclesiastical and political
structures. Indeed, while she lived willingly within the structures
of Church and society, her colleagues, members of the clergy and

of the broader society, recognised her as a woman of immense charm and determination, often quite autocratic and capable of acting independently while mouthing conformity. While she lived in Rome, she was considered Gallican, and when in Paris, Ultramontane. Nevertheless, despite the vast amount of material available on Madeleine Sophie Barat, especially the large number of letters which have survived, she remains a distant figure, reticent and even reluctant to be seen. She rarely speaks directly about herself and is often cryptic when she does so.

The General Archives in Rome contain extensive material pertinent to all these themes and aspects of the life of Madeleine Sophie Barat: her origins in Joigny, in the department of Yonne (the most Jansenistic region of France); her family and childhood experiences; her early years in Paris, at the height of the French Revolution, 1795-1800; her relationship with her brother, Louis Barat, both in Joigny and Paris; the influence of Paris, where she lived most of her life; and the gradual assumption of leadership of a small group of women.

Furthermore, there are extensive archives on key questions: the houses, communities and schools founded by Madeleine Sophie Barat during her lifetime (these extended to France, Belgium, Italy, Austria, Poland, Germany, Ireland, England, Spain, America, Latin America, Canada and north Africa); her negotiations with the governments of the day, especially in France and Italy; her negotiations with the Roman Catholic Church, with popes, bishops and clergy; her relationship with the communities, with the students and with the families of the members of the congregation. Moreover, the development of a curriculum and of plans of studies for the schools are preserved in several editions, as well as school journals for each house established. Each house and community has records of its history, especially its foundation, as well as its own journal, letters and accounts. Inevitably, there were legal cases involving property, family rights, inheritances as well as the personal grievances of those members who left the congregation. All this material provides insight regarding Madeleine Sophie, especially her manner of governing, her educative vision, her dealing with financial problems and the legal niceties involved.

As the membership of the congregation which she established increased, the instinct to record its history grew and there are several contemporary histories of the Society.[8] Short biographies of members were written on their deaths and these contain useful information, though by their nature they tend to be eulatory and rather general in comment. Far more useful to the historian are the

notes on individuals sent by members and which were later used
to compose the obituaries. These notes are preserved in the General
Archives. From 1806, the minutes of the general meetings of the
congregation were kept and these record the administrative life of
the Society during the lifetime of Madeleine Sophie. Two general
council meetings stand out as crucial for Madeleine Sophie Barat,
that of 1815 and that of 1839. The material on these general council
meetings is extensive and they show both the size and rapidity of
the congregation's growth in the early nineteenth century, as well
as the gradual adoption of organisational methods of government
to deal with these realities.

In addition to her letters, Madeleine Sophie also wrote circular
letters to the communities, which were printed in two volumes
after her death. She gave conferences regularly and these were
written up from her notes and the notes of those who heard her
speak.[9] Those who governed with her, assisting her in her work,
have extensive archives also and this material provides insight into
how contemporaries within the congregation viewed Madeleine
Sophie Barat. Among those who worked closely with Madeleine
Sophie was Adèle Cahier, who was employed as her Secretary
General (1843-65). It is due to the industry and archival skills of
Adèle Cahier that the General Archives in Rome are so extensive
and well preserved. On the death of Madeleine Sophie and in
preparation for the beatification/canonisation process, Adèle Cahier centralised all the letters of Madeleine Sophie and created a
detailed catalogue of them which is still invaluable. In addition she
recorded in a series of small exercise books, working from the
letters preserved, exactly where Madeleine Sophie was at any
given time from 1800 to 1865.[10] Adèle Cahier was a meticulous
recorder of events, particularly of the 1839-1851 period in the
history of the congregation which was critical for its growth and
which certainly moulded Madeleine Sophie's own views and outlook. Adèle Cahier records every point of view, commenting only
in the margins that the reader must read all the documentation
before passing judgement. It is no exaggeration to say that her hand
rests over the bulk of the archival material, yet it is restrained and
respectful of the reader.

Finally, there are extensive records of the process of beatification
and canonisation, which began in 1872 and ended in 1925.[11] The
most important stage, of course, was at the beginning when memories were still alive and personal. However, bearing in mind the
purpose behind the examination of the life and the writings of
Madeleine Sophie Barat, it is clear that these records are of limited

value. Yet the integrity of the witnesses demands our respect, for their depositions were made under oath of secrecy which could only be relieved by papal dispensation. This responsibility was taken seriously and many found it a burden and strain. On the other hand, the criticisms and queries (known as the work of the 'devil's advocate' and called the *animadversiones*) which followed the depositions of the witnesses contain some insight into Madeleine Sophie herself and into the views of her critics. Thus while there are valuable insights to be gleaned from this body of material, especially when the life and context of the deponents are known, it is to be read with caution and reserve.

The material held in the General Archives, Rome is complemented by the holdings in the archives of the French Province of the Society of the Sacred Heart at Poitiers.[12] This archive contains further, detailed accounts of the communities and schools established during the life of Madeleine Sophie and these are indispensable for any study on Madeleine Sophie Barat. However, any documentation dealing directly with Madeleine Sophie, or any of her correspondence, is retained in Rome. The archives in Poitiers are well catalogued and accessible and in the main follow the system of Charles Molette.

These two archives in Rome and Poitiers contain the major resources within the congregation for a study of the life of Madeleine Sophie Barat. However, documentation on Madeleine Sophie and the Society of the Sacred Heart in nineteenth-century France is substantial within libraries and archives in France and in Rome. The National Archives of France contain extensive dossiers on religious communities in nineteenth-century France. These can be discovered by consulting documents on religious congregations during critical political periods in nineteenth-century France, as well as during the several crises in the field of education at this time. Within these collections there are dossiers on the houses and schools of the Society of the Sacred Heart founded in France during the lifetime of Madeleine Sophie. In addition, when the religious communities were expelled from France by the law of 10 July 1904, the acts of expropriation often contain histories and legal documentation pertaining to the houses, schools and indeed to Madeleine Sophie herself. Further documentation is contained in the responses of the French bishops to the several governments of the day commenting on religious communities who resisted inspection, including the Society of the Sacred Heart. Finally, the National Archives of France contain material on the department of the

Yonne, and these are completed by the departmental archives held in Auxerre.[13]

While the archives of the archbishop of Paris contain a limited amount of material under the name of Madeleine Sophie Barat, the archive of Archbishop de Quelen (1778-1839) contains extensive dossiers on the Rue de Varenne, founded in 1820 by Madeleine Sophie Barat and where she lived for prolonged periods of her life. This archive is well documented and accessible, and it pertains to Paris only. The archive of Archbishop Affre (1793-1848) contains further, but much less, material on the Society of the Sacred Heart in Paris. The archives of the Jesuits in France are held in Vanves, in the suburbs of Paris, and they contain two dossiers which are directly concerned with Madeleine Sophie, that of her brother, Louis Barat (1768-1845), and of her friend and guide, Joseph Varin (1768-1850); both men became Jesuits when the order was restored in France after the Revolution.

The archives of the Ministry of Foreign Affairs in Paris contains material on the foundation in Rome of the Trinité des Monts, a French foundation which Madeleine Sophie undertook at the request of Pope Gregory XVI and King Charles X. Dossiers on this and on the affairs of the Society of the Sacred Heart in Rome are extensive and indicate the level in society at which Madeleine Sophie operated. This is clearly brought out in the correspondence between the French Ambassador to the Holy See and the Minister of Religion in Paris, between 1839 and 1843. Comments exchanged on Madeleine Sophie herself and on her mode of government are enlightening and show how she was judged outside of her inner circle.[14] The National Library of France contains printed material on the Society, as well as many of the manuals of instruction written and used by the congregation in the nineteenth century. Most of these are duplicates of works held in the General Archives, Rome and in the archives of the French province in Poitiers. Obviously, the vast amount of material in the National Library is essential for any research on the life of a Frenchwomen.

Finally, the Historical Library of the City of Paris holds useful material on the Rue de Varenne and on the de Gramont family. This family, with its several branches, traced its origins to the early middle ages in France, belonged to the nobility and suffered greatly during the French Revolution. Three of the de Gramont family entered the Society, two sisters and then their mother. One of them, Eugénie de Gramont, was a close friend of Madeleine Sophie until her death in 1846. In all, some 1024 letters of Madeleine Sophie to Eugénie de Gramont, and just twenty-five of Eugénie de Gramont to Madeleine Sophie, exist and are central to tracking a relationship which was sorely tested at the two most critical periods in the life of Madeleine Sophie, 1812-1815 and 1839-45. In addition to these letters, the private papers of the de Gramont family are accessible in the National Archives of France in Paris.[15]

In Rome, the Vatican Archives contain material on the Society of the Sacred Heart and specifically on Madeleine Sophie herself for the period 1837-1850. Over fifty manuscript documents exist and these were used extensively during the process for beatification/canonisation. Some of Madeleine Sophie's letters are included in the dossier, but most of the material consists of letters and documents exchanged between Cardinal Lambruschini, Secretary of State in the Vatican and the Inter-Nuncio in Paris, Monseigneur Garibaldi, with a few from Archbishop Mathieu of Besançon and from Cardinal Pedicini, Cardinal Protector of the congregation.[16] Like the documents in the Ministry of Foreign Affairs in Paris, these papers in the Vatican Archives are a commentary on Madeleine Sophie herself and on the several crises which she handled during the period in question. They deal in particular with the period 1841-1843 when the congregation seemed to be heading towards destruction, deeply enmeshed in the polarities of Gallicanism and Ultramontanism at the level of both Church and government in France.

Two other archives located in the Vatican City contain material on Madeleine Sophie Barat. One is the Congregation for Saints, which has some of the printed and hand-written versions of the beatification/canonisation process and some miscellaneous documents which are of interest. The other is the Congregation for Religious where there are documents on the history of the congregation during the lifetime of Madeleine Sophie, as well as detailed documentation on several crises which she handled, especially between 1837 and 1851.

The archives of the French Ambassador to the Holy See, held in Rome, contain several key documents on the Society of the Sacred Heart and this material is the other side of the correspondence held in the archives of the Department of Foreign Affairs in Paris.[17] It also contains documents pertaining to the foundation and development of the Trinité des Monts, established in 1829, with some original letters of Madeleine Sophie Barat. The archives of both the Roman houses of the Society of the Sacred Heart, the Trinité des Monts and the Villa Lante, contain material which is pertinent both to Madeleine Sophie and to the growth of the Society of the Sacred Heart in Italy.[18] Finally, the General Archives of the Jesuits in Rome have a significant dossier on the Society of the Sacred Heart and on Madeleine Sophie herself. Some years ago, many of the documents pertaining to the Society of the Sacred Heart were gathered into one collection and so are easy to locate and provide clues to other material in the archive itself, as well as complementing the extensive dossiers on the Jesuits in the General Archives of the Society of the Sacred Heart in Rome.

These then are the resources available for a biography of Madeleine Sophie Barat. Many biographies have already been written, in several languages. While most of them are based partially on the material printed internally by the congregation, all have relied basically on two sources: the life by Adèle Cahier written immediately after the death of Madeleine Sophie but not published until 1884;[19] and the life written by Louis Baunard and published in 1876 specifically for the beatification process which was initiated in 1872.[20]

For the writing of her book, Adèle Cahier relied entirely on the documents to which she had complete access, both in her capacity as Assistant General and as the former Secretary General of the Society for 22 years. It was ready to go to press when it became clear that it would be politically incorrect for a member of the Society to publish a life of Madeleine Sophie Barat at a time when the process of beatification was about to begin. The choice of an outside biographer became necessary in view of this situation and a young priest, Louis Baunard, a doctor in theology and in literature, was asked to undertake the biography in view of the process. Cahier had already spent at least three years writing her text and many more amassing the material needed both for the biography and for the beatification process.

Thus the work of Adèle Cahier was sacrificed to the extent that the leadership in the Society chose to appoint Louis Baunard as the official biographer of Madeleine Sophie and asked Adèle Cahier to hand over her material to him. This cost her greatly and she did it most reluctantly, since she did not trust his integrity as a historian. It is clear that she felt a sense of violation, of piracy over the way her work was absorbed into the study of Baunard. She clashed again and again with her colleagues and continually represented her misgivings.[21] When the two-volume life of Madeleine Sophie was published by Louis Baunard in 1876, Adèle Cahier was vindicated to the extent that she saw his errors in print. For her own professional satisfaction and integrity she recorded them in detail and deposited these papers in the General Archives.[22] Even though she was basically ignored at the time, since the process with Rome was considered the most essential task in hand, Adèle Cahier was greatly heartened when a historian in Germany refused to translate the work of Baunard because of its inaccuracies. Nevertheless, Baunard's work became the best known and standard life of Madeleine Sophie for many decades. It was reprinted several times and translated into many languages, while Adèle Cahier's life remained less well known in the Society and scarcely known outside the congregation.

It is clear that there is extensive material for a biography of Madeleine Sophie Barat. The quality of the primary sources and their accessibility in France and Italy makes the task of the researcher both heartening and daunting. Madeleine Sophie lived to a good age and she had an exceptionally long period in leadership, 1800-1865. There are so many approaches and contexts within which to study this woman, for biography sets out to tell the story of a human life, of its beginnings, it development, its flowering and expression, its pain and sorrow, its successes and failures, its gradual moving into maturity and death, its legacy and memory. This story has already been told, officially, for the purpose of canonisation. Basically it was an examination of a life to see if it conformed to pre-set criteria, established exclusively by men, and this was generally accepted in this period as both correct and true and entirely valid. Our consciousness is different today and we seek other ways to discover the truth of another human being: simply by writing their story as closely as we can with their own voice. So another story of Madeleine Sophie has to be written, as far as possible by herself, through the extensive amount of material she left behind in the form of letters and records.

But no one is neutral and, while the historical records are respected in their integrity, biographers can only think, select and write out of the age in which they live themselves, with its particular accent and consciousness, especially in the field of historical research. At present there is great interest and development in the art of women's biography, of examining a woman's life on its own terms, with all that implies of women's experience both defined and judged within a male-dominated world. For if Madeleine Sophie Barat had to run the gauntlet of established criteria in order to pass the test of sanctity with the Roman Catholic Church tradition, her experience is not very different from other women whose greatness or otherwise has been evaluated by male standards and norms, as firmly set down as any beatification/canonisation process.

In 1939 the central council of the Society of the Sacred Heart commissioned a new, critical biography of Madeleine Sophie

Barat.[23] This will appear in the year 2000 to celebrate the bicenten-
ary of the Society. Only time will tell if this new story of Madeleine
Sophie will be substantially different from the old one which has
been told and re-told over many years. Will there be a very big
difference, or indeed a split, between the public and private
woman, and did these ever come together, and if so what enabled
this to happen? How did she establish her identity? Was she
content and fulfilled in her work? Did it ever become easy? Did she
value what she achieved and was it worth all the pain and effort?
Did she own it and acknowledge her part in it? How did she value
her relationships? How did she deal with her feeling world? Why
did she talk so much about her health? What did she believe in?
What motivated/energised her? All these questions and more may
become clearer as the biographer re-reads her life, consciously
removed from the previous constrictions enshrined in hagiography. In December 1871, Adèle Cahier wrote to tell a friend how her
book on Madeleine Sophie was developing. She expressed concern
as to how much to include in the text, especially since it was such
a short time since the death of Madeleine Sophie. She also felt
constrained by the beatification process and concluded that she
must preserve all the material and await the time and circumstances when the full story could be told.[24] In some strange way
she must have sensed that it would be another time, another day,
beyond her lifetime.

A Natural Tenderness:
The Ideal & the Reality of Eighteenth-Century Female Philanthropy
Rosemary Raughter

An anonymous author, commenting in 1795 on the upsurge in philanthropic activity which characterised the final decades of the eighteenth century, made particular mention of the involvement of 'some excellent women' in a range of contemporary initiatives. Institutions such as the Leeson Street Magdalen Asylum, the Female Orphan House and the Bethesda Lock Penitentiary had, he noted, been singled out by 'some good ladies of rank and fortune ... as the peculiar object of female protection, and therefore worthy to receive the first fruits of their charity'.[1] Another observer, writing a few years later, similarly recognised women's prominence in charitable effort, remarking that

> In Ireland there are numerous occasions which call for the exercise of benevolence, and by the female part of society these opportunities are never neglected ... This disposition is a conspicuous trait in the female character in that country; and when I add that the ladies are benevolent, it must be understood in its more enlarged sense, including all those acts which are the result of humanity and charity united.[2]

Women's involvement in philanthropy was not, of course, novel to the eighteenth century. Charity, as a central tenet of the teaching of all Christian confessions, and as an aspect of women's role within the home and the community, was already a well-recognised element of the female sphere of activity, and throughout the century women of all social classes continued to address themselves privately and informally to the relief of distress within their own immediate locality. However, women's benevolence did during this period assume a new dimension, with the growing importance after mid-century of associated and institutional philanthropy. The female contribution to this process was at least equal to that of men, as women involved themselves at all levels in a wide range of philanthropic organisations. From the first, however, charitable women claimed for themselves certain specific areas of endeavour, which, while they accorded with accepted views of the female role and nature, also offered a significant, if largely covert, challenge to those views. This essay will examine the ideal and reality of the female charitable role in relation to women's involvement in institutional philanthropy. It will consider the extent to which cultural prescriptions of womanhood shaped that philanthropy, the qualities and concerns which women themselves brought to it and the implications which women's involvement in organised charity had for their place within society.

Demographic expansion, it has been said, 'is the basic fact of the eighteenth-century Irish experience',[3] and the doubling of the population which occurred between 1700 and 1800, concentrated as it was in the poorest labouring class, could not fail to have damaging implications for the prosperity and living standards of the least affluent sectors of the community. Increased pressure on land and rural under-employment combined with periodic agricultural crises and, later, the decline in domestic industry, to intensify poverty in the countryside. The influx of poor into rapidly growing urban centres, such as Dublin, Cork and Belfast, aggravated the incidence of destitution, and stretched available charitable resources in those areas to their limits. The severity of the problem prompted concern among members of the propertied classes, which found expression in calls for better legislative control of beggars and the homeless poor, and for the provision of improved systems of relief for certain categories of the needy.[4]

While Irish women took little part in the mid-century debate on the causes and treatment of poverty, at any rate in terms of published works on the subject, the female participation in the charitable initiatives of the period is clear evidence that they shared its preoccupations. Eighteenth-century female philanthropy was practical rather than theoretical in its approach, and women demonstrated their concern through their involvement in a multiplicity of benevolent ventures, both private and public. Thus, individual women took a prominent part in the charity school and voluntary hospital movements, the two most notable instances of associated philanthropy in the early part of the century, while also offering patronage and support to a range of male-run charities, within which, however, they could rarely expect more than a peripheral role. The Charitable Musical Society, for instance, founded in 1757 with the aim of providing interest-free loans to distressed families, was 'composed of ladies patronesses, and of ladies and gentlemen'. Yet, while women members subscribed to the Society and performed in its fund-raising concerts, they were denied the right, granted to their male colleagues, to vote or to enact or change statutes of the association.[5] The Sick and Indigent Roomkeepers' Society, established in 1790 by a group of Dublin tradesmen, allowed female subscribers to recommend cases for assistance. However, the officers were all men, and women could exert influence within the organisation only at an informal level.[6] A similar body, the Strangers' Friend Society, founded in 1790 by a Methodist minister, 'to visit and relieve distressed strangers and the resident sick and industrious poor of Dublin', excluded women from full membership until 1883, while admitting the generous support which it received from a number of benefactresses, and employing at least one woman as a visitor for several years.[7] There were, of course, instances in which individuals of sufficient standing and force of personality could circumvent the limitations customarily placed on their sex. Thus, Lady Arbella Denny was able to obtain from the governors of the Dublin Foundling Hospital the right to direct the officers and servants of that institution, and in due course received the thanks of Dublin Corporation and of the Irish House of Commons for her work in improving conditions within the hospital.[8] In general, however, it is clear that women were almost invariably relegated to a subordinate and supportive role within male-run organisations and, where they were not absolutely denied membership, were excluded from all administrative and policy-making functions. It was possibly in reaction to this fact, and certainly in response to perceived needs for which charitable women felt a particular sense of responsibility, that there emerged from mid-century a distinctively female brand of philanthropy, characterised by a primary concern for the welfare of poor women and children and operating through bodies established, managed and largely supported by women themselves.

One of the earliest examples of organised female philanthropy in Ireland was the Magdalen Asylum, founded in Leeson Street in 1766 by Lady Arbella Denny for the reception and reform of penitent prostitutes. Managed for many years by Lady Arbella herself with the assistance of her deputy, Mrs Usher, the institution was under the supervision of a committee of ladies, whose members visited and took a personal interest in the inmates, instructed them in moral and spiritual matters and in useful skills, and helped them to find employment on departure. The Asylum was one of the best-known and most fashionable charities of the period. Operating under the patronage of Queen Charlotte, it attracted considerable public interest and support, and may well have served as a model, both in terms of organisation and in its focus on the needs of poor women, for later female-run charities. Certainly, a number of those whose names appear as benefactors or friends of the institution were subsequently associated with other benevolent ventures: these included ladies of the Latouche family, who in the course of the following decades, and indeed into the next century, were to become notable for their involvement in a whole range of charitable and educational bodies, and Mrs Theodosia Blachford, who played a leading part in the establishment of the Female Orphan House and subsequently founded a refuge for unemployed and homeless young women.[9] However, Lady Arbella's enterprise was less a cause than an indicator of an increasing commitment on the part of upper- and middle-class women to organised philanthropy, and its foundation coincided with the establishment of a number of other female charitable initiatives. These included Nano Nagle's poor schools and other charities, established in Cork from about 1755, and the school and orphanage founded by Teresa Mulally at George's Hill in Dublin, as well as the Female Orphan House, established in 1790 by a group of concerned individuals who included Mrs Margaret Este, Mrs Edward Tighe and Mrs Blachford. Other such institutions were the Townsend Street Penitents' Asylum, the first Catholic-run institution for 'fallen women', founded by Mrs Bridget Burke in 1798, and Mrs Blachford's House of Refuge, opened in Baggot Street in 1802. All of these charities were managed largely or entirely by women, all were concerned with the care of abandoned, destitute or otherwise needy women and children, and all relied heavily on the generosity of a body of female support. Their example and their appeals, addressed specifically to female sympathy and benevolence, intensified the interest and involvement of growing numbers of women in charitable activity, creating an awareness, not only of the need for relief, but of the duty and the capacity of women to supply it.

The conventional eighteenth-century moral ideal of womanhood incorporated qualities which theoretically predisposed and fitted women to engage in charitable activity. Thus, Elizabeth Hamilton, author of a number of novels and didactic works on the subject of education and on the condition of the poor in her native Scotland, listed the 'female virtues' as

> meekness, gentleness, temperance and chastity; that command over the passions which is obtained by frequent self-denial; and that willingness to sacrifice every selfish wish, and every selfish feeling, to the happiness of others, which is the consequence of

subdued self-will, and the cultivation of the social and benevolent affections.[10]

The belief that women had an innate aptitude and vocation for beneficence was a widespread one, voiced by both male and female philanthropists. Sarah Trimmer, in her widely-popular and influential *Oeconomy of Charity*, published in Dublin in 1787, cited 'the tenderness which is allowed to be natural to our sex' as women's primary qualification for philanthropic activity, and the male-run Society for Promoting the Comforts of the Poor regarded 'ladies in the middle ranks of life' as having a particularly valuable contribution to make to schemes for the encouragement of 'the good habits, the industry, the welfare, and the happiness of the lower orders of the community', on the grounds that 'they have the most humane dispositions, and a lively feeling for the distresses of the poor.'[11]

Women, therefore, by virtue of those qualities deemed to be inherently feminine, were believed to be more tender and compassionate, more likely to be moved to pity and to benevolence by evidence of distress. At the same time, charitable women claimed a particular responsibility and understanding for the condition of those with whom their own life experience gave them a certain, albeit often tenuous, affinity. Thus, Teresa Mulally, in soliciting support from the Catholic parishioners of St Michan's for her school for poor girls, placed her 'chief dependence' on 'the ladies, whose usual tenderness for the poor in general cannot but show a particular feeling for the distressed members of their own sex.'[12] This principle applied even when the objects of charity were less conventionally 'deserving' than Mulally's 'poor children of the female sex ... many of them orphans ... the rest, by the helpless condition of their parents, scarce better than orphans.' Thus, the initiators of a scheme to establish an asylum for penitent females in Dublin addressed their appeal especially to 'the ladies of this kingdom ... who, with compassion equal to their own superior virtue, will certainly patronize an undertaking designed to restore many fallen and unhappy persons of their sex to chastity, decency and competence.'[13]

The response to such appeals, as revealed in institutional records, shows the confidence of activists in their own sex to have been well placed. While women did support male-run organisations such as the Association for Discountenancing Vice and the Strangers' Friend Society, their contribution was significantly greater in the case of societies run by and for women. Thus, 77% of subscribers to Mulally's charity during its first five years of existence were female, as were 56% of those to the Female Orphan

House during its first decade (1791-1803), and 77% of those whose names appeared on the subscription list of the Baggot Street House of Refuge for 1802-3.[14] On the other hand, women's sense of duty towards the unfortunate of their own sex cannot be taken as indicating any concept of 'sisterhood' or any recognition of a correspondence in the condition of charitable women and their female charges. Indeed, any suggestion to this effect was likely to be counter-productive in terms of enlisting support. The fashionable congregation at the chapel attached to the Magdalen Asylum, for instance, felt themselves grossly insulted by a visiting preacher, who placed them 'on a level with the unhappy daughters of uncleanness' who were the objects of their charity, and who warned them, with more zeal than tact, that 'the hearts of all men were alike, that they were deceitful above all things and desperately wicked, and though not guilty of such acts of sin, yet ... the seeds of the same depravity ruled in the hearts of all.'[15]

The spirit in which philanthropic women approached their work was, in fact, one of maternalism rather than of sisterly solidarity. The image of charitable women as 'perfect mothers to the poor' was, after all, a constant of female philanthropy, given visible expression in Cramillion's contemporary figure of Charity in the chapel of the Dublin Lying-in Hospital, which depicted her as a mother with an infant at her breast and two children playing nearby,[16] and the charitable woman was conventionally seen as offering to the poor and needy a care comparable to that which she gave to her own family within the home. Indeed, personal experience of maternity was assumed to make women more responsive to the needs of children and the helpless in general. Thus, Sarah Trimmer, in seeking support for the recently-established Sunday school movement, questioned whether 'a woman accustomed to the exercise of maternal affection towards her own beloved offspring' could 'be indifferent to the happiness of poor children, who have no means of learning their duty but what these schools afford', and it was observed of Mrs Margaret Este, founder of the Female Orphan House, that 'sympathy called on her especially to reflect on the sufferings of desolate female children, for she had herself been the nurse mother of many females.'[17]

Yet the maternal role implied authority as well as solicitude, and women commonly assumed a quasi-parental and arbitrary control over the objects of their concern. In her association with a charity school in Belfast, for instance, Mrs Martha McTier found it necessary 'to adopt a rule I long ago urged, but was then supposed harsh ... "Not to allow the girls to visit their parents on Sunday".'[18] Teresa Mulally imposed a similar restriction on her pupils, abolishing the holiday which had previously been granted at Christmas when she found that some of them failed to return at all, while others absented themselves for so long that they 'forgot what they had been taught and came in worse than when they had first entered.'[19] Indeed, as these examples suggest, charitable women wielded a power more formidable than that of a biological mother over her children, since they fulfilled towards those in their care a dual parental role, combining in their relations with them the functions both of a father and a mother. Thus, the author of a 'monody' published shortly after the death of Lady Arbella Denny describes her as a surrogate and omnipotent parent to those rejected by family and by respectable society:

> No father's arm to shield her from dismay –
> No mother's hand to wipe her tears away –
> A prey to sad disease, to want, and shame –
> A soul without a hope, a form 'without a name'...
> To you, her power a father's arm supplied,
> Strong to protect, and skilful to provide;
> To you her fondness gave a mother's care,
> And smooth'd the tear-worn furrows of despair.[20]

Inseparable from the parental role, whether real or assumed, was the obligation to provide moral and spiritual instruction, to inculcate in the objects of charity acceptable values and standards of behaviour. As the acknowledged guardians of purity and propriety within the home, women were regarded as having a special contribution to make in this regard, and societies concerned with the moral condition of society, and particularly of its lower orders, recognised the relevance of this role to their own aims and encouraged women's participation in their efforts. Thus, a member of the Association for Discountenancing Vice and Promoting the Practice of Religion and Virtue wrote with enthusiasm of women's potential contribution. 'Theirs,' he wrote,

> is the empire of softness, of address, of complacency. 'Tis theirs to promote the cause of virtue and religion, by rescuing their own sex from misery and destruction. 'Tis theirs to discountenance vice, by setting their faces against every dissipated suspicious character, and banishing them from their company.[21]

Through their charitable endeavours, therefore, women could exert their influence for good in an arena beyond the narrowly domestic, and could contribute to the moral regeneration of society as a whole. As was pointed out in relation to the training provided to the inmates of the Female Orphan House,

> It is not to be overlooked that in proportion as females trained to
> industry, regularity and religious conscientiousness are sent into
> the community, those influential principles will be diffused
> which constitute the truest elements of general melioration; and
> by the multiplying of which alone, the rude mass of our popula-
> tion can ever be humanized or made respectable.[22]

The character and focus of eighteenth-century female philanthropy, then, were in part determined by idealised and sentimen-
talist concepts of the nature and role of women, which allowed
their influence within the domestic sphere to be extended into a
more public arena. However, this was far from being their sole
qualification for such work. The benefits conferred upon women
by their involvement in charitable activity have been noted in a
number of recent studies of the topic. Their engagement in such
work, it has been argued, offered them an opportunity to acquire
'practical experience and responsibility ... heightened their self-
confidence and self-respect', and equipped them with skills which
were to be deployed in the campaigns for emancipation and female
suffrage.[23] It should not be forgotten, however, that women, in
entering the field of organised philanthropy, brought to it a not
inconsiderable expertise and experience of their own. The practical
domestic skills of rearing and educating children, of nursing the
old and sick, of managing a household and supervising servants
and of keeping household and personal accounts were, after all,
precisely those most relevant in the relief of distress and in the
administration of institutions and societies. As Sarah Trimmer
pointed out, 'women are undoubtedly best able to judge of the
faults and mis-managements of their own sex, and of their peculiar
wants; which in many instances are unavoidably overlooked by
those who are unacquainted with the minutiae of domestic business.'[24] Similarly, it was reported that Lady Arbella Denny, in
taking over the supervision of the Dublin Foundling Hospital and
in proposing the appointment of a committee of lady visitors,
considered that 'the wants of young children, the negligence of
nurses, and the general management of such an institution, fell
more within their sphere of observation than of any gentlemen,
however wise or discerning they might be.'[25] Nor were the skills
which women brought to philanthropy solely domestic. Denny
herself, for instance, had a long involvement with the Dublin
Society, established in 1731 for the encouragement of Irish agriculture, manufacture and trade, and had been instrumental in efforts
to foster textile and other industries. Described as 'having a remarkable capacity for comprehending great principles and attending at the same time to matters of minute detail and management',

she also enjoyed the advantage of ready access to those in power in Church and State.[26] Lower down the social scale, Teresa Mulally had enjoyed a successful career as a milliner before deciding to devote herself wholly to charitable work, in which, like Denny, she proved herself a capable administrator. Recalled by one of her colleagues as 'a very keen woman', possessed of 'a cool head and a masculine understanding', Mulally was a careful manager of the financial and legal affairs of her charities; she personally supervised the complicated negotiations for the purchase of a site for the building of a new school, successfully petitioned the Privy Council for exemption from parochial taxes and continued to take charge of the business of the George's Hill establishment following its transfer to the Presentation Order until her death in 1803.[27]

Women's qualifications to engage in organised philanthropy, therefore, were much more than merely theoretical. While such activity was regarded as conforming to correct models of female behaviour and as drawing on qualities defined as quintessentially feminine, it did also utilise a battery of skills acquired by women in the course of their daily lives, and reflected the varied experiences of individuals as apparently different as Denny and Mulally, the former a self-assured and well-connected aristocrat, the latter a member of the Catholic bourgeoisie and a working woman, who for many years acted as the family breadwinner. What these two, and all charitable women, did share, of course, was a disadvantaged position within a patriarchal society, a position inevitably reflected in the attitudes of men and of women themselves to female philanthropy.

Elizabeth Hamilton, in noting the equation of virtues regarded as innately feminine and truly Christian, regretted the tendency of 'this unfortunate association' to bring 'religion itself ... into disgrace; devotional sentiment is considered as a mere adjunct of female virtue, suitable to the weakness of the female mind, and for that reason, disgraceful to the superior wisdom of man.'[28] By a similar process, the association of the prescribed female virtues with those appropriate to charitable activity led some observers to devalue female philanthropy. On the one hand, the usefulness of women's contribution to the relief of distress was acknowledged, the efforts of those 'excellent women' who engaged themselves in voluntary charitable work were applauded and presented to other women as examples worthy of emulation. On the other hand, the abilities necessary, and the difficulties and demands involved in such work were dismissed as inconsiderable. The Society for Promoting the Comforts of the Poor was among the organisations anxious to enlist women in its schemes to relieve distress and provide instruction and training at a local level. 'Females in the higher ranks of life,' it was noted, 'cannot be more usefully employed' than in the supervision of such plans in their own neighbourhood. Elsewhere, the society in seeking women's support declared that

> The lady who will employ a few hours in the week, in overseeing the execution of a well-digested plan for enabling the poor to relieve themselves will do the most important good ... For this work ladies are often better qualified than men; as they are more accustomed to domestic management, and have a greater quantity of time at their own disposal.[29]

Yet the society, while enlisting women's assistance in the running of its various schemes and acknowledging their actual and potential contribution to its stated purpose of promoting 'the good habits, the industry, the welfare, and the happiness of the lower orders of the community', also implicitly denigrated the effort involved. 'It is a mistake,' women were reassured, 'to suppose that much time or talent is required for the undertaking. In almost every parish, some may be found possessing ample means and qualifications.'[30] Other observers apparently regarded female benevolence as little more than a genteel occupation for otherwise idle hours, which also offered, in the words of a contemporary ladies' periodical, 'the delightful pleasure of feeding the hungry and clothing the naked.'[31] In a similar vein, the author of a public letter to Mrs Peter Latouche, patroness of the Female Orphan House, urged her to

> Endeavour to make the benevolence of your female friends a little more active ... Tell them that active benevolence is its own reward ... that the moment their fine feelings shall become interested ... they will thank you for relieving them from the *ennui* of an insipid morning visit ... that the acts of charity of the morning give a poignancy to the pleasures of the evening.[32]

In his examination of early nineteenth-century English female philanthropy, Prochaska has noted that the increasing pressure put on privileged women to engage in philanthropic activity had the unlooked-for effect of turning it into a fashionable pastime, of making it, in fact, a form of 'outdoor relief for leisured women'.[33] For some of those involved benevolence was, without doubt, little more than a convention, while for others the initial charitable impulse clearly did not long survive close involvement with the realities of distress. Of the ladies who joined Lady Arbella Denny in forming a committee to oversee the care of the children at the Foundling Hospital, for instance, only Denny herself apparently persevered in her interest.[34] On the other hand, it does seem safe to assume a high degree of concern and commitment in those Irishwomen who chose to engage personally in organised philanthropy at this early stage of its development, given that the number of activists involved was still relatively small, and that the problems encountered were of a magnitude and nature likely to deter those merely in pursuit of diversion or sensation.

In seeking the motivating factors behind such efforts, the testimonies of those concerned are of special relevance and interest. In this regard, the personal writings of Nano Nagle and of her contemporary, Theodosia Blachford, are a particularly valuable source of information, throwing light both on the concerns and achievements of the individuals themselves, and on the philanthropic movement in which they played a principal part. Divided by religion, and operating in isolation from one another, Nagle and Blachford nonetheless had much in common, both with each other and with the majority of the women, in this and in the next century, who engaged in voluntary charitable activity.

Born in 1718, Honora Nagle belonged to one of the leading Catholic gentry families in Munster. Disadvantaged by their religion and Jacobite associations, the Nagles had, however, managed to retain some of their lands, and had, in addition, various mercantile interests in Ireland and on the Continent. Nano's upbringing, therefore, was a relatively sheltered and comfortable one and, like many girls of a similar background, she was sent to France for education. According to her earliest biographer, she first became aware of the scale and implications of need in Ireland while visiting the poor in the neighbourhood of her father's estate. Horrified by her discovery of the 'ignorance of the lower classes ... their consequent immorality, and the ruin of their souls', but believing that her lack of fortune, her 'delicate' constitution, and the restraints imposed by the penal legislation prevented her from doing anything to remedy the situation, she chose instead to withdraw from the evidence of such deprivation and to enter a convent in France.[35] After only a few months, however, she determined, with the approval of her confessor, to return to Ireland in order to undertake what she herself regarded as a mission of charity to the poor. 'Nothing would have made me come home,' she told a friend many years later, 'but the decision of the clergyman that I should run a great risk of salvation if I did not follow the inspiration', and she attributed the ultimate success of her project to having acted in accordance with that inspiration. 'I began in a poor humble manner,' she wrote, 'and though it pleased the divine will to give me severe trials in this foundation, yet it is to show that it is His work and has not been effected by human means.'[36]

For Nagle, then, philanthropy was primarily an expression of her religious faith. Her initial concern was prompted as much by a realisation of the spiritual deprivations which distress implied as by the material conditions of the poor, and the education provided in her schools, although not exclusively religious, placed a heavy emphasis on religious training. Pupils were taught the catechism, as well as reading, writing and ciphering, heard mass every day and were taken to confession and communion.[37] Nagle herself supervised this spiritual instruction, and saw her foundations as having a missionary function far beyond their immediate sphere of influence. 'My schools are beginning to be of service to a great many parts of the world,' she wrote in 1769, ' ... and my views are not for one object alone. If I could be of any service in saving souls in any part of the globe, I would willingly do all in my power.'[38]

For Theodosia Blachford, too, charitable effort was initially a response to religious feeling, and continued throughout her life to be the primary expression of her faith. Born in 1744, Blachford was the daughter of William Tighe, a substantial landowner and member of parliament. An intelligent and introspective child, she received a conventionally pious upbringing, but at the age of seventeen had what she regarded as a spiritual awakening, as a result of which she resolved, in her own words, to 'renounce the world, leave *all*', and, as proof of the sincerity of her intention, to dedicate all the money she possessed at the time – one guinea – 'to the poor as His representative.' Like Nagle, although, as a Protestant, in different circumstances, Theodosia found that withdrawal from the world failed to satisfy her needs. Married in 1770 to the Reverend William Blachford, she was widowed three years later, and thereafter she devoted herself to the care and education of her two children, to good works and to a search for spiritual fulfilment.[39] In about 1777 she 'fell in with the Methodists', becoming one of the leading figures in the movement in Ireland: John Wesley, noting her services to the cause, described her as 'one of our jewels'. Other influences included Jeanne de Chantal, founder of the Visitation Order, whose *Life* Blachford translated into English, and the author and religious mystic, William Law, who in about 1740 established a small community, dedicated to pious reflection and charitable works, at King's Cliff in Northamptonshire, and to whose writings Blachford was introduced as a young woman.[40] The religion which Law preached was one of the heart, centering on the concept of God as 'all love ... and the Christian religion is nothing else but an open full manifestation of His universal love towards all mankind', and this was the creed to which Blachford referred throughout her life as underpinning all her beneficent efforts.[41]

In background and motivation, therefore, Blachford and Nagle were in a number of respects typical of this first generation of women to be involved in organised philanthropy. Both, for example, belonged to the middle to upper ranks of society, and drew on family traditions of responsibility towards their social inferiors and dependants: Nagle's sister, Ann, was also celebrated for her generosity to the poor and, in establishing her own projects, Nano received substantial support from her relatives, while Blachford's brothers, Edward and Robert Tighe, and her sisters-in-law, Mrs Edward and Mrs Sarah Tighe, were all active in a variety of benevolent causes and organisations.[42] Both were women of 'vivacity' and 'eagerness' of spirit, who found in philanthropy an outlet for their frustrated energies and abilities.[43] Both, too, chose to concentrate their attention on areas of activity typical of female charity in general, that is, on the education and care of children and on the welfare of poor women, and to do so in co-operation with other concerned members of their own sex. Finally, both in their enterprises drew strength from, and contributed to contemporary movements of renewal within their respective confessions. Historians have noted the vital part played by women in the expansion of Methodism, as well as the opportunities which such movements of religious renewal and the associated 'feminisation' of religion provided to women, who increasingly discovered within the confines of their church an arena where they could meet and co-operate with others of their own sex.[44] Blachford's interest in the philanthropic careers of de Chantal and Law suggests that she may have been attracted to the idea of a sisterhood linked by shared spiritual values and a dedication to charitable work, and her journals and the record of her philanthropy reveal her membership of an informal network of pious and socially-concerned women, such as Mrs Margaret Este, Mrs Elizabeth Latouche and Mrs Sarah Tighe. For Nagle, as a Catholic, the female religious orders provided a ready model for a framework within which such charitable women might organise themselves for action, although not without some sacrifice of autonomy and independence.[45] The Ursuline and Presentation Orders which Nagle established in Ireland were a significant aspect of the Catholic revival of the second half of the century, and of the part played by women, lay as well as religious, in that process, while also signalling the beginning of the expansion of the female

religious orders, which in the next century was to be one of the most
noteworthy features of that revival.

The personal accounts of Nagle and Blachford leave no doubt
that religion was overwhelmingly the most important driving force
behind their benevolence. Yet such clear-cut evidence is unusual
in a matter which is, in any case, essentially internalised. Religion
was certainly the most readily-avowed motive for women's philanthropy, and the revivalist movements which existed in the two
main branches of Christianity in the final decades of the century
clearly acted as an impetus to charitable endeavour, by stressing
the religious and moral duty of the individual and, in the slightly
longer term, by creating a climate of competition between the sects
in the practice of charity. On the other hand, religious zeal did not
preclude other motivations for the relief of distress. The founders
of the Female Orphan House, for example, were impelled to action
by a variety of considerations, which included a 'humane design'
that 'little deserted females' should have 'some earthly place of
refuge ... from want and misery', disapproval of the perceived ill
effects of indiscriminate almsgiving, and disquiet about the threat
posed by the lawlessness and moral degeneracy of the poor to the
structures of society.[46] While the initiators of this particular charity
were uniformly members of the ascendancy, such concerns were
not confined to this class. Teresa Mulally, whose 'extraordinary
piety' was a crucial element in her benevolence, was equally concerned about the social implications of ignorance and destitution.
The poor children on whose behalf she sought assistance suffered,
she wrote,

> all the hardships of extreme poverty; but their poverty, extreme
> as it is, is not the worst of their miseries. Their chief misfortune
> is to be without any means of instruction; for want of which they
> grow up in such habits of ignorance, idleness and vice, as render
> them for ever after not only useless, but highly pernicious to
> themselves and the public.[47]

Christian duty and humanitarian feeling, therefore, combined with
more pragmatic considerations in the relief of poverty. These considerations, rarely absent from eighteenth-century philanthropy,
were given greater urgency by the impact of the French Revolution
in Britain and Ireland, and by growing domestic instability and
political and sectarian polarisation during the 1790s. The noted
preacher, the Reverend Walter Blake Kirwan, in his 1796 charity
sermon on behalf of the Female Orphan House, cited the preva-
lence of revolutionary doctrine and the unsettled state of the country as reasons for providing instruction to the lower orders of

society, and lamented that such measures had not been taken earlier. Had they been,

> The mischievous doctrines of a Paine would not have taken root in your soil ... You would not now be obliged to fly to your capital for protection ... You would not have clubs of conspirators deliberating upon murder in every corner of your country ... You would not now be reduced to the necessity of strong and extraordinary exertions of power, to restrain sedition and treason from reducing the beautiful fabric of society to a mass of ruin.[48]

Charity, therefore, might serve as a means of safeguarding the established order, by improving relations between the classes and by instilling in the poor sentiments of deference, gratitude and affection towards those above them in the social scale. Women were seen as having a particularly valuable role to play in this process. Their charity, insofar as it was largely practical, allowed them to form close relationships with those whom they assisted, and to exert influence over the young and impressionable. Thus, the 'familiar intercourse' between the pupils at Derryloran Sunday School and the ladies who superintended it was declared to have created

> a reciprocal attachment between them ... which even extends to the parents, who, as far as we can judge, have been in every instance fully sensible of, and gratified for the benefits their children have derived, and so far from encouraging levelling principles, it increases respect, founded on gratitude and esteem.

Such schemes, it was argued, convinced the poor

> that their interests are an object of affectionate concern with their wealthier neighbours ... and by making them feel inequality of rank and wealth as the immediate source of blessings and comforts, must furnish the best practical answer to all factious declamation on the equality of mankind.[49]

The standards which philanthropic women sought to instil in their charges, therefore, were far from radical, nor did they seek to challenge the subservient position of their own sex, either on behalf of poor women or on their own account. Objects of female charity were encouraged to acquire the approved feminine virtues of tenderness, purity and obedience, while the education offered to poor girls reinforced the idea of separate and unequal male and female spheres of activity. Thus, while Nagle's boy pupils learnt to read, write and 'cypher', her girls apparently learned only to read and to 'work'.[50] On the other hand, charitable women did set out to provide young women with skills which would enable them to support themselves. Teresa Mulally was particularly insistent on this point, perhaps because her personal experience had demon-

strated its importance, and the girls in her school were instructed
in a variety of crafts which included knitting, quilting, mantua-
making and plain work, 'whereby they may be rendered useful to
society and capable of earning honest bread for themselves.'[51]
Other philanthropists also recognised the urgent need to provide
poor women with a means of livelihood at a time when many
occupations previously open to them were being usurped by men.
Poverty and unemployment were acknowledged to be major factors in driving women to deviate from the social and moral norm,
and the Magdalen Asylum, for instance, placed a strong emphasis
on the necessity to provide those in its charge with training which
would enable them to earn a living without resorting again to
prostitution. During their term in the house, inmates learned a
variety of skills, most especially those which would fit them on
departure for work in the clothing trades or in domestic service,
currently the two chief areas of female employment. Charitable
women also recognised the peculiar vulnerability to exploitation
and need for protection of certain categories, such as orphaned and
homeless girls and destitute and unemployed young women, for
whom a number of institutions were established in the final decades of the eighteenth and the early years of the nineteenth century.
One such was the Baggot Street House of Refuge, principally
intended for 'young women out of employment who have been
brought up in charity schools' or 'who are either orphans, or have
their parents so circumstanced, that they cannot afford them necessary protection.' As a report on the charity observed, 'there is
perhaps no class of human beings more destitute of resource, or
more helplessly exposed to the temptations of vice, and the arts of
designing villainy.'[52]

Charitable women's recognition of poverty as the root cause of
the social evils whose effects they were attempting to mitigate, and
of the disadvantaged position of women within the general body
of the poor, did not, however, find expression in any meaningful
critique of the basic structures of a patriarchal and hierarchical
society. Indeed, the religious and politically conservative views of
the great majority of activists made any such questioning extremely
unlikely. It would seem, then, that the reality of the female charitable role offered little challenge to the ideal, and it might be
argued, indeed, that philanthropic women through their work,
their teaching and their example actually reinforced the existing
structures of society and stereotypical notions about the female role
and nature. Yet, for the practitioners themselves, participation in
institutional charity could hardly fail to have implications which

would distance the ideal from the reality. Women had themselves chosen the objects towards whom their charity would primarily be directed, they had designed the machinery through which it would be administered and had organised to achieve their ends. By the final decade of the eighteenth century, philanthropic women of all confessions were active at every level in a range of institutions, catering primarily for the needs of poor women and children. Admittedly, the short-term impact of these initiatives in terms of relieving distress was far from dramatic. The number of women involved was as yet extremely small, and the institutions through which they operated were severely limited in their scope. All, for instance, were located in urban areas, and most in the larger metropolitan centres. Moreover, even within those areas, institutional charities, however efficient or effective, could reach only a tiny proportion of the needy. Thus the Leeson Street Magdalen Asylum, during the first thirty years of its existence, admitted a total of 388 penitents, and on that basis can hardly be credited with making a substantial contribution to curbing the incidence of prostitution in Dublin.[53] The same reservation might be applied to any one of the institutions mentioned: when Teresa Mulally's orphanage opened in 1771, for example, five girls were admitted; in 1783, just twenty children were lodged in the house.[54] The larger and better-funded Female Orphan Asylum could accommodate between 150 and 170 girls, a not unimpressive total, but one absolutely unequal to the scale of the problems which the institution had been founded to address.[55]

The significance of eighteenth-century women's philanthropy, therefore, did not lie in the numbers involved, either as dispensers or as objects of relief, but in its achievement in casting light upon previously disregarded areas of need and in initiating new fields of philanthropic endeavour, and in the implications which such activity had for charitable women themselves. Ultimately, indeed, it is impossible not to feel that philanthropic women gained from their charity at least as much as they gave. For the great majority, reward must have lain not only in a consciousness of duty done, but also in the sense of purpose and direction which such activity conferred. Sarah Scott, in her highly-popular contemporary novel, *Millenium Hall*, depicted philanthropy as a source of relief for the 'sisterhood' of benefactors as well as for the beneficiaries,[56] and it is clear from the evidence of some such practitioners that their benevolent pursuits brought them a sense of achievement and fulfilment which they could currently have attained in no other sphere of activity. Thus, Nagle wryly remarked to an associate that

'I often think my schools will never bring me to heaven, as I only take delight and pleasure in them,' and Blachford, writing towards the end of her life, declared her work to have been 'a providential blessing ... compelling me to some mental and physical exertion, which has kept me for the last ten years from dwelling on anxieties few can imagine, and still saves me from stupid indolence.'[57]

For these, as for growing numbers of other women, organised philanthropy offered a new field of activity and gave access to experience and to influence outside the home. Ultimately, it was to force women to engage with social problems and to question the place of women in society. In the short term, it offered a sense of usefulness and achievement, of escape from the narrowness of the domestic sphere and from the 'stupid indolence' to which women of the propertied and affluent classes were increasingly being condemned. According to the approved concept of womanhood, upheld both by religion and society, true happiness and fulfilment lay in service and in sacrifice. Yet women's involvement in philanthropy, while seemingly conforming to this ideal, covertly challenged it, constituting, in effect, an assertion of women's right to self-expression as individuals, and of the right of the sex to a place in public life. The significance of this advance was obscured, however, by the lack of radical content and, indeed, the resolute conservatism of virtually all contemporary philanthropy. Ironically, it was these very characteristics which made the achievements possible. It was precisely because the reality apparently offered no challenge to the ideal, because women's new public role grew logically out of functions which they had traditionally fulfilled within their own homes and in the local community, that organised female philanthropy had freedom to develop and to flourish.

Women & Politics in Nineteenth-Century Ireland

Maria Luddy

It is generally assumed that nineteenth-century Irish politics were a function of public life, a male activity in which women played little if any role. Political historians pay scant attention to the role of women in political life, seeing it as either peripheral, or of small consequence.[1] Women, of course, were not voters,[2] nor did they have access to high political office in the nineteenth century. Although individual women such as Isabella Tod and Anna Haslam can be regarded as politicians, for most of the nineteenth century Irish women were excluded from formal male political culture. The ideology of 'separate spheres', the world of work and politics advocated for men, and the world of domesticity advocated for women, played some part in limiting their political aspirations. The concept of the ideology of 'separate spheres' which has had such an impact on historians of women was less distinct and less limiting than once believed.[3] Public and private life interacted in complex ways in the nineteenth century and political activity took on a wide variety of forms.

In this paper I would like to extend the boundaries of what we consider to be political by looking at a range of informal and formal political activity engaged in by Irish women in the last century. I want to examine a number of issues around women and politics. On one level I wish to describe political activity by women. They were involved in indirect and direct action at local and national level. They also played a role in political parties and pressure groups, such as anti-slavery and temperance societies. For some women, formal political activity culminated in the suffrage campaign, while for others it involved more nationalistic aims. The political aspirations of women activists were not necessarily for the benefit of other women. Arguments about gender difference abounded in the nineteenth century and these played a role in shaping women's political involvement. Particular constructions of gender difference arose in the arguments which informed women's political activities. Women were not a homogenous mass and their politics differed according to their class. Women's role in politics in nineteenth-century Ireland was diverse and involved women from all social classes. Women as well as men expressed political opinions, played a part in political rituals, and created a role for themselves in public political life so that their political presence had become commonplace by the end of the nineteenth century. Women's historians who have shown some interest in politics have concentrated on women's attempts to secure the parliamentary franchise. Other areas of interest have been the Ladies' Land League and, of course, women's involvement in nationalist organisations.[4] I want to move beyond these issues to reveal the variety and wider meanings of women's political activity. Historians have underestimated the extent and significance of political involvement by Irish women. In order fully to understand political life in nineteenth-century Ireland, it is necessary to become aware of the contribution made by women during that period.

I will first examine informal political activity by women, and will then discuss women's political role in organisations and societies which were directed at improving the position of women in Ireland or which attempted to use women's influence to alter codes of conduct in society. The activities selected for detailed consideration are anti-slavery societies, the campaigns to repeal the Contagious Diseases Acts and to gain women's admission to local and national franchises. I would like to start with a working definition of 'politics'. I will use the term 'politics' to include any action by an individual or group, in a formal or informal way intended to affect or alter either the policy of government, or the behaviour or beliefs of individuals or groups within the local community, for the apparent benefit of a particular group or community. Clearly activity that is carried out by an individual for individual ends is not part of this definition.

Taking this wide definition allows a number of areas to be investigated. Looking at women's informal political activity reveals that they were exercising political power long before they won the franchise. It is clear, for example, that some wives and daughters could exert influence over the male members of their families, Daniel O'Connell's wife, Mary, being a case in point.[5] Such influence is an aspect of informal activity which deserves more sustained study than can be incorporated into this piece. Here I am going to concentrate on the involvement of women in agrarian disturbances and in riots throughout the century.

Agrarian disturbances were a feature of Irish life from the 1760s. We have little information on the role played by peasant women during the eighteenth century in such societies. There is evidence to show that Lady Arabella Jeffrys of Cork did play a leadership role in the Rightboy movement of the 1780s, though this appears to have been a singular case of such involvement.[6] During the nineteenth century there are documentary references to women participating in such societies. A.G.L. Shaw, working from the records of transported convicts, noted that a number of women were sentenced as 'incendiaries', a crime associated with agrarian outrages.[7] In 1843 for example, Bridget Maher was arrested and tried for attempting to burn down the house of one Thomas Coughlan as part of a Ribbon conspiracy. Another young woman was arrested on suspicion of burning stacks of turf in an agrarian outrage in the 1840s[8] and there are other examples of such outrages being committed by women. Women's involvement in violent activities during the tithe war of the 1830s is also recorded. For example, in 1833 two tithe proctors were murdered in County Cork, with a number of women being involved in the murder which was particularly brutal.[9] As James Donnelly has shown, many of the agrarian outrages which occurred in pre-Famine Ireland were carried out by groups of individuals with the official or unofficial sanction of their local community. In the majority of instances, such disturbances reflected resistance to imposed economic changes by communities whose structures of economic interdependence encouraged group action. Such activities were generally conservative and sought to preserve the status quo concerning the group's particular economic arrangements.[10] It is clear from the available evidence that in such activities women acted with men to achieve benefits for their community, those benefits being primarily of an economic nature.

As yet we are unaware of the scale of women's involvement in these societies. It is not clear, for example, if women could be sworn. Though most of the violent activity was carried through by men, women were not barred from such activity. While women's involvement in agrarian outrages is sparsely documented, enough evidence is available to raise some questions about women and secret societies. What is the relationship, for example, between communal action and gender issues? What is interesting is that these societies appear to have been unconcerned with gender differences. There seem to be no political, economic or social aspirations which are gender specific. Such activity was communal activity, for the benefit of all. There is no political consciousness of difference between men and women. If we are to fully understand the complexities of peasant life, we need to explore further how decisions were made within households, not only in terms of how individuals contributed in financial or work terms to the family, but also of how decisions affecting political involvement were made. It seems unrealistic to assume that all decisions on whether or not to join agrarian secret societies were totally left to the male members of the family. Since communal ends were sought, it seems likely that women also played some role in encouraging or dissuading their menfolk from such activity.

Election mobs, as K. Theodore Hoppen has shown, offered those without a formal political voice a variety of roles within the world of politics.[11] He has shown that women could achieve local political influence. For example, a Miss Forrest of the Gort Hotel in County Galway was described in 1872 as the MP Sir William Gregory's 'right hand man'.[12] Anne Brien was a Dungarvan mob leader in 1868; the Claddagh fishwives constituted guards of honour for Michael Morris in Galway in 1872; and there is ample evidence that numbers of women negotiated their husbands' election bribes.[13] A Mrs Elizabeth Brown of Derry told a select committee in 1833 that she had promised her husband's vote to a particular candidate in return for money.[14] Lady Anne Daly, of Galway, canvassed the tenants on her husband's estate in Galway in 1872 and received an anonymous and threatening letter denouncing 'her wonderful achievements in canvassing for votes amongst your peasantry.'[15] Occasionally appeals were issued by candidates to women to help them persuade their spouses to vote in the 'right' direction or to urge women to force others to do so. In 1852 Lord Eglington, writing to J.H. Walpole, noted, 'The non-electors, women and children have been invited in the chapels to attend every polling place and mark the men who voted against their religion.'[16]

Women's enthusiasm at election time often attracted commentary from public officials, particularly when they became involved in riots. Women were noted, in the pre- and post-Famine periods, for taking a prominent part in such disorders. Perhaps poorer women found the riots one way of asserting their needs in a society which allowed them no formal political voice. Hoppen has noted that women-only mobs were common and that women led and organised mobs composed of men and women. Women rioters were described by officials as savage and violent.[17] For example, a reporter at an election riot in Cashel in 1865 noted '... a fearful scene ... where well-looking, well-dressed girls, one a perfect Amazon, bared their arms, wound their shawls tightly around them, and

rushed with the mêlée.'[18] A number of Donegal magistrates writing
to the Lord Lieutenant in 1852 informed him that at a recent
election, the local priests requested their parishioners, male and
female, to prevent the attendance at the election of any who would
vote against their supported candidate. As a consequence, the
magistrates noted, 'at day break ... enormous crowds of men,
women and children assembled at different points on the road from
Ballybofey to Lifford, and all voters supposed to be favourable to
the old members were by force and violence prevented [from]
going to Lifford.'[19] The mayor of Limerick, writing to Dublin Castle
in 1852, noted that 'a riotous mob, principally composed of females
taking advantage of the temporary withdrawal of the military and
police, attacked some houses – broke the windows and furniture
and destroyed property in the shops and houses.'[20] Some of this
activity, of course, may have opened opportunities for opportun-
istic looting, but attacks directed at private houses, very much a
carry-over from agrarian tactics, generally had a political motivation. Commentators were well used to this type of behaviour from
women rioters and surprisingly little is made of the fact that it is
women who are engaged in such violent attacks. It appears that it
was not until the era of the Land League that men publicly re-
nounced riotous activities by women on a broad scale. By the 1880s,
particular gender expectations had become part of political life.

Women were observed with banners and placards supporting
or denouncing particular candidates, and were also to be found in
large numbers at political demonstrations. For example, a demon-
stration for the release of Fenian prisoners took place in Drogheda
in 1868 and it was noted that 'women had their bonnets trimmed
in green, or their hair bound in the national colour. From their necks
flowed thin stripes of the green silk, in almost every instance some
portion of their dress was rendered conspicuous by the introduction of the prevailing colour.'[21] Women were thus making a visible
public display of political activism. Disenfranchised women were
as adept as disenfranchised men at utilising whatever power they
had, through rioting, accepting bribes, demonstrating and becoming involved in violent activities to affect the political climate of the
period. They expressed allegiance to causes, such as Fenianism,
through these public displays. They heckled and rioted at election
times and in the process contributed to the vibrancy of political life.
Such women were not involved in any way in developing a feminist agenda of action. But, in terms of the assertion of a female
presence and its display in demonstrations and riots, these women
offered more of a challenge to assumptions about the female role,

and female behaviour, than did the first women voters of the twentieth century. As Hoppen notes, such activity also offered women far
more political opportunities than the suffrage campaign ever would.

Apart from being involved in riots and mobs at elections,
women were also prominent in the food riots which occurred
throughout the century. During the Great Famine in particular,
such action was necessary to stave off starvation. James Donnelly
has noted that food riots and similar disturbances were an attempt
to bring the plight of the people to the attention of authorities and
force them to act in their favour. Rising unemployment and increasing food prices led to hundreds of men, women and children
venting their anger on local landlords and relief committees. A
large crowd of men, women and children, for example, marched
into Macroom in County Cork in September 1846, striking terror
into the townspeople and shopkeepers.[22] In May 1847, a Cork
newspaper reported the following:

> On Wednesday as seven cartloads of flour, from the concern of
> Sir David Roche, at Carass, and four loads of Indian meal, from
> the mills of James D. Lyons, Esq., were being conveyed to Ballin-
> garry under an escort of four police, a mob of about 500 men and
> women attacked the carriers near Kilmacow, and despite the
> exertions of the constabulary in charge, carried off the entire of
> Sir David's property; but on being told that the other carts were
> the medium of transmitting provisions for the use of the Relief
> Committee of Ballingarry, the marauders were content with
> relieving only one horse of its load.[23]

Similar disturbances occurred in those parts of the country which
suffered most during the Famine years. Outbreaks continued until
the autumn of 1847. Donnelly notes that these riots seem to have
ended at the close of 1847, when the poorest and most affected
groups became incapable through starvation and debilitation of
carrying out mass protests.[24] Similar rioting was to occur at other
times of crisis. The harsh winter of 1879 and the fears of famine also
led to disturbances. In January 1880, for example, it was reported
that an 'immense crowd of men, women and children' had attacked
a bread cart in Mayo on its way to a workhouse.[25] Whether these
outbreaks of rioting were premeditated or spontaneous remains
unclear. From the evidence available they do not seem to have been
particularly the province of women. Again the evidence suggests
collective action on a large and small scale for group purposes.

Even during times of extreme crisis, like the Famine, women
were capable of encouraging a more formal political campaign. For
example, *The Chronicle and Munster Advertiser* of 22 September 1847
published a letter addressed to the 'virtuous women of the county

of Waterford', urging them to set up a female Tenant League which would look after the interests of their tenant husbands. The author of the letter argued that the men seemed incapable of taking action and it was up to the women to do so. The women of Ireland, it was declared, would form a movement which would 'shame the men into action. We'll insist on love of country and kind in the tender hearts of our children. We'll control our husbands and command our daughters. We'll make a solemn vow not to rest our heads on the same pillow with our husbands until they become ardent members of the Tenant League.'[26] Whether this letter resulted in women forming an organisation remains unknown.

When we are looking at these informal associations and political activity, it seems clear that political action by poorer women and men takes the form of pragmatic action undertaken particularly on economic grounds. There is little, if any, concern with gender difference in the sense that such difference became a uniting principal in those organisations set up to fight for various rights for women from the 1860s. Yet these individuals and informal groups were exercising political power. It was via secret societies and through mob violence that the private concerns of families and communities confronted the public power of the law, landlords and the State.

There are still numerous questions which need to be asked about these areas of informal political activity. Are issues which relate specifically to women addressed in these actions? How and when, if ever, was a political consciousness which accounted for gender difference developed in the lower classes? Is there a discourse which takes account of gender difference to be found anywhere in the rhetoric of secret societies, or election mobs? Do issues concerned with gender aspirations surface in any of the range of secret societies in different parts of the country? If it is difficult to ascertain a sense of the import of gender difference in informal political activities, that concept was developed in the more formal political activity in which women engaged from the beginning of the nineteenth century.

When associated with nationalist uprisings of the last century, such as those involving the Young Irelanders, or the Fenians, women are generally seen in symbolic terms and rarely acknowledged as playing an active role in the practical or theoretical formulations of these organisations. The structure of many of these organisations was laden with culturally constructed concepts of gender, which in turn helped to define clear gender specific roles. While the male members of Young Ireland held definite and idealistic ideas of women's place in the nationalist arena, those beliefs echoed the ideal of women as mothers inculcating the virtues of the nation state in the nation's children. Of secondary importance to the male leaders was women's contribution to national debate in the forms of letters, articles and particularly poetry which appeared in *The Nation* newspaper. Women were not ignored in these organisations but they were kept in a subordinate role. Within the Young Ireland movement, women such as Ellen Mary Downing, Mary Eva Kelly, Jane Francesca Elgee and others played a role in helping to create a sense of national identity. Whilst helping to create this identity, the writers were also consciously or unconsciously appealing to specific gender constructions. Ellen Downing, for example, writing in 1848, appealed to Irish women, as consumers, to support Irish industry. 'I have striven,' she noted, 'with my weak endeavours to work for Ireland, because she is my country and 'twas right to love and serve her. Won't you begin too, and let us all work together? ... and if all of us would unite it would be a great step towards nationhood.'[27] This attempt at politicising women's purchasing power was reminiscent of campaigns urged by members of anti-slavery organisations in Ireland and dates back to the late eighteenth century. Boycotting British goods was not just a symbolic act; it was also an attempt to encourage native industry.

Women played a role, not only in creating a sense of national identity through their writings, but also through the practical support which they gave to these organisations. Women, for example, carried despatches between the local leaders of the Fenian movement in the 1860s.[28] In October 1865, a group of women formed the Ladies' Committee to aid the families of imprisoned Fenians and that work continued until 1872, when a general amnesty was announced for the prisoners.[29] The organisational pattern of men's and women's leadership roles was not equal in these nationalist societies. Equality between men and women was rarely advocated. Where women's groups were affiliated to male groups, they tended to be placed in an hierarchical relationship to the male society. We need to look no further than the Land League and the Ladies' Land League to see this in action.[30] Many women accepted subordination and the attendant roles they were expected to play as natural, but others such as Anna Parnell created modified positions of authority for themselves.

The Ladies' Land League was established in New York in October 1880 for the purpose of collecting money for the Land League. On 31 January 1881, Anna Parnell presided over the first official meeting of the Ladies' Land League in Dublin. From that time until its formal dissolution on 10 August 1882, the women of the League raised funds, oversaw the housing of evicted tenants and took a very visible role in the public and political life of the country. We have little information on how the Ladies' Land League operated in the different counties. It does appear that leadership within branches was confined to the middle classes, but it is also clear that peasant women played a part in protests organised by the League. In 1881, for example, Adam Mitchell, the sessional crown solicitor for King's County, reported of a 'very bad case I prosecuted not long ago in Tullamore in the petty sessions, in which nine women were charged with violently beating a process server, taking the processes from him and throwing him into the canal. They battered his face.' Nine women were charged and six of the nine were sent to prison for a month.[31]

Women who involved themselves in the Ladies' Land League had to act against prevailing ideas of women's place. The famous pronouncement of Archbishop McCabe, telling the clergy in his diocese not to admit these women to sodalities, placed Irish women in subordination to the Church and advocated their removal from politics.[32] The editor of the *Belfast Newsletter* echoed similar sentiments, noting that 'Sensible people in the North of Ireland dislike to see woman out of the place she is gifted to occupy, and at no time is woman further from her natural position than when she appears upon a public platform.'[33]

The Ladies' Land League was not formed with any specific intention to advance the cause of women, but it did provide some women with an opportunity to take part in mainstream politics. A number of women were certainly radicalised by their experiences in the League. Jennie Wyse Power and Hannah Lynch, for example, went on to become important nationalist figures. There are many unanswered questions concerning the Ladies' Land League. We need to ascertain the geographical and occupational distribution of women active in that organisation. What difference did women's participation in the Ladies' Land League make to the participation of women in Irish political life, especially to Irish nationalism? What was the legacy of women's experience in the Land War for later feminist and radical politics? The role of women was conceived as auxiliary to that of the men. Public discussion on women's role in the Ladies' Land League asserted that the rightful place for women was in the home, and that their involvement was a temporary measure, resulting from extraordinary circumstances. It appears that the women of the Ladies' Land League were predominantly Catholic. Catholic women were more active in nationalist organisations than in societies or groups which organised and campaigned for social change, a fact which may be linked with their relative inactivity in philanthropic organisations. They appear to have been more willing to become politically involved through nationalism, than through social activism. During the nineteenth century, large-scale public Catholic philanthropy was taken over by nuns, and lay Catholic women were relegated to a supporting role, primarily as fund-raisers. For a number of Quaker and Protestant women, on the other hand, involvement in charitable societies was to have a radicalising effect, and a small number went on to participate in societies such as the Dublin Aid Committee (later the National Society for the Prevention of Cruelty to Children), which lobbied for legislative change to improve the lot of the poor.[34]

The patriarchal structure of society led naturally to women's subordination and to their exclusion from the body politic. Women in nineteenth-century Ireland were denied a legal and political identity. Single women and widows (*femme sole*) had full legal capacity, but married women were legally dependent on their husbands (*femme covert*). The control of women's property through the idea of 'coverture' and the increasing implementation of primogeniture in post-Famine society significantly affected women's economic and political claims. The state, through legislation, reinforced traditional gender roles for men and women and thus prevented equality. From 1857 women lobbied parliament in an attempt to alter the property laws, but change was slow in coming. Discrimination in the area of property rights led women to campaign, not only for changes in these laws, but also for the right to make political claims based on property qualifications. This formed the basis of their claim to the vote and thus political equality with men.

Protestant middle-class women created a political identity for themselves in the nineteenth century based on ideas of civic duty, just as peasant women had created their political identity through ideas of communal rights. Political organisation by middle-class women was more formal and structured than that of peasant women. Philanthropic activity provided middle-class women with an enhanced public role in society and a number of women philanthropists entered the public world of politics through their charitable work.

When we look at women's formal political activity, that is in societies specifically organised by women for a clear political end, we can see the formation of distinct political outlooks. We can also witness the development of concepts of gender difference. Women's involvement in formal politics is something which develops very strongly in the nineteenth century. The concept of difference is not developed by women alone. There are other influences which also need to be examined, such as Catholicism, and particularly the spread of convents, and its impact on the lives of women. The concept of gender difference was not new to the nineteenth century, but women activists of that century used the concept to argue for political rights on a scale previously unknown in Irish history. Irish women developed a strong public voice, particularly from the 1860s, arguing for the advantages that gender difference would bring to public and private life.

Some of the earliest formations of difference can be discerned in the anti-slavery societies which were organised by Irish women from at least the 1830s.[35] The information available on anti-slavery societies is quite scant, but the committees of those societies for which we have information were composed almost entirely of women.[36] Although it is impossible to ascertain with any degree of certainty the religious affiliations of the members, it appears, from some of the available membership lists, that the majority of members were Quakers, and Quaker women were to the fore in campaigning for women's rights in Ireland during the nineteenth century.

The primary objective of these anti-slavery societies was to raise the consciousness of the Irish people as to the horrors of slavery. To this end some societies annually distributed thousands of copies of a leaflet entitled 'Address to Emigrants' to emigrant offices in Dublin, Belfast, Cork and Derry. The dubious effect of such a paper blitz was noted in an annual report of 1860, when the committee was obliged to 'regret to acknowledge that hitherto our Irish emigrants have done small credit to the land of their birth and have generally thrown their influence into the pro-slavery side.'[37] They also invited speakers from America to address the Irish public on the issues of slavery. An anti-slavery petition presented to Queen Victoria in 1838 was signed by 75,000 Irish women.[38] So even if the membership of the organisations was small, they were certainly able to muster support when necessary. The female committees of these societies sought support for their cause primarily by appealing to other women. They accepted the status of wife and mother as a universal bond uniting all women and they used this to harness sympathy for their cause.

In an appeal from the Dublin Ladies' Association, published in 1837, Irish women, it was declared, as wives and mothers free from slavery, must empathise with their slave-bound sisters, who as a '... wife may be torn from the husband of her choice forever', or as a mother have no '...right of maternal property in her offspring.'[39] The concept of gender difference could not be more forcefully made than by appealing to the maternal privileges of women. The belief in the innate moral superiority of women was also revealed, a sentiment expressed again and

again by all the voluntary philanthropic organisations of the nineteenth century. 'Let us not,' the appeal continued, 'be deterred
because we are women – but let us remember that oft times God
uses the weak things of the world to confound the things that are
mighty.' 'Motherhood' and 'womanhood' were the powerful inte-
grating forces which allowed women to cross class and international boundaries. Through their work, anti-slavery activists fashioned
a rhetoric which was echoed in all other public organisations and
societies established by women in the nineteenth century.

The debates taking place in Ireland from the 1860s concerning
women's education, employment and status in society were profoundly influenced by ideas about appropriate behaviours and
expectations for women. While rigid role prescriptions existed for
women and men in the nineteenth century, women were adept at
politicising domesticity for their own purposes. The ideology of
domesticity, which argued that women's primary function was to
act as wife and mother, is viewed by historians to have been part
of the formulation of the 'public/private' dichotomy which it is
claimed existed in the last century. However, the division between
public and private was not as exclusive as has been believed, since
public and private life interacted in complex ways.

The debates concerning women's roles and status in Ireland
were not formulated in a vacuum and were affected, amongst other
things, by debates occurring in the English women's movement.
The immediate connecting point for some of the views being
expressed was the National Association for the Promotion of Social
Science. When Isabella Tod, the pioneer of most feminist organisations of nineteenth-century Ireland, first entered public life at the
age of 31, it was under the auspices of the National Association for
the Promotion of Social Science, which held its annual meeting of
1867 in Belfast. This society was developed by members from the
British Association for the Advancement of Science in 1857 and
attempted to create a 'social science' of society which would help
to alleviate the social problems of society.[40] The NAPSS provided
an important platform for activists, many of them women, who
wished to reform the position of women in society. It was this
association, Tod later wrote, which gave her her first experience 'of
direct political effort for a social purpose, and [I] was also first led
by it to speak in public.'[41] From this meeting, Tod undertook the
formation of the first consciously feminist group in nineteenth-century Ireland when she organised a small committee to press for
changes in the married women's property laws. Shortly afterwards
Tod also instituted committees to actively campaign for improve-

ments in the educational opportunities, at both secondary and university levels, available to women.[42] These societies and committees were consciously political.

The 1860 meeting of the NAPSS was held in Dublin and aroused considerable debate around the public role of women. Among the women to speak at the meeting was Anne Jellicoe, a pioneer in women's education and founder of Alexandra College in Dublin, and Sarah Atkinson, writer and philanthropist.[43] Women activists from England also spoke at the meeting, among them being Emily Faithful and Bessie Parkes. That there was some public unease about women speaking in public can be gleaned from a newspaper report, which stated 'that the appearance of women as orators addressing a public and mixed audience is not an experiment which merits encouragement, but an innovation, which calls for suppression.'[44] Women preachers had been involved in preaching to the public at the turn of the century,[45] but by the 1860s the public appearance of women on platforms was limited to those who sat on platforms when the annual reports of their various charitable organisations were read to the public. The NAPSS was influential in allowing women a public platform to debate issues relating to women's status in society. It provided a vital link between women activists in Ireland and England, and was the starting ground for many campaigns around women's issues.

The late 1850s and 1860s witnessed a more sustained public debate on women's place in society. Irish society generally reinforced traditional gender roles. Women's greatest role was to care for children. As an article published in the *Dublin University Magazine* in 1859 pronounced, 'The mother is the educator of the race. The child is father of the man. The nation is the result of motherhood.'[46] Similar views about the role of women in the home were expressed by clerics who sermonised on the duties of women to their families.[47] Linda Kerber has argued that the idea of 'republican motherhood', an ideology evolved in the early American republic which stressed that women's major civic role was to raise sons for the State, defined women's civic duty.[48] A similar view is to be found in Ireland, particularly in the nationalist organisations, such as the Young Irelanders and the Fenians. The nationalist and Gaelic Leaguer, Mary E. L. Butler, was arguing at the turn of the century that woman's primary role in revitalising the Irish language lay in her ability to teach and use the language in her domestic setting.

> Most earnestly is it to be desired that in the life and death crisis through which the country is now passing, the women of Ireland may not be found wanting; that they will turn the enormous

influence which they wield to good account, that they will shake themselves free from the dead hand of denationalisation which has weighed down on them in the past, and frozen the best in their nature, and that, becoming imbued themselves with true nationality, they will, one and all, make their homes centres of Irish life. They will have the proud consciousness of knowing that in making the homes of Ireland Irish they will be doing the best day's work that has ever been done to make Ireland a nation in the fullest, truest sense of the word.[49]

Such a view, however, denied women direct access to political power. Middle-class women, many of whom did not become mothers, found an outlet for their political aspirations through benevolent action. This in turn led to a small minority of women challenging inequalities based on sex. Activists of the nineteenth century who espoused women's rights claimed that their special status and moral and spiritual nature entitled them to participation in the affairs of the nation. While women activists called for political equality with men, many also believed that women were morally and spiritually superior to men. They used this argument of superiority to claim the franchise at both local and national levels. Isabella Tod, who had campaigned for the municipal franchise in Belfast, which was granted to women in 1887, was to note that:

For the first time in Ireland women in our town possess the most important of local franchises. We hope, and from the experience of our friends in Great Britain, we have good reason to hope, that they will care less for party politics than men do, and more for the great social and moral questions which ought to be the end for which party politics are only the means.[50]

Tod was not alone in arguing for the importance of gender difference and the complementary talents which women would essentially bring to public life. Activists also argued that social, economic and gender distinctions, which kept women from the arena of political power, were detrimental to the country. Work in benevolence was to bring many women into organising political groups. Women began to mobilise themselves through their charity work, by campaigning for changes to women's education, by publicly questioning the sexual double standard and campaigning for the franchise. But it was not until the formation of the Irish branch of the Ladies' National Association for the Repeal of the Contagious Diseases Acts in 1870 that an organised and extended political campaign, based on a perception of sexual oppression and the rhetoric of gender difference, operated on a national scale.

In 1864, parliament passed the first of three statues which permitted the compulsory inspection of prostitutes for venereal disease in certain military camps in both England and Ireland. The three Acts of 1864, 1866 and 1869 were introduced to control the spread of venereal disease among the soldiery.[51] In Ireland the areas designated 'subjected districts' were Cork, Cobh and Curragh camp. Any woman believed to be a prostitute (there was no definition of 'prostitute') could be asked to submit to a medical examination; be forcibly detained in a Lock hospital which treated venereal diseases; and be registered as a prostitute. The Acts were based on the idea that while men 'contracted' venereal disease, women transmitted these diseases.

Opposition to the Acts became organised from 1869. A number of associations were established to enforce their repeal. Amongst these were the National Association for the Repeal of the Contagious Diseases Acts, formed in 1869, and the Ladies' National Association, formed also in 1869 by Josephine Butler. Both of these organisations had branches in Ireland. By 1871 three branches of the LNA had been established, in Belfast, Dublin and Cork. Both Isabella Tod and Anna Haslam were involved in the campaign from the beginning and Tod also served on the executive committee of the London-based LNA until 1889, when Haslam took her place. They both served on the general council of the NARCDA, although this society was run by men and women council members had little impact on policy.[52]

The LNA in Ireland was a very localised and small affair. Throughout its active period, from 1871 to 1885, it never had more than forty-nine subscribers, the majority of whom were residents of Dublin, Cork and Waterford. Although the association was small, its very existence marked a new departure for Irish women. For the first time, they were willing to discuss openly matters pertaining to sexual morality and to initiate a public campaign to question and alter the sexual double standard which existed. For the women involved in the Irish campaign, there was an attempt made at redefinition and representation of women and their relationship to men. The women involved in the campaign in Ireland used those typically middle-class campaigning strategies which were to become such a part of the suffrage campaign. Petitions, meetings, letters to MPs and deputations formed the core activities.

Isabella Tod, who opposed the Acts, saw their implementation as an affront '... to the decency and purity of society – the dignity and independence of every woman in the land.'[53] While the women of the LNA were active in Ireland, their campaign never reached a mass audience. The subject matter of the Acts made it a delicate one to bring to public attention. It was also the case that many women did not wish to be involved in issues which related to sexual morality. Those who were involved felt an imperative to organise, to protect the status of women and to promote a higher standard of morality amongst men. Their civic duty now extended to protecting the morals of the nation. It was 'womanhood' in the guise of selfless, moral women who would bring about change in society. For many other women, and indeed men, women's moral nature gave them a reason for public and political action. This imputed 'moral' superiority, expressed also in many forms of philanthropic work, became the primary element in the concept of gender difference which emerged in the last decades of the century.

The demand for suffrage was the principal means whereby women fought for political involvement on the same terms as men in the late nineteenth and early twentieth centuries. A sizeable majority of those women who began the suffrage campaign in Ireland had activist roots in various philanthropic organisations. Tod, for example, established the first suffrage society in the north of Ireland in 1872, and Haslam organised a similar society in Dublin in 1876. The demand for enfranchisement in nineteenth-century Ireland was grounded in one principle – equal treatment of men and women. These Irish suffragists also believed that reform was achievable only in stages. The methods used were 'genteel'. Drawing room meetings, petitions, letters and the like, were the means preferred to lobby politicians or win public favour. It was not until the establishment of the Irish Women's Franchise League in 1908 that more vigorous or militant methods were entertained, and ultimately adopted. The suffrage issue in nineteenth-century Ireland received little widespread support. Membership of the two suffrage organisations remained small. In 1896 the Dublin Women's Suffrage Association, formed twenty years earlier, could only claim 43 members.[54] A number of issues prevented the suffrage cause from achieving wider support. There was little public interest in suffrage. The Land War had overtaken the country in the 1880s, and the Ladies' Land League had caused controversy over women's public role. Suffragists of the nineteenth century expected the democratic procedures of petitioning and lobbying to advance their cause. They did not recognise the extent to which party divisions would hamper the passage of the requisite legislation. Suffragists generally did not ally themselves to any one party. However, the introduction of the Home Rule Bills forced some Irish women activists to associate themselves with either the Liberal Unionist or Conservative camps.

The introduction of Gladstone's first Home Rule Bill in 1886 had a profound impact on a number of women in Ireland. In Belfast,

Isabella Tod reacted with horror to the Bill, seeing in it the seeds of the destruction of all her work. Tod, on the announcement of the Bill, organised a Liberal Women's Unionist Association. She suggested that Ulster should have a

> separate jurisdiction. If we can keep some degree of political freedom, such as is totally impossible for Ulster in a Parnellite Parliament, we can continue to do some good for the rest of Ireland. But no conceivable good for any created being could come from our being crushed under such a parliament.[55]

Anna Haslam, also a staunch Unionist, established a branch of the Women's Liberal Unionist Association in Dublin. The suffrage issue in the north was overtaken by the Home Rule issue. The Ulster Unionist Women's Council was formed in January 1911 to support male unionist politicians. By 1913 it was claimed that membership of the Council stood at anything up to 200,000,[56] a figure which makes the suffrage campaign appear very small. In 1893, a memorial addressed to Queen Victoria opposing Home Rule had 103,000 female signatures. Another petition sent at the same time from Ulster women had 145,000 signatures.[57] If there was a mass movement of women in nineteenth-century Ireland, it was to be found amongst unionist rather than nationalist or suffrage women.

Unionist women were extremely adept at organising themselves, a fact that has been little recognised by historians. This involved lobbying, mass letter-writing, petitions to Queen and parliament, public speeches, with Tod even taking to the election campaign trail in England to support the Liberal Unionist candidate and suffrage supporter, Leonard Courtney.[58] By the 1890s women were certainly expressing strong political preferences as to how they expected their country to be governed. Liberal women in England saw the Home Rule crisis as something which had roused women in particular to political action. A meeting of the Birmingham Women's Liberal Association in 1899 were told that:

> The Irish question has done more in the last two or three years to settle definitely the long-contested question of women's mission and women's place in politics than the patient and laborious efforts of the last twenty years past has done. It was like the national crisis which in old times had produced a Judith, a Boadicea, and a Joan of Arc. Many women who once personally disapproved of women taking an active part in politics had, during the last few months, not only attended but spoken at meetings on the Irish question.[59]

That Irish women were as affected by the Home Rule issue as English women is clear from the petitions they organised. Some Irish women found expression for their political convictions in the

Conservative party, through involvement in the Primrose League. The League, organised in England in 1883, had a number of branches in Ireland, and women appear to have played a significant role within these. In Cork, for example, Lady Mary Aldworth was convenor of the Mitchelstown branch of the organisation, while her sister-in-law held the same position in Bandon.[60] It has been argued that in England, Liberal women were encouraged much more in their participation of politics than Conservative women.[61] It is unclear whether the same was the case in Ireland.

There were other organisations and societies which claimed the allegiance of women during the period of the suffrage campaign. By the end of the nineteenth century vigorous campaigning, mainly by women involved in the suffrage issue, secured a place for women in local government. Women began to seek admittance to workhouses as visitors soon after the establishment of the poor law system in the 1830s. It is difficult to gauge the extent of philanthropic women's involvement in these institutions. It was not until 1880 that the North Dublin Union Board of Guardians allowed Catholic and Protestant women to 'visit the sick of their own persuasion'.[62] It seems that women had already been allowed to visit in the South Dublin Union. Where women were allowed to act as visitors, they dealt only with other women and children. By 1899, the government officially recognised that women did play an important role as visitors to the workhouse. In that year, the Local Government Board requested that all workhouses which boarded out children should form ladies' committees to oversee the boarding-out system, and by 1900 there were fifteen such committees in existence.[63] Women played a key role in the Irish Workhouse Association (1897) and the Philanthropic Reform Association (1896), two of the few charitable organisations in which men and women had an equal share in management. Both organisations lobbied to bring about changes in the workhouse system. The IWA, for example, had succeeded in persuading the government to employ one trained nurse in every union by the early twentieth century.[64] Organisations such as the IWA and the PRA encouraged and lobbied for women to become poor law guardians. It was not, however, until 1896 that a bill was passed which allowed women with certain property qualifications to serve as poor law guardians. In that year two women guardians were elected; by 1897 this had increased to twelve, by 1899 to eighty-five. This, although a significant advance for women, only made up a tiny proportion of the over 8,000 guardians elected in those years.[65]

Irish women never sat on poor law boards in any significant numbers, and consequently did not exert any great degree of influence on decisions made by these boards. It was expected that women poor law guardians would look after the interests of women and children and 'the training of girls for service, and the food and sanitary arrangements'.[66] Anna Haslam, philanthropist and suffragist, who had campaigned for women as poor law guardians for a number of years, asserted in 1899 that valuable work was being done by women, although this appears to have been limited to extending, in six unions, the practice of boarding out children.[67] Women had little, if any, control over the financial allocations made by boards of guardians. Women, through the 1898 Local Government Act, also won the right to vote and sit on district councils, but it was not until 1911 that Irish women could become county councillors. Haslam was to write in 1898 that the passing of the Act represented 'the most significant political revolution that has taken place in the history of Irish women'.[68] In the 1899 elections, of the eighty-five women elected as poor law guardians, thirty-one were also returned as rural district councillors, and four as urban district councillors.[69] As the first decades of the twentieth century dawned in Ireland, poor law boards became an important arena for the articulation of political allegiances, whether nationalist or unionist. Some commentators assumed that electors would find women candidates more attractive as rising 'above sectarian prejudices'.[70] However, women were as ready as men to associate themselves with particular political affiliations, especially in the increasingly hostile political climate developing in Ireland in these years. Lady Dockrell, who sat as an urban district councillor in Dublin, was a Protestant and unionist. She believed that the granting of local government to the Irish would 'steady' Irish nationalists. She argued that 'they will gain the courage of responsibility, and will weed out or restrain the more uncontrollable members of their party.' Invoking the moral and spiritual nature of women, she noted that upon them

> devolves the task of reconciling the opposing forces, softening asperities, and cementing all classes, so that peace and harmony shall reign in our land, and that truth and justice, religion and piety, may be established among us for all generations.[71]

It is clear from the records of the Association of Women Poor Law Guardians, which was actively involved in the movement to reform the workhouse system, that women developed a sophisticated political analysis of the role of the State in welfare provision. However, women played very little role in changing the fundamental nature of the workhouses. Unlike the situation in England, local government and the voluntary sector were not conceptualised as extensions of the family. In Ireland they were part and parcel of national politics and arenas where national politics were played out, leaving women with very little opportunity to make a strong impact.[72]

Local politics in nineteenth-century Ireland provided the only continuous and effective channel through which nationalist and unionist politicians could exert practical power. Local government thus constituted a key forum for the development of political ideology and was a primary means of distributing power amongst political élites. During the late nineteenth century opportunities for Catholics to stand for local office became more numerous. As the century progressed, the deliberations of local bodies to which Catholics were admitted in significant numbers increasingly became the scene of party conflict and manoeuvring. The Local Government Act of 1898 established elected county councils to conduct county administration, and rural and urban district councils, and poor law boards. It represented a major alteration in local administrative structures and, at county level in particular, heralded a wholesale transfer of power to the Catholic majority, excluding, of course, the Ulster counties. The eligibility of women to stand as councillors and their impact in the council chamber has gone unremarked by historians.

This brief survey of women's political involvement shows the diversity and range of activity by women which crossed class boundaries. There are still many questions to be answered about this involvement. What factors, for example, impeded or supported women's commitment to politics in the nineteenth century? What were the primary issues which were of concern to them? Are the political interests of men and women really substantially different? How did they develop a sense of political identity? Where, for example, did the women of the Ladies' Land League emerge from? What gave unionist women their attachment to empire? Attempting to answer some of these questions should lead us to a deeper understanding of the complexities of nineteenth-century political life in Ireland. Clearly women's political involvement was substantial. That historians of Irish politics need to accept the participation of women as a significant aspect of political life seems beyond doubt. Once their contribution is incorporated, a more complete picture of Irish political history will emerge.

Asenath Nicholson & the Famine in Ireland
Maureen Murphy

Had you been travelling in Ireland in 1844-1845, you might have seen – or heard about – an extraordinary American woman who was walking through the countryside singing hymns, reading the Bible and distributing religious tracts drawn from the depths of her large, black, bearskin muff. She wore Indian rubber boots, a polka coat, a bonnet and – when they weren't missing – silver-rimmed spectacles. A number of doctors offered to remove the large wart on her face. She recorded, with some indignation, that people stared at her. She was Asenath Hatch Nicholson: teacher, reformer, abolitionist, writer and traveller, and she had come to Ireland to investigate the condition of the Irish poor. Her account of her travels, *Ireland's Welcome to the Stranger* (London, 1847), is one of the most valuable records we have of Ireland on the eve of the Famine. She left Ireland in the fall of 1845, just before the first sighting of the potato blight was reported. She returned at the end of 1846, determined to do what she could to relieve the suffering.

The story of this remarkable woman begins in Chelsea, a village in the White River valley of eastern Vermont, where she was born, on 24 February 1792, to pioneering settlers Michael (c.1747-1803) and Martha (c.1748-1837) Hatch. Her name was prophetic. It appears in the Book of Genesis as the name of the daughter of the Egyptian high priest of On who was given by the pharaoh as a wife to Joseph. She shared Joseph's life while he managed the food supply so that the Egyptians did not starve when the famine came. Asenath Hatch would face a famine in her own time and devise her own plan to manage her resources to provide relief to the Irish poor.

Vermont was a centre of social reform in her youth. As early as 1789, the Republic of Vermont forbade the sale of slaves. In 1828, the abolitionist William Lloyd Garrison became editor of the *Journal of the Times* in Bennington. Closer to home, her parents provided examples of charity and tolerance. Nicholson's mother, Martha

Hatch, '... remembered the poor, and entertained strangers; hated oppression, scorned a mean act and dealt justly by all.' Her father, Michael Hatch, '... hung no Quakers, nor put any men in a corner of the church because they had a coloured skin.'[1] Her father also had a special feeling for the Irish. 'Remember, my children,' he told his family, 'that the Irish are a suffering people and when they come to your doors never send them empty away.'[2] Trained as a teacher, Asenath Hatch taught first in Chelsea, perhaps in her own District #2 schoolhouse, where she was remembered 'as a famous teacher' by Thomas Hale in his address celebrating Chelsea's centennial in 1884.[3] Like many of her generation, Asenath Hatch left rural Vermont for the city in 1831; she turns up in the *New York Directory*, listed as the schoolteacher wife of merchant Norman Nicholson.

Both Nicholsons followed the regime of Sylvester Graham, the New England temperance reformer turned diet crusader, whom Ralph Waldo Emerson called 'the poet of bran and pumpkins'. Graham warned against the enormous dinners fashionable at the time, with their courses of meats, fried foods and hot breads, and instead advocated strict vegetarianism. While diet was his obsession, he also concerned himself with other matters of health: sanitary food preparation, regular bathing, exercise in the fresh air, sensible dress and sexual hygiene.[4]

Grahamite boarding houses opened to house and feed the faithful. The movement reached its climax in the late 1830s, a decade when the Nicholsons' Grahamite boarding houses operated at 79 Cedar Street (1833-1834) and at the corner of Wall Street and Broadway (1834). Between 1835 and 1841, Asenath Nicholson was listed as the proprietor of boarding houses at 118 Williams Street and at 21 Beekman Street. While the *New York Directory* does not identify the Nicholsons' establishments as Graham boarding houses, they were certainly run along Grahamite principles.[5]

Nicholson's first book, *Nature's Own Book* (1835), outlined the Spartan regime of her household. She believed, for example, that Adam and Eve had a physical as well as a spiritual fall from grace in the Garden of Eden and that vegetarianism was the means of physical atonement.[6] Her book warned against the evils of tobacco, alcohol, coffee, tea – which she believed caused the *delirium tremens* – and hot chocolate.

Nicholson's boarding-houses were situated near the old Five Points, a section considered the worst slum in the city. Located on the site of the present New York City Court House, the Five Points was an area rife with crime, disease, gang warfare and vice. Poor Irish immigrants began settling in the Five Points in the 1830s. By the time the Civil War began, Famine immigrants were the over-whelming majority of residents of the eighty-six acres that made up the Sixth Ward.

While running her boarding houses, Nicholson joined the re-formers who tried to work among the poor of the Five Points. In the late 1830s the Central and Spring Street Presbyterians sent missionaries into the district, and in 1840, the Congregationalists founded the Broadway Tabernacle on Broadway near Worth Street. However, the Irish regarded Protestant missionaries as proselytisers and their institutional efforts were unsuccessful.[7] Nicholson, however, chose to work alone as she later would in Ireland. Recalling those years, she said, 'It was in the garrets and cellars of New York that I first became acquainted with the Irish peasantry and it was there I *saw* that they were a suffering people.'[8] Her work with those Irish informed her sense of mission. When the circumstances of her life changed – she was listed as a widow in the 1842 *New York City Directory* – she left aboard the *Brooklyn* in May 1844, for a fifteen-month trip to Ireland. It was a courageous adventure for an arthritic widow of fifty-two.

Nicholson spent six months 'investigating' conditions in rural Ireland before she began her self-appointed mission to bring the Bible to the Irish poor.[9] She filled two bags with Bibles supplied by the Hibernian Bible Society, attached the bags to a stout cord twisted under her polka coat and set off in her Indian rubber boots to distribute Bibles to those who could read and to read herself to those who could not. Her mission was not as straightforward as it appeared. In fact, she moved in a kind of vacuum between the Irish poor – predominantly Catholic – and the Protestant Anglo-Irish gentry and the Protestant missionaries who were actively prosely-tising in the countryside. Her position was not enviable: the Catholics were suspicious of any Bible-reading strangers while the missionaries suspected her broad tolerance and her democratic ideas.

She was shown the door at the Ventry Mission in Dingle and, while not mentioned by name, she was the subject of a hostile account in the Reverend Nangle's anti-Catholic paper, *The Achill Missionary Herald and Western Witness. A monthly journal exhibiting the principles and progress of Christ's kingdom of the anti-Christ commonly called the papacy; together with a practical exposure of the civil, social and political delinquencies practiced by the pope's emissaries in attempting to re-establish his wicked usurpations throughout the world generally and especially in this kingdom:*

During the last month this settlement was visited by a female who is travelling through the country. (We traced her from Dingle to this place.) She lodges with the peasantry and alleges that her object is to become acquainted with Irish character, she states that she has come from America for this purpose. She produced a letter purporting to be addressed by a correspondent in America to a respectable person in Birmingham; but in answer to a communication addressed by the writer to that individual, he stated that he has no acquaintance with her either personally or by letter. This stranger is evidently a person of some talent and education; and although the singular course which she pursues is *utterly* at variance with the *modesty and retiredness* to which the Bible gives *prominent place* in its delineation of a *virtuous* female, she professes to have no ordinary regard for that Holy Book. It appears to us that the principal object of this woman's mission is to create a spirit of discontent among the lower orders, and to dispose them to regard their superiors as so many unfeeling oppressors. There is nothing in her conduct or conversation to justify the supposition of insanity and we strongly suspect she is the emissary of some democratic and revolutionary society.[10]

Nicholson's curiosity and outspokenness were probably a trial to people she met. However, one can be certain that her only revolutionary idea was her egalitarianism. For Nicholson, it was tolerance and charity that counted, and she records with approval the evangelists working among the poor without regard to their willingness to convert, the instances of co-operation between Catholic and Protestant clergy and the work of Catholic religious among the poor.

Reaction to Nicholson was – above all – curiosity. She often complained of people staring at her, but she was an unusual sight. They wondered why she had travelled so far and usually attributed her presence among them to one of two traditional notions: to the saint's visit or to the penitential pilgrim. 'It was difficult,' she said, 'to make them believe I was not some holy St. Brigid going on penance.'[11]

Both ideas, favourite themes in medieval literature, were part of the folklore of the Irish countryside. The saint's visit, a parable of hospitality, is a popular religious legend while the pilgrimage to holy sites like Croagh Patrick and Lough Derg continues down to our own time. (Nicholson did, herself, climb Croagh Patrick. Scrambling down the Reek, she was convinced that her difficult descent was a judgement on her frivolous trip to the top to view the scenery.) *Ireland's Welcome to the Stranger*, Nicholson's account of her 1844-1845 travels, is valuable to the social historian, for it offers a panorama of Irish country life on the eve of the Famine: people, social movements, calendar customs and the ordinary life of the cottier class, the class that was scattered by the Famine diaspora. There are unforgettable vignettes: a description of a dance held in her honour near Urlingford, her duet across a Kerry mountain with a herd boy, a gathering around bonfires to celebrate Daniel O'Connell's release from prison, but there is always the *leitmotif* of unemployment.

Nicholson believed that Ireland needed work more than Repeal. As the fires blazed, a country woman said to her:

> It's many a long day that we have been working for that same to do somethin' for us, but not a hap'orth of good has come to a cratur of us yet. We're atin' the pratee today, and not a divil of us has got off the rag since he began his discoorse.[12]

When she went into a cabin in County Cork and saw two old women and their daughters spinning and carding, she remarked:

> This was an unusual sight, for seldom had I seen, in Ireland, a whole family employed among the peasantry. Ages of poverty have taken everything out of their hearts preparing and eating the potato and they sit listlessly upon a stool, i.e., on their straw, or saunter upon the street, because no one hires them.[13]

Even when there was employment, Nicholson was concerned with the working conditions – particularly those involving women and children. Watching Kerry women gather seaweed standing chest-deep in freezing water, she raged, 'Woman here is worse than a beast of burden because she is often made to do what the beast never does.'[14] Nicholson was among the first to bring the conditions of women's work to readers' attention. Later in the century, engravings and photographs would document her observations. Margaret MacCurtain's essay, 'The Real Molly Machree', contrasts the reality of women's work lives which Nicholson described with the colleen iconography of Victorian Ireland, an imagery that at once sentimentalised and exploited women.[15]

Nicholson's concern for the Irish was informed by her genuine charity and her efforts to help those among whom she travelled. When she returned to Ireland during the Famine, it was not as a Bible reader, but as a relief worker. She was unique in that she was the only woman who travelled to the afflicted areas of the west and who left us an account of her work among the poor. Hers is the lone voice that speaks to women's work and lives. Many of her views about famine relief programmes, employment and proselytism have been validated by the work of later historians and social workers.

She arrived in Dublin on 7 December 1846, armed with the promise of help for the poor from friends in America and from England. As she described the character of the Irish poor in *Ireland's*

Welcome to the Stranger, she described their suffering in *Annals of the Famine* (1851). Her return to Ireland was informed by her sense that she was on a Divinely-appointed mission. She paraphrased Luke 22:42: 'Father, if you are willing, remove this cup from me, nevertheless, not my will but Yours be done.'

Her previous experience in Ireland gave her a unique understanding of the poor as they coped with the catastrophe of the Famine. Once again, Nicholson brought to the country her singlemindedness and her sense of mission that involved bearing witness to the suffering and explaining not only how the Irish suffered, but why they suffered. She challenged absentee landlords and the land system, the government and the Churches' stewardship of resources entrusted to them for those starving; she rebuked them for their attitudes toward the poor. No hurler on the ditch, her own personal Famine relief effort was marked equally by practical and sensible practices and by a spirit of Christian charity.

Landing in Kingstown, she went to work immediately dispensing food from the house where she lodged.[16] Her first image of the Famine was one of special horror: the story of a woman cooking a half-starved dog with potatoes she had gleaned from a harvested field.[17] She despaired that she could do so little:

> I would not say that I actually murmured but the question did arise, 'Why was I brought to see a famine and be the humble instrument of saving some few alive, and then see these few die, because I had no more to give them?'[18]

Providentially, a parcel arrived from New York with money for her work and the promise of more help. The letter was not only a means of providing practical relief, it was a sign:

> I adored that watchful Hand that had so strangely led and upheld me in Ireland and now, above all and over all, when my heart was sinking in the deepest despondency, when no way of escape appeared, this heavenly boon was sent![19]

Nicholson moved into Dublin in the new year. On 23 January 1847, the Central Relief Committee of the Society of Friends established a soup kitchen in Charles Street, Upper Ormonde Quay.[20] Between January and July, when the Temporary Relief Act was passed and the soup kitchen was closed, the Quakers sold soup, an average of l000 quarts each day, for a penny a quart. They also sold soup tickets that could be distributed to the poor.

The Central Relief Committee was alone in providing relief to the poor. The government had decided to abandon its public works relief scheme in favour of direct distribution of food to the poor, but there was a gap between programmes in the spring of 1847. Mary Daly has observed that this break '... during one of the most difficult periods of all – one marked by extremely high death rates – was one of the most serious inadequacies in the whole government relief programme.'[21]

The male narrators of the Quaker records tell us little about women's work. While Jonathan Pim's letter of 2 July 1847 to Jacob Harvey in New York mentions that it was 'generally ladies' who were distributing cooked rice to the sick and to the children, it is Nicholson who described the Quaker women at work in their soup shop. 'Quaker matrons and their daughters with their white sleeves drawn over their tidy-clad arms – their white aprons and caps, all moving in that quiet harmony so peculiar to that people.'[22]

The official Quaker Famine report, *Transactions of the Central Relief Committee of Society of Friends* refers to ladies forming associations in towns for making, collecting and distributing clothes and its Appendix 15 suggests something of the enormous work of the Sub-Committee for Clothing, but it lists only the names of the men of the Central Relief Committee who were the Sub-Committee officers.[23] Nicholson left vignettes of women in Belmullet and Ballina working to provide clothes for the poor.

Although Nicholson admired the Quaker women working together in their soup shop, she went her own way establishing her own *modus operandi* in the spring of 1847. There is a letter from Nicholson to the Central Relief Committee written from 45 Hardwicke Street in July 1847; however, she described herself lodging in a house overlooking the Liffey during the early months of 1847. Walking through Dublin each morning with a large basket, she distributed slices of bread along the route from her house to her own soup kitchen on Cook Street, which was also called Coffin Street because there were sixteen coffin-makers or undertakers in Cook Street in 1847. There were also two tenement houses at number 19 and at number 55.[24] As was her custom, Nicholson located herself in a place selected for its poverty.

Officially, the Quakers ran their soup shop on a purchase system. Nicholson gave her food *gratis* although a system of triage obtained. She decided that £10 divided among one hundred helped no one, so she committed herself to a limited number of families for whom she cooked daily. During the six months that the Quakers ran their Charles Street soup shop, Nicholson cared for her small group of Dublin poor.

The English Quaker William Bennett met Nicholson during the first week in April 1847, at the home of his 'earliest friend in Ireland'. While Bennett does not mention him by name, his friend was probably Richard Davis Webb, the Dublin Quaker who would have shared Nicholson's commitments to abolitionism and to temperance. In the spring of 1847, Nicholson was correcting the proofs for *Ireland's Welcome to the Stranger*; Webb was her printer. Bennett's description of Nicholson shows that he was familiar with her text. He recounted her mission and then told of his impression of Nicholson struggling with meagre resources – heroic and hopeful.

> I found her with limited and precarious means, still persevering from morning to night in visiting the most desolate abodes of the poor, and making food – especially of Indian meal – for those who did not know how to do it properly, with her own hands. She was under much painful discouragement, but a better hope still held her up. Having considerable quantity of arrow-root with me, at my own disposal, I left some of it with her, and five pounds for general purposes. [25]

Like the Quakers, Nicholson relied on the help of English and American supporters to help her relief efforts. Nicholson suggested that she was the agent for a New York relief fund. What relief fund remains a mystery. Even straightforward organisations like the American Quakers' Relief Committee present difficulties. Jacob Harvey, who emigrated from Limerick, was the driving force in American aid, working regularly with the Central Relief Committee, but he was disowned in 1829 by the New York Quakers, both the Orthodox and the Hicksites, for marrying out.[26]

New Yorkers met to found the General Irish Relief Committee at the Mulberry Street House. It was not a Quaker meeting house, but the African Free School at 2 Mulberry Street. Quakers would have been involved with the school but locating a meeting at the School meant that it was not an official Quaker enterprise. Nicholson is not mentioned in the 1848 *Report of the General Irish Relief Committee of the City of New York* nor is she mentioned in the *Transactions*.

Nevertheless Nicholson did receive aid from supporters in New York. The records of the New York Quakers' Meeting for Suffering held on 22 May 1847 indicates that a committee collected the sum of $4013 to purchase food for the Irish and that food was aboard the U.S. Frigate *Macedonian* which arrived at Haulbowline on 16 July 1847.[27] In the shipment consigned to the Quakers were fifty barrels of Indian corn meal for Maria Edgeworth. Boston children sent one hundred and fifty pounds of flour and rice to her for her poor.[28] Along with the food for Maria Edgeworth were five barrels of Indian meal, flour and biscuit for Asenath Nicholson.

There is no record that the two remarkable ladies ever met although they shared similar views about the Irish poor: their criticism of absenteeism, their concern that poverty not take away the dignity of the poor and, more than anything, the need for employment. Edgeworth wrote to the Central Relief Committee about her district in County Longford petitioning the Committee's Clothing Committee for shoes for her tenants working in drainage projects.[29]

Nicholson was told that she would have to pay the costs to have her food in the barrels on the *Macedonian* shifted to sacks purchased from the government. (While the British government underwrote the expense of transporting relief supplies, they required that stores be shifted from barrels to sacks.) Nicholson criticised the practice on two grounds: that the meal stored in sacks became damp and mouldy and that the sacks cost money that could be spent for food.

In her usual way, Nicholson simply refused to comply. When her sacks were delivered through the Central Relief Committee, she did not pay the charges. Her letter to the Committee, dated 7 July 1847, from 45 Hardwicke Street, began with an apology for troubling them but went on to say firmly:

> Your clerk told me when I received your order that I must pay for the sacks but if they are returned in good order, this money would be refunded. When this was refused, he denied the engagement saying I should pay freight if not pay for the sacks. This I am willing to do if it is just, but the donors in New York sent me notice that all they sent me was freight free *and* sent in barrels and I quite *prefer* them because sacks will not keep the meal so well as much that I had was seriously injured.[30]

The Central Committee responded that she did not have to pay for the sacks.

Before the five barrels of food on the *Macedonian* arrived in Cork, Nicholson left for Belfast. Her last Dublin donation was a 'few barrels' sent under the auspices of the Central Relief Committee to Nicholson from the children of a pauper school in New York.[31] Nicholson brought the meal to an appropriate destination, '... to a school in the poorest convent in Dublin [that] was in a state of the greatest suffering.'[32] It is likely that the school was the Presentation school at George's Hill, founded for the children of the Dublin poor in 1789. Its location near the Four Courts puts it in the vicinity of Nicholson's Cook Street soup kitchen. Nicholson would have had an entrée to the Presentation nuns through her friendship with the Irish temperance crusader, Father Theobald Mathew, who was related to the foundress of the order, Mother Nano Nagle. During her first stay in Cork, Father Mathew took Nicholson to the golden jubilee of Mother Clare Callaghan at the South Presentation Convent.[33]

Nicholson noticed the kinds of distances that separated the nuns from the world: the grating which set the nuns apart from where she stood in the chapel, the nuns sitting with Father Mathew and Nicholson but not sharing the breakfast they had prepared for their guests, and the unwrinkled face of the old jubilarian which had been untouched by life – '... not a furrow had old Time made in her plump, placid face.'[34]

When she returned to work for Famine relief, she recognised that, while the nuns lived cloistered lives, they were nonetheless very much involved with the world. Caitriona Clear characterises Irish women's religious life between the 1770s and 1840 as Irish congregations with a broad mandate to work among the poor that included schools which fed and clothed their children.[35] Nicholson shared their vocation. She had answered her own call to help the suffering. En route from the west to Dublin, she stopped at the Presentation convent school in Tuam where she found, for the first time in her Famine travels, a school where the 400 children had normal affect and appearance. When she returned to Cork in 1848, she visited the Presentation convent again and recorded the work that the 'indefatigable' nuns did to feed about 1300 children.[36] She may have found religious life as incomprehensible as Catholic theology, but she responded to the good works of religious women.

With the last of her Dublin stores distributed and the Central Relief Committee closing its soup shop when the government set up soup kitchens under the Temporary Relief Act, Nicholson left Dublin by steamer, on 6 July 1847, for Belfast. She was going to see the Belfast Ladies' Association for the Relief of Irish Destitution, founded in January of 1847. She contrasted their work with their Dublin counterparts':

> *Here* was a work going on which was paramount to all I had seen.
> *Women* were at work; and no one could justly say that they were
> dilatory or inefficient. Never in Ireland, since the famine, was
> such a happy condition of all parties, operating so harmoniously
> together, as was here manifested. Not in the least like the women
> of Dublin, who sheltered themselves behind their old societies –
> most of them excusing themselves from personal labour, feeling
> that a few visits to the abodes of the poor were too shocking for
> female delicacy to sustain; and, though occasionally one might
> be prevailed upon to go out, yet but a few days could I ever
> persuade any to accompany me. Yet much was given in Dublin;
> for it was a city celebrated for its benevolence, and deservedly so,
> as far as giving goes. But *giving* and *doing* are antipodes in her
> who has never been trained to domestic duties.[37]

In Belfast Nicholson found an organisation of about 150 ladies of all denominations working in different aspects of Famine relief. She was especially impressed with their Ladies' Industrial School and with their involvement in the Connacht Industrial School.[38] Nicholson's analysis of the group's success turned on their energy and on their spirit of cooperation, for there was '... none of that desire for who should be greatest.'[39] Nicholson observed just the characteristic that contemporary feminist historians identify with the success of women's organisations that put cooperation before competition.

Nicholson's trip north, which took her to the coast of Antrim and to Donegal as well as to Belfast, was the prelude to an extended journey to the west of Ireland. She returned to Dublin briefly to collect some money and a box of clothing and to arrange that a grant that she expected be given to Mrs Hewittson, a Donegal friend who could make the best use of the funds.[40] Then she set out by coach for Tuam and from there by open car to Newport, County Mayo, a place she had visited in 1845. Finding western Mayo '... misery without mask,' she stayed until April 1848.

While she knew Mayo from Westport to Achill, Nicholson was unfamiliar with the area of greatest destitution: from Ballina west to the Erris peninsula. She followed the route of the Quakers William Forster, James Tuke, William Bennett and Richard Webb. She refers to Forster's extensive tour, from 30 November 1846 to 14 April 1847, which sounded the Famine alarm and mobilised the Quakers. It was also the opportunity to locate people in the afflicted areas who could be counted on to minister to those in need. Nicholson would have had Bennett's advice for her travels. She wrote with praise for his scheme that distributed seeds for green crops in the west and noted its success on Aranmore. Distrustful of institutions, even one as praiseworthy as the Central Relief Committee, she noted with approval that Bennett acted as an individual, not as a member of a society.[41]

Richard Webb would probably have been the most helpful to Nicholson as she planned her own visit to Mayo. She does not mention Webb's tour in *Annals*, but he visited Mayo and Galway in May 1847, stopping in the places and meeting many of the people that Nicholson mentioned or described in *Annals*. When Webb returned to Erris in February 1848, it is likely that they met in Ballina. Webb wrote to the Central Relief Committee from Ballina on 18 February 1848.[42] Nicholson recorded that she was in Ballina in February and left for Castlebar on 28 February 1848.[43]

In Newport, Nicholson set about bearing witness to the suffering. Her *Annals* differs from the compassionate accounts of her Quaker male contemporaries in that she combines documentary with other forms of discourse including parables, dramatic scenes and dialogues written in the cadences of the Old Testament. While the men focused on the problems of famine relief, Nicholson looks to the human face of suffering. On 28 November 1847, she described a scene that anticipated Synge's *Riders to the Sea*. A fisherman's widow journeyed twenty miles to 'prove' her husband who had been washed ashore and buried without a coffin. She bought a white coffin and with her hands, she dug him from his grave and 'proved' him by the leather button she had sewn on his clothes.[44]

In recording such scenes, Nicholson made it clear that she believed that the Famine was not a Divine judgement, but the failure of man to use God's gifts responsibly. Nicholson considered herself as 'acting entirely as a passive instrument; moving because moved upon', but there was nothing passive about her indictment of the government and the Established Church for failing in their stewardship of their relief resources and in their attitude toward the poor for whom they were responsible. She distinguished between hired relief officials, whom she dismissed as bureaucratic, hierarchical and self-serving, and local volunteer relief workers, whom she lauded as compassionate, egalitarian and selfless.

Scrupulous herself about her own expenses, she reported that she allowed herself twenty-three pence a day for food – a diet of cocoa and bread – and that she dispensed with her sevenpence-worth of cocoa, milk and sugar when she was running short of stores for her poor. She continued to ask herself whether she was doing enough to economise, so she was critical of official relief officers who lived well while those they were charged to care for went hungry.

She attacked government relief officers for putting record-keeping before the hungry, and described the dying poor turned away and told to return another day to be first entered on the roster and then fed. She described two orphans, aged seven and five, who were sent from Newport by relief officials to the poorhouse at Castlebar. They walked ten miles through the rain and arrived late at night. The little girl was accepted but the boy was turned away and walked the ten miles back to the door of Nicholson's friend, Mrs Arthur, the widowed postmistress of Newport.[45] Nicholson intervened and brought the boy to a school where he was fed and clothed for the winter.

It has often been charged that the government allowed food to be exported while Ireland starved. Nicholson looked at the matter of diverted food sources from another angle: she charged that grain used for distilling alcohol could have fed the Irish poor. Elizabeth

Malcolm says very little about alcohol and the Famine in *Ireland Sober, Ireland Free*, except to note that duty on spirits increased and that in 1847, with grain prices sky-high, the consumption of legal spirits fell only about twenty-five percent, from approximately 8,000,000 gallons to about 6,000,000 gallons.[46] The 60,000,000 pounds of grain or 30,000 tons of grain used to distil 6,000,000 gallons of eighty-proof spirits could have provided more than 300,000,000 servings of grain-based cereal.

Even with consumption reduced, Father Mathew complained to the assistant secretary to the Treasury, Charles Edward Trevelyan, that make-shift drink shops were erected at some relief work sites and presumably condoned by officials. In at least one case, a publican member of a local relief committee recommended men for work only on the condition that they spent part of their wages on drink.[47]

Concerned as she was about stewardship, Nicholson was far more interested in the attitude of the relief workers toward the poor. Over and over she contrasted the lack of charity on the part of officials with the compassion of the volunteer workers. The lack of charity on the part of officials appears to have been based, in part, on their opinion – part Malthus, part Darwin – that the Irish brought their troubles on themselves. Christopher Morash has observed, in his study of the literature of the Famine, that contemporary accounts often cited Malthus in trying to explain the Famine. Morash also argues that Malthusian doctrine informs the fictional representation of nineteenth-century Ireland in Anthony Trollope's *Castle Richmond* and in William Carleton's *The Black Prophet*.[48]

Critical as she was about government relief officers, Nicholson was quick to praise the generosity of coast guards and their families stationed in the west of Ireland toward their poor neighbours. Many guardsmen were recruited by the Quakers. The Coast Guard Inspector General, Sir James Dombrain, who shared their view of the poor Irish, supported their work. Having experienced the 1839 Famine, Sir James prevailed on the relief officer at Westport to issue free meal, and he directed the captain of the government steamship *Rhadamanthus* to take 100 tons of meal to the Killeries where, on 22 June 1846, the cutter *Eliza* was met by a boatload of starving men begging for food.

Sir Randolph Routh, who had the responsibility for distributing the Indian corn, complained about Sir James to Trevelyan.[49] Seamus Heaney based his poem 'For the Commander of the *Eliza*' on the episode; his closing lines articulate the Malthusian/Darwinist bias of the speaker:

Sir James, I understand, urged free relief
For famine victims in the Westport sector
And earned tart reprimand from good Whitehall –
Let natives prosper by their own exertions;
Who could not swim might go ahead and sink.[50]

As far as Nicholson was concerned, the problem was not that the
Irish avoided exertion, but that they had no employment. On 31
October 1847, she wrote to an English friend from Belmullet: 'Every
effort of the friends of Ireland is battled by the demoralising efforts
that feeding a starving peasantry without labour produces,' and
went on to observe that the condition of the resident landlords in
the west had an adverse effect on local relief efforts:

> You sir, who know Erris, tell, if you can, how the landlord can
> support the poor by taxation, to give them food, when the few
> resident landlords are nothing and worse than nothing, for they
> are paupers in the full sense of the word.[51]

Nicholson anticipated Mary Daly's argument one hundred and
fifty years later, that relief work – subject as it was to the variables
of local lobbying efforts and administrative skills to propose projects and to apply for funds – meant that the number and power of
local resident landlords accounted for the great differences in
expenditure on public works. The amount spent between April
1846 and January 1847 in Erris was 4.00-4.99 pounds per family,
while in north Clare the amount was 10 pounds per family.[52]

Nicholson made her own case for local employment and, as
always, she took a special interest in work for women and in work
women were doing:

> I must and will plead, though I plead in vain, that something must
> be done to give them work. I have just received a letter from the
> curate of Bingham's Town saying that he could set all his poor
> parish, both the women and the children, to work, and find a
> market for their knitting and cloth, if he could command a few
> pounds to purchase the materials. He is young and indefatigable,
> kind-hearted and poor and no proselyte. Mrs Stock has done well
> in her industrial department. The Hon. William Butler has pur-
> chased cloth of her, for a coat to wear himself, which the poor
> women spin, and gave a good price for it.[53]

While Nicholson's witness to suffering and challenges to the
authorities on behalf of the Irish poor are, in themselves, of interest,
it is her own active efforts to offer aid and comfort that command
our attention. She distributed her supplies of food and clothes. She
visited the distressed and brought their stories to the world. She
helped the relief workers she admired and left a record of their
names and service. The Quakers left us some account of relief
workers, but it is Nicholson who tells us about remarkable women

like Mrs Stock, who ran a soup kitchen from the Belmullet rectory and who organised a women's clothing industry, the charitable Mrs Arthur of Newport, and Mrs Garvey who forgave her suffering tenants their rent.

Above all, she was moved by the generosity and kindness of the suffering Irish to one another and to strangers. The hospitality of the Irish countryside was a theme of *Ireland's Welcome to the Stranger*; in *Annals*, it was the generosity of the Irish to one another. Irish oral tradition down to our own time describes the charitable woman who gives her last measure of meal to a beggar at her door, and is rewarded with an inexhaustible supply of food.

Always, she read the Bible. Nicholson read the Bible to the Irish to save them from the superstitions of Rome, so she was – in principle – supportive of the efforts of Protestant missionaries; however, she wanted conversions to be the result of reason, not coercion. It is not surprising, therefore, that she condemned proselytisers:

> It requires the Irish language to provide suitable words for a suitable description of the spirit which is manifested in some parts to proselyte *by bribery* obstinate Romans to the Church which had been her instrument of oppression for centuries.[54]

She predicted accurately that proselytisers' gains would be short-lived, and quoted children who told her they would be going back to their own chapel when the stirabout time was over. What was more common in Nicholson's experience was co-operation among many of the clergy of different denominations who worked together to help the poor.[55]

She left Ireland in the fall of 1848, when she felt that her work there was over. There is the suggestion that she was planning to return to America; however, she left Dublin for England where she wrote the first edition of *The Annals of the Famine*, called *Lights and Shades*, in London in 1850. She reported on the Crystal Palace Exhibition, joined the American pacifist Elihu Burritt's delegation to the International Peace Conference in Frankfurt, and travelled on the continent before she returned to America in 1852.

One might argue that Asenath Nicholson was a woman ahead of her time, a Shavian new woman. She was certainly a kindred spirit: vegetarian, teetaller, outdoor exercise enthusiast. What's more, she was a forerunner of Shaw's heroine, St Joan. Certainly, she was not the androgynous teenager with a mission, but she was another androgynous critter: the middle-aged widow with a mission.

Critical of the superstitions of Rome, she certainly would *not* have heard saints' voices, but her books speak of her sense that she was on some Divinely-appointed mission. She too challenged the system, marshalled resources to accomplish her ends, and, if she did not demonstrate her subversiveness by cross-dressing – though her appearance was, in its way, extraordinary – her straightforward questions, impromptu sermons, impassioned letters and candid books marked her, by some like the Reverend Nangle of the Achill Mission, as a dangerous fomenter of discontent among the lower orders.

Asenath Nicholson, was not, of course, imprisoned, tried and burned at the stake. Had she been brought to trial, she would have read the Bible to her fellow prisoners, defended herself with the same spirited clarity as Joan, but like her fellow New Englander, Mark Twain's Connecticut Yankee, she would have found a way to escape the flame. No doubt she would have talked her way out of it. She certainly would have had the last word.

No, she was not burned at the stake. Instead, she shared the fate of other worthy women: she was ignored. Her name appears on one or two lists; she is praised in an article in the *Cork Examiner* in August 1848, and William Bennett praises her work for Famine relief in his *Narrative of a Recent Journey of Six Weeks in Ireland* (1847); but, in the end, she speaks for herself in a book that has never been reprinted.

During her first stay in Ireland, while travelling the road from Oranmore to Loughrea, Nicholson rested to ease her blistered feet and thought of her prudent friends who had cautioned her against her reckless adventure. Did she wish to be in her own parlour in New York? She did not.

> Should I sleep the sleep of death, with my head pillowed against this wall, no matter. Let the passerby inscribe my epitaph upon this stone, *fanatic* who then? It shall only be a memento to that one in a foreign land loved and pitied Ireland, and did what she could to seek out its condition.[56]

'To Bounce a Boot Off Her Now & Then ...': Domestic Violence in Post-Famine Ireland[1]
Elizabeth Steiner-Scott

In 1878 Frances Power Cobbe published in *The Contemporary Review* the seminal piece on wife-beating in the nineteenth century: 'Wife Torture in England.' She informed her readers that: 'In the worst districts of London ... four-fifths of the wife-beating cases are among the lowest class of Irish labourers – a fact worthy of more than passing notice ... seeing that in their own country Irishmen of all classes are proverbially kind and even chivalrous towards women.'[2] In the same year that Cobbe deplored Irish emigrants' barbarous treatment of their wives and applauded Irishmen's apparent kindness to their wives at home, *The Irish Times* and *The Cork Examiner* reported weekly cases of wife-beating that were heard before the local Magistrates' Courts. And between 1853 and 1920 in the Criminal Index Files in the National Archives in Dublin, there are recorded 1,012 appeals by men convicted of beating their wives, mothers and sisters lodged before the Lord Lieutenant of Ireland, seeking to have their sentences reduced or dismissed.[3] These cases revealed that women in Ireland were being abused at the hands of their husbands, fathers and brothers to such an extent that Cobbe's assessment of Irishmen's alleged 'kindness' and 'chivalry' to their womenfolk must be questioned.

However, even though people could read almost daily reports of harrowing incidents of abuse of women, there was virtually no outcry against wife-beating and domestic violence in Ireland. There were no editorials condemning it in either *The Irish Times* or *The Cork Examiner*. There was no demand to extend the 1853 Aggravated Assaults on Women and Children Act to Ireland. And a series of reforms widening the availability of divorce and judicial separation also were not extended to Ireland during the nineteenth century. When divorce was absolutely outlawed by the Irish Constitution of 1937, it merely copper-fastened a long-accepted reality for abused wives in Ireland: there was legally no way for them to leave their abusive husbands.[4] There was a virtual silence about a phenomenon that was so widely reported that the historian can only surmise that there existed some kind of collective wish either to ignore this social crime, or to accept it as commonplace. It was not until *The Irish Citizen*, Ireland's first avowedly feminist newspaper, began to publish articles condemning domestic violence in the first decade of the twentieth century that the reality of many women's lives was brought home to a largely middle class and urban Irish public. And even then, these articles were submerged among the greater concerns of the First World War and the struggle for national independence. With the founding of the Irish Free State in 1922, silence surrounding domestic violence returned until well into the 1970s and the emergence of a second wave of Irish feminism.

Why was this issue shrouded in silence? Why did the British feminist campaign against wife-beating in the nineteenth century fail to make an impact in Ireland? What recourse did Irish women have to the law? What role, if any, did the Irish Temperance Movement play in affecting Irish people's perception of domestic violence? How did abused wives respond? Did the community restrain abusive husbands or did the unwillingness of the community to get involved provide protection for those husbands? How did class issues intersect with domestic violence? What connections, if any, can be established between the emerging Irish nationalism of the late nineteenth century and an unwillingness to address serious social problems? These are a few of the questions which provide a framework within which an investigation of Irish women's domestic life in post-Famine Ireland can be undertaken.

In recent years, a number of historians – Anna Clark, J. Lambertz, Linda Gordon, Elizabeth Pleck, Nancy Toames – have looked at the various campaigns against wife-beating in nineteenth-century England and the United States.[5] They have shown that public concern about wife-beating did not correlate with the actual incidence of the crime, but increased when domestic violence became symbolically linked with other concerns, such as temperance and women's suffrage. By the mid-nineteenth century when the British Parliament passed the 1853 Act for the Better Prevention and Punishment of Aggravated Assaults upon Women and Children, popularly known as the 'Good Wives' Rod', violence in general had become less publicly acceptable. Despite traditional liberal distaste for interfering in the intimate private sphere of the family, the State found itself forced by a variety of interested groups, including feminists, to take increasingly interventionist actions. The Act, while not extended to Scotland or Ireland, allowed for cases of assault against any female or male child under 14 years of age to be heard before two Justices of the Peace at Petty Sessions or before a Magistrate at any Police Court. The Act allowed magistrates to impose a maximum six months' sentence with or without hard labour or a fine not exceeding 20 pounds. It also granted the magistrates the right to demand that the convicted offender be bound over to keep the peace for an additional 6 months.[6]

Anna Clark and Jan Lambertz have both shown that this Act was the result of a concerted 'moral purity' campaign waged in the press in England and largely directed against working class husbands.[7] Wife-beating was seen as a predominantly working class phenomenon which required punishment by law. Working class husbands who beat their wives were 'barbarians' who appeared untouched by the niceties of middle class Victorian culture and civilisation. Their wives, perceived as largely uneducated and pathetic creatures, required protection by the State since they could not rely on their husbands' protection. In 1853 and 1856 many members of Parliament called for flogging to be imposed as punishment for abusers, and the press largely agreed with this view. In an editorial of 20 August 1852, *The Times* of London called for education to 'elevate' the lower orders, but went on to say that 'if we will not teach we must punish, and the lessons which ought to be impressed by reason must be inculcated by fear.'[8] Flogging wife-beaters was demanded but ultimately not included in the 1853 legislation.

The Aggravated Assaults on Women and Children Act did very little to deter husbands from abusing their wives and children. It simply punished briefly, by imprisonment, those few husbands whose wives were brave enough, or battered enough, to testify against them in the Magistrates' Courts. Most wives, because of their economic dependency, fear of reprisals, and distrust of the law, were unwilling to prosecute. As long as the very basis of marriage remained an inherently unequal arrangement that left husbands with the power to control, harass and beat their wives with impunity, domestic violence was inevitable.

In the 1870s, the need to highlight the appalling conditions of many married women remained a priority for feminists. The well-known social reformer and journalist, Anglo-Irish-born Frances Power Cobbe, published a series of articles that documented what she called an epidemic of 'wife torture' in Britain. She also highlighted the judicial double standard that occurred whenever abused wives attempted to retaliate against brutal husbands. She horrified her middle class readers by reporting the case of an

Irishman who had murdered his wife 'under circumstances of exceptional brutality and who had from first to last gloried in his crime' and was set free after a week's imprisonment. At the same time, a woman who accidentally killed her husband during a drunken row was sentenced to be hanged. As a result of Cobbe's campaign in the newspapers, the woman's sentence was commuted, and she was released.[9]

Cobbe seemed particularly sensitive to the fact that so many of the cases of wife-beating that came to her attention were perpetrated by emigrant Irishmen. In 1878, when she published 'Wife Torture in England', she argued that wife-beating was especially endemic among the artisan and labouring classes, and, even more especially, among the Irish. She indicated that Liverpool, where the Irish had settled in huge numbers in the immediate post-Famine decades of the 1850s and 1860s, was perhaps the worst city in England for wife-beating. She quoted Mr Serjeant Pulling, writing in the *Transactions of the Social Science Association* in 1876: 'Nowhere is the ill-usage of woman so systematic as in Liverpool, and so little hindered by the strong arm of the law; making the lot of a married woman, whose locality is the "kicking district" of Liverpool, simply a duration of suffering and subjection to injury and savage treatment, far worse than that to which the wives of mere savages are used.'[10] Employing encoded references which her Victorian English readers would easily decipher, Cobbe endorsed this view of the Irish labourer as a 'savage'. According to her, the Irishman in England lived outside the pale of civilisation; he was a brute incapable of reasoned behaviour; he was the victim of a system of cruel, capitalist exploitation that made him impervious to the 'delicate courtesies of humanity'.[11] In so doing, Cobbe merely echoed the common stereotype of the brutal Irish labourer which frequently appeared in *Punch* and other English satirical magazines. A typical example appeared in 1874. With his readily recognisable simian features, the Irish husband taunted his beaten and cowering wife with the words: 'Ah! You'd Better go Snivelin' to the 'Ouse o' Commons, You Had! Much They're Likely to do for Yer!'[12]

In comparing the battered wife to the oppressed slave 'on a Southern plantation before the war struck off their fetters', Cobbe was clear where the blame lay: not entirely, she argued, in the abusive character of the husband, but in the lack of civil rights of the wife. 'The position of a woman before the law as wife, mother and citizen, remains so much below that of a man as husband, father and citizen, that it is a matter of course that she must be regarded by him as an inferior.' This situation 'exposes women to an order of insults and wrongs which are never inflicted by equals upon an equal, and can only be paralleled by the oppressions of a dominant caste or race over their helots.' Finally, Cobbe stressed that there was a direct connection between male concepts of ownership and the reality of violence: 'The notion that a man's wife is his PROPERTY, in the sense in which a horse is his property ... is the fatal root of incalculable evil and misery ... It is even sometimes pleaded on behalf of poor men, that they possess *nothing else* but their wives, and that, consequently, it seems doubly hard to meddle with the exercise of their power in that narrow sphere.' She concluded 'that the common idea of the inferiority of women, and the special notion of the rights of husbands, forms the undercurrent of feeling which induces a man, when for any reason he is infuriated, to wreak his violence on his wife.'[13] It was clearly Cobbe's conviction that the question of marital brutality was inseparable from the negative view of the female sex that was at the heart of the Woman Question. Cobbe's campaign culminated in the passage of the Act to Amend the Matrimonial Causes Acts of May 1878. The new law paved the way for separation orders to be granted in cases where the wife could prove that her husband had been abusive to her or her children. According to William Duncan, writing in *The Irish Jurist* in 1972, there is some confusion about whether the 1878 Act ever fully applied to Ireland. 'Whether the 1878 Act did or did not apply to Ireland, it is quite clear that the general policy of the Westminster Parliament in legislating for matrimonial causes was to treat Ireland as a separate entity having different requirements or no requirements at all.'[14] None of the landmark English Acts of the latter half of the nineteenth century increasing the matrimonial jurisdiction of the Magistrates' Courts was, in fact, extended to Ireland.[15]

There has been considerable debate among historians as to the extent of marital violence in the second half of the nineteenth century. Whereas the public remained convinced that the problem was endemic, especially in working class communities and in immigrant Irish communities in England and the United States, the actual incidence is difficult to determine. It was certainly the case that contemporaries saw wife-abuse as continuing to pose a profound social problem, in spite of so-called reforming legislation like the 1853 Act and the Matrimonial Causes Act of 1878. It is also true that increasing community intolerance of domestic violence in England and the U.S., as well as sustained community interest in it, affected marital relationships. Nancy Toames endorses this view in her study of the actual level of aggravated assaults on women in working class London in the latter half of the nineteenth century. She concludes that the nineteenth century witnessed a genuine decline in marital violence as respectable values defined such conduct as unmanly and therefore unacceptable.[16] A. James Hammerton, in *Cruelty and Companionship: Conflict in Nineteenth-Century Married Life*, agrees with Toames and stresses that there was indeed a decline in official convictions for aggravated assaults on women, including those between husband and wife. He emphasises, however, that this was consistent with the more general decline in violent crime in the nineteenth century.[17] But the extent to which such a decline represented a genuine decrease in domestic violence remains unresolved, and, perhaps, unresolvable. There is consistently a disparity between recorded and actual domestic assaults. V.A.C. Gatrell argues persuasively that 'the gap between the real incidence of the *less* serious forms of violence and their recorded incidence must have been, and still is, very large indeed ... most trends in recorded violence, especially petty violence, may be profoundly affected by changes in public attitudes to violence.'[18] This was certainly the case in Ireland, where crime statistics for 'petty' crimes are sketchy and the historian must rely on the more anecdotal evidence from court reports in the newspapers.

When looking at Ireland in the latter half of the nineteenth century, it is possible to recognise profound differences in the community's attitudes to crime, violence, notions of respectability and marriage.[19] The emphasis until very recently has been for historians of Ireland to concentrate on the political and economic struggles of this period. A few historians of women have begun to broaden the historical agenda, and we are now in a better position to speculate on the extent to which Irish women's experience of marriage diverged, if at all, from their British sisters'.[20]

Irish readers of British papers saw Irish men accused of beating their wives in England, and they could be easily reassured that this was because these men had undergone the dehumanising effects of emigration and the worst ravages of industrialisation. They might comfort themselves with Cobbe's assurance that in Ireland, Irish men treated their wives chivalrously. However, this view was clearly contradicted in the police reports in Irish newspapers daily. In an investigation of *The Irish Times* and *The Cork Examiner* for 1878 and 1885, one can find detailed accounts of wife-beating and domestic violence cases that were heard in both the Police Courts and Petty Sessions. Also, an investigation of appeals seeking mitigation of sentences by men convicted of domestic violence sent to the Lord Lieutenant of Ireland's office (the highest level of appeal open to an Irish prisoner before the foundation of the Irish Free State), reveals the nature and extent of domestic violence in Ireland in the latter half of the nineteenth century. The details reported both in the papers and in the petitions for clemency give a valuable insight into the extent and serious nature of the abuse, the attitude of the magistrates who heard the cases, the inadequacy of the law in Ireland to extend any protection to abused wives, the sentencing patterns of abusers, and the recidivism of the abusers. These cases underline the fact that wife-beating was, certainly, as widespread and as brutal as it was in England. Women in Ireland had to endure daily beatings, verbal abuse, psychological torture, and grinding poverty which made it often impossible for them to escape their tormentors.

The Irish Times covered the Police Courts and Petty Sessions as well as any divorce cases heard before the Probate and Matrimonial Division of the High Court for the city and county of Dublin as well as neighbouring counties. 1878 began with a report on 4 January of John Heffernan who was charged before the Co. Kildare Quarter Sessions at Naas with grievously assaulting his wife and attempting to drown his daughter at Robertstown. At the same Sessions, John Wall was also charged with grievously assaulting his wife at Athy. Both men were convicted and awaited sentencing.[21] On 7 February, Michael Dodd, carpenter, was indicted for the wilful murder of Catherine Dodd, his wife. He allegedly stabbed his wife in the breast with a poker on 25 October in Bride's Alley, in a working class district of Dublin. He was also indicted for man-slaughter. He indicated through his lawyer that he would plead guilty to the manslaughter charge and was remanded on the lesser charge awaiting his sentence.[22] A report from Limerick City on 11 March told of a father, Richard Hickie, who pleaded not guilty to a charge of stabbing, cutting and wounding his daughter 'while under the influence of drink.' The jury found him guilty, and he was remanded to await his sentence.[23] There were an additional thirty-nine cases reported in *The Irish Times* for the remainder of 1878.

In many cases, the abused wife protested vigorously that she did not wish her husband to be prosecuted, but that she simply wished him to be warned by the magistrate, not punished. This was also borne out in the many petitions sent to the Lord Lieutenant's Office asking for a mitigation of sentence for convicted abusers. Many of these appeals – or 'memorials' – were written by wives asking that their husbands be released before the completion of their sentences. Often the wife stressed the dire nature of her economic situation which resulted from her husband's imprisonment. One such appeal recorded in 1872 was on behalf of William Skelly, a 34-year-old wire worker from Dublin, who was sentenced to three months with hard labour for severely beating and cutting his wife. At his trial, his wife testified: 'When he asked me for spirits and when I gave him none, he locked me in the room and struck me five times with a form and cut me five times severely. He has frequently beaten me on other occasions. He tore the eye out of his own child last night thinking she was I.' But in her 'memorial', she asked that he be released because the family was in such a state of distress due to destitution. She went on to state that she gave him great provocation and that he had never beaten her before. The appeal was dismissed, and William Skelly had to serve out his three-month sentence.[24] In a similar case in 1873, Hugh Martin, a 27-year-old tradesman from Newry, received six months' hard labour for beating his wife. He had one previous conviction for assault, and it was stated in the Court that he 'frequently was in the habit of beating his wife who was afraid of her life from his violent conduct.' His wife had made several complaints about his conduct in the past, and she stated in testimony before the Court that he spent most of his wages on drink, leaving her to be supported by her mother. Nevertheless, Mrs Martin appealed that her husband's six-month sentence be reduced. The magistrate, in denying the petition, remarked that: 'Wives are invariably in the habit of memorialising for the release of their husbands. The reason is obvious.'[25]

Magistrates also used the occasion of the appeal to comment on the frequency of such cases. For example, in 1886 Hugh McKerr, 34 years old, from Lurgan, was convicted of assaulting his wife and sentenced to six months' hard labour. At his trial, his wife Rose testified: 'I have been married to the defendant about two and a half years, and from about three months after our marriage, he has behaved cruelly towards me. I cannot count the number of times he has beaten me ... I do my best to please him, and I work hard as every one of the neighbours knows but nothing will please him ... About three weeks ago he beat me badly, and I was coming to town to complain about him, but he promised to behave kindly to me and I forgave him. Yet that very night he never ceased abusing and threatening me and would not let me go to bed ... He often said that he had another way of killing me than murdering me ... He threatens me that if I cry out or make a noise he'll choke me. I am afraid now to go home, and I fear he will kill me and be the cause of the death of our child unless he is brought to justice.' In her memorial, some weeks later, on Rose's behalf, it was stated: 'Since his imprisonment she [Rose] has scarcely been able to support herself and her infant child and as she is now expecting her confinement within a month, she fears she will have to break up her home and go into the workhouse unless her husband is released.' In denying Rose's petition, the Magistrate stated: 'As the practice of wife-beating is very prevalent in the locality where this offence was committed, the Magistrate's report is that this case is not one deserving clemency.'[26]

These petitions represent a rich source of information for the historian. Not only do they provide verbatim testimony by victims, they also record the abuser's age, occupation, and residence. Depending on who was making the appeal, they also offer an insight into the attitude of both abuser and victim. The magistrate in each case is asked for his opinion as to whether or not the convicted abuser is deserving of a mitigation of his sentence, and, in giving his judgement, he often uses the occasion to comment on the frequency of such cases and the possibility of the abuser re-offending. Roughly half the appeals were dealt with favourably, which indicates that prisoners in these cases felt that it was well worth attempting an appeal. It is impossible to estimate what percentage of wife-beating cases out of the total were represented by these appeals. However, if one is to believe the comments of the magistrates, then one must hazard a guess that these 1,012 cases represented only a small proportion of those cases heard daily in the Police Courts throughout Ireland. The appeal files also permit a preliminary investigation into sentencing policy in wife-beating cases. For the period 1853-1920, the average length of sentence was three months, and 22% of those petitioning received a sentence of six months with hard labour. It is also clear from the files that the rate of recidivism was relatively high. For example, in the case of Thomas Higgins, 24 years old, from Limerick, who was sentenced in 1891 to three months' hard labour for assaulting his mother, it was noted that the prisoner had eight previous convictions for drunkenness and disorderly behaviour including assault. His mother testified that on this occasion 'he caught me by the hair of the head and knocked me down and pucked me with his head into the teeth and mouth and cut me and I bled a lot ... He often assaulted me before but I never prosecuted him. I gave him no provocation ... I swear that I am afraid of my life that he will assault me again.' Thomas Higgins' petition for a mitigation of sentence was denied.[27]

The reports in the newspapers augment the evidence of the appeals files. An interesting case was reported in *The Irish Times* on 11 April 1878. At the Courthouse, Green Street, Dublin, David

Quaid, a 'respectably dressed man', was indicted for assaulting his wife. The evidence showed that Mrs Quaid was the owner of some chemical works at Black Pitts. A widow with four children, she had only been married to Mr Quaid for four years. It was stated that he had repeatedly assaulted her during those years, and had been bound over to keep the peace on one previous occasion. He had never supported her. Her children assisted her in her business, and it was stated that on one occasion Mr Quaid had so seriously assaulted one of his stepdaughters that she had to remain in bed for a fortnight. On the night of 17 February, he came to his wife's house and 'conducted himself in a very disorderly manner. He beat her in the face with his fist and threatened to strike her with the tongs and a candlestick.' A neighbour intervened, and the police were sent for and Mr Quaid was arrested. Mrs Quaid testified that she did not want him to be punished, but only to be bound over to keep the peace. Mr Quaid said that his wife wanted him to sign a document transferring property to her son. The jury found him guilty as charged, and he was sentenced to six months' imprisonment with hard labour.[28]

This case is particularly revealing. Not only was Mrs Quaid financially independent with her own business, she also lived with her children from her previous marriage in her own house. In spite of this, her husband continued to beat her throughout the four years of their marriage, even on one occasion beating his step-daughter. His testimony attempted to show that she provoked him because she wanted him to sign over property to her son. This attempt to establish provocation – a defence often used – was, in this case, ignored by the jury, and he was convicted. It should also be noted that Mrs Quaid sought to prevent her husband being sentenced to jail, and instead wished to have him bound over to keep the peace. Perhaps her relative financial security made her feel less vulnerable – although to judge from his past behaviour, she should have been wary of him. Also, it is important to note that in this case a neighbour intervened, thus pointing to the possibility that there was some community disapproval, or at least concern, for such behaviour.

There are a number of cases both in the appeals files and the newspapers where husbands prosecuted their wives for assault and which they invariably blamed on their wives' drunkenness. On 13 August 1878, for example, before Dr Kaye, Q.C. of the Northern Division, Dublin, Mrs Young of 19 Upper Dorset Street was prosecuted by her husband, John, for having used abusive and threatening language towards him. He testified that his wife was drunk and when he refused to give her his wages, 'on account of the condition she was in', she 'used abusive and threatening language, threw on him some boiling tea, and when he pushed her away, she struck him on the forehead with a tin teapot inflicting a serious wound on him.' Mr Young went on to say that his wife was a woman of 'bad character', and that he had frequently preferred charges against her but had each time withdrawn them. Mrs Young was remanded until a later date.[29]

This case is useful for highlighting the expectations that married men and women had of each other. She was expected by her husband to be sober, compliant, and use lady-like language; he was expected by her to hand over his wages. By withholding his weekly wages, he apparently provoked her into a temper which resulted in her retaliating with a teapot. It is doubtful that his injury was too serious, in spite of his testimony, since the charge brought against her was not one of assault but of using abusive and threatening language. Clearly both Mr Young and the Court believed that she had transgressed acceptable and respectable marital expectations. Joanna Bourke, in *Husbandry to Housewifery: Women, Economic Change and Housework in Ireland, 1890-1914*, corroborates this attitude by arguing that most domestic violence 'centred increasingly on accusations of poor housework. Assaults were admitted by husbands ... but excused because the woman was not performing her duties adequately.'[30]

A similar scenario occurred in Cork in March 1878. In a case heard before Magistrates Macleod and Honan on 8 March, and reported in *The Cork Examiner*, Eugene Forde, a quay porter, was charged with having assaulted his wife. Mrs Forde testified that she had asked her husband for some money on Tuesday evening when he was taking tea at her brother's house. He assaulted her violently by pulling her hair and kicking her in the side. Under cross-questioning by her husband's counsel, she denied that she prefaced her request by throwing a cup at him. She did acknowledge, however, that she had a stone in her hand at the time and that she did break a window with the stone. She also admitted that she was 'under the influence of drink', but excused her behaviour by saying that she had acted in self-defence since her husband 'was in the habit of assaulting her in this way.' In this case, it is interesting to note that the Magistrates ruled that it would be better for both parties if the couple agreed to live separately with Mr Forde giving his wife 5s. a week in maintenance and keeping custody of their eldest son.[31] This solution was uncommon, since most magistrates did all they could to maintain the family intact.

Husbands rarely expressed regret or sorrow for their behaviour before the courts. *The Cork Examiner* on Tuesday 3 September 1878 reported that Isaac Johnson was charged before Magistrates Hall and Scott with violently assaulting his wife, Bridget, who appeared 'with her face in a dreadful state scarcely a feature being distinguishable.' She testified that she lived in Harpur's Lane and had only been married since February – eight months. Her husband threw her down and kicked her about the head and body. She said that she 'gave him no provocation and that it was usual for him to beat her that way.' The Head Constable testified that three months ago Isaac Johnson was charged with the very same offence, but on that occasion his new wife forgave him. Magistrate Hall, before sentencing him to three months with hard labour, commented: 'He is a brute and he doesn't deserve the name of a man.' As he was being led away, Isaac Johnson declared: 'I am as good as a husband as were [sic] took charge of a woman.'[32]

Similarly, husbands also tried to blame their wives for their injuries. On 23 March 1878, before Magistrate O'Donel of the Northern Division in Dublin, a Mr Molloy was charged with 'having violently assaulted his wife who appeared in court with black eyes.' Mrs Molloy testified that her husband had bitten her on the shoulder, 'boxed her in the face and blackened her eyes.' When Mr Molloy gave evidence, he 'denied the truth of the charge and said his wife beat herself in the eyes with her closed fists in order to get him punished.'[33] His ludicrous claim was rejected by the Court, and Mr Molloy was held in jail awaiting sentence.

In the Criminal Index Files between 1853-1920, there are a total of fifty-six cases of women appealing for mitigation of their sentences. Seven cases involved women who had assaulted their husbands; seven involved the murder, either of husbands or children; three involved women who had assaulted their mothers-in-law, brothers-in-law, and sisters. The majority of the cases concerned women who had either assaulted or ill-treated their children. The charge of 'ill-treatment of children' was a common one in the years after 1894, when, following the passage of the Prevention of Cruelty to Children Act, inspectors from the Society for the Prevention of Cruelty to Children (S.P.C.C.) often made depositions to the Courts on behalf of the child. For example, Bridget Prendergast, 26 years old, from 3 Upper Mercer Street, Dublin, was convicted on 27 August 1897 and received two months' hard labour for ill-treating her three children. The deposition from the inspector of the S.P.C.C. stated that he had found Bridget's three children, aged seven, four, and one and one-quarter years, 'alone and almost naked in a shocking state of filth. The room had only a table, chair and orange box, the bed a piece of sacking which was wet ... The husband was away with the Militia ... She said her husband allows her 16/ a week and that it was all her own fault through drink – pawning things for drink.' Bridget was pregnant with her fourth child and both she and her mother appealed for remission of her sentence because they feared her giving birth in prison. She had two previous convictions for assault due to drunkenness. Her petition was turned down.[34] In the majority of these cases, especially where the woman's behaviour was implicated by drink, the magistrates rarely granted the appeal. It is clear that women's ill-treatment of children, particularly when perceived to be as a result of intemperance, flew in the face of contemporary notions of respectability for women, especially mothers. Comments by the middle class magistrates adjudicating on these cases indicated a particular loathing for such behaviour. Men's abusive behaviour was often excused by claiming alcohol as a contributory factor; similar behaviour in women was almost always punished harshly. This remark by a magistrate in 1908 in the case of Mary Fitzgerald, 40 years old from Killarney, who received a sentence of six months' hard labour for ill-treating her child, reflected contemporary feelings of disgust: 'The prisoner is of drunken habits and in every respect a woman of doubtful character. The children are better off than in her charge.'[35]

Domestic violence cases were heard daily in the Police and Magistrates' Courts among other cases of 'petty' crimes, such as: stealing a watch; stealing rope; illegal possession of a woman's waterproof cloak; stealing forage from an employer's stable; operating an unlicensed house with 24 bottles of porter; and stealing a cow. Many of the perpetrators of these crimes received sentences of two to four months' imprisonment, the same as that received by a husband convicted for assaulting his wife. Similarly, a man convicted of assaulting another man received, on average, a four-month sentence with hard labour. Crimes against property, particularly theft from employers, often carried longer sentences. Gatrell quotes D.H. MacFarlane, writing in 1881, that 'property was better defended in English law than the person ... when a man was flogged for robbery with violence, he was flogged for the robbery and not for the violence.'[36] Men who committed violent crimes were considered less amenable to the deterrent effect of lengthy prison sentences. 'It was generally felt that by virtue of the very impulsiveness of their acts these men could not be *deterred* from violence by the anticipatory threat of arrest or punishment.'[37]

Therefore, the leniency with which wife-beating was treated by the courts must have led battered wives to question the wisdom of seeking the protection of the law. The fact that their situation was reported in some detail in the papers for all to read was particularly humiliating, and many wives, after completing preliminary reports to the police, refused to testify in court against their husbands. The law and subsequent sentencing did not act in any way as a deterrent to prevent domestic violence. The Irish newspaper-reading public, despite extensive reports over many years, remained indifferent to the fact of the widespread nature of such domestic violence.

Recourse to the courts was an uncommon occurrence for working class women. It was estimated by Anna Martin, a social reformer who lived and worked with working class women in London in the first decade of the twentieth century, that 'for every case reaching court there were probably as many as fifty aggrieved wives who did not pursue such action.'[38] However, middle class women often sought relief from abuse by seeking separations in the Matrimonial Division of the High Court in Dublin. The middle class wife could sue for a divorce *a mensa et thora* (judicial separation) on the grounds of cruelty perpetrated by her husband. Sometimes the husband counter-sued, accusing his wife of intemperance or of using abusive language and/or violence. In some cases, the couples agreed to settle their differences; on other occasions, the judge refused the wife's petition, claiming there was insufficient evidence of cruelty. These cases provide substantial information about middle class Irish marriages. Wives were expected by the judge in such cases to catalogue details of their marital relationships. Husbands frequently complained of their wives' improprieties. Financial arrangements within marriages were also exposed under the glaring light of the court proceedings. In this respect, it took some courage for wives to sue for judicial separations, when they knew that they would have to reveal the extent of their humiliation before a very interested public. Divorce cases were followed avidly by the press. Therefore, the very act of petitioning for separation was, in the words of A. James Hammerton, 'an act of resistance or defiance – the last desperate attempt, for those able to afford it, to escape from an intolerable marriage.'[39] A great deal more research is required to unravel this story of middle class domestic violence in Ireland, but the cases heard before the Matrimonial Division of the High Court provide the historian with a useful avenue for investigation.

Considering the extraordinary number of wife-beating cases reported in the daily press, why was there no outcry in Ireland against this crime? Criminally abused Irish women in the latter half of the nineteenth century were quite literally 'beneath notice.'[40] Contemporary commentators on the law justified not dealing with certain acts of violence against the person, in particular 'the whole series of offences relating to the abduction of women, rape and other such crimes. Their history possesses no special interest and does not illustrate either our political or our social history.'[41] Therefore, even though wife abuse was a criminal offence, it appeared 'to be outside the sphere of the criminal law in some intuitive way.'[42] This was, of course, a very turbulent period in Irish history. Momentous events were occurring that profoundly shaped Ireland's future: post-Famine emigration continued to drain away over half of Ireland's population in the space of fifty years; Irish tenant farmers were engaged in a protracted Land War with largely absent English landlords in an effort to secure land reform; Parnell and his Irish parliamentary colleagues showed remarkable skill in manipulating Parliament and the British government to consider Home Rule for Ireland. The daily papers were full of stories concerning campaigns by the Land League, including, by 1885, reports of so-called agrarian outrages that occurred regularly throughout Ireland. Burning hay-ricks, maimed cattle, boycotts and evictions made the headlines, as did visits by Queen Victoria and her royal household. Abused wives, unless they were murdered, found their stories buried amidst reports of petty crimes such as adulterating milk, watering pints, stealing fruit, wrenching knockers off doors, and breaking the licensing laws. The very ordinariness of these crimes deserves attention. Wife-beating appears to have been perceived as just another petty, daily occurrence.

A few temperance campaigners did attempt to raise public awareness on the issue, but their emphasis was on the benefits that sobriety would bring to the family, rather than on the gross violation that individual women and children suffered as a result of abusive husbands and fathers. It should, however, be noted that Father Mathew – the Cork priest who is best known for his total abstinence campaigns of the 1840s – issued a Temperance Certificate to individuals who took the pledge to abstain from drink that illustrated vividly the detrimental effects of drink on the family.[43] According to Colm Kerrigan in his recent biography of Father Mathew: 'The message is simple. If a drunkard would only spend his money on the necessities of life rather than on drink, there would be no poverty and domestic violence.'[44] It seems clear from both leading historians of Irish temperance, Elizabeth Malcolm and Colm Kerrigan, that wife abuse, while featuring prominently in English and American campaigns, did not really become part of the first- and second-wave temperance campaigns in Ireland. Malcolm suggests that Irish women were not given the opportunity to play an independent role in the Irish temperance movement, since it was largely controlled by either priests or Protestant evangelicals who were suspicious of women's activities outside the home. The few female temperance organisations that did exist in Ireland, mainly in Dublin and Belfast, were, according to Malcolm, 'firmly under male control.'[45] Malcolm also suggests that Parnell, while declaring himself in favour of temperance, was always careful to introduce a disclaimer as to the seriousness of the drink problem in Ireland. He felt that it was unfair to say that the Irish were any less temperate than the English or the Scots, and Malcolm points out that Parnell, like other Home Rule Nationalists, 'did not like to see Liberal or Conservative Irish M.P.s portraying the Irish people before the British Parliament as peculiarly prone to drunkenness.'[46] By the 1890s, proponents of Gaelic nationalism in Ireland were claiming that traditional Irish society had been sober, and that it was the English conquest which drove the Irish to drink.[47]

This reluctance to expose Ireland's social ills, particularly at a time of heightened nationalist activity, is a possible explanation for the silence that greeted the problem of wife-beating and associated domestic violence in the latter half of the nineteenth century. Could it have been that such a phenomenon was seen as a peculiarly 'English disease'? Frances Power Cobbe certainly thought so, as she sought to explain Irishmen's violence in Britain as a symptom of the degradation associated with advancing industrialisation and poverty. Furthermore, Ireland was very often portrayed in the Irish media as the mythical 'Mother Ireland', or 'Hibernia', or 'Erin' – a beautiful, dark-haired and wide-eyed woman whose innocent virtue was threatened by a macho John Bull.[48] Increasingly, Irish virtue was defined as the inevitable victim of English vice.

David Cairns and Shaun Richards, in *Writing Ireland: Colonialism, Nationalism and Culture*, suggest that this personification of Ireland as 'woman' and 'mother' also necessitated that 'the purity of that image was maintained on all levels for, in order to maintain its mobilising force, "Woman" could only ever be an eternal essence beyond the physicality which suggested other, darker, demands and desires.'[49] This idea found an earlier exponent in Irish feminist and nationalist Maud Eden, who wrote in 1919 that Irish marriages were more 'pure' than their English counterparts. This was the reason, she argued, that divorce was not a necessity in Ireland: 'We require education in comradeship to fit men and women for marriage, not divorce ... We have to avoid imitating England in this matter ... [their] national characteristics are producing endless unhappy marriages. That is why Irish marriages, even the commercial bargains of the countryside, are so much happier than the average British love-match.'[50]

There was, indeed, a strong Catholic wish to maintain the indissolubility of marriage in Ireland. However, David Fitzpatrick suggests that this was as a result, not just of Catholic doctrine, nor Irish nationalism, but rather the widespread practice of 'the match' or arranged marriage that existed in rural Ireland. 'Wherever the "match" prevailed,' according to Fitzpatrick, 'divorce followed by remarriage was socially and economically dysfunctional ... It was these structural impediments to divorce which gave force to the moral objections [to divorce] ...'[51] Therefore, if Fitzpatrick is correct, Irish couples had a compelling economic reason to stay married, even in the face of appalling domestic violence. However, Fitzpatrick also claims, in an earlier essay in *Marriage in Ireland* (1985), that there exists little evidence to back up the suggestion that 'the male Irish may have been a race of drunken wife-beaters or even passionate suitors,' stating that 'the records of outrage and disputation give little hint of either proclivity.'[52]

Contrary to Fitzpatrick's claim, the evidence clearly shows that many nineteenth-century Irish men beat their wives with impunity. It seems immaterial to those battered wives whether it was the system of arranged marriages, or the doctrine of the Catholic Church, or nationalist ideology that locked them into abusive marriages. What is clear is that there was no concerted public campaign to release battered wives from their marriage vows in Ireland. It is William Duncan's opinion that 'the stagnation of the civil law has probably not been the product of a conscious policy of deference by the State to the Church. More probably it results from the slowness of legislators to recognise the social need to develop civil law remedies.'[53]

Many Irish feminists believed that when the suffrage was extended to women, their status would guarantee them new respect from their fellow Irish men. *The Irish Citizen*, newspaper of the Irish Women's Franchise League, which was published weekly and then monthly between 1912-22, ran articles that criticised the exclusion of women from all ranks of the judiciary and even called for a women's presence in the police that would provide support for women wishing to see their husbands prosecuted for wife-beat-

ing.[54] Many articles made a clear connection between a woman's
lack of civil rights and her subsequent vulnerability in the private
sphere. However, the attitudes expressed in the feminist *Irish
Citizen* reinforced essentialist notions of the relationship between
the sexes that were prevalent at the time. Man was seen as a
'natural' protector of woman. When the woman could no longer
depend on him for protection, only then should the State intervene.[55]

At the height of the struggle for independence in September
1919, *The Irish Citizen* carried a comprehensive account by L.A.M.
Priestly-McCracken entitled simply 'Wife-Beating', in which she
deplored the ability of husbands to beat their wives with impunity
behind the closed doors of the family home.

> An age-old tradition prevails that in matrimonial affairs what
> transpires in the home must be carefully concealed from the
> world without. The quarrels and differences ranging from 'in-
> compatibility of temper' and wrangling, to physical violence and
> giving of black eyes must be kept strictly secret ... This natural
> shrinking from exposure gives a sense of security to the stronger,
> fiercer, and more dominant partner, the husband, in ill-treating
> his wife.[56]

Priestly-McCracken went on to explain that wife-beating was a
common occurrence in which the victim remained silent because
of her social or financial position. This need to keep it hidden only
served to increase the husband's power. If a wife was courageous
enough to go to Court and her husband convicted, the magistrate
usually imposed a short sentence or light fine, as so many cases
reported in the press corroborated. Priestly-McCracken indicated
that the wife's economic dependency actually amounted to 'tacit
encouragement to the wife-beater: the husband's importance as a
breadwinner is set off against his cruelty.' She concluded by calling
on recently enfranchised Irish women 'to seek to have the personal
safety of the wife adequately and effectively secured ... until the
relations between husband and wife shall be that of civilised and
independent human beings and not that of ruthless tyrant and
hapless victim.' Her final plea was that a society to prevent cruelty
to wives 'at the hands of their natural protectors – their husbands'
be set up.[57]

Following the foundation of the Irish Free State in 1922, reports
of wife-beating declined in the press. The new State showed in
many ways that it was reluctant to inquire too closely into what
was considered to be the private domain of the family, largely
taking its lead from the Catholic hierarchy who considered such
intervention to be indicative of socialist, and even communist,

social policy. Indeed, the Irish Free State proceeded to pass a series of laws in the 1920s and 1930s designed to reinforce Irish women's isolation in the home as wives and mothers.[58] In the 1920s, the American anthropologists Arensberg and Kimball carried out their field work in Co. Clare. They reported that in country districts where a wife was found to be barren (and it was believed that this was the wife's problem solely), it was perfectly acceptable for the husband to beat her: 'To bounce a boot off her now and then for it,' was how they reported one husband explaining his actions.[59] Domestic violence in Ireland was only 'rediscovered' by the Women's Movement in the 1970s, and the State had to be forced to respond by helping to subsidise a number of refuges for battered wives. Reluctant to accept new feminist theories about the nature of domestic violence, the Irish government continued to emphasise that the problem stemmed largely from an abuse of alcohol, not power.[60]

Ironically, late-nineteenth-century readers of daily Irish newspapers had more opportunity to read about domestic violence than contemporary readers. This made the Irish public more aware of the daily occurrence of such crimes, but, simultaneously, those same readers appeared unwilling to mobilise against domestic violence. Perhaps they were anaesthetised to the grim details; perhaps other daily reports of agrarian outrages, evictions, faction fights and political murders represented the stuff of 'real' violence. After all, wife-beating and other domestic crimes were treated in the courts as little different from stealing a door knocker or breaking the licensing laws. Perhaps, as David Lloyd suggests, in the nationalist campaigns to forge an Irish identity, a 'negation of recalcitrant or unassimilable elements in Irish society' was required.[61] Or perhaps, as J.J. Lee provocatively suggests: 'The self-image of "traditional" Ireland was, it may be suggested, characterised less by hypocrisy than by a capacity for self-deception on a heroic scale. It was this that gave it such enormous emotional power, and could achieve such resonance even among those who might objectively be regarded as the victims.'[62] As Irish women and men sought to 'imagine' the new Ireland at the turn of the century, it was imperative that Frances Power Cobbe's myth that Irishmen at home were in general 'kind and chivalrous towards women' be incorporated into that new identity. A gendered history of post-Famine Ireland demands that the reality of domestic violence be acknowledged.

A Problematic Relationship:
European Women & Nationalism 1870–1915
Cliona Murphy

Nationalism has been an enduring theme in modern Ireland's historiography. It was not, therefore, surprising that, with the advent of women's history in the late 1970s, the relationship between the nationalist and women's suffrage movements would occupy historians. Margaret MacCurtain considered it in 1978 in her article in *Women in Irish History: the Historical Dimension*.[1] The topic was also taken up by Beth McKillen in two articles in *Eire/Ireland* in 1982[2] and by Rosemary Cullen Owens in *Smashing Times* in 1984.[3] This writer too has noted the relationship of interest and has discussed it particularly in connection with the Irish Parliamentary Party.[4] The theme has also threaded its way through the work of a number of other historians such as Margaret Ward, Mary Cullen and Dana Hearne.[5] Nationalist women themselves have also received much attention (most notably from Ward).[6]

Studies which have examined the relationship between nationalists and suffragists have asked whether or not the nationalist movement damaged the suffrage cause in Ireland, and if Irish suffragists were at a unique disadvantage because they lacked a national parliament to petition for the vote. Others have asked if the nationalist movement became more pro-women's suffrage and if parts of the suffrage movement, particularly the Irish Women's Franchise League, became more nationalist from approximately 1914 onwards.

These questions and others have emerged out of analyses of the Irish women's suffrage movement which have outlined the history of a movement which had its origins in the nineteenth century.[7] In 1872, Isabella Tod founded the Irish Women's Suffrage Society in Belfast and the Haslams founded a society in Dublin in 1876, which later became known as the Irish Women's Suffrage and Local Government Association. By 1914, the movement had proliferated and included numerous organisations which reflected the diversity of religious and political opinion in the country. Among them were the Munster Women's Franchise League, the Conservative and Unionist Women's Franchise Association, the Church League for Women's Suffrage (Anglican), the Irish Women's Reform League (which also focused on trade-unionism) and the Irish Catholic Women's Suffrage Society, which was founded during the war. The Irish Women's Suffrage Federation was set up in 1911 as an umbrella organisation to which some of the other organisations were loosely affiliated. The Irish Women's Franchise League (IWFL), founded in 1908 by Hanna Sheehy Skeffington, Margaret Cousins and their husbands, Frank Sheehy Skeffington and James Cousins, stands out from the others in its visibility, its membership and its militancy. The *Irish Citizen*, its weekly newspaper, has left historians with a detailed account of its activities, views and dilemmas.

While it claimed to be apolitical, the IWFL's orientation was decidedly pro-Home Rule and its members did their best to get a women's suffrage amendment attached to the third Home Rule Bill in the years between 1912 and 1914. They were also active in pursuing other suffrage legislation in parliament, including the Conciliation Bill in 1911 and 1912 and the Dickinson Bill in 1913. The majority of the members of the Irish Parliamentary Party did not take heed of the IWFL, as they feared that a women's suffrage amendment to the Home Rule Bill would damage its passage and that other suffrage legislation might result in the election of a Conservative government and the downfall of the pro-Home Rule Liberal government.[8]

The relationship which the IWFL had with the revolutionary nationalists was even less satisfactory. For the latter, independence was a priority and women's suffrage was at best a distraction and at worst a dangerous, foreign movement undermining Irish nationalism. The IWFL experienced strained relations with female and male nationalists and there was much name-calling and accusations about having chosen the wrong cause. However, there were defections in both directions. Nationalist women who became disillusioned with restrictions placed upon them by their organisations joined suffrage groups. On the other hand, women initially interested in suffragism, like Mary MacSwiney, eventually made nationalism their cause as it became politically more important.[9]

The interest which historians have shown in the relationship between Irish nationalists and Irish suffragists provokes the larger question: were Irish suffragists the only ones to experience this tug of loyalties between nationalism and feminism, or was it evident elsewhere? While clearly there were differences between Ireland and the other European countries in relation to its colonial status, nationalism was a phenomenon which was apparent all over Europe. Examining the experiences of women in selected European countries in the late nineteenth and early twentieth centuries will help shed light on the extent to which colonialism was responsible for Irish women's dilemma. To some degree this last question has been tackled in recent studies on women in the Irish Free State by Frances Gardiner and Maryann Gialanella Valiulis. Gialanella Valiulis has shown that women's position improved very little and very slowly under independence.[10] However, this article is concerned with the pre-suffrage and the pre-independence period and thus will be investigating the question in that context.

An examination of the European context of Irish nationalism and the suffrage movement leads to another pertinent question about the study of women in Irish history and its general historiography. To what extent is Irish women's history being examined in isolation and apart from the general European, and indeed world, context? While it is necessary to specialise within certain geographical and historical areas, an ignorance of the larger picture can lead to false conclusions and an exaggeration of the uniqueness of the Irish situation. This is particularly true in relation to women's history, where women may experience certain phenomena in a similar manner in different countries simply because they are women. Is women's history in Ireland being dictated too much by the confines of Irish history, indeed Irish nationalist history? Have historians of the suffrage movement been involved repeatedly in the same debate over the last two decades? Could a new perspective be given to the debate by comparing Irish women's experience with that of other European women?

This article will endeavour to place the nationalist-suffragist debate in the European context. It will attempt to show that the Irish situation was far from unique, that suffragist women across the European continent also had their nationalism questioned, that they also experienced the same tugs of loyalty, and that they were accused of the same misconduct. The argument will be made that this tense relationship was not peculiarly Irish, but rather an inherent part of the women's struggle. It was inevitable that the suffrage movements would clash, sooner or later, with the predominant national ethos which prevailed in many European countries and which ignored their aspirations.

It is still difficult to find detailed studies on the topic of women's suffrage and nationalism, despite the wealth of material on European women's history. While some information can be gleaned in specialised studies (not always focused on either nationalism or suffrage),[11] in general studies of European nationalism, women, suffragists or otherwise, are barely visible.[12] This is not surprising since the study of nationalism usually comes within the parameters of mainstream political and military history, and to a lesser extent cultural history, and has often been written by historians within their own national settings. Women have not been their concern. Their endeavour has been to explain the origins and evolution of nation states, to examine conflicts of groups, both inside and outside those states, and to look at the question of identity.

Not only is there a problem with sources, there is also a problem with terminology. The difficulty of relating women to nationalism is connected with how the term was understood. It was largely associated with male issues: war, politics and government. Men were unifying states, men were fighting for independence, and feared or were aggressive towards men of other nations. Nationalist activities were carried out by men because women were denied access to political, administrative and military positions which would have involved making national decisions. Women hardly came within nationalists' vision (not to mind the historians'), and when they did, they were on the periphery in a reproductive and supportive role.

However, in the last quarter of the nineteenth century, it became increasingly difficult for nationalists to maintain their frozen image of the role of women. Nationalist and suffragist territory increasingly began to overlap. With the unification of Germany in 1871, nationalism was intensified throughout Europe. The balance of power had been upset and many countries, fearful of the German Empire, became acutely aware of threats to their national security and the possibility of a future European war. Germany needed to defend its new borders. France desired revenge for the Franco-Prussian war and feared further German encroachments. Britain had to adjust itself to the new continental situ' ' ᵕ‑ᶜᶜᵉss its relationship with Germany. Austria-Hungary mies both within and without its empire. Itạ fragile position. Nationalist fervour develop(of the nineteenth century and war seemed ir

At the same time, women were becomin suffrage movements were appearing all ov each other and also by the movement in women's convention at Seneca Falls in N Stuart Mill's failed attempt to get a wome

to the 1867 Reform Bill and his subsequent essay, *On the Subjection of Women* (1869), the unpopularity of the Contagious Diseases Acts in Britain and contemporary writings on the suffrage movement, all served to publicise the cause and create an international atmosphere of encouragement and reinforcement.[13] When women were granted the vote in the American territories from 1869 and in New Zealand in 1893, further impetus was given to the movement world-wide.[14]

The women's suffrage movement, therefore, became vociferous at a time of heightened nationalism. Not surprisingly, the two movements conflicted for many reasons but not least because the suffrage movement crossed national borders and to some extent was international in nature. Nationalists also wanted women to play a particular (but not an equal) role in the State. The suffragists' demand for the vote had profound implications beyond the franchise: women wished to participate equally within the State and thus become an integral part of that State. This was a problem, as there was a great deal of legislation in place which prohibited women from participating fully in political life. For example, in a number of countries women, besides not being able to vote, were denied the right to join political parties. This prevented them from fully realising their nationalism. If they were not allowed to participate within the political system how could they ever be full citizens? In 1867, women were banned from joining or forming political associations in Austria. A similar ban lasted in Germany until 1908. In Britain, women could join auxiliary organisations of the Liberal and Conservative parties but, as in other countries, they could not participate in elections nor could they sit in parliament, while in Italy, a law of 1861 excluded women from voting for parliament in the new State. Even though many women in Europe lived in independent states, national independence was irrelevant to their personal position and freedom. It did not provide them with a more emancipated life, as Irish women would find out after independence.

The core of the problem was that nationalism was not truly national. It was a narrow ideology, which, apart from the fact that they were needed to perpetuate the race, did not embrace women within its boundaries. Had it been truly national, women's rights would not have been dismissed as separate or as 'women's rights' would have been included in the rights of the citizens of the Advocates of nationalism believed that women's primary the domestic or private sphere. Nationalism was concerned with issues as politics, defence, insurrection – issues which were all in the public sphere, i.e. the men's sphere. It was very difficult, if not impossible, for women to play a role in these areas since, in theory at least, they were relegated to the private sphere.

However, the reality was that women did not live exclusively within the private sphere. Their lives were very much moulded by the fact that they lived within a particular nation. They were not immune from national forces which also affected men. They, too, could experience love of country, hatred of an oppressor, and a desire to defend borders. Women also felt emotion when they saw their national flag or heard patriotic music, and felt sadness and grief when their soldiers died and fought in wars. These were not sentiments peculiar to men. When girls began to receive elementary education in Europe (from about 1870 in many countries), they were subject to all the national propaganda which was also directed at boys. Governments realised the importance of education as a medium for controlling people and creating loyal citizens who could be called upon in times of war. At school children were taught national history and geography, to love the flag, the government, the culture, to fear the oppressor or belligerent neighbour and to be proud of their country's overseas colonies. Females as well as males could hardly come out of this pedagogic process without developing an attachment to their nation.[15]

As a result some European women, like some Irish women (albeit a minority who were politicised), believed that they were entitled to participate in the public life of the nation. While there may not have been equivalent organisations to Cumann na mBan or Inghinidhe na hÉireann on the mainland of the continent, there were European women who were involved in nationalist movements. Though rarely leaders, women were active in salons, reform movements, and revolutionary organisations. They fought in the 1848 revolutions in Germany and France; they were involved in Mazzini's unification movement in Italy, in the German women's nationalist organisations before and after unification in 1871, in the Paris Commune of 1870, and in nationalist groups in the Balkans. When their nations were at war, they made ammunition, provided safe houses, treated the wounded and took over the farms and workplaces. But while women could experience and respond to nationalist emotion, their gender prevented them from fully realising their nationalist potential. However fervent their nationalism was, they could not participate on the same level as men. They were denied the right to be national leaders or representatives, to make national decisions, and to be regarded as full citizens of the nation.

Such restrictions led some women into the feminist movement and specifically the suffrage movement. For example, women who were politicised during the Italian unification struggle subsequently became teachers and from there they went into the feminist movement. While the unification of Italy did not realise their ideals, it provided them with a national language through which they could reach out to each other. They could read women's literature, radical newspapers, feminist newspapers and participate in political debate.[16]

Women in the German nationalist organisations after unification also confronted the reality that unification and the creation of a new state did not dramatically transform their status. Bismarck's nationalist ideal was a narrow one. The German Women's Association for Eastern Marches (established in 1895) worked for the expansion of German influence in the eastern provinces of Prussia, where there were ethnic conflicts between Germans and Poles. These women set up German businesses and helped promote German culture, but discovered also that their power was limited and that they were unable to have any administrative or political influence in the organisation. The men 'had more control of arduous tasks.' The Naval Association of German Women (auxiliary of the German Naval League) helped finance the construction of battleships. However, they were repeatedly confronted with limitations to their nationalism since the men always viewed them in the role of helpers rather than political leaders.[17]

This inequity of opportunity for women in the nationalist organisations led to frustration and convinced some that the only way to advance in the nation was to pursue the suffragist path. Irish suffragists frequently voiced their indignation about the position of women nationalists. Frank Sheehy Skeffington's oft-quoted judgement on the women in Cumann na mBan, as 'slavish with regard to the men at the head of the movement' and of showing 'a crawling servility', expresses the suffragists' repugnance at the women supporters of the nationalist movement and the futility of their subservience.[18]

Dismissal of women's suffrage by nationalists was perceived as perplexing by suffragists, who were continually pointing out parallels between the nationalist and suffragist causes. Members of the Irish Women's Franchise League were at a loss as to why members of the Irish Parliamentary Party and other nationalist groups did not see the similarities. Both causes were about self-determination; both were about civil rights; both were about fighting for a political cause; and both were about identity and self-respect. Members of the IWFL hoped that women's rights could be achieved within the context of the nation. Yet, while it seemed very clear to them that the ideologies of the two movements overlapped, nationalists did not see the same parallels nor did they share the same sentiments.

Hanna Sheehy Skeffington pointed to the irony that nationalists failed to sympathise with the suffragists when they both had similar goals:

> Here were good Irish rebels, many of them broken into national revolt, with all the slogans of Irish revolution and its arsenal of weapons – Boycott, Plan of Campaign, Land for the People, and so forth, the creators of obstruction in Parliament – yet at the whisper of votes for women many changed to extreme Tories ...[19]

A writer to *The Irish Times* echoed Sheehy Skeffington and asked: 'Have Catholic Irishmen lost their sense of chivalry? Because they suffered so recently from political disabilities, should not their imaginations be fired by the passionate struggle women today are making to win what they won?'[20] In Italy, similar wry observations were made by the feminist Anna Maria Mozzoni. As early as 1864, she compared the nationalist and women's movements and asked 'how men who conspired for freedom, suffered in Austrian dungeons, and defied the gallows in order to be citizens, not subjects, could not imagine that women also would not be subjects?'[21] Nationalists did not see the parallels. In fact, they often considered that the two movements were in total opposition.

Clearly some goals of nationalists and suffragists were in direct conflict and any amount of eloquent statements on their similarities could not contradict that fact. In Ireland suffragists, particularly the IWFL, learnt that they could not adhere to both causes without putting a strain on one or the other. Fighting for Home Rule meant giving up pestering a British parliament for votes for women and it meant believing the nationalist men when they said that they would be catered to after independence. When women chose the suffrage cause and still claimed to be nationalistic, these claims were looked upon with suspicion and even hostility.

In Britain, France, Germany and Italy the clash of interests was even more apparent and its consequences were even more pervasive throughout society. Though quite different from the Irish situation, this conflict illustrates once more that what may have been seen as in the interests of nationalism was not always seen as in the interests of women. Between 1870 and World War I, the biggest clash of interests between nationalists and suffragists revolved around the role of motherhood and the population question. Producing and raising children were seen by nationalists as the most important duties which women could perform for the

State. This is not surprising, considering that women were denied other ways of expressing themselves. Governments were concerned with the birth rate for defence reasons. If there was to be a European war, soldiers were needed to defend their borders. It was vital, therefore, that the birth rate should not fall. There were fears that the population would decrease and that a country would be overwhelmed by its enemies. The increasing popularity of the new pseudo-science of eugenics, which was concerned with both the quantity and the quality of population, meant that the production and rearing of children was increasingly coming under scrutiny.[22]

Feminists in general, as well as suffrage organisations, were concerned with the birth rate because it interfered with women's lives. They, therefore, were interested in propagating information about birth control. The two outlooks were in direct conflict. Women's efforts to limit their families and improve their own lives were considered unpatriotic by nationalists. National security thus touched at the very heart of the family and the idea of there being two separate spheres of life for men and women was eroded. Women's concerns were not just with the private sphere and men's concerns embraced more than the public sphere. The spheres were inextricably linked. If the mothers were unwilling to have children, then the security of the State was thought to be at risk. Much of the responsibility for the undermining of motherhood was thrust upon the women's movement. Its support for birth control, abortion and encouragement of women to enter higher education and the workplace was thought to be undermining the State.

Contemporary observers and politicians frequently voiced concerns about the women's movement and the population question. Advocates of birth control, or neo-Malthusianism, were seen as committing 'the ultimate act in civil disobedience'.[23] Despite the fact that it had the third highest birth rate in Europe, there was concern in Italy about the declining birth rate and the 'degeneration of family'. One Italian nationalist declared 'Maternity is the patriotism of women.'[24] In Germany, it was argued that women's attempts to be politically and professionally active 'brought upon Germany the double curse of declining birth rate and impending racial degeneration.' In 1909, a government commission report found the women's movement partly responsible for the decline of the birth rate,

> either by encouraging women to take jobs which removed them from their function as child bearers, or by persuading them to lead an independent existence outside the family, or by spreading ideas about free love, contraception and abortion, and leading them to neglect their duty to produce children.[25]

In France, the 1895 census indicated that the birth rate was lower than the death rate. This caused concern because of Germany's larger population, and it was argued that if woman's intellect was over-developed she would be less fit to bear children and 'motherhood was a more useful function for France than women receiving the baccalaureate.'[26]

In Ireland, similar language on motherhood and the women's movement came from the Churches and from nationalists, and the same conviction was expressed that the traditional role of mothers was part of the national identity. In his pastoral letter in 1912, Bishop O'Dwyer of Limerick pointed out that 'there has been for some years a movement to draw women from their homes and to engage them in occupations which an older generation thought entirely unsuited to them.'[27] John Dillon, deputy leader of the Irish Parliamentary Party, declared that 'women's suffrage will, I believe, be the ruin of our Western Civilisation. It will destroy the home, challenging the headship of man, laid down by God.'[28] In the Irish Free State, similar attitudes informed legislation regarding women and undoubtedly contributed to Eamon de Valera's thinking when he drew up the 1937 Constitution.

Suffragists, whether they were concerned with the population question, as in Europe, or Home Rule or independence as in Ireland, did not conform to the nationalists' ideals. Consequently, there was much antagonism shown towards them in this period. In Ireland, nationalist hostility to the suffrage movement was expressed in numerous ways ranging from verbal castigation to physical violence.[29] Irish suffragists were accused of being unpatriotic, pro-British and part of an international movement. They were told to wait for the vote until independence was achieved. Opposition to women's suffrage on traditional grounds was one reason for the hostility. However, even nationalists who were amenable to the idea[30] opposed the suffragists' goals because they saw them as undermining the goals of nationalism. Moreover, nationalists believed that it was up to them to decide whether or not their women should get the vote.

While nationalists in other countries were not looking for independence, they still gave priority to nationalism at the expense of the women's cause and accused suffragists of disloyalty. Suffragists were told to wait until unification was achieved or until stability or security was established. The reason depended upon each country's circumstances, yet the outcome was the same: the nationalist cause was always given priority over the suffragist cause. The nationalist cause was always just out of reach and the suffragist one was always subservient to it.

In Italy before unification, women were reassured, 'First the republic – then we'll get to you immediately.'[31] The fact that the new unified Italy was a monarchy and not a republic probably made no difference (although it has been suggested that if the new Italy had been the one which Mazzini envisioned, women would have been better off). Nevertheless, it was a long time before women were 'got to' in the new Italy. There were always other excuses. They did not receive the vote until 1945. In Austria-Hungary, certain nationalities feared women's suffrage because there were other nationalities which the Austrians wished to keep entirely disenfranchised and they could hardly enfranchise their women.[32]

It was argued in the French Third Republic, in the decades before World War I, that the introduction of women's franchise would lead to the collapse of the Republic. Supporters of the government 'were loathe to enfranchise a mass of women they saw as cleric-dominated and conservative' (i.e. enemies of the republic who would bring back the monarchy).[33] The demand for suffrage was viewed as undermining the Republic. If the republicans' opponents from both the left and the right had been in power, they too would have found valid 'national' reasons to prevent women from getting the ballot.[34]

A continual accusation against Irish suffragists, especially the IWFL, was that they were part of a British movement. The fact that they were in touch with organisations from many other countries was ignored. The English connection was focused upon. One letter to the *Catholic Bulletin* argued that 'Granted that an Irishwoman wants a vote, she wants something else more; to nationalise her land, to keep it Ireland not west Britain. The suffrage movement is turning thoughts of the average Irishwoman Englandwards. That is its greatest danger in the present state of this country.'[35] Hanna Sheehy Skeffington, Margaret Cousins and others were very outspoken in denying these accusations. In her autobiography Cousins declared, '... the Nationalist Party had been taught by the press to regard us as opponents to Irish freedom, which we certainly were not, but opponents to the opposite of freedom in Ireland as anywhere else ...' However, she added that 'No self-respecting woman can be satisfied with any government which makes her sex a disqualification for citizenship ...'[36] Sheehy Skeffington objected strongly to the British Women's Social and Political Union setting up a branch in Ireland and she expressed this view in strong terms to one of its leaders, Christabel Pankhurst.[37]

Despite the protests of some suffragists, it is not difficult to see why nationalists believed that the suffrage movement was pro-British. Irish women were clearly inspired by the larger British movement. Indeed, after a visit by Mrs Pankhurst, suffragist Deborah Webb wrote a poem which contained the lines: 'To us an inspiration thou hast been ... To somewhat of thy zeal we would aspire.'[38] When Pankhurst's daughter, Christabel, visited Dublin in 1911, it was said of her visit: 'She came, we heard and saw, she conquered.'[39] Some Irish suffragists had undergone training in England, even members of the more nationalist IWFL. The Irish movement was largely middle-class and there were a number of Irish suffragist organisations that had unionist sympathies, most notably the Conservative and Unionist Women's Franchise Association, but also certain members of the Munster Women's Franchise League.

Elsewhere in Europe there were also accusations that, in the pre-World War I world of extreme nationalist tensions, the suffrage movement was viewed not only as anti-national and indicative of subversive forces within many European countries, but also as coming from 'abroad', and consequently it was considered even more suspicious and insidious. In France, feminism was linked to 'internationalism' and 'cosmopolitanism' and feminists were seen as being in league with the Jews, Protestants and Freemasons. Anti-feminist nationalist writer Theodore Joran asserted that 'Feminism, like Socialism, is an anti-French malady!'[40] August Provost depicted 'feminism as a new secular religion, international in scope and utterly foreign to France.'[41] In Germany, too, the suffrage movement was perceived as part of a Jewish conspiracy and labelled 'anti-national' in spirit.[42]

Welsh suffragists had to come to terms with being perceived as part of a 'foreign' English movement. Most of the suffrage societies in Wales were branches of the English organisations, the Women's Social and Political Union and the National Union of Women's Suffrage Societies. While it does not seem that Welsh feminists had a problem with this, other Welsh people did. The movement was seen as English, because the Welsh women who were involved tended to be from the English-speaking towns and they were often visited by English suffragists. In every country there were peculiarities. In the Welsh case, Welshman Lloyd George, a prominent member of the Liberal party and later Prime Minister of Great Britain, was frequently accosted by the suffragists. This caused a problem for many Welsh people who were proud of Lloyd George's achievements. The fact that he was regularly the target for bags of flour thrown by the suffragists did not add to the popularity of the women's movement in Wales.[43]

The English connection was also a problem in Italy. When Italian feminists cultivated ties with women's associations abroad, particularly with English militant suffragists, they were criticised and told that feminism was alien to Italian soil. The feminist newspaper, *La Donna,* was attacked for its 'foreign' model of the woman citizen.[44]

Nationalists' suspicions of the internationalism of the women's suffrage movement were reinforced in April 1915, when suffragists and other feminists met at The Hague for the Women's Peace Conference. The dilemma confronting the women delegates was twofold. How could they attend a peace conference when their country was fighting a war? How could they claim to be loyal citizens if they were seen mixing with enemy women and apparently undermining war efforts? Such was the resistance to women's efforts to discuss peace that many governments did not allow their women to attend the conference. As Rosemary Cullen Owens indicates elsewhere in this volume, Irishwomen were among those whom the British government prevented from travelling to The Hague. A number of German delegates were arrested when they returned home. The names of others appeared in intelligence reports.[45]

Repeatedly the suffrage movement was viewed as an import from abroad; it came from somewhere else. It was as if nationalists could not conceive of their own good women coming up with such ideas; suffragists were tainted by foreign ideas which were a threat to the stability of the State and the *status quo.* Nationalism was essentially based on ideas of male citizenship. The women's movement was labelled not only as unpatriotic but 'international'. Women were perceived as 'other' or as 'outsiders' in their own nation. This was particularly the case if they did not conform to the predominant male view of what their role in the nation should be. Accusations that the Irish movement was pro-British were not just a consequence of the colonial context of Ireland, but formed part of the general experience of suffragists everywhere.

In such a climate of nationalist fervour, women involved in the campaign for suffrage had to constantly proclaim and establish their nationalism to opponents. In the words of historian Karen Offen, they were 'nationalising their feminism'. They wished to assure nationalists that they, too, were patriotic. In the titles of their organisations and newspapers, the national context was often emphasised. For example, the suffrage newspaper of the Irish (note, Irish) Women's Franchise League was *The Irish Citizen* (established 1912). The word 'citizen' underlined the main point of their organisation. Their nationality was an integral part of their womanhood.

Likewise, in France the feminist newspaper was *La Française* (established in 1906) and a number of women's organisations had *Française* in their titles.[46] German women who were aware of the antagonism defended themselves against accusations of disloyalty by using 'the language of patriotism to buttress opposition'.[47] In Sweden, where the word 'emancipation' was also viewed as a foreign import, the feminist *Home Journal* urged women to seek political influence by encouraging patriotism and ran articles on Swedish national defence as Bismarck's Prussia expanded.[48]

Even in England, suffragists felt compelled to assert their loyalty and argue that women's suffrage was for the benefit of the country and the Empire. Mrs Fawcett, the leader of the National Union of Women's Suffrage Societies, pointed out in 1909 that 'the first Commonwealth countries to give the vote for women had also been the first to offer dreadnoughts as free gifts to the Mother Country, threatened by German naval development.'[49] It was argued that if women were enfranchised, they could greatly contribute to the Empire. A year after World War I began, the British suffragist newspaper *The Suffragette* changed its title to the more nationalistic, militaristic and aggressive title *Britannia*. The new title also reflected Britain's changing world position and self-perception since it was now at war with Germany. Members of the Women's Social and Political Union channelled all their energy into the war effort.[50] It is clear that women were continually being obliged to prove their patriotism.

Suffragists also pointed to their national history to justify their claims for the vote. In France, they cited the Revolution and the Declaration of the Rights of Man and Citizen as a starting point for their movement. The strong position of women in Celtic and pre-colonial Ireland was stressed by Irish suffragists, who indicated that Irish women had lost their rights because of colonisation and that with independence they would revert to the old ways. Imprisoned Irish suffragists who went on hunger strikes placed themselves in the tradition of Irish nationalist hunger strikers. These appeals to national histories were attempts by the women to place themselves strongly within the national context and to contradict the accusations of unpatriotic behaviour and internationalism.

Nationalism in Europe presented a formidable obstacle to the advancement of women in the period covered by this article. It was

vehemently opposed to the suffrage movement which was perceived as an anathema to the very ideals of nationalism. Patriotic
women who loved their country, and yet were discontented with
the limitations which were placed on them because they were
women, were in a dilemma. They viewed the vote as the key to
changing their situation and to becoming full members of the
nation. With the franchise they would be able to change laws and
improve their position. Yet in their very attempt to become part of
the nation and in their pursuit of the vote, they were barraged with
accusations of being disloyal, unpatriotic and in collusion with the
nation's enemies. How could they then advance the cause of
women without appearing to be undermining the nation? There
was no satisfactory answer. Whether they were in Ireland petitioning the British government, or in Europe petitioning their own
governments, the problem was the same. The demand for women's
suffrage was not only viewed as outside the nationalist goals, it was
considered to be in opposition to them. Thus women's dilemma
was that, if they wished to be seen as loyal members of their nation,
they could not demand equal citizenship with men, nor could they
fully participate in the affairs of that nation. The implications of all
of this for Irish women's history is that, when the European context
is investigated, the Irish situation becomes part of a much wider
pattern. Perhaps this is also the case in other areas of Irish women's
history?

Engendering Citizenship:
Women's Relationship to the State in Ireland & the United States in the Post-Suffrage Period
Maryann Gialanella Valiulis

Writing in one of her early essays in women's history entitled 'The historical image,' Margaret MacCurtain discussed the initial years of the Free State. She wrote:

> Historians have tended to explain the illiberal legislation and stifling provincialism of the post-Civil War decades in the Irish Free State by referring to the value system of a tradition-minded, rural-orientated society. Rarely, if at all, is allusion made to the total exclusion of woman from public life, and from responsibility for public morality. Woman's place was in the home.[1]

Implicit in this statement is the question: if historians had taken notice of women's exclusion from public life, had taken notice of the gender legislation of the period, would their interpretation have been any different? Or to put it another way: does an understanding of women's history change or alter our understanding of Irish history? Equally significant is the reverse of that question: does an understanding of Irish history contribute to our understanding of women's history?

In both these cases, I would argue that the answer is yes. We will have a more complex reading of both Irish history and women's history if we apply the insights we garner from one to another.

Let me illustrate. First, I will look at Ireland in the 1920s. The question I would pose is: is the traditional interpretation which characterises the years immediately following Irish independence as a turning inward to create and celebrate a rural, conservative culture accurate? Focusing on women and the gender legislation of the 1920s and 1930s demonstrates the need for a more complex understanding of this period, because what was happening in Ireland was not simply a turning away from the modern world but rather was also part of a more universal trend in Western countries.

Clearly, the climate of the Free State was conservative. It obviously suited the needs and aspirations of the male political élite, of the ruling Catholic middle class. But it was not necessarily a parochial response which tried to shut out the modern world. This, I believe, is the myth which has been foisted upon us by literary scholars, who point to censorship as the defining moment which stigmatises the Free State as inward-looking, provincial and narrow. The reality is more complex. The history of women reveals this complexity.

Equally illuminating for women's history is the experience of Irish women in the post-suffrage period. Far from seeing suffrage as the climactic point after which the women's movement splits asunder, the reality is revealed to be somewhat different, again more complex. In the Free State, in the 1920s and 1930s, various women's groups/feminist groups – women who were conscious of the status of women and were working together for the betterment of women – joined together to work towards the goal of full and unfettered citizenship. There were indeed many issues, from jury service to employment to the 1937 Constitution, in which these groups – groups like the Irish Women Workers' Union, the Irish Women's Citizens' Association, the Irish Women's International League, the Federation of University Women, to name but a few – came together to challenge the government. Therefore, in terms of women's history, what we learn from the Irish experience is that the divisions which are said to be typical of the women's movement are not characteristic of the Irish women's movement. Certainly, what divisions did exist did not prevent these women from working together. Thus, the generalisation concerning splits and differences within the women's movement must be tempered in light of the Irish experience. What current research in women's history has demonstrated is that the divisions between women in both Britain and the U.S. were not so stark as at first appeared. While some women's groups in both these countries emphasised women's right to equality and others chose to highlight the differences between men and women as the basis for a programme of political change, there were many areas of common concern. When we add the Irish experience, the generalisation about the splintering of the women's movement in the post-suffrage period becomes less tenable and more in need of qualification.

What is interesting when we analyse the official discourse of the period in Ireland and the U.S. is that the group which was promoting the split between the equality and difference groups was the dominant male political élite. For example, in their arguments over the issue of jury service, it was the government of the Free State which chose to emphasise the difference element in regards to women and women's claim to citizenship. The very quotable Minister for Justice, Kevin O'Higgins, said very clearly that 'a few words in a Constitution do not wipe out the very real differences between the sexes, either physical or mental or temperamental or emotional ...'[2] Lest we think this is a peculiarly Irish sentiment, the same ideas were expressed by politicians in the U.S. From a report of the state of Massachusetts came the same claim: '... it has been recognised by everyone that women differ from men; and despite the clamour of the most ardent contender for equal rights between the sexes the fact remains that women are, and always will be, different from men.'[3]

Feminist groups, on the other hand, rejected this dichotomy and argued that women were both equal to men and different from them. Both arguments were employed to further their claims for full citizenship. Thus, our understanding of the post-suffrage period is indeed enhanced by turning to Irish political history.

The issue I would like to examine from this dual perspective of Irish political history and women's history is that of citizenship as it is illuminated in the debates on jury service. What I would like to focus on is not the issue of jury service itself, but rather the ways in which women's relationship to the State was defined in the political debate on jury service, and to uncover the way in which citizenship was being defined for women and how women were defining it for themselves. In addition, I would like to add a comparative dimension because – despite obvious and real limitations – I think if we analyse the experience of women in Ireland and the United States, what is revealed is that a similar gender ideology prevailed in Western cultures despite differences in geographical size, population, levels of industrialisation and cultural ethos. Perhaps this is due to the ubiquitous nature of patriarchy. There is, however, one caveat I would note. By the 1920s, Irish American men had come to dominate urban centres in the northern states. Their sentiments, however, were echoed by non-Irish male political leaders from all over the country. Regardless of the differences, when we analyse what was happening in the 1920s in Ireland and in the U.S., two points become clear: 1) that the Free State was not unique in its attitude towards women; and 2) that citizenship for women was not a simple matter.

Certainly this is not unexpected. Women have had a very different relationship to the State than men. As historians have demonstrated, traditionally women's relationship to the State has been derivative, indirect. It is the male (husband, father) who had a direct relationship to the State and women were subsumed under their civic identity. Republican motherhood – whether in the U.S., France or Ireland – offered women a limited role in exercising her civic responsibilities and obligations. But, despite some attempts to keep it alive,[4] for many women, this indirect style had lost its appeal. Indeed, in the U.S.,

> the role of the republican mother who enacted her civic obligations through her service to her family, merging private choices with political obligations, had been marked as retrograde as early as the 1840s by Elizabeth Cady Stanton and her colleagues.[5]

The quest for the ballot, for suffrage, was clearly a repudiation of the indirect relationship of women to the State and an endorsement of the individual rights of women, of the direct relationship of women to the State. The granting of suffrage was a major step in defining women as citizens with rights and obligations to the State directly. It was not, however, the end of the story – or the end of the argument.

Over the issue of jury service – an issue which comes to the fore in Ireland and the U.S. in the 1920s – women's relationship to the State was renegotiated. Embedded in the political discourse surrounding this issue was: 1) the question of whether women were able to claim a direct relationship to the State or whether a woman's relationship to her husband/father/family took precedence over the obligations which she had to the State; and 2) whether women had a right to participate in the public sphere, in the political life of the State. Or, to put it another way: was the kitchen or the jury box to be the symbol of the post-suffrage woman?

Theoretically, there did not need to be a discussion. In 1922, the Irish Free State enacted a Constitution which gave women total and complete rights as citizens. In 1920, 36 states of the United States ratified the 19th Amendment granting women the right to vote. Yet, despite these assertions of political equality and the promise of full citizenship implicit in the granting of suffrage, restrictions and impediments characterised women's relationship to the State. For example, the right to free and unfettered jury service – a right which is fundamental to the exercise of citizenship – was denied to women until 1976 in Ireland and did not become a reality in all 50 states of the United States until 1979.

The Irish inherited jury service for women. According to the terms of the British Sex Disqualification (Removal) Act of 1919, which at that time applied to Ireland, women had complete access to jury service. In 1924, the Irish government enacted legislation which, while retaining women's right to serve on juries, gave them exemption upon demand. Just by notifying the appropriate official, women – simply because they were women – could be exempt. Few women were empanelled; fewer actually served. The Irish government was still not satisfied. In 1927, it proposed the rather extreme step of removing women from jury service altogether. Its reasons for so doing – administrative efficiency and financial savings – were not compelling. Its arguments were not convincing. In the end, the government accepted an amendment which exempted all women from jury service, but allowed women to serve if they so chose. Thus, under the 1927 Act, women could opt in and volunteer to serve on juries.

In the U.S., the situation was obviously much more varied. In a number of states, on becoming voters, women automatically qualified for jury service, for example, in Michigan (1918); in other states, it required a specific act of the legislature to allow women in the jury box, for example, in New Jersey (1921), or in the case of the District of Columbia, an act of the Congress of the United States (1927). In addition, not all states offered women jury service on the same terms as men. In some, women were excused upon request – much like the 1924 bill in Ireland. In others, like Louisiana, women's names were not entered on the jury rolls except upon written request – which was similar to the situation of Irish women after the 1927 legislation.[6]

Before analysing the common elements surrounding the issue of jury service in both the U.S. and Ireland, there are glaring differences which need to be stated. In the U.S., issues of race, class and ethnicity played a significant role in the arguments about jury service in a way in which they did not in Ireland. In Ireland eligibility for jury service for both Irish men and women was tied up with property rates and valuation.

In the U.S., anti-black and anti-immigrant feeling surfaced quite clearly in the debate over jury service. Those who opposed jury service for women held out the spectre of women sequestered with black men and immigrant men. One member of the House of Representatives asked quite bluntly: 'Does the gentlemen want his daughter ... to be locked up for a week, night and day, on a jury where there are at least three or four coloured [*sic*] men?'[7] Or to participate on juries in which there is 'not a name on the jury list that has an American sound?'[8] To be sure, the issue of women being sequestered with any man received a great deal of play, but it was given greater potency when issues of race and class were added.

American feminists were also guilty of class bias. They bemoaned the fact that when men alone were in the jury pool, the juries were made up of 'inferior personnel'[9] and claimed that:

> The best type of men frequently cannot leave their work or business without great sacrifice in order to serve for any continuous period upon a jury. However, women of equal intelligence and ability have more time to serve without such sacrifice.[10]

And, if there were any doubt as to who the best type were, they were defined as those with 'education and higher standing in the community.'[11] Thus feminists argued that 'having women serve on juries was one way in which a great improvement could be made in the class of jurors which it would be possible to secure.'[12] This type of argument obviously excluded large segments of the population and identified jury service as a middle- and upper-class issue.

Even within this restricted view, the issue of jury service took on a degree of importance which, in other cases, it lacked. For example, the right/obligation to serve on juries had been granted as a natural consequence of suffrage in the U.S. And, under the British system, this right was tied up with property qualifications. Jury service flowed naturally as part of the right to participate directly in the body politic.

Women then were the obvious exception. Not only was the right to serve on juries not simply viewed as part of their newly defined status, it became a hotly debated issue. In the words of the American activist, Gladys Harrison, Executive Secretary of the League of Women Voters, speaking in 1930: 'Getting the word "male" out of jury statutes is requiring something very like a second suffrage campaign – laborious, costly and exasperating.'[13] Her Irish counterparts would echo her sentiments.

The gender dimension in this discussion is obvious. For those who opposed jury service for women, this issue provided the opportunity to negate the implication of suffrage – that women had a direct relationship to the State – and reassert that women's primary obligation was to their husbands/fathers/families. On both sides of the Atlantic, women were, once again, being defined in terms of their reproductive capacity, as bearers of children, and as nurturers, keepers of the hearth and home. These two functions, it was argued, were of such primary and defining importance that they superseded any other claims that the State might make on women or that women might claim for themselves. Thus, Kevin O'Higgins referred to women's reproductive capacity as 'women performing the normal functions of womanhood in the State's economy.'[14] One of his colleagues, Sir James Craig, spoke of women having 'a much more important duty to perform to the State than service on juries, that their functions were motherhood and looking after their families ...'[15] In the U.S. Congress, one opponent of jury service drew the following scenario for his colleagues in the House of Representatives:

> I cannot conceive in my family of any time for 25 years when my wife had the time or the inclination to go off and serve on a jury in a murder case or a felony case while her children roamed the streets in her absence. Why, every child when it comes home from school, every older child when it comes home from work, why even the old man himself when he opens the door asks, 'Where is mother?'; shall the answer be, 'She is off on jury duty somewhere'? [Laughter and Applause][16]

The Representative's comments bring up another issue. After locating women's primary function in her reproductive capacity, her second primary function was care not only of these children, but care of the husband, the family, tending the home. Again O'Higgins voiced a common sentiment when he said:

> A man can be absent for a day or a couple of days, from his household, as a rule, without any serious consequences occurring to anybody. He can lunch out, and it does not follow that the other members of his household have to do without their lunch. He is not, as a rule, charged with the care of young children ...[17]

This was the point of 'sharp discrimination between the sexes' – women cooked and men did not.[18] Evident throughout this argument was the idea that jury service as an obligation/right of citizenship and as an exercise of activity in the public sphere was superseded by what was defined as the more primary one of familial obligations in the domestic sphere.

Moreover, this relegation of women to the domestic sphere was justified by the dominant male political figures and their allies as a function of the 'natural and normal' gender divisions of society. As one Dáil deputy claimed: 'We also know that the normal woman will have no desire ... to serve on a jury, and she never will serve on a jury if she can avoid it.'[19] From Massachusetts came the statement that 'a good housewife or mother' had no inclination to serve on juries nor, asserted one Congressman, did the 'good women' of Washington.[20] Most women, according to the *Irish Independent*, 'desired to be left in their homes to do the work that best fits a woman's nature.'[21] Or as this same newspaper claimed, 'real' women did not want to serve on juries, did not want to be dragged away

> from the bosoms of their families, from their cherished household duties, from the preparation of their husbands' dinners ... to take their places on juries to decide matters entirely foreign to their experience and often beyond their comprehension.[22]

From the U.S. Congress came the injunction that

> we should at least show some consideration for the hard-work-
> ing, intelligent, and home-loving women of our Nation. I believe
> we should avoid trying to get them to do men's work and change
> their sex through legislation.[23]

This same speaker went on to castigate the 'manhood' of those men
who supported jury service for women:

> I say to you that unless you are a henpecked husband, unless you
> have an absolute fear of a few women who are in the gallery, you
> are not going to impose upon the decent women of this District
> so onerous a duty ...[24]

Thus for both men and women, attitudes towards jury service
indicated gender correctness. Real men and normal women would
not countenance this 'monstrous' and 'repugnant' attempt to put
women in the jury box.[25]

For feminists, indeed for all women who were prepared to serve
on juries, the issue became more invidious. It was not only about
being 'good' women. In Ireland, all those who were prepared to
serve on juries were derogatorily categorised as abnormal with 'the
implication that only abnormal women were prepared to serve
upon a jury.'[26] And, in the United States, it was claimed that 'good
women' did not want to enter courthouses, 'only poor white trash
would want to serve,' as they said in Georgia,[27] or, put another way,
only those undesirables who are attracted by the service fee would
want to serve. Invoking the concept of abnormal during the 1920s
and juxtaposing it with words like monstrous and repugnant can
be seen to have as its subtext the charge of lesbianism. It is precisely
in this period that lesbianism is identified and defined as an abnor-
mality. Clearly, this type of attack was meant to discredit feminists
and all those who challenged the dominant male political élite.

The good women – the women who stayed safely in the domestic sphere – were not only normal, but on them was cast the
crowning epithet of the gender ideology – they were ladies. Unfortunately, those who used this term failed to define it more completely. In this case what it seemed to mean was those who never
had 'the least desire to enter the jury box.'[28] This was amply
demonstrated in the following burst of chivalric rhetoric in which
one Dáil deputy advised his colleagues to:

> Consider the unsuitability of such services for a lady. We all know
> that ladies are entitled to respect and attention and I must say I
> appreciate very much this great privilege the Minister has given
> them of not being compelled to go on jury service.[29]

Ladies and chivalry – women on the pedestal – emerged as a strong
theme in the discourse of U.S. political leaders – from the Florida

courts to the Congress of the U.S. to the Massachusetts legislature. 'Women on the pedestal' is an interesting phrase in this particular context because women who are on the pedestal have no mobility and, in effect, have no way of entering the public sphere. Perhaps this was the intent. A Congressman from Massachusetts certainly voiced this concern:

> I am a little old-fashioned. I am afraid, if women go into jury service, they will not occupy that high pedestal which they have in the past. I personally feel women should not serve on juries for that reason.[30]

The courts echoed this sentiment:

> The legislature still has the power to prescribe the qualifications of jurors, and to impose this burden upon men alone if it sees fit so to do ... The spirit of chivalry, and of deep respect for the rights of the opposite sex, have not yet departed from the heads and hearts of the men of this country.[31]

In other words, a House of Representative member explained, 'they still have sufficient chivalry out there ... to give the women more privileges than are given to men.'[32]

This statement spoke to a central, key issue in the debate about citizenship. It was a question of privilege – the privilege of not serving on juries which was given to women by the Irish government and the U.S. courts and legislatures. Citizenship for women was not a question of rights and obligations. In the case of women, government was claiming that it had the right to decide what aspects of citizenship women should enjoy, that citizenship was in its gift. Kevin O'Higgins explained the common dominant male position:

> The case is this: the vast majority of the women citizens of this country, as in most countries, dislike this work, dislike it intensely, and would be grateful to the Government that would relieve them from it. We can afford to relieve them from it. There is not the necessity of putting this unpleasant duty on the women section of the country's citizenship.[33]

Women could be exempt because, O'Higgins explained, government had no duty to impose the burdens of citizenship equally. Government, he claimed, was not 'constitutionally bound to impose an absolutely equal burden of citizenship on all its citizens.'[34] Government thus became the arbiter of citizenship, the mediator between women and the State. Because government positioned itself as the intermediary between women and the State, it thus reinforced the derivative, indirect nature of women's citizenship.

Moreover, women were defined not as individuals who had specific rights and obligations, but rather only as part of the wider community. The wider community would suffer if women were allowed access to the public sphere, claimed one U.S. politician, and hence he opposed jury service.[35] This refusal to acknowledge women's individual rights again reinforced the idea that women occupied a position which was circumscribed by their domestic responsibilities.

From the dominant male political discourse of the period, it becomes apparent that full, direct and complete citizenship was thus reserved for those who did not give birth, did not tend to the hearth and home. In essence, it was reserved for men. It was 'the men who should be patriotic citizens.'[36] Thus governments were erecting a barrier between the domestic and public sphere, a barrier which women – because of both biological and social conditions – were defined as incapable of crossing.

Not surprisingly, feminists defined citizenship for women differently. Indeed, for a variety of groups of women, jury service in particular and citizenship in general became a *cause célèbre*. In Ireland, women formed a broadly-based coalition which included such diverse groups as the Irish Women Workers' Union, the Irish Women's Citizens' Association, the Irish Women's International League. In the U.S., jury service was the one issue on which the numerous women's groups – such as the National Women's Party, the League of Women Voters, the Women's Bar Association, and the Women's City Clubs could unite.

Feminists on both sides of the Atlantic rejected the idea that women's primary obligation was to the home and not to the State. Indeed feminists claimed the right to full and unfettered citizenship in their own right – not as wives, mothers or daughters but as citizens of their respective nations.

Women, feminists argued, were equal under the law and thus had a right to participate in the public life of the country – in this instance, a right to serve on juries. It was, they claimed, their constitutional right. In the Irish context, women charged the government with violating the Constitution which, they believed, established the principle of complete equality between men and women. Access to jury service, they argued, was a 'constitutional right which no Minister can tamper with without violating Article 3 of the Constitution of the Irish Free State.'[37]

Across the Atlantic, U.S. women argued that suffrage made them citizens and that jury service was a complement of citizenship, 'one of the most obvious and most useful of the civic duties.'[38] Women pointed out that 'all kinds of people' had, in the past, been added to the electorate, and with it came the right to serve on juries. Only women were different.[39] And only 'peculiar masculine reasoning,' they claimed, 'interprets persons and citizens to include women at one time and not to include them at another time.'[40]

Equality was thus one theme of feminist discourse. Another theme centred on the issue of difference, much noted, as we have seen, in the dominant male political discourse of the day. An analysis of feminists' discourse demonstrates that they did not challenge the assumption that women were mothers or that in their society in the 1920s, women had the primary responsibility for the hearth and home. But they interpreted these facts quite differently from their male colleagues.

In the first place, feminists challenged the equation that womanhood equalled motherhood equalled derivative citizenship. Feminists pointed out that women were mothers for only part of the time, that 'they did not have children clinging all their lives.'[41] Hence to exclude all women for all time on the rationale that they had a more important service to perform to the State was illogical.

Moreover, feminists repudiated the implicit assumption in the dominant male political discourse that there was a barrier between the public and private spheres which prevented women from crossing from the home to the courtroom. They strongly disputed the notion that if a woman were a wife and a mother, she could not be an active public citizen. They rejected the assumption that care of husbands and families restricted women to the domestic sphere. In Ireland, feminists ridiculed 'the poor, dinnerless husband who manages to survive in this country as an argument against almost any kind of progress ...' (masculine imagination apparently could picture no greater calamity).[42] This sentiment was echoed in the States:

> The home has not suffered ... because women have sat on city councils, or on boards of directors ... family life has not been destroyed; children have not gone in greater numbers than before, breakfastless to school. There is no recorded increase in the burning of soups.[43]

In addition, following in the tradition of nineteenth-century women's rights advocates, feminists argued that because of 'difference,' because of their different roles in society, women had something unique to contribute to the public realm. They would bring to the public sphere 'an element of sincerity, honesty, and righteousness which was not present in the same extent before.'[44] Women, feminists asserted, would 'raise the standard of our juries ... [and] add dignity to the courtroom.'[45] Thus the government's and indeed the court's position, that women could be excluded from juries and nothing would be lost, was patently false.

Because men and women were different, feminists maintained, the interests of justice demanded that there be mixed juries. Justice, they argued, was 'more likely to be achieved when the mental qualities of both sexes are brought to bear on the evidence.'[46] Or, as one women argued,

> Men are always at their best in the presence of good women; hence with mixed juries one usually can expect from the men a more earnest and serious consideration of the questions involved than from a jury composed entirely of men.[47]

For similar reasons, feminists stressed that women's presence on juries was vital in cases concerning other women and children, '...for whose suffering and whose needs women have a special understanding.'[48] As one woman asked:

> ... Would any mother be capable of wishing her child to appear in a court of law composed exclusively of men? Surely, ordinary common decency of feelings demands that there should be women on the juries which try these cases.[49]

Nor was it only children and adolescents who needed women on juries. Other women involved in the judicial process also needed the presence of women in the jury box. What was at issue was the right to be tried by one's peers. And feminists reiterated time and again that only with women on the jury could women truly be tried by their peers.[50]

Difference also demanded women's presence on juries because feminists claimed that women, as a result of their role as child-rearers and nurturers, had insights denied men. 'We want,' one League of Women Voters publication rather exuberantly proclaimed, 'the mother instinct which is used in the closeted nursery to be used also in the big troubled nursery of the world.'[51] These women used society's argument about natural roles to further their own ends, to assert their unique public value in a patriarchal society which devalued their political personas.

Nor did feminists accept the wreath of protection, the attitude of chivalry which male politicians offered them. Women's groups rejected the myth of women as the fair sex who needed protection from the harshness of real life. As a representative from the Women's Trade Union League in the United States pointed out to the legislators in the state of New York:

> We don't need to be shielded ... sometimes because of a mistaken sense of chivalry you think you are protecting us. You have been protecting us for years and years, and we have appreciated the motives behind that protection, but we do doubt its wisdom.[52]

Women, feminists claimed, could deal with the realities of life. They were not 'such tender plants as the Victorians pretended, and, indeed, some men are far more shockable ...'[53]

Finally, in Ireland, feminists claimed that they had earned the right to citizenship because of the role they had played in the revolutionary struggle. Senator Jennie Wyse Power's now familiar speech in the Senate, in which she reminded her colleagues of the enormous contribution which women had made, castigated the government for its current treatment of women.

In sum, feminists conceptualised citizenship as direct and complete. For them, women had a dual role to play in society: as citizens in the public sphere and as mothers/nurturers in the private sphere. Neither role excluded the other.

Feminist discourse used the language of rights and individualism but did not abandon women's role within the larger group; the dominant male discourse spoke only of the needs of the family, of the community. The dominant discourse turned difference into inequality, inferiority; feminist discourse embraced the concept of difference. Indeed, an analysis of feminist discourse reveals that their arguments turned a misogynistic emphasis on difference to their own advantage.

On one level, feminists' emphasis on the positive side of difference was strategically sound, at least in the short term. Arguments for equality were certainly much more threatening to those who opposed jury service and complete citizenship for women and would, most likely, lose rather than gain allies. Many more would rally to ideas such as 'mother's instinct' than would accept claims of equal intelligence, equal rights and so on.

With hindsight, however, the strategy of concentrating on difference rather than equality, of arguing for women's unique contributions rather than their rights, weakened women's ability to withstand the conservative onslaught of the 1920s and 1930s. This failure to emphasise equality, to emphasise women's right to exercise the full complement of citizenship, undermined women's claims to a direct relationship to the State.

There is, I would argue, a direct link between engendering citizenship so that women's relationship to the State is superseded by their relationship to the family and the conservative onslaught of the 1920s and 1930s. Because women's primary function was defined as being in the home, women's right to employment could be restricted through such devices as the marriage bar – a restriction which operated in both countries. Because, according to the dominant male political discourse, women were to occupy only the domestic sphere and not the public sphere, the 1937 Irish Constitution could enshrine women's place in the hearth and home. And by discursively defining women in such a way, the reality of women's lives – that many women did not marry, did not have children, needed to work to support themselves and others – did not impinge upon subsequent debates.

Patriarchal power provides a key to understanding much about citizenship for women. Perhaps the idea of jury service for women became such a battleground because the dominant male political élite saw it as yet another threat to patriarchal power. Such power was premised on male control of the public sphere and restricting women to the private sphere. And this separation was under attack, as women made their way onto local governing bodies, into the ballot box, into the legislature. Any further undermining of this separation of public and private spheres would loosen a bit more the underpinnings of patriarchy. Restricting jury service thus bolstered patriarchal power. Engendering citizenship increased the power of a male patriarchal élite, disadvantaged women and deprived the State of alternative voices in the public sphere.

In conclusion, I return to the beginning, to ask the question implicit in Margaret MacCurtain's analysis: if historians had taken notice of women's exclusion from public life, had taken notice of the gender legislation of the period, would their interpretation have been any different? The answer, I believe, is that an analysis of the common beliefs and attitudes surrounding women's right to citizenship provides a more complete, more complex, more nuanced historical construction of the period.

Women & the Politics of Equality:
The Irish Women's Movement 1930–1943
Caitriona Beaumont

On 6 February 1943, the twenty-fifth anniversary of Irish women receiving the parliamentary franchise,[1] an article appeared in the *Irish Times Pictorial* entitled 'Women must fight on!: From tubs to parliament'. Anna Kelly, an *Irish Times* journalist, recalled that twenty-five years earlier

> women of political reason were able to put on their hats, grasp their umbrellas, take one last look at their homes and babies, and heedless of their husband's appeals, march out to face the ballot paper for the first time in their lives. And what happened? What, after all the dreadful prognostications, came to pass? Nothing. Women voted and returned home to normality.[2]

The failure of the Irish women's suffrage movement to evolve into a dynamic campaign for women's equality was lamented by Kelly. She bemoaned the fact that in 1943, there were only three female representatives in the Dáil and women had not yet achieved equal status with men. The republican Nora Connolly echoed Kelly's frustration when she wrote that the women of her generation 'having won the right to share in the dangers of war ... had relinquished their right to share in the dangers of peace and returned without protest to their domestic role.'[3]

The participation of a small but influential number of Irish women in the suffrage movement and women's involvement in the nationalist struggle heightened expectations about the status of women in an independent Ireland.[4] These hopes were sustained by the guarantee of equality contained in the 1916 Proclamation and the 1922 Free State Constitution. The Easter Proclamation asserted that Irish men and women were entitled to equal citizenship, equal rights and equal opportunities. Following the War of Independence and the establishment of the Irish Free State in 1922, the Free State Constitution extended the franchise to women over the age of twenty-one. This meant that Irish women were now entitled to the same rights of political citizenship as men, the right to vote.[5]

Article 3 of the 1922 Irish Constitution ensured that 'every person, without distinction of sex, shall ... enjoy the privileges and be subject to the obligations of such citizenship.'[6] In spite of this guarantee, legislation was passed during the 1920s and 1930s which indicated that the State envisaged very different roles for men and women in Irish society. Men were expected to work and support their families, while women performed their 'normal and natural' function as wives and mothers. As Eamon de Valera put it, 'everyone knows there is little chance of having a home in the real sense if there is no woman in it, the woman is really the home-maker.'[7]

Recent research has highlighted the role played by women's organisations in protests against restrictive legislation, including the 1927 Juries Act and the 1936 Conditions of Employment Act.[8] These campaigns were organised by a number of Dublin-based societies determined to defend the citizenship rights of women. Yet to focus exclusively on protests against discriminatory legislation has diverted attention from other activities undertaken by the women's movement during this period. Throughout the 1930s and early 1940s, societies for women called on the government to introduce social and economic reforms which would benefit women and children. Their demands included family allowances, the appointment of women police and adequate health care. Women were encouraged to work together to achieve these goals and learn about their rights and duties as citizens. Membership of a women's organisation also gave women and girls the opportunity to meet for talks, classes and social activities, away from the responsibilities of home and family.

This paper argues that there was an active women's movement in Ireland during the years from 1930 to 1943. Organisations for women during this period persistently campaigned against legislation which discriminated against women. At the same time, women's groups did much to highlight the needs of women, both in the home and the work-place, so that the health and welfare of all women would be improved. Women's organisations were not just political pressure groups reacting to restrictive legislation. Instead, they addressed a wide range of inequalities and hardships endured by many thousands of women in the Irish Free State.

Within ten years of the establishment of the Irish Free State, it was already clear that women in Ireland were not considered equal 'without distinction of sex'. The 1925 Civil Service Regulation (Amendment) Bill and the 1927 Juries Act showed that the Cumann na nGaedheal government was willing to exclude women from participating in public service.[9] Although a career in the civil service was the preserve of a minority of middle-class women and many women had taken up the option of having their names removed from jury rolls,[10] it was the fact that women alone were being singled out for discrimination which so angered women's organisations.

A number of women's groups came together to protest against the enactment of the 1925 Civil Service (Amendment) Bill and the 1927 Juries Bill.[11] As part of their campaign, three leading feminist societies, the Irish Women's Citizens' and Local Government Association, the National Council of Women and the National University Women Graduates' Association wrote to members of the Dáil and Seanad outlining their objections to the proposed legislation. Protesting against the Civil Service Regulation (Amendment) Bill, the Irish Women's Citizens' and Local Government Association insisted that when recruiting civil servants the question asked should not be 'are these candidates men or women, but are they competent to do the work.'[12]

Asserting the right of women to jury service, the Irish Women's Citizens' and Local Government Association argued that 'women had no right to evade any duties and responsibilities involved in citizenship ... it would be unfair to men citizens and derogatory to women if women could escape sitting on juries due to sex alone.'[13] Senator Jennie Wyse Power, former President of Cumann na mBan, was an active member of the Irish Women's Citizens' and Local Government Association during these years. Along with fellow ·Senator Eileen Costello, Wyse Power condemned the government for trying to deprive women of their rights and duties as citizens.[14]

The campaign against these legislative proposals was relatively successful. Following its defeat in the Seanad, the Civil Service Regulation (Amendment) Act was suspended. Although the 1927 Juries Act became law, an amendment was added which allowed women to sit on juries, but only if they specifically applied.[15] In spite of this compromise, the Cumann na nGaedheal government had by the late 1920s sent a very clear message to Irish feminists. The struggle for women's equality in the Free State was far from over.

Feminist opinion at this time was, as noted, represented by the Irish Women's Citizens' and Local Government Association, the National Council of Women and the National University Women Graduates' Association. These groups recognised the imbalance of power between men and women in society and tried to secure equal rights for women in the Irish Free State.[16] With no religious or party-political affiliations, feminist societies attracted educated middle-class women, many of whom had been involved in the suffrage movement. It was the status of leading members, Hanna Sheehy Skeffington, Mary Hayden and Mary Macken to name but a few, which guaranteed political recognition and media attention for feminist organisations during this period.

When the parliamentary vote was extended to women in 1922, the Irish Women's Citizens' and Local Government Association[17] expressed its intention to unite 'Irish women of all politics and all creeds for the study and practice of good citizenship.'[18] Yet in spite of efforts to recruit women in rural areas, the Association remained a small Dublin-based society throughout the 1930s and 1940s.[19] As in many feminist organisations during this period, the difficulty in recruiting members was in some ways overcome by having well-known and respected women involved in the organisation. Membership of the Association included Senator Jennie Wyse Power and Mary Hayden. Professor of Modern Irish History at University College Dublin, Hayden was a committed feminist who was appointed Vice-President of the Association in the late 1920s.[20] Through her writings and her involvement in numerous women's organisations, Mary Hayden was an outspoken critic of every kind of discrimination perpetrated against women during the 1920s and 1930s.

One of the principal aims of the Irish Women's Citizens' and Local Government Association was to lobby the government on legislation affecting the lives of women and children. Weekly meetings were held to discuss current legislation and members were encouraged to support 'enlightened legislation especially in those spheres which concern the lives of women and those dependent on them.'[21] The introduction of family allowances was one example of progressive legislation which interested the Association. At a public meeting in December 1925, members were told that family allowances paid to the mother would not only improve their children's standard of living but give wives 'a sense of contributing to her share of the family exchequer.'[22]

The Irish Women's Citizens' and Local Government Association was affiliated to the National Council of Women, set up in 1924 'to promote co-operation among women all over Ireland interested in social welfare'.[23] Membership of the National Council included non-feminist societies such as the United Irishwomen and the Mothers' Union.[24] The fact that feminist and non-feminist women's organisations co-operated within the National Council of Women is noteworthy. It illustrated the willingness of disparate women's groups to work together on issues which affected the welfare of women and children.

Mary Hayden, President of the National Council of Women, also served as President of the National University Women Graduates' Association from 1913 until 1942.[25] Representing women graduates from the three national universities of Cork, Galway and Dublin, this organisation catered for a minority of Irish women who had benefited from a university education.[26] In spite of its limited membership, the National University Women Graduates' Association proved to be one of the most influential women's societies of the 1920s and 1930s. Leading members included some very distinguished Irish women. Hanna Sheehy Skeffington, a founding member of the association, was a woman with impeccable credentials.[27] A suffrage campaigner, she set up the Irish Women's Franchise League in 1908 with her husband Francis Sheehy Skeffington. As well as being an advocate of women's rights, Hanna Sheehy Skeffington was a republican and nationalist. A former member of the Sinn Féin executive, she was elected as a Sinn Féin representative to Dublin Corporation in 1918.

Mary Macken, Professor of German at University College Dublin, and Agnes O'Farrelly, Professor of Modern Irish at the same university, were two other prominent members of the Women Graduates' Association. Both women were respected academics who, like Hanna Sheehy Skeffington, were committed to both the feminist and the nationalist cause.[28] The National University Women Graduates' Association is best known for its leading role in the campaign against the draft 1937 Constitution. It was, however, involved in numerous activities throughout the 1920s and 1930s. The Association helped set up an employment bureau for female graduates and spoke out in favour of equal opportunities in the civil service, pointing out that many of its members were qualified for the higher grades.[29]

When Fianna Fáil came to power in 1932, feminist societies had already demonstrated their determination to campaign against legislation discriminating against women. The new government, led by Eamon de Valera, did little to reassure feminists that women would be treated more equitably under a Fianna Fáil administration. The 1934 Criminal Law (Amendment) Act, the 1935 Conditions of Employment Act and the 1937 Constitution revealed the government's inclination, supported by a majority of deputies in the Dáil, to differentiate between the citizenship rights of men and women.

In March 1935, the Joint Committee of Women's Societies and Social Workers was set up when representatives of nine voluntary organisations met to discuss the 1934 Criminal Law (Amendment) Bill.[30] Concerned with the welfare of women and children, these groups were disturbed by a number of clauses included in the proposed legislation. In cases of indecent assault, the Bill proposed to raise the age of consent from thirteen to fifteen. This clause was criticized by women's groups, who argued that to safeguard children from indecent assault the age of consent should be raised to at least seventeen years of age.

Senator Kathleen Browne, a member of the Irish Country-women's Association, accused the government of providing 'less protection to our young girls than the governments of Great Britain and Northern Ireland.'[31] In the Seanad, a special Seanad Committee, which included Senator Jennie Wyse Power, was established to discuss the implications of the proposed Bill. This committee recommended that the age of consent in cases of indecent assault should be eighteen. The government, however, declined to accept the recommendations of either the Seanad committee, women's societies or the advice of social workers and stood by its original proposals.[32]

The Joint Committee of Women's Societies and Social Workers also objected to the clause in the Bill which proposed to increase the penalty for women convicted of prostitution from a fine to six months' imprisonment.[33] Not only was the prison term considered too severe, but the fact that male clients were rarely charged with any offence was condemned by the Joint Committee. The Committee maintained that the penalties for solicitation should be the same for both men and women. This view was supported in the Seanad by Kathleen Browne and Kathleen Clarke who attempted, unsuccessfully, to amend this section of the Bill.

It is noteworthy that the Joint Committee of Women's Societies and Social Workers raised no objection to Section 17 of the Criminal Law (Amendment) Act, which prevented the sale and importation of birth control devices in the Irish Free State. In 1929, the Censorship of Publications Act had prohibited the distribution of literature advocating the use of birth control.[34] Now under the terms of the Criminal Law (Amendment) Act the sale of the contraceptives was to be banned. For what appeared to be a controversial clause, signifying State interference in family life, it is interesting that women's organisations did not object to this ban on contraceptive devices.

In a country where the vast majority of the population were practising Catholics and the influence of the Catholic Church was predominant, the fact that women did not publicly oppose a ban on contraceptives is not so surprising.[35] Any organisation advocating the use of birth control would have been condemned by the Catholic Church. This meant that large numbers of women, themselves devout Catholics, would have found it impossible to remain members of a society denounced by the Church. Another factor which hindered the debate on this issue was the fact that any discussion of sex and questions relating to sexual practice was taboo in Ireland at this time. Because of this, it was unlikely that women's organisations or any other group would speak out in favour of the use of birth control devices.

Even societies representing the interests of Protestant women did not object to Section 17 of the Criminal Law (Amendment) Act. In 1930, the Church of England had sanctioned the use of birth control when there was a 'moral obligation to limit or avoid parenthood'.[36] Yet in spite of this ruling, the Mothers' Union and the Girls' Friendly Society frowned upon artificial methods of birth control. According to the Mothers' Union 'a selfish refusal of children is wrong ... all artificial checks to conception are against the laws of nature.'[37] As a result, the one section of the Criminal Law (Amendment) Act most relevant to the lives of Irish women was passed virtually unnoticed.[38]

Having avoided the controversial and divisive issue of birth control, the Joint Committee of Women's Societies and Social Workers went on to represent fourteen organisations on 'matters of mutual interest affecting women, young persons and children.'[39] One of the first campaigns launched by the Joint Committee was for the appointment of women police in the Irish Free State. The Committee supported the employment of women in the police force because it was felt that women were best suited to deal with police cases involving women and children.[40] As early as 1925, the National Council of Women had sent a deputation to the Minister for Justice urging him to appoint fully-trained policewomen to the Irish police force. The Cumann na nGaedheal government, however, appeared unwilling to take the matter further and it was not until 1935 that the issue was raised once again. The Joint Committee then approached the Fianna Fáil government hoping for a more favourable response to the concept of female police officers.

In December 1935, the Joint Committee presented its proposals to the Minister for Justice urging him to sanction the establishment of a force of trained, educated women, officered by women, with the status, powers of arrest, and remuneration of their male colleagues. This body would operate within the general police force.[41]

The Minister was informed that the duties which women police could perform, working alongside their male colleagues, included taking evidence from women and children, searching women prisoners and dealing with cases involving domestic violence.[42]

Following this meeting, the Minister promised to look into the question of women police, but it soon became clear that the government had no intention of appointing women to the police force. In December 1939, the Minister refused a request to meet with representatives of the Joint Committee, informing them that 'the agitation for women police is an artificial business without any real roots in the country.' He added that funds needed to employ women police were not available 'at a time when there are so many heavy demands on the public purse'.[43]

Numerous letters and requests for meetings were sent to the government and the Garda Commissioner calling for the appointment of women police.[44] Yet in spite of persistent pressure from women's societies including the Joint Committee, the Women Graduates' Association and the Mothers' Union, it was not until 1959 that trained policewomen were finally appointed to the Garda Síochána. As the campaign for women police continued throughout the 1930s, women's organisations had to contend with further legislative measures restricting employment opportunities for women. In 1932, a marriage bar was introduced which excluded married women teachers from the workforce.[45] This practice, already established in Britain, was one way of protecting job opportunities for men during a time of severe economic depression. The fact that the majority of Irish women did not work outside the home after marriage was not disputed by Irish feminists.[46] The marriage bar was condemned, however, on the grounds that it discriminated against single women interested in pursuing a career in the public service. Mary Kettle, future chairman of the Joint Committee of Women's Societies and Social Workers, argued that the marriage bar hindered the promotional opportunities of single women. Employers were unlikely to promote women who, if they ever married, would be forced to resign.[47] This meant that single women, even if they had no intention of getting married, would find it difficult to gain access to higher grades in the public service.

The 1935 Conditions of Employment Act was seen by Irish feminists as yet another attack on the right of women to work outside the home. Employment opportunities for women in industry increased significantly during the 1930s with the establishment of new manufacturing industries. There were fears, however, that the rising demand for low-paid female workers would result in male unemployment. The government, submitting to pressure from the male-dominated trade union movement, agreed to restrict the employment of women under the terms of the 1935 Conditions of Employment Act.[48] Section 16 of the Act gave the Minister for Industry and Commerce the right to limit the number of women working in any given industry.[49] The Irish Women's Workers' Union saw this as a blatant attempt to deprive women of their choice of work in order to safeguard the employment of men. Equal pay, the Union argued, would be a more just way of protecting job opportunities for both men and women. The Union launched a protest campaign against the implementation of Section 16, but without the backing of trade unions or the Labour Party, their efforts proved futile.[50]

Although the campaign against the Conditions of Employment Act ended in failure, it strengthened links between individual women's societies. The Irish Women Workers' Union, in defending the principle of 'equal rights ... equal democratic opportunities for all citizens and equal pay for equal work',[51] was backed by feminist societies including the National Council of Women and the Women Graduates' Association. Two years later, these organisations joined forces once again to protest against the enactment of the 1937 Constitution.

In May 1937, the draft of the new Irish Constitution was submitted to the Dáil for its final reading. While this debate was taking place, women's societies met to discuss the implications of the draft Constitution for women. Following a meeting of the Women Graduates' Association on 10 May 1937, it was reported that

> the omission [from the draft] of the principle of equal rights and opportunities enunciated in the Proclamation of 1916 and confirmed in Article 3 of the Constitution of Saorstat Éireann was deplored as sinister and retrogressive.[52]

The following day the Joint Committee of Women's Societies and Social Workers passed a resolution calling the attention 'of all women voters to the manner in which their rights have been undermined in the draft Constitution.' Articles 40.1, 41.2 and 45 were singled out 'as an attack upon our fundamental rights as human beings and contrary to the principles of the founders of this state'.[53]

Articles 9 and 16 were also condemned because they did not guarantee the right to Irish nationality and citizenship 'without distinction of sex'. On 14 May 1937, the Taoiseach, Eamon de

Valera, met with representatives from the National University Women Graduates' Association, the Joint Committee of Women's Societies and Social Workers and the National Council of Women to discuss the draft Constitution. De Valera informed the deputation that the term 'without distinction of sex' was 'otiose, redundant and indeed meaningless'.[54] Yet, in spite of his insistence that the political rights of women were not in danger, de Valera agreed to allow amendments to Article 9 and 16. These changes ensured that Irish nationality and citizenship could not be withdrawn on the sole ground of sex.[55]

The Joint Committee of Women's Societies and Social Workers and the Irish Women Workers' Union were successful in lobbying the government to amend Article 45 of the draft Constitution. This Article proposed to protect the 'inadequate strength of women and the tender age of children' and ensure that women and children would not have to 'enter avocations unsuited to their sex, age or strength.'[56] In a letter to the Executive Council the chairman of the Joint Committee, Mary Kettle, wrote that

> the question of the adequacy or inadequacy of strength for any particular work is one which arises in the case of men, as much as in the case of women. Secondly, we fear that this article could be used to limit women's legitimate choice of occupation, on the grounds that their strength is inadequate.[57]

In light of objections raised by the Irish Women Workers' Union and the Joint Committee, Article 45 was amended and the offending phrase 'inadequate strength of women' removed.[58] Although the Irish Women Workers' Union was satisfied with this change, the Joint Committee of Women's Societies and the Women Graduates' Association continued to object to the inclusion of the word 'sex' in Article 45. Excluding workers from employment 'unsuited to their sex' could, it was argued, still signify discrimination against working women.

On 14 June 1937, the draft Constitution was ratified in the Dáil and 1 July was the date chosen for a national referendum. All efforts by women's societies to have Article 40 and Article 41 either deleted or amended had failed. Article 40.1 guaranteed that all citizens were equal before the law but that 'this shall not be held to mean that the State shall not in its enactments have due regard to the differences of capacity, physical and moral, and of social function.'[59] The National University Women Graduates' Association claimed that this clause left it open to the legislature and the courts to 'restrict the legitimate liberties of any group or class of citizens'.[60]

Objecting to Article 40.1, Louie Bennett, Secretary of the Irish Women Workers' Union, suggested in a letter to the *Irish Press*

that others besides ourselves would find in this statement authority for discrimination in regard to women, especially in view of
the extreme solicitude for the physical powers of women displayed in other sections of the document and the emphasis laid
upon her social function as mother.[61]

Bennett expressed her fear that women, as wives and mothers,
would be judged to have an inferior social status, thus allowing the
government to 'impose legislation upon women which they themselves strongly disapprove'.[62]

Article 41.1.1 recognised that 'by her life within the home,
woman gives to the State a support without which the common
good cannot be achieved.' The Irish Women Workers' Union saw
no reason for 'special recognition of women as fulfilling the natural
duties of the mother' when no mention was made of the work done
by women outside the home.[63] The Union also objected to the
phrase 'by her life within the home'. It was suggested that 'her
work for the home' was a more accurate description of the tasks
performed by housewives and mothers.[64]

The fact that Article 41.1.1 referred to the service women performed in the home was in itself very significant. The majority of
Irish women at this time were housewives and it was important
that their contribution to society was officially recognised. De
Valera, in his defence of Article 41.1.1, had stated that 'the duties
women perform, of looking after the children and educating them,
is work of fundamental importance to the State.'[65] Yet it would
appear that, in spite of such accolades, the work done by women
in the home was not to be rewarded in any way. During the Dáil
debate on Article 41.1.1, no mention was made of measures such
as family allowances, free health care or home helps for mothers,
reforms which would have doubtlessly enhanced the lives of thousands of women.

Article 41.2.2 asserted that 'the State shall, therefore, endeavour
to ensure that mothers shall not be obliged by economic necessity
to engage in labour to the neglect of their duties in the home.'[66] The
National University Women Graduates' Association objected to
this clause on the grounds that it suggested

> interference on the part of the State with the affairs of the family.
> We consider that the husband and wife, knowing best what is
> necessary for the support and happiness of the family, should
> decide what work is necessary to these ends.[67]

The Joint Committee of Women's Societies and Social Workers
argued that this article could be used to confine women to 'their
duties in the home'. In a letter to the Taoiseach, Mary Kettle wrote
that

Women fear that this article may foreshadow an extension of such
legislation as Section 16 of the Conditions of Employment Act,
legislation which would limit the opportunities of women in the
economic field, and which could be passed under Article 40.1.[68]

When the draft Constitution was ratified in the Dáil, with Article
40.1 and Article 41 intact, the Joint Committee of Women's Societies, the Women Graduates' Association and the National Council
of Women launched a campaign urging voters to reject the new
Constitution. Public meetings, letters to the papers and advertise-
ments in the national press alerted women to the dangers of Article
40.1, Article 41 and Article 45. A handbill distributed by the Women
Graduates' Association concluded with the words: 'women are
human beings with a personal destiny, and demand to be treated
as human beings with full rights and responsibilities. Do not vote
away these rights.'[69]

De Valera was clearly perturbed by the women's campaign. At
election meetings held before the 1937 general election, taking
place on the same day as the Constitutional referendum, de Valera
told voters that

> there is nothing in the Constitution which is an attack on women's
> rights, there is nothing in it to cause woman to fear that she will
> be denied any opportunity of earning her bread.[70]

The National University Women Graduates' Association rejected
de Valera's assurances at a meeting attended by 1,500 women in
Dublin.[71] It would appear, however, that the majority of women
voters were either unaware or unconcerned about their status
under the new Constitution, which, when put to the country, was
accepted by 685,105 votes to 526,945.

There are many reasons why the majority of women did not vote
against the 1937 Constitution. Traditional party loyalties, de
Valera's reassurances and the manifestation of Catholic social principles in the Constitution are all factors to be considered.[72] It is also
vital to remember that for many women, equality was an abstract
concept which had little to do with the everyday necessities of life.
For women who struggled to feed and clothe their families, a
political debate raging in Dublin about women's equality was of
little relevance.

The importance of reaching out to these women was not lost on
those who had campaigned against the Constitution. In November
1937, representatives from the Joint Committee of Women's Societies and Social Workers, the National University Women Graduates' Association and the National Council of Women met in
Dublin to consider their position. Aware that the campaign against
the draft Constitution had attracted little support from women

voters, a decision was taken to set up an independent political party for women.

The new party, named the Women's Social and Political League, proposed to organise women voters throughout the country and increase awareness about the rights and duties of citizenship. As a political organisation, the League intended to support the election of independent women candidates to the Dáil. It was hoped that independent candidates, free of all party loyalties, would champion the cause of women's equality.[73] However, without substantial funding and a nationwide network of support, any plan to set up a new political party was particularly ambitious. Within a year, the Women's Social and Political League was forced to abandon its plan of becoming a political party for women. Having changed its name from Political to Progressive, the League took on the more conventional guise of a voluntary women's society.[74] Despite its intentions to organise all women voters, by the early 1940s it was clear that the League was another small, Dublin-based feminist society.[75]

While feminist groups appeared unable to attract widespread support amongst women during the 1930s, the Irish Countrywomen's Association began to recruit significant numbers of rural women.[76] This organisation, whose work has traditionally been associated only with handicrafts and cookery, encouraged a wide range of activities undertaken by rural women. Advice on poultry farming, bee-keeping, domestic science classes, music and drama all featured in weekly guild meetings throughout the 1930s and 1940s. By 1940, the I.C.A. had set up seventy guilds in rural areas which had a membership of over 2,000 women.[77] Aware of the loneliness experienced by many women living in the countryside, the I.C.A. gave members the opportunity to meet for weekly classes in domestic science, traditional handicrafts and farming skills. Lectures and debates as well as music, dance and drama were organised to recruit new members and provide some light relief from the everyday drudgery of life.[78] Women were also encouraged to get involved in local government and many guilds campaigned for the introduction of school meals and nursing schemes in their areas.[79]

The Irish Countrywomen's Association represented women who worked within the home and who accepted their domestic role as wives and mothers. As the editor of the *United Irishwomen*, the Association's journal, explained, 'the value of the women's movement does not necessitate the women leaving their homes.'[80] Never in any doubt that a woman's first duty was to her children, the Association hoped that

> through membership of an organisation such as the I.C.A. they will be enabled to continue to take an interest in the questions of the day so that when years of leisure come to them they will be in a position to place their valuable contributions of wisdom, experience and sound common sense at the service of their local community and their country.[81]

Although the Irish Countrywomen's Association was not an egalitarian feminist society, it maintained close links with the National Council of Women, the Irish Women's Citizens' and Local Government Association and the Women's Social and Progressive League. The I.C.A. shared the desire of these feminist groups to improve the quality of women's lives and represent women as intelligent and responsible members of society.

Towards the end of the 1930s, the Joint Committee of Women's Societies and Social Workers also began to consider ways in which the opinions of housewives and mothers could be better represented. In 1940, the Committee joined forces with the National Council of Women and the Catholic Women's Federation of Secondary School Unions to give evidence before the Commission on Vocational Education.[82] These three societies hoped to organise the 'home-makers' of Ireland and ensure that they too had a voice in public life. In evidence to the Commission, it was suggested that housewives and mothers

> by the work they have to do in the home, and the different number of things about which they have to know, have got a particular point of view and a particular competence to speak as regards problems concerning the home and family.[83]

It was hoped to encourage housewives to link up with other women in their area and set up local action groups. Joining these groups would not only encourage a sense of civic responsibility in women, but give them the opportunity to express their opinions as wives and mothers.[84]

W.R. O'Hegarty, secretary of the Joint Committee of Women's Societies and Social Workers, remarked that the women's perspective on health and housing was essential: 'I do not think that they [women] are satisfied to leave to the men things about which they know a great deal more.'[85] Maternity clinics, nursery schools, cheap housing and general health care provision were amongst the services demanded by women working within the home. The Joint Committee hoped that local women's groups would empower housewives and encourage them to lobby local authorities to provide these essential services.

The Irish Housewives' Association also sought to consolidate and support women working at home. Set up in Dublin in 1942, the aim of this new society was to 'unite housewives so that they shall recognise, and gain recognition for, their right to play an active part in all spheres of planning for the community.'[86] The Association's primary objective during the early 1940s was to urge the government to introduce price controls and rationing. Their aim was to ensure that housewives could buy essential foodstuffs at affordable prices to feed their husbands and children.[87]

It is significant that when Hanna Sheehy Skeffington stood as an independent candidate in the 1943 General Election, she included a series of social welfare reforms in her election manifesto. Family allowances,[88] higher pension rates and school meals were listed, together with more traditional feminist demands for equal pay and equal opportunities.[89] It is also noteworthy that Sheehy Skeffington's campaign was endorsed by both feminist and non-feminist societies.[90] When the election took place in June 1943, Hanna Sheehy Skeffington and the three other independent women candidates were all badly defeated.[91] Yet in spite of this defeat and the failure once again to capture the women's vote, Hanna Sheehy Skeffington remarked optimistically that 'the challenge to the party-system has at least been made by the independent women; their election campaign has set the public thinking.'[92]

Traditionally, the 1930s and 1940s have been regarded as a low point in the struggle for Irish women's equality. Following the success of the suffrage movement, the 1930s and early 1940s are seen as a time when women acquiesced to an ideology of domesticity and did nothing to challenge the restrictive legislation passed during these years. This essay has endeavoured to show that twenty-five years after the extension of the franchise, there was still an active and vibrant women's movement in the Irish Free State. It is true, as some historians have suggested, that most women's societies were run by educated middle-class women. It is also true that these organisations found it difficult to win the support of the vast majority of Irish women. Nevertheless to dismiss or render insignificant the aims and activities of feminist and non-feminist women's groups during these years is to overlook an important period in the history of the Irish women's movement.

During the 1920s and 1930s, feminist societies consistently defended the right of women to equal citizenship in the Irish Free State. Although unable to prevent the enactment of all discriminatory legislation, objections raised by women's societies did result in a number of crucial changes. The suspension of the Civil Service Regulation (Amendment) Act and the amendment of the 1927 Juries Act were considerable achievements. Even more significant was the inclusion of a guarantee of equality without distinction of sex in Articles 9 and 16 of the 1937 Constitution. At the same time, non-feminist women's societies, including the I.C.A. and the Joint Committee of Women's Societies and Social Workers, highlighted the contribution that women as 'home-makers' could make to Irish society. These organisations recognised that housewives were in need of representation to ensure that their work within the home was not only acknowledged but justly rewarded. Working together, feminist and non-feminist women's societies defended the right of all women, workers and mothers, to equal citizenship in the Irish Free State. They called on the government to introduce social welfare reforms which would enhance the lives of many thousands of Irish women. In doing so, women's organisations active during the 1930s and early 1940s provided a vital link between the suffrage campaign and the women's liberation movement of the 1970s. It is crucial, therefore, that their achievements are included in any history of Irish women and the politics of equality.

No Feminine Mystique:
Popular Advice to Women of the House in Ireland 1922–1954
Caitriona Clear

It is reasonable to assume that the value of food and other materials consumed in the average household is not less than £2 5s a week ... it is clear that the value of food and other materials consumed in the average household is £60m, and that the difference between good and bad housekeeping is measured by a sum of £14m per annum.[1]

> When friends come unexpected do I fuss and tear my hair
> Even though there's only meat enough for two?
> No; I walk into my pantry with a calm unruffled air,
> I pick a tin of bully beef that's waiting for me there,
> I mix it with an onion and a fervent grateful prayer,
> And for dinner we have savoury ragout.[2]

'The modern idea is to get as much pleasure with as little trouble as possible,' said the *Catholic Bulletin* in 1937. The tone was one of hearty approval. The subject? Picnics. Bean a' Tighe, who wrote the regular 'For mothers and daughters' column in this popular monthly magazine, sang the praises of thermos flasks and sliced pans, happily waving goodbye to the inconveniences of picnics before these marvels.[3] Her enthusiastic embrace of the modern way of keeping house and its labour-saving devices would have been cheered to the echo by most writers of cleaning, cooking and catering advice to Irish women in these years. Members of Oireachtas commissions, and some politicians and social observers in this period, male and female, would have found Bean a' Tighe's apparently flippant attitude to effort worrying. 'The workman's wife buys her loaf from the baker; treats her family (unfortunately) to dinners the chief ingredients of which have been extracted from cans; smears her children's bread with bought jam,' wrote feminist Mary Hayden in 1940. Home production, she said, was diminishing, and 'unless there are quite young children around her [the woman of the house] has not nearly enough to do.'[4] Hayden used this argument to support the development of durable interests outside the home for women – such as work and public life – and her view of working-class women as bad housekeepers (whether through their own 'fault' or not) was shared by many. Indeed, it was often extended to all women of the house, and used by feminists and non-feminists alike to illustrate the need for more intensive and wide-ranging domestic training of girls. 'In this country at least 75% of women find themselves sooner or later responsible for the care of a home,' wrote Maire McGeehin in 1943. 'One would expect in these circumstances to find a marked bias towards home-making in the training of girls, yet such is far from being the case.'[5] McGeehin, like Hayden, also believed in an extended public role for women.

The subject of women's relationship to the work involved in maintaining a house was not a matter of hot debate in these first three decades of independence. When it was discussed, it usually came up in the context of the pressing economic and social problems of the era – public health, employment and unemployment, housing, population and emigration. Nobody dissented from the view that household work was women's particular province, though many who whole-heartedly supported this view argued that this was all the more reason for giving them a stronger voice in politics and public life. There was a certain amount of debate about whether it was right to bar all women or married women from certain kinds of work, and some voices called for the setting up of crèches for children whose mothers were forced to work outside the home. There were also objections to the constitutional identification of women with 'the home' in 1937.[6] Broadly speaking, however, those who addressed themselves to the topic of women's relationship to household work in popular publications in this period did so without questioning the inevitability of this relationship, and their tones were either gloomily anxious or cheerfully pragmatic. There was a precedent for the gloom. Katharine Tynan, when she blamed excessive drinking on 'the cold hearth and the miserable feeding at home' in 1924, was echoing the tones of George Russell (AE), Ellice Pilkington and other promoters of domestic reform in the early twentieth century. 'Irish women have seldom learned to love housecraft,' Tynan wrote, 'they think it is drudgery; whereas it is the sanest, the sweetest, the most satisfying of arts.'[7] Arland Ussher, scholar and philosopher writing thirty years later, shared Tynan's view:

> [N]o Irishwoman, it would seem, has any suspicion that cookery is an art worthy of her attention. There are, I am aware, cookery classes in our technical schools, but our teachers apparently

specialize in the making of cakes and not very imaginative cakes at that; seedcakes, scones and what have you? The crown of every girl pupil's ambition is the wedding cake, which, ill-equipped as she is for captivating a husband, she may never be called upon to make.[8]

His poor opinion of the average Irish woman of the house was shared by many in this thirty-two-year period, bounded at one end by political independence and at the other by the beginning of serious government concern about de-population. Publications which were intended for popular consumption by the woman in charge of a house herself, however, maintained an upbeat tone. Typical is an article in the *Irish Press* in 1936: 'Grandmother envies the housekeeper of today.' 'The party around the Christmas fire agreed that although the good old times had many advantages, they had extremely bad old apparatus, as far as women were concerned anyhow.' The article also acknowledged that the labour-saving resources it extolled – electricity, gas, piped water, stainless steel, linoleum floors – were not available to all Irish households, though there was a note of hope that they would be, soon.[9] Between the contempt of the pessimists for the old, and the headlong rush of the optimists for the new, a lot of traditional Irish cookery and housekeeping knowledge must have been lost.

Examination of the political status of Irishwomen in these years and the constitutional references to them could lead us to believe that there was a strongly-held shared set of beliefs and values about women's household work in Ireland in these years, a discourse of domesticity subscribed to by all who opposed, in one way or another, or questioned, women's civil and political equality. No such discourse existed. The spectacle of women in politics, in pressure groups, and in some occupations certainly aroused opposition from some quarters, but these opponents did not have an alternative way of life clearly marked out for women. At the very top, lip-service was certainly paid to the ideal of the 'domestic' woman, as in de Valera's Constitution of 1937, but very little attention was paid to the practical attainment of this ideal. The numbers of itinerant and stationary cookery classes provided by the Department of Agriculture fell significantly between 1922-3 and 1929-30, despite the fact that there was demand for this kind of class.[10] When the Dublin vocational schools began to run evening classes in cookery in Parnell Square in 1931, they were so inundated with female applicants that they had to run overflow classes from 5 p.m. to 7 p.m., and women attended these classes straight from their office jobs, postponing their evening meal to do so. About two-thirds of those attending classes were from outside

Dublin. This enthusiasm – from office workers, 'stay-at-home girls', prospective domestic servants and others – seems to belie the contention that Irish women had no interest in cookery.[11] The promotion of domestic education was not, however, a priority with any government department in these years. It was certainly taught in secondary schools, but only a minority of girls attended up to Leaving Certificate. There were specialised domestic science secondary schools, e.g. the Irish Training School of Domestic Economy in Stillorgan, Dublin, the Munster Institute in Cork, Coolarne in Galway, but these were for students who could either pay or win scholarships, and they were most often attended by those who wished to make a career in the catering industry or in domestic science teaching. Arland Ussher complained about girls being over-interested in making wedding cakes, but the commercial possibilities of such a skill do not seem to have occurred to him. The same commercial impulse might have motivated many of the girls and women flocking to cookery classes in Dublin in 1931. Apart from the very basic *Cookery Notes*, published by the Department of Agriculture in 1924 and constantly revised up to 1944, 'originally prepared for use in schools and classes for girls working under the schemes of the Department of Agriculture' and used in secondary schools in the 1940s, I have not come across any government publication of any length on the care and maintenance of a house and its inhabitants. When Josephine Redington brought out the ninth edition of her *Economic Cookery Book* in 1927, she made it clear in the preface that she was doing so 'as quite a private undertaking'. This book was still in use in at least one domestic science college in the 1940s. *The Bluebird Cookery Book for Working Women* by Margaret Roper and Ruth Duffin was brought out in 1939 and published by the Educational Company of Ireland, a publishing company, and the Sisters of Mercy in Callan, Co. Kilkenny brought out their own basic and practical cookery books for 'first year' and 'second year' students, in Irish and in English. Maura Laverty's *Flour Economy* (1941), a book of potato and oatmeal recipes, was intended to preserve wheat and enlist the help of the 'conscientious housekeeper' in doing so. It had an introduction by John Ingram, the Chief Inspector of Technical Schools, but it was in no way intended as a cookery book, and there was no information on processes or principles of cooking in it.

Government commission after government commission insisted on the need for girls of all classes to be systematically trained in the care and the running of a household.[12] They were more or less ignored. Changing government and intellectual (or, if you like, 'élite') opinions on women's household work in this period and the impact of these opinions on legislation, and on the realities of women's work within the house and outside it, need a discussion to themselves. What follows here is a necessarily speculative discussion of the various tones used to address or to describe women of the house in accessible publications – magazines, books, schoolbooks – in these years.

A Vocation and a Social Service: Some Perspectives on Women's Household Work

'Gran was different to most other women in Ballyderrig in that she took a great interest in food,' wrote Maura Laverty in 1942 in her elegiac, autobiographical novel, *Never No More: the Story of a Lost Village*.[13] Good, wholesome, plain cooking is one of the aspects of life in County Kildare in the 1920s and early 1930s documented by Laverty. 'Gran' was a fictional character but the food – the ingredients and the processes of cooking are described in loving detail – is real. Was this expertise passed on to the author by her mother? She suggests as much in *Kind Cooking* (1946), but disentangling fact from fiction is a difficult task, as some of the fictional characters referred to in *Never No More*, such as Moll Slevin and the Reddins of the bog, feature in this book too.[14] Laverty herself had no cookery qualifications. It is possible that she got recipes from her mother, who in turn got them from itinerant cookery classes in the 1880s, 1890s and 1900s. There are some similarities between *Never No More* and *Economic Cookery Book*, first published in 1905 – ling stew (ling was a type of dried fish), pot-roasted rabbit, mock goose/duck, and Laverty's 'Gran' also used Indian (yellow) meal quite often, as recommended by Redington, who deplored the popular prejudice against it. (*Cookery Notes* does not mention it at all.) Other *Never No More* dishes include coddle (a popular Dublin dish), mushroom ketchup, ashcakes and boxty pancakes, and many more which cannot be found in either Redington, *Cookery Notes* or Kathleen Ferguson's 1903 *Lessons in Cookery and Housewifery*. Laverty's maiden name was Kelly, and her antecedents came from the west. She claimed that this was where 'her' boxty pancakes originated, so there must have been some transmission of skills from one generation to the next.[15]

Taking a great interest in cookery was, however, according to Laverty, unusual. How accurate was her perception? Was taking an interest in cooking seen as modern, even 'new-fangled', kind of behaviour? One of the only other two cooks that Laverty mentions as coming near her 'grandmother's' standard was a Quaker friend

of the family.[16] Most of the public figures associated with the
campaign to improve Irish housekeeping in the early twentieth
century were either Protestant or unionist or both – Horace
Plunkett, AE, Ellice Pilkington, Countess Aberdeen, Lady Fingal
and others. The Irish Countrywomen's Association, formerly the
United Irishwomen and founded in 1911, had to reassure the
Commission on Vocational Organisation in 1940 that they were not
'ladies of the manor', that their organisation was democratic and
of the people. The lady of the manor, they joked, would be very
welcome indeed if she placed her motor car at the disposal of the
organisation, but, 'we get on well without her'.[17] The fact that the
question was asked in the first place was significant, and it was
Maura Laverty, again, who made a satirical connection, in 1946,
between variety in diet and non-Irishness:

> In our place we were acquainted with only six kinds of vegeta-
> bles; onions, cabbage, turnips, boiled potatoes, roast potatoes and
> potatoes steamed in the baker. The only people who grew such
> rarities as peas, beans, parsnips and carrots were the Protestant
> peelers. I think that it was this fact that kept the rest of us from
> moving with the times and introducing health and variety into
> our diet ... we felt it couldn't be good or lucky.[18]

Laverty loved to exaggerate for the sake of a good story, but still,
her belief that growing a wide variety of vegetables was not common practice is supported by evidence from other sources. Hers
was one of many voices urging Irishwomen to make more use of
fresh vegetables, but urging them in a mild, humorous sort of way.
She reserved her strongest criticism for mothers who would not
share what she saw as the adventure of cooking with their small
daughters, probably because this was how she herself had learned
all she knew.[19] 'For mothers and daughters' was the title of the
women's page in the popular periodical *The Catholic Bulletin* in the
1920s and '30s, and as the opening quotation of this article suggests,
it had a relaxed tone. Women of the house were advised to get out
and about as much as possible, and also to have an 'engrossing
indoor hobby'. There was something 'a little sad' about the woman
who could think of nothing but house and family all the time. To
this end, daughters were encouraged in August 1929, in what was
a regularly recurring piece of advice, to give mothers a good long
break of at least two weeks, and even if she could not get away from
home, to ensure that she had 'both leisure and amusement'.[20] For
the most part this women's page, like women's pages in newspapers, featured useful and seasonally appropriate household-main-
tenance information. Childcare rarely, if ever, featured.

There was a small section devoted to childcare in *Women's Life,* an extremely interesting and attractive Irish women's magazine of the 1930s and '40s. It sold more copies in Ireland than any other Irish or British women's magazine, cost 2d and appeared weekly. Its articles on cookery and home management carried no hint that women of the house needed to be brought up to a certain standard, except for occasional exhortations about fresh vegetables. In the 1930s, it carried lengthy interviews with women about the work they did. A trade union secretary, a factory worker, a radiographer, a street-seller, a commercial traveller, two Gaiety chorus girls and a nurse were only some of those featured. A 'wife-and-mother' was included along with the others, without any comment to indicate that she was seen as any less a worker than the others. Mrs Curran, who lived in a suburban house without any maid and a number of children, had literally no time to spare from her daily round. She was very grateful for 'switches and buttons' – modern methods of cooking and cleaning – and 'she simply cannot believe that the modern girl is not interested in men.' When pressed, however, she herself admitted that marriage and motherhood were not romantic, were in fact, quite tough – but rewarding.[21] All the working women interviewed professed not to be waiting around for marriage. The trade union secretary said that working every day with men would make her think twice about settling down with one, while the greatest ambition of the packer in Brown and Polson's factory was to win the Sweep and see the world.[22] The magazine also carried articles on health and beauty and on famous people including Madame Elizire Dionne (mother of the quintuplets), and Maureen O'Sullivan, film star, and never failed to headline the achievements of women in culture, politics, the arts or sport.[23] 'Mrs Wyse' who answered problems, told a 50-year-old woman whose husband never talked to her or took her out to get all dressed up and go out with her women friends. She advised an assisting daughter on a small mortgaged farm to let her labourer boyfriend go away to earn money for them both. 'I have nothing to offer him but debt,' she lamented.[24] Those who sent in problems ranged from those who were domestic servants to those whose families had motor cars, and the household hints seem to have been aimed at women who did most or all of their own housework. The magazine might have carried pictures of the Fingals at the Meath hunt, and of the wedding of Mr Desmond Fitzgerald, son of the former Minister for Defence, and that of Miss Ray Gore-Grimes,[25] but its readers seem to have come from a variety of social and geographical backgrounds. Most women's magazines then as now aimed at as wide a readership as possible.[26] *Woman's Mirror,* a precursor of *Woman's Life,* ran an article in 1932 on how to make up a special soothing bath 'when tired or irritable as a result of an overdose of sport or dancing,' but it also told readers how to get onion smells off their hands, and how to clean enamel.[27] The 'Happy Irish Babies' whose photographs, along with their names and addresses, were sent in by readers, are the clearest indication we have that the readers of *Woman's Life* came from a variety of social and geographical backgrounds (as are the addresses of 'Dawn Beauty contests' and film-star lookalike competitors). This column and the accompanying doctor's article on childcare were the only prescriptive notes in the whole magazine. Mothers and guardians sent in photographs of babies, toddlers and small children, with details on how the babies were 'reared' or fed – 'naturally' (i.e. breast-fed), on cow's milk, on Sister Laura's food or Neave's food (about half of the babies whose pictures were sent in were being or had been breast-fed). Cod liver oil, orange juice and Virol, a popular tonic of the period, were often mentioned. Inclusion of these details reflects contemporary concerns about infant health and infant feeding. The doctor regularly congratulated the mothers on what was seen to be their fine achievement in this regard. His/her own articles on child health and welfare are very practical in today's terms (for example, the belief that breast-feeding was the best method but a clean bottle would do; fresh air and roughage were also considered very important, and children should be encouraged and not frightened). The mothers who sent in their babies' photographs were no doubt doing so from a variety of motives – to show off the babies, to show off the photographs – but to all intents and purposes, it looked as if they were writing in for the doctor's approval on the babies' condition.

Other writers on health and welfare in this period would have approved heartily of mothers looking for doctors' advice on the care and 'management' of their babies. The *Irish Nurses' Union Gazette* in 1930 wrote:

> Our [health visitors' or public health nurses'] teaching should fit the mother to manage her affairs alone and not be obliged to turn to her neighbours and to kind-hearted old women who are learned in all the old superstitions, who are sure to find the doctor's treatment too difficult to carry out and who will replace it with those old women's recipes which can be so dangerous.[28]

The world-wide concern about maternal and infant health at this time also reverberated in Ireland. A conference of public health and local government representatives in Dublin in 1930 emphasised that mothers 'were the most potent factors for good in the nation's health' and had to be encouraged to bring their children for medical treatment, and that it was important for the mother to be present when her child was being examined, for the child's reassurance and the mother's information.[29] Annie M.P. Smithson, public health nurse, novelist, and secretary for many years of the Irish nurses' trade union, drew attention to the difficulties experienced by mothers living in tenements in Dublin, in 1925, and lamented the habit of babies under one year being fed ice cream off street-barrows, and fizz-bags, by 'little mothers', sisters or brothers scarcely twice the size of them and in sole charge. Her horror at a child of one year being given 'the run of the supper table' – i.e. eating what the rest of the family was eating – would not find many echoes today, when parents are encouraged to adapt family foods for babies, though we might share her disapproval of the ice cream, the fizz–bags, and the 'little mothers'.[30] The subject of public discourses on infant and maternal health would need an article to itself, but in the context of popular advice to women it can be noted that many historians of motherhood and health in the early twentieth century believe that mothers appreciated practical and practicable advice on children's health, especially if this were available in a place to which they could choose to go. 'Baby nurse' in St Andrew's Baby Club in Dublin in 1937 seemed to understand the realities of life for the mothers who attended with their babies, noting that all their husbands were unemployed, that the women themselves were undernourished, and that créches were needed for children whose mothers were forced to go out to work.[31]

It is an indication of developing concern about health and nutrition that the revised *Cookery Notes* of 1944 carried information about vitamins, carbohydrates and minerals, and mild recommendations about diet: 'The opportunities afforded to persons of limited means of raising food by cultivation of allotments should be availed of to the fullest extent. Special attention should be devoted to green vegetables and salads,' it recommended, and elsewhere it commented: 'A dietary of tea, bread and factory-made jam, supplemented only occasionally by potatoes and meat, is far too prevalent.'[32] The National Nutrition Survey carried out in the 1940s drew attention to the appearance of 'bread and spread' at almost every meal, in most working-class and lower-middle-class households. The Irish Countrywomen's Association, when asked about country people's diet in 1940, emphasised the need for education and the availability of packets of seeds: 'Very often in the country they have not got the vegetables to cook.'[33] *Cookery Notes* in 1944 provided recipes using all kinds of vegetables, including some adapted to

'Present Emergency Conditions' – potato salad dressing, potato and oatmeal rissoles, potato pudding, potato pastry, potato rock cakes and a (miraculously potato-free!) economical fruit cake. It also included two pages of information on scullery and kitchen work – how to wash dishes, how to clean a stove and to set a fire (the common practice of throwing paraffin onto the fire was condemned as 'not only extravagant but dirty and very dangerous') and how to clean cutlery.[34] Josephine Redington's cookery course, to be carried out on an itinerant or evening basis, was far more comprehensive on what she called 'hygiene and housewifery'. Redington was a teacher at the Irish Training School of Domestic Economy in Stillorgan, Dublin, up to 1936. There were lectures on expenditure of wages, care of invalids, treatment of cuts, scalds and burns, simple ventilation, dangers of drinking impure water, care of household furniture, 'best way to sweep earthen and other floors', care of kitchen utensils, making beds, personal cleanliness ('a weekly bath. Hair washed once in six weeks'), simple menus for a working man's family, general management of household wastes, feeding of infants before cutting teeth, care of clothes, laying of table for breakfast, dinner and tea. These were accompanied by practical demonstrations (although 'how to clean windows' was to be attempted 'only if building is one storey high'). It could be argued that Redington's course was more detailed than *Cookery Notes* because the former was published in 1927, when housekeeping was more onerous and before modern conveniences were widespread. Still, the first edition of *Cookery Notes*, in 1924, contained even less information on housekeeping than the 1944 edition, and in any case, all the recipes and advice in *Cookery Notes* at both dates were aimed at houses with no running water, where cooking was done on the fire. In 1946, 48% of Irish households did not have piped water, so this was a realistic assumption.[35] If it was widely believed at the time that young females needed detailed and intensive instruction in cookery and housekeeping – and I have not come across any contemporaries who did not believe this – then government publications on the subject failed to respond positively to this belief.

Redington's book also went into great detail on household economy, including, as well as recipes and basic cookery information, sample weekly menus for a labourer's family, and advice on spending money: 'Family, Father, Mother, 4 children under 15 years. The father a rural labourer earning 39s a week (1927). 3 meals per day. 1.5 loaves i.e. 3 lbs of bread allowed each day, besides scones and tea-cakes.' Tuesday's menu, to give an example, was:

Breakfast, tea, bread and butter, 4 salt herrings (fried) for all. Dinner, 1.5 lbs of ox liver, stewed with vegetables and plenty of gravy, potatoes in jackets or bread. Tea, scones etc. for father and mother – Butter for all – Buttermilk and Indian meal scones or thick oatcake for children.

Redington was realistic enough to give the cup of tea its due, and to include lots of comfort foods like fried bread. She also assumed, as she did in all her recipes, that cooking would be done on the fire. She seems to have thought that some of her recommendations were a little unusual:

In the above list of meals the food is more varied and nourishing than that usually provided by a rural labourer's wife and though, perhaps, more troublesome to prepare, the gain in health and physique to the members of her family would quite compensate the careful housewife for any trouble she might have.[36]

The onus to inform herself and to take trouble on herself for her family's good was placed firmly on the woman of the house. It was, and is, a common theme in much of the prescriptive literature about childcare and housekeeping. Other observers and commentators throughout this period agreed. Amy Lisney, commenting on Dr James Deeny's paper to the Statistical Society in Dublin on the health of married women factory workers in Lurgan, commented that 'the workman's wife, she and her fellows make up a large proportion of the population in every country, and for *years* people have not bothered about her'. These women, she went on to say, needed company and guidance:

she had known houses, side by side, where the incomes were the same, £2 10s a week. In one case the house was untidy, children ill and husband irregular in his work. Next door they seemed to have more and the house was clean and tidy. That shows how one must educate this huge class of women and teach them how to manage.

Deeny's point, however, was that the cleaner the house and the more 'upwardly mobile' (as we would call it) the family, the worse the health of the mother, because 'managing' took such a toll of her health.[37] In any case, thrifty and economical households were very often, according to a study of a Dublin working-class suburb in 1943, 'beyond the scope of the average housewife'. This was not an insult to the housewife's capabilities but an understanding by the writer, Charles Clancy-Gore, of how these households were run. Shopping was done in bits and pieces, every day, at highly-priced local shops – lack of affordable transport, of storage space at home and simply of sufficiently large sums of money at any given time, prevented the housewife from doing otherwise. Besides, Clancy-Gore argued, the breadwinner could hardly be expected to surrender all his wages without keeping back some for his own entertainment and personal use.[38] There is a common theme to be discerned in this prescriptive literature from urban and rural communities, and that is the belief in the unchangeability of the male and the total responsibility of the female for management of the household economy at the working-class level of society. However, Clancy-Gore's approach is typical of the new understanding by middle-class people of the genuine difficulties experienced by working-class people in the 1940s. Emergency shortages, the pressing need felt by dependent-burdened middle-class people for a comprehensive health service and for affordable housing, all seem to have brought about awareness of the even greater deprivations undergone by working-class people. The Irish Housewives' Association, set up in 1942, was composed entirely of middle-class women, most of them based in Dublin, but it concerned itself with a wide range of social issues, many of them of great concern to working-class women and to rural women of all classes but the very wealthy: tuberculin-tested milk, housing, conditions in rural National schools, high prices, food shortages, the treatment of juvenile criminals, housing, urban and rural, and hygiene in grocery shops.[39] There was nothing new about middle-class women – or men – being concerned with the living conditions and lives of working-class and labouring people. The Irish Housewives' Association insisted, however, that these issues affected women of the house of all classes in one way or another. Like other women's organisations, the IHA also thought of itself as feminist, supporting Hanna Sheehy Skeffington's candidature in the 1942 general elections, and incorporating into itself the Irish Women's Citizens and Local Government Association in 1947. Louie Bennett, veteran trade unionist and feminist, who had objected vigorously and vociferously to Article 41.2.1 in de Valera's constitution, wrote in the first issue of *The Irish Housewife* in 1946:

> Woman herself is still seeking her real place in the world, and for those of us who belong to an older generation it is difficult to foresee what part she will play in the revolutionized and mechanized world we are entering upon. One line of hope lies in a new approach to the home and the domestic sphere, and if the new generation accept homekeeping as a vocation and a social service I believe that they will blaze a trail towards a finer civilization than we have yet known.[40]

The IHA, like the ICA, the Joint Committee of Women's Societies and Social Workers, the National Council of Women in Ireland and the Federation of Catholic Secondary School Unions, believed this, and they also insisted that women should be politically and civilly equal to men and active in public life. Seth Koven and Sonya Michel, writing about women's welfare work in the first half of the twentieth century in Europe, America and Australia, describe this approach as 'maternalist politics'. Maternalism, they suggest, 'always operated on two levels; it extolled the virtues of domesticity while simultaneously legitimating women's public relationships to politics and the State, to community, work-place and market-place'.[41] And as a result of this paradoxical approach, Koven and Michel point out, 'maternalists' often experienced hostility from the male-dominated centre of power. This was certainly true in Ireland. Bishop Michael Browne accused three of the above organisations, when they were giving evidence to the Commission on Vocational Organisation in 1940, of wanting to get mothers out of the home and into the workplace because they planned to set up 'Baby Clubs' and crèches for children whose mothers had to go out to work due to widowhood or male unemployment. Fr Edward Coyne, S.J., another of the Commissioners, who was more sympathetic to the women, was wary of what he believed to be their claims to 'put forward being a woman as a special vocation'.[42] While the Report of the Commission on Vocational Organisation (1943) warmly commended the women's organisations for their good work and presentation of evidence to the Commission, it only allowed one place for 'home-makers' on the proposed National Vocational Assembly, and that place a co-opted one, a fact which caused Maire McGeehin and G.H.C. Crampton to issue addenda to the Report. McGeehin believed that 'home-makers', due to their strength in the population, needed at least fifteen permanent seats on the proposed Assembly.[43] The journal of Catholic sociology *Christus Rex*'s 'As I see it' column in the late 1940s regularly sniped at the IHA, questioning their claim to speak for Irish women as a whole.[44] None of these were popular publications: they are included in this discussion simply to show that those who were closest to developing a 'feminine mystique'[45] – an elaboration of the meaning of household work for women – in Ireland in these years, were also those who were constantly on the alert to defend women's political equality. Is this one reason why governments and government departments were so slow to act on the regular recommendations that they implement country-wide comprehensive schemes of domestic education for females? Was there a fear that such schemes would extend the range of women's participation in local and national politics? Writers of household advice in books, magazines and women's pages shared with the ICA, the IHA, and the various other organisations a distaste for household work undertaken for its own sake, and a firm rejection of any idealisation of it. 'There is something both pitiful and revolting about anybody who makes a god out of work,' wrote May Laverty (not Maura, though she would have agreed) in the *Irish Press* in 1935, and Margot Moffett in *The Irish Housewife* eleven years later recommended doing away, if possible, with the bother and dirt of the coal or turf fire: 'Deep down in our honesty we know that the open fire is hardly more than a cheerful decorative feature whose charm is precariously balanced against the almost automatic self-sacrifice of the housewife.'[46] There is no contradiction between this and Louie Bennett's view, quoted earlier, which can be read as a plea for a woman-controlled and woman-defined domestic space, the work of which is no more or no less idealised than that of any other space – 'a vocation and a social service'.

There is precious little idealisation of the home-maker's lot in Ann Hathaway's *Homecraft Book*, published in Dublin in 1944. This is a practical compendium of household knowledge, aimed at a household where there is 'no maidservant, and no Hoover'. Running water and electricity are not taken for granted either. 'Every housewife should organise her work as a man organises his business,' Hathaway points out at the beginning. If there were babies and small children in the house 'all rules and regulations must be considered subject to the attentions necessary to their special needs,' though 'half the battle is won if the planned routine is adhered to strictly with the children as with every other activity.' This is the only mention of childcare in the book, though there are sections on health and beauty. The emphasis on regularity might seem to imply an elaboration of household work for the sake of it, or, as we would see it today, a neglect of 'essentials' (e.g. attention devoted to children) for 'peripherals' – care of the house. However we should remember that, in the 1946 census, over one-fifth (21%) of all women 'engaged in home duties' were single. Childcare was not, therefore, by any means an inevitable part of household work for every woman of the house.

The range of the advice gives us an insight into the huge amount of work necessary to maintain even a modestly-sized household, to economise on resources, and to dispose of waste (incidentally, questioning Hayden's assertion, quoted earlier, that the woman of the house without small children 'has not nearly enough to do'). Hathaway insisted that the woman of the house was not to be an uncomplaining slave. All other family members over the age of four had to be trained to put away clothes and belongings after use: 'It's something worth having a row about!' She was also on the alert for the possibility of the over-elaborate household creating more and more work for the unwary housekeeper, advising: 'Go over every inch of your house and remove ornaments or any other article you can do without.' The object of all this was to save time, so that the evening could be spent relaxing: 'In the presence of friends' company, the desultory family conversations and fireside dreaming may be found every recompense for the day's extra efforts and the rigid adherence to rules.'[47] Here again is the familiar emphasis on women having time to themselves. Most of the advice in the book is concerned with making and mending, and saving money and effort in the long run. Wellington boots could be mended with a bicycle puncture repair kit; and electricity could be saved by regularly washing dirty light bulbs in warm soapy water. Egg-water and egg-shells had many uses, while candles could be made to last longer by being coated in white varnish and put away for two days to harden. Shoulders could be whitened 'for an evening' by rubbing in warm milk and oatmeal, and then applying 'the usual complexion powder'; neuralgia could be eased by putting half a teaspoon of brandy in the palm of the hand and 'taking it up through the nose'.[48] The domestic environment envisaged by Hathaway was, if not an urban one, at least a non-agricultural one, though the farm woman would surely have found a lot of her strategies and information relevant. *Woman's Life* had a regular 'Letter to a farmer's wife', giving her advice about poultry-keeping and electrification. The magazine certainly had rural readers, judging by the problems and the addresses of the 'Happy Irish Babies', but it cannot have endeared itself to many rural hearts by comments like this one:

> Compare the average countrywoman of 35 with her city sister and what do you find? The countrywoman looks at best ten years older. The balance should be on the other side, seeing that the woman who lives on the farm gets plenty of God's fresh air, sane sensible food and regular hours.[49]

As well as being insulting, this betrayed an invincible ignorance about agricultural life. There was little that was regular about farm working hours, and God's fresh air was often bitterly cold and sharp, and not very kind to the complexion. Was there a patronising attitude to country people among town and city-dwellers at that time? The ICA had to assure the Commission on Vocational Organisation in 1940 that their members did not mind the term 'countrywomen' – 'They are charmed to be called countrywomen.' It could also be argued that the ICA itself was misunderstood and treated dismissively by many people, among them feminists, for many years.[50]

Conclusion

'To see the peace of a home properly you must see it threatened temporarily, as when the woman of the house, hearing a knock, jumps up shouting; "Hide your boots and I'll carry out the clothes-horse,"' wrote the widely-read columnist John D. Sheridan in 1954.[51] In the popular publications which aimed at or described them, women of the house loomed large. They were physically strong, with loud voices, and they were as much a part of the house as the fireplace and the front door. It could be argued that this was a deeply conservative view, which saw these women as utterly bound up with and inseparable from the houses they ran, but if it was a conservative view, it was certainly not an idealistic or a romantic one. This was why there were so many exhortations to these women to take it easy, to get as much rest as possible, to acquire as many labour-saving devices as they could, not only because there was no virtue in work for its own sake, but also because there was no escape from it, otherwise. This in turn partly explains the strong resistance to anything which was seen to be glorification of women's household work, a resistance which came not only from those who supported women in public life, but from those who opposed them also. The article concerning women and the home in de Valera's Constitution aroused the opposition of women's organisations, but the feminist IHA also aroused opposition and ridicule. Hilda Tweedy claims that the organisation adopted the term 'housewife' to defy critics who jeered at them for being housewives.[52] There was, in certain quarters, an attitude of hostility and ridicule towards both representations and representatives of women in charge of households. Three cartoons by Charles E. Kelly which appeared in *Dublin Opinion*, between 1937 and 1951, underline the uneasiness about the idealisation of women's household work and the lip-service paid to it. The first (for our purposes) and best-known appeared in 1937, and depicted a large and strong-looking tenement-dwelling mother-of-many calling her large and unruly family to order, while her husband reads out of the newspaper: 'Will yiz shut up, all o' yiz, while your father explains me position under the new Constitution!' Is Kelly poking fun at the supposedly grandiose aspirations of Dublin working-class people (a common theme in Irish comedy), or at the government's presumption in paying such feeble lip-service to such an obvious figure of authority, or at the woman herself for presuming that the Constitution will change her life? The second cartoon appeared in 1951 and it shows the statue of a round, happy, cheerful-looking woman washing dishes on a pedestal in a park, with 'Bridget O'Halloran, Housewife' inscribed on it, and one male onlooker saying to another: 'I believe she's no one in particular. She's just symbolic ... erected by a committee of grateful husbands.' Is it the idea that such a committee would ever exist that is funny here, or is Kelly making fun of the idea that an archetypal house-wife exists? I suspect both. The third cartoon also appeared in 1951, and it too can be read a number of ways. My favourite way to read it is as a defiant assertion of a totally different scale of priorities, at a time when certain elements in Church and State were placing great emphasis on the sacred duties of parents. Why not end a discussion of popular perceptions of women of the house with a portrayal which explodes anarchically any notion of the responsi-ble keeper of the household? The scene is a street of run-down tenement houses, and one untidy-looking woman is rushing along, saying happily to another untidy-looking woman: 'Where does the morning go? Half-eleven and I'm only going down to get the bets on.'[53]

'Turn on the Tap':
The State, Irish Women & Running Water
Mary E. Daly

In the years immediately following the end of World War II, the continuing decline in the population of rural Ireland became a cause of growing concern. Prior to 1921 the problem could be blamed on British mis-rule in Ireland; after more than twenty years of self-government, this excuse began to lose credibility. During the 1950s, the *Report of the Commission on Emigration*, and the controversy aroused by the book *The Vanishing Irish*,[1] focused public attention on government policies towards rural Ireland and on the relationship between emigration, late marriages and the quality of rural life. Nowadays it is widely appreciated that this crisis had a specifically gendered dimension. While there was a minimum of five single farmers' daughters to every single male farmer in both 1926 and 1936, this ratio fell sharply after 1951, until by the end of the 1950s, as Hannon has shown, 'every local girl had, on average, two farmers to choose from.'[2] A majority of the 'vanishing Irish', who emigrated to English cities in the decade following the end of World War II, were women. Many other women flocked to Dublin and to other Irish towns and cities. By 1951 rural Ireland contained 868 women for every 1000 men, the lowest ratio since the Famine.[3] This female exodus has generally been explained in terms of lack of employment opportunities or the rejection of the social constraints associated with traditional rural life, such as poor marriage prospects or having the choice of a husband determined by matchmakers or by parents. However, the widening gap in material standards between urban and rural life may also have played a part. In 1946 the overwhelming majority of urban houses had access to electricity; few rural homes had this service. (No accurate figures exist.) In the same year almost 92 percent of urban homes had access to piped water and 35 percent had a fixed bath. By comparison, over 91 percent of rural homes were forced to rely on a pump, a well, a stream or some other unspecified source for domestic water supplies and less than 4 percent of rural homes contained a fixed bath.[4] Lack of electricity in rural areas was seen as a major national challenge. Addressing this shortcoming became a major priority for post-war Ireland and in 1947, the Electricity Supply Board (ESB) began its rural electrification campaign. By March 1956, the ESB had connected 163,000 consumers under this scheme, or over half of all rural households.[5] Where water and sanitary services were concerned, however, the gap between town and country probably widened during the 1950s. By 1961, 97 percent of urban homes were supplied with running water and 60 percent had both a fixed bath and a hot water tap. In the country-side, however, only one house in eight had running water, roughly the same proportion as those with a fixed bath and a hot water tap. Many of these rural water supplies were less than adequate, often drawn from a roof tank or a nearby well; data from the 1956 census suggest that only 3 percent of rural households were connected to a public water supply. [6]

This paper examines some of the reasons for the contrasting rate of progress in providing electricity and piped water to rural areas, with a specific focus on what it reveals about gender in twentieth-century Irish rural society. In a recent article examining the growth of ownership of modern appliances in both Britain and the United States, Bowden and Offer show that ownership of time-using or leisure appliances such as televisions, radios and videos has spread much more rapidly than ownership of time-saving appliances such as washing machines or vacuum cleaners, and they conclude by noting that 'The task of engaging idle minds has proved more amenable to technology than the challenge of keeping house.'[7] The difference between time-using and time-saving improvements provides a useful analytical tool for examining the diffusion of electricity and running water supplies throughout the Irish country-side. Although occasional token references were included to the value of electricity as an aid to modern farming, there is little doubt that it was seen primarily as a means of improving leisure and social facilities – brightening the long winter evenings or guaran-teeing that rural households could listen to the All-Ireland Final – rather than as a mechanism for reducing the toil involved in housework. In 1947, the Dublin City Engineer proposed that all new houses constructed by Dublin Corporation would be provided with one light socket in each room, plus one plug per house. The solitary plug was earmarked for use for a wireless or electric radio. Each house would have a maximum supply of 150 watts of elec-tricity, sufficient to have 2 to 3 lights burning at any one time, though if people were listening to the radio there would only be sufficient power for one electric light. The Dublin City Engineer apparently assumed that families living in Corporation housing would not be interested in using either an electric kettle or an electric iron, not to mention having a ready supply of hot water.[8] Electric radios were undoubtedly the first appliance bought by most Irish households. They meant an end to the fears and uncertainties caused by batteries failing in the middle of important football matches or during evening music programmes. A survey carried out by the ESB in 1953 in seventeen typical rural areas, which had been connected to electricity for some time, revealed that 77 percent of households owned an electric radio against 69 percent with electric irons, 42 percent owning an electric kettle and 23 percent owning an electric fire. Only one household in five had an electric cooker.[9] We can therefore suggest that just as leisure appliances such as radios, or in more recent times television and hi-fi, spread more rapidly among consumers than labour-saving devices such as washing machines, so electricity, which was associated with leisure, spread more rapidly to rural households than rural water. The fact that leisure products were used by men, while household appliances were primarily of benefit to women, is an important consideration in this argument.

If households have proved slower to buy labour-saving appliances such as washing machines or vacuum cleaners than to invest in leisure products, it is also apparent that the spread of labour-saving household gadgets has not necessarily brought a reduction in the number of hours devoted to housework. In the United States, the average amount of time spent on housework actually rose during the first half of the twentieth century, despite the proliferation of gadgets. Purchasing a washing machine simply meant that people washed their clothing more frequently; buying a vacuum cleaner meant a lower tolerance of dusty floors and a greater tendency to install fitted carpets.[10] However, the trend towards higher standards of housekeeping appears to have pre-dated the spread of modern household appliances; Joanna Bourke has suggested that standards of housekeeping in rural Ireland were improving substantially from the turn of the century, long before the emergence of so-called 'labour-saving' devices. The advances reflected the construction of bigger and better houses, many containing a parlour, and the transmission of new standards of health, hygiene and domesticity.[11] Rising incomes meant that families could afford better furnishings and non-essential items such as china crockery and ornaments. Rural women would have become increasingly aware of new and higher standards of housekeeping as a result of attending classes in domestic economy, given either in schools or by itinerant instructors.[12] Reading women's magazines or women's columns in general-interest newspapers and magazines provided another source of ideas. Many country women had also worked for a number of years as a domestic servant in a middle-class or upper-class house in a town or city, and they carried some of the standards of these households back home when they married.[13]

Higher standards of housekeeping posed a considerable strain on rural women, because they required generous quantities of water. In 1911 Mrs Harold Lett, president of the United Irishwomen – a women's organisation established by Horace Plunkett, the founder of the Irish co-operative movement and the ancestor of the modern Irish Countrywomen's Association – claimed that an 'ordinary family' would require about nine gallons of water a day with an extra nine gallons on washday,[14] though this seems an overly-ambitious figure. Fetching water for domestic use appears to have been regarded as women's work, both in Ireland and in most traditional societies. It remains one of the most time-consuming tasks of African women – taking up to four hours per day in parts of Ethiopia. Few men participate; African society shows a strong prejudice against men carrying water on their heads or backs, though it is acceptable for them to work as commercial water sellers, and African men only appear to have fetched water for household use if their wife was sick or absent.[15] Little precise evidence survives about the amount of time which Irish rural women spent fetching water. Arensberg and Kimball's sympathetic account of the working day of a farmer's wife in the 1930s merely makes a passing reference to the 'many trips she makes in and out of the kitchen doors for fuel, or water ...', though they also note that women were responsible for the household laundry and for washing up after meals.[16] The Limerick rural survey, which was carried out over the years 1958-64, noted that drawing water was the only household task in which boys regularly participated,[17] but it gives no indication as to who carried out this task in households which lacked sons who were strong enough to fetch water but not old enough to have graduated to more adult tasks. Folklore records are equally paltry, though there are frequent references to the obligation on women to leave clean water available in the house at night, as in the reference from Dun Chaohn to '*cailin na .... an tuisce glan intigh sa tigh aici instoiche,*' or Henry Morris's account that

> No woman in Farney[18] would go to bed without leaving the
> hearth swept and clean water in the house and numerous are the
> stories of a woman, who remembered only when in bed that there
> was no clean water in the house so she got up again, went to the
> well, and brought in clean water and then retired to bed with a
> satisfied mind.[19]

More prosaic images of women carrying water emerge from photographic collections; their frequency perhaps testifying to the fact
that this was a regular task.[20] Although nineteenth-century public
health policy was very conscious of the importance of clean water,[21]
and the Irish Local Government Board put pressure on Boards of
Guardians to provide water pumps in most villages,[22] convenience
of access does not appear to have been a major concern. In 1911,
Mrs Lett of the United Irishwomen complained that some modern
labourers' cottage schemes erected by local authorities were over
half a mile from the nearest water supply.[23] In 1911, rural labourers
and farmers were not unique in facing difficulties in having access
to sufficient supplies of clean water; Dublin tenement dwellers[24]
and many women living in cottages in Irish towns and villages
were also forced to fetch water from a distance and the available
supplies were often polluted. A Department of Local Government
inquiry into a proposed new water scheme in Tubbercurry, Co.
Sligo in 1928 was told that existing water supplies were both
inadequate and polluted with the result that there were only two
courses of action remaining: to provide a new water scheme or to
evacuate the town.[25] By the 1950s, however, most of the problems
in urban areas had been resolved and it could be argued that the
gap in living standards between town and country had actually
widened, at a time when women were more conscious of the
importance of such amenities.

Whereas a nationwide scheme for rural electrification was given
a high priority in the government's plans for post-war Ireland,[26]
there is no sense that providing piped water to rural, or indeed to
urban, homes was seen as equally important. Nor did the concern
shown during the 50s for the survival of rural Ireland – which led
to higher spending on local roads, houses and other forms of
infrastructure such as parish halls – give rise to any obvious interest
in providing running water. In 1947 Sean MacEntee, the then
minister for Local Government and Public Health, established a
committee to report on the possibility of supplying piped water in
areas, particularly rural districts, where no supply existed. When
he addressed the committee's first meeting in September 1947, he
linked the issue with the need 'to make the conditions of life in rural
areas, particularly for those who work on the land, less onerous

than in some respects they now are, so that our country people may enjoy as many as possible of the advantages which town dwellers expect as a matter of course.'[27] James Deeny, chief medical adviser to the Department of Local Government and Public Health, was almost unique in insisting that a piped water supply and the 'further refinement' of a domestic hot water system should be regarded as basic amenities in all new houses. However, it is interesting that Deeny associated supplies of hot water or running water with the quality of women's lives.

> Men, all over the world, are singularly lacking in thought for the welfare of their womenfolk. While any drudgery or inconvenience in man's work will soon be lightened by invention or improvisation, for women little or no effort is made to ease the burden of their monotonous household tasks. All over the country hundreds of thousands of women depend for every drop of water on half-filled cans – drawn laboriously from surface wells sometimes hundreds of yards away. Therefore for the plain and simple reason that of all the people in this country the mother or housewife deserves most from the community, the provision of piped water and better still a domestic hot water system should be our first consideration in household planning.[28]

Deeny and MacEntee's awareness of the importance of running water supplies was not widely shared. The Committee on piped water, which MacEntee established, was disbanded early in 1948 immediately following the change of government. Neither the incoming Minister for Local Government, T.J. Murphy, nor his successor appears to have shown any interest in water schemes. Both preferred to devote their energies to improving housing standards; nor do they appear to have recognised that the two issues were related. The *Commission on Emigration and Other Population Problems* commented on the drudgery of rural life resulting from the lack of power, light, water and sanitation. However, it contented itself with recommending that such facilities 'should be provided as widely and as speedily as possible in rural areas ...', subject to financial considerations'.[29]

Between 1950 and 1959 three government departments, Agriculture, Local Government and Lands (a scheme restricted to houses in the Gaeltacht), each provided grants for the installation of water in rural homes. Yet by 1959 only sixteen thousand households had availed of these schemes, hardly a spectacular number.[30] This was a tiny fraction of the number of rural households who had availed of government grants to construct new homes or to extend and improve existing houses. In 1955, a departmental committee contrasted the lack of progress in the provision of piped water with the achievements in other European countries and concluded that success could only be achieved by 'vigorous policies' which were 'strongly directed'. It added that the limited improvement since the end of World War II in the number of rural homes with running water had 'not however been inspired by any overt policy for the comprehensive improvement of the rural water supply'.[31]

A role model of how to promote the gospel of running water existed in the Electricity Supply Board's (ESB) rural electrification drive. This had involved an extensive campaign throughout rural Ireland to promote the benefits of electricity, which was carried out by a team of men – there is no evidence that any women were employed in this capacity – who were described as rural area organisers. They canvassed the Irish countryside, parish by parish, persuading reluctant families to bring electricity into their homes.[32] The ESB also enlisted the aid of local voluntary groups such as Muintir na Tire and Macra na Feirme, together with supportive local priests, though some parish priests expressed hostility because they believed that electricity would be the first step towards an undesirable modern lifestyle.[33]

Although promoting the adoption of running water was not within the immediate remit of the ESB, it was undoubtedly the organisation with the greatest capacity to undertake such a campaign. From an early stage in the rural electrification campaign, the Board preached the message that electricity would make it possible to pump water into most rural homes. At the 1949 Royal Dublin Society Spring Show, the ESB display promoting rural electrification featured a kitchen complete with taps and sink – with running water available courtesy of electricity. In November 1950, the Annual Fair of the Irish Countrywomen's Association included a special display mounted by the ESB rural electrification office which had running water as its central theme. By 1950 the Board was showing a promotional film entitled 'Rural Water' as part of the rural electricity campaign.[34] In 1955, the ESB contacted the Department of Local Government with the proposal that its publicity drive for rural electrification should be extended to include material advertising the merits of installing running water in rural households. This suggestion aroused no enthusiasm in the Custom House, probably because the Department of Local Government was conscious that there was a shortage of capital for its existing housing and road programmes, and it would have been reluctant to embark on another costly programme. However, it agreed to provide the ESB with details of the various government grants available for meeting some of the cost of installing running water and these were included in subsequent ESB brochures on rural electrification. The ESB's interest in running water was not entirely disinterested; the organisation foresaw a promising market selling water pumps, water-using domestic appliances and the electrical current to drive them. In 1950-51, the Board sold only 150 water pumps to rural customers and demand remained sluggish in later years.[35] When the Board approached the government in 1955 with a view to promoting rural water schemes, they had concluded that lack of running water made it difficult to extend the market for electrical appliances and was one factor explaining the low level of electricity usage in rural households. Only 13 percent of rural households had a washing machine, and only 7 percent owned a water boiler.[36] Moreover, by 1955, the rural electrification scheme was beginning to wind down,[37] and under-employed officials would have been in a position to devote time to promoting the merits of piped water.

The extension of running water into rural homes was undoubtedly handicapped by the fact that this was the responsibility of passive government departments, or perhaps county councils, as opposed to a proactive and dynamic semi-State company. It also seems probable that politicians and government officials showed a limited interest in extending access to running water, perhaps because piped water was seen as primarily benefiting women. When the ESB sought to persuade women of the benefits of electricity, they appear to have presented electricity as a means of providing rural kitchens with running water.[38] (Bathrooms feature little if at all in the publicity, which raises many questions about Irish standards of personal hygiene.) As we shall see, whereas male organisations, or groups containing male and female members, were active in the campaign to promote electricity, the cause of rural water appears to have been seen, almost from the beginning, as a matter of concern only to women. This appears to suggest that most of the benefits of running water would accrue to women: women (and children) carried water from the well; women were solely responsible for laundry, washing-up and other domestic cleaning. The major farm task which would benefit most from running water, dairy hygiene, such as cleaning milk utensils, also appears to have been primarily a woman's chore. Hence the onus for promoting the spread of running water in rural areas fell on the Irish Countrywomen's Association, the largest women's organisation in Ireland.

Although the the ICA did not became actively associated with the government's effort to promote rural water schemes until 1960, the Association's concern with this issue was of much longer

standing, as the speech by Mrs Lett, president of the United Irishwomen, the ICA's ancestral organisation, suggests. A speaker at
one post-war ICA council meeting compared 'the simple process
of washing up after dinner in town and country'. For the country-
woman, without running water, this involved eight separate op-
erations – filling and refilling a kettle, heating successive supplies
of water, throwing out dirty water. A townswoman merely 'stands
at her sink and turns on her hot and cold tap as required'.[39]
However, as already noted, the ICA's concern was slow to arouse
political support. Throughout the 50s most grants for rural water
schemes outside Gaeltacht areas were awarded by the Department
of Agriculture, which appears to have been more concerned with
agricultural production and prices rather than with the quality of
rural life. In addition, the Department of Agriculture and (male)
farming organisations were utterly opposed to any increase in
taxation on farmers. Agricultural interests feared that a campaign
to promote rural water would mean additional borrowings by local
authorities and higher rates charges on farms.

The Department of Local Government appears to have shown
little interest in the matter until 1958, when a report from a committee which examined sanitary services in both rural and urban
areas focused attention on the lack of bathrooms and toilets in rural
homes. Unlike the committee which laboured unnoticed during the
1940s, the timing of this report's publication ensured that it was not
ignored. By 1958, the post-war housing drive had been largely
completed and the Department of Local Government needed another cause to occupy its attention and the time and energy of its
officials. Moreover, a recent polio epidemic, a disease spread by
polluted water, had focused attention on the quality of water
supplies, though the report on sanitary services noted that 'few
people are sufficiently aggrieved by water pollution to take action.'[40] (Times have certainly changed!) While a polio epidemic and
the winding-down of the post-war housing campaign were arguments favouring a major drive to install running water in rural
homes, the publication of the white paper *Economic Development*,
also in 1958, was a less favourable coincidence. *Economic Development* and the related *Programme for Economic Expansion* both emphasised the need to switch investment from social expenditure, on
items such as housing or water, to more productive purposes
which would generate growth in exports and in national income.
The report of the committee on sanitary services emphasised that
if 'vigorous policies' were adopted to promote rural water, they
would require generous subsidies from central government; how-

ever, it was difficult to argue this case at a time when government policy was planning to divert money from housing to items such as a fertiliser factory. The Department of Finance opposed the committee's proposals to introduce a major programme of government grants and subsidised loans to cover the cost of rural water schemes on the grounds that this was merely social investment which could not be justified on public health grounds, though they were prepared to continue the existing programme of modest grants provided by the Department of Agriculture. The Department of Local Government ultimately won the argument by replacing references to the quality of rural life and benefits to human health with purely economic arguments: memoranda now argued that adequate rural water supplies were essential if bovine TB was to be eliminated and the quality of Irish dairy products improved. Both these objectives were seen as central to increasing Irish agricultural exports. It was also argued that the development of tourism in rural areas was dependent on ready access to running water.[41]

The Department of Local Government enlisted the aid of the Irish Countrywomen's Association in a campaign to spread the gospel of piped water, which one senior civil servant described as 'the first and greatest of domestic labour-saving devices'. A joint committee was established to plan and launch a national campaign, and although it included other rural groups such as Muintir na Tire, the main momentum was carried by the ICA. At a conference held in ICA headquarters, An Grianan, in October 1960, Minister for Local Government Neil Blaney blamed Irish men for the poor standard of amenities in rural homes and told the assembled ICA members that 'now that the cause has been taken up by your association, we may assuredly look forward to the breaking down by the farmer's wife and daughters of the farmer's traditional conservatism in this matter.'[42] During 1961, the ICA and the Department co-operated in organising the 'Turn on the Tap' exhibition, which toured Ireland spelling out the benefits of running water in rural homes. In a style reminiscent of the rural electrification campaign, the Department of Local Government commissioned a documentary film, *Water Wisdom*, by Colm Ó Laoghaire, which had its première at the 1962 Cork Film Festival. The campaign benefited considerably from close personal links between the ICA and the Department of Local Government: Mrs Aine Barrington, a key figure in the 'Turn on the Tap' campaign, was the wife of Tom Barrington, a former senior official in the Department of Local Government. The 1961 general election gave a further boost to the campaign to install running water in country homes. Taoiseach Sean Lemass in one speech during the election campaign described it as 'perhaps the most significant measure ever taken to improve the conditions of people in rural areas,' and cited a recent encyclical by Pope John XXIII – *Mater et Magistra* – which called for an equalisation of public services between town and country.[43] Although Lemass believed that the new rural water campaign would prove a major vote-winner, not everyone agreed and the ICA's efforts to promote the benefits of running water were not universally welcome in the Irish countryside. Most vocal opposition came, somewhat ironically, from the National Farmers' Association (NFA), who objected that the government's scheme would result in farmers being forced to pay higher rates on agricultural land and on farm buildings.[44] Their opposition would appear to have included a considerable measure of self-interest; the organisation was dominated by larger farmers, who were more likely to be among the minority of rural households which were already provided with running water.[45] NFA members in several areas passed resolutions which asserted that farmers who would not directly benefit from the rural schemes (presumably because they had installed their own water supplies) should not be required to pay the higher rates resulting. When this demand was conveyed to him by the Minister for Agriculture, Patrick Smith, Local Government Minister Neil Blaney replied that he was 'frankly puzzled as to the purposes of the correspondence'. Blaney pointed out that most ratepayers already paid for services from which they would not directly benefit, such as local authority housing.[46] In addition to a clash between male and female rural organisations – the NFA versus the ICA – the dispute also carried connotations of class difference and inter-departmental power politics. The 1960 campaign was a missionary campaign, designed to bring water to all rural households, rich and poor. Only the more prosperous rural households had taken advantage of the grants scheme previously operated by the Department of Agriculture, because much of the cost remained to be borne by the consumer. In addition the dispute highlighted the contrasting attitudes of Patrick Smith, who echoed the views of conservative farming interests, and the clear commitment to improving rural amenities shown by Neil Blaney. This may also mark a generational and cultural divide within Fianna Fáil: between Blaney, seen as representative of the modern Lemass-style of ministers, derided by Kevin Boland and others as 'mohairs' – a reference to the lighter mohair suits which they wore – and the more traditional Smith.[47] Although Smith had served as Minister for Local Government during the years 1951-54 and again for some months in 1957, there is no evidence that he showed any interest in improving rural water supplies during these years.

The opposition which Smith and the NFA displayed towards the rural water campaign was not without influence. The Department of Local Government initially proposed to bring water to most rural areas via major regional water schemes, and work started on several of these projects during the early 1960s. However, the repeated assertions by the NFA that regional water schemes were too elaborate began to bear fruit, and from 1962, they were gradually abandoned in favour of group water schemes, many of them organised on a co-operative basis. A memorandum presented to the Cabinet in 1962 emphasised that individuals could contribute their share of the overall cost in the form of labour, with cash outlays reduced to token payments which could be as little as approximately £5. In the case of old age pensioners and other impoverished households, this could be waived altogether.[48]

Lemass' 'rising tide' did not lift all boats during the first half of the 1960s. This proved a difficult time for Irish farming; export markets proved unattractive until after the Anglo-Irish trade agreement of 1965 and farmers became increasingly dependent on government subsidies to achieve higher prices and increases in income. Farmer resentment against poor economic conditions was expressed in a variety of ways, including a wave of protests against the rising cost of local authority rates, which was partly blamed on the government's rural water campaign. It is ironic therefore that the resentment expressed by (male) farmers against stagnant or slowly-rising incomes, at a time of increased national prosperity, held back improvements in rural domestic life. The public relations campaign to promote the merits of running water in rural homes proved a major casualty of farmer/ratepayer hostility and it petered out at a relatively early stage. The shift from regional schemes to less elaborate group schemes was not particularly successful. Government expenditure on water schemes peaked in 1962-63 and the number of rural houses with running water on tap fell below the targets set by the Department of Local Government in the *Second Programme for Economic Expansion*. Efforts to promote tap water in country homes suffered a further blow in 1965 when a difficult budgetary position brought severe cutbacks in expenditure for housing and sanitary services. Although both categories were linked in the expenditure cuts announced by government, housing escaped relatively unscathed and water schemes bore the brunt of the reduction. Expenditure of over £2.5m in 1964-65 fell to less than £900,000 in the following year. By the late 60s, when the budgetary situation had again eased, attention had shifted to the demands of urban Ireland as rapid population growth in towns, cities and suburbs meant water shortages. As a result, the capital available under this heading was increasingly directed away from the countryside. The *Third Programme for Economic and Social Development, 1969-72* noted that built-up areas would be given priority, though the demand for money for rural water schemes would 'continue to be met as far as possible'. Although conditions in rural homes improved substantially during the 1960s, the 1971 census revealed that over 42 percent of rural homes continued to lack any supply of running water – even an outdoor tap – and less than one-third of rural households contained a fixed bath. Moreover the shift in emphasis from large-scale regional water schemes to smaller group schemes transferred much of the initiative for promoting rural water schemes away from central government to the local community, where women were forced to assume an even more active role – canvassing neighbours, collecting down payments, and raising consciousness of the value of such amenities. As women's involvement in this area pre-dated the emergence of a Women's Movement within Ireland, the campaign was not able to benefit from the wider support which would be available if a similar campaign were needed today.

Running water undoubtedly reached Irish homes at a slower pace than would have been possible, if the government programme had not been opposed by major farming organisations. With the exception of a brief period in the early 60s, the provision of running water in country homes never assumed the political momentum associated either with the post-war housing drive or with rural electrification. The contrast between the attention given to rural water and rural electrification and the slow rate of improvement in rural water supplies reveals much about the status of women in rural Ireland at this time. When Hannan and Katsiaouni surveyed several hundred farm families in the west of Ireland in 1970, only half of the households had piped water, though most of these households also had a bathroom, a gas or electric cooker and a television set.[49] Households with piped water and a washing machine also tended to have a separate sitting room. Hannan concluded that the wide variation in amenities between different households could not simply be explained by income levels; rather it reflected prevailing values and attitudes. Better material standards were found in households containing younger wives and women with higher educational standards, who had worked outside farming and outside rural Ireland prior to marriage.[50] Such families also tended to display less rigidly-defined sex roles and more egalitarian relationships.[51] The unmodernised households, those without running water and other modern amenities, were those which were doomed to disappear; most were inhabited by ageing bachelors whose lifestyle was rejected by modern Irish women. Would a more active government campaign to promote the gospel of running water have carried wider benefits, such as a lifestyle and domestic environment more attractive to women?

Women & Pacifism in Ireland
1915–1932
Rosemary Cullen Owens

In her study of feminism and anti-militarism in Britain, Jill Liddington describes as inadequate and misleading any history of feminism which does not include a study of the links between feminism, anti-militarism, peace ideas and campaigns.[1] From an Irish perspective, the history of feminism has been well documented over the past decade – mainly by women historians encouraged and nurtured by Margaret MacCurtain. Interaction between peace campaigners and feminists, and the effect of militarism on the Irish women's movement, however, need further examination. This article seeks to raise questions concerning the connections between Irish feminism and pacificism: was there a recognisable pacifist element in Ireland on the outbreak of war in 1914? How did women react to the growing militarist atmosphere within Ireland from 1915? What was the nature of discourse on the significance of militarism for the women's movement? How did committed feminists and pacifists cope with often radically different priorities for peace and/or freedom?

The outbreak of war in 1914 had serious repercussions for the women's suffrage movement worldwide. The movement had become increasingly international in outlook after 1904 with the formation of the International Woman Suffrage Alliance (IWSA) by women from the United States, Australia and Europe.[2] Within the following ten years a series of international congresses were held, with ever-increasing representation from member countries. Irish suffragists were kept informed of developments through the suffrage press. In 1913 the 7th – and largest – such conference was held in Budapest. Among the 300 official delegates from 22 countries were three Irishwomen – Hanna Sheehy Skeffington from the Irish Women's Franchise League (IWFL), Louie Bennett from the Irish Women's Suffrage Federation (IWSF), and Lady Margaret Dockrell from the Irish Women's Suffrage and Local Government Association

(IWSLGA). The list of attendance at this meeting of prominent women activists reads like a 'Who's Who' of the early women's movement.[3] Contacts made or renewed in Budapest would strengthen the internationalist stance of many suffragists during the war years ahead.

With the outbreak of war in 1914 a significant section of the international suffrage movement adopted a pacifist stance, causing division within most national women's organisations. For example, in the same month in 1915 nationalist German women cancelled the 9th IWSA congress planned for Berlin, while anti-war German suffragists published an Open Letter extending their hand 'to our sister-women ... above the war of the nations'.[4] Following an American tour by feminist campaigners Rosika Schwimmer (Hungary) and Emmeline Pethwick-Lawrence (England), a Women's Peace Party was formed in the U.S. in January 1915 by Carrie Chapman Catt (President of the IWSA) and Jane Addams.[5] These developments were followed with close interest in Ireland.

Unlike many suffrage organisations worldwide, the three Irish associations represented at Budapest continued throughout and after the war of 1914-1918, but this did not reflect a unified stance vis-à-vis the war. In fact, there was a wide variety of opinion as to the correct stance for women in Ireland at this time, particularly in the early war period. An Emergency Council of Suffragists was formed in Dublin in August 1914 to provide a forum wherein women could engage in relief works without abandoning the suffrage campaign. The IWSF – and its Dublin branch named the Irish Women's Reform League (IWRL) – initially supported this Council, suspending active suffrage propaganda for some months. Among the projects engaged in was the organisation of workshops in Dublin employing 100 girls.[6] The IWSLGA was primarily involved in war relief works, ranging from the making of bandages to an endowment of a hospital bed for wounded soldiers. Jingoistic references in their annual reports to 'our brave soldiers and sailors' offended nationalist women and feminists who considered such activities inconsistent with the aims of suffrage societies. The action of the Cork branch – the Munster Women's Franchise League (MWFL) – in presenting an ambulance to the military authorities forced the resignation of Mary MacSwiney, who declared that the majority of members were 'Britons first, suffragists second, and Irishwomen perhaps a bad third'.[7] The IWFL did not join the Emergency Council and remained firmly opposed to such activities, commenting in the suffrage paper *The Irish Citizen* that 'The European war has done nothing to alter our condition of slavery.'

Small wonder that Louie Bennett should write to Hanna Sheehy Skeffington in despair that women's groups were: 'like sheep astray and I suppose when the necessity of knitting socks is over – the order will be – Bear sons, and those of us who can't will feel we had better get out of the way as quickly as we can.'[8]

Early in 1915, the IWSF changed its policy regarding the suspension of suffrage activities. Commenting that its objective was the enfranchisement of Irishwomen and that all philanthropic activities were of secondary importance, it urged members to work for attainment of women's suffrage before the end of the war. Louie Bennett, writing in *The Irish Citizen* that 'Women should never have abandoned their struggle for justice, war or no war,' probably had a strong influence on such a decision.[9]

Responding to the Christmas 1914 message from anti-war German suffragists, the IWSF rejoiced that 'the bond of international sisterhood has risen above the fierce struggle in which our nations are engaged'.[10] Shortly afterwards, the IWRL suggested to the IWSF executive that a campaign be initiated to educate public opinion against the prevailing militarist spirit. Louie Bennett – the proposer of that motion – asked in *Jus Suffragii* (Journal of the IWSA): 'Are we right to tolerate in silence this modern warfare, with all its cruelty and waste? ... More and more the conviction grows that it is full time that women rose up and demanded a truce for reflection.'[11]

In *The Irish Citizen*, she appealed to all suffrage societies to organise meetings and study groups on the issue. The IWFL strongly supported these developments. Weekly articles and editorials in *The Irish Citizen* kept women informed of developments. One article suggested that women should hold a congress of their own at the same time as any proposed peace settlement conference.[12]

Following the German withdrawal of its invitation to host the 1915 congress, IWSA President Carrie Chapman Catt cancelled the Congress entirely. Many members vigorously disagreed with this decision. In response, a group of Dutch suffragists organised a meeting with women from Belgium, Britain and Germany at Amsterdam in February 1915. From this emerged a plan for an international women's peace conference in The Hague on 28 April 1915.[13] Developments were being monitored in Ireland through regular reports in *The Irish Citizen*. At a conference held to discuss possible Irish participation, fears were expressed that such activity might imply disloyalty to those fighting at the front. Recording 'hot debates on the Peace Congress Scheme' at committee meetings of the IWRL, Lucy Kingston concluded Ireland would not be represented 'simply because of ultra Loyalists' objections'.[14] Similar sentiments were being expressed throughout Europe. In the British press, intending participants were derided as 'pro-Hun peacettes' going to 'pow-wow with the fraus' and their desire for a negotiated peace was opposed as treachery.[15] Almost all governments tried to prevent their women attending The Hague. German delegates were stopped at the Dutch border, but 28 women managed to get through. No French or Russian woman was able to attend. The American delegation of 41 was delayed on government orders in the British channel for three days, delegates arriving just after the Congress started. From a total of 180 British delegates, only 24 were – very reluctantly – granted travel permits by the Home Secretary, an action almost immediately negated by the announcement that all cross-channel travel was suspended indefinitely. Only three British women reached The Hague – two who had crossed some days earlier and Emmeline Pethick-Lawrence, who had travelled with the U.S. contingent.

In his study of European feminism and pacifism, Richard Evans has pointed to the close link drawn at the Hague Congress between women's subjection and the triumph of militarism. Feminist pacifists took the commonly cited argument that women's suffrage would have a civilising influence on society and radicalised it, to claim that the granting of the vote to women was the quickest way to end the war.[16] One week before the Congress, a book entitled *Militarism Versus Feminism: an Enquiry and a Policy Demonstrating that Militarism Involves the Subjection of Women* was published by Allen and Unwin in London. It argued that the level of militarism in any society affects the liberty which women might enjoy. Jill Liddington has noted that whereas previous propaganda for suffrage and equality had helped to obscure gender differences, militarism raised different issues. While keenly pro-suffrage, *Militarism Versus Feminism* placed emphasis on gender difference and patriarchal institutions rather than equality, declaring that:

> Militarism has been the curse of women, as women, from the first dawn of social life ... War has engendered and perpetuated that dominance of man as a military animal which has pervaded every social institution from Parliament downwards.[17]

Women's marginalisation, the authors argued, might give women's protest a powerful platform. As Liddington points out, the authors' indictment was not of men, but of militarism. Bennett argued in the *The Irish Citizen* in February that year:

> Suffragists of every country must face the fact that militarism is now the most dangerous foe of woman's suffrage, and of all that woman's suffrage stands for. The campaign for enfranchisement

involves now a campaign against militarism. And if we are to
conquer militarism we cannot postpone doing so for any 'whens'
or 'untils'. If women do not at once decide to use all the forces of
their organisations against militarism, then there is grave reason
to fear that in the European settlement militarism will once more be
a dominant factor and humanitarianism, which includes feminism,
will be discredited.[18]

The emergence of feminist peace campaigners during the war years
caused much dissension among women's organisations world-
wide. Throughout Europe, feminist organisations espousing pacifist views at the beginning of the war quickly lost members.[19] The
overwhelming majority in all countries supported the war effort.
French feminists commented that 'Duties called louder than
rights,' while in Britain suffrage leader Millicent Fawcett declared,
'Let us prove ourselves worthy of citizenship, whether our claim
is recognised or not.' Thus, Evans points out, 'Feminist pacifism
was the creed of a minority, of a tiny band of courageous and
principled women on the far-left fringes of bourgeois-liberal feminism.'[20] While feminist groups in combatant countries adopted
varying degrees of nationalist rhetoric, the situation in Ireland
posed particular difficulties. Initial differences within Irish suffrage
societies reflected pro- and anti-war stands, either on loyalist or
feminist grounds. Despite opposition, an Irish committee was
formed to promote Irish representation at the Hague Congress and
decided to send seven delegates.[21] Outlining the reasons why the
IWFL wished to attend the Congress, Hanna Sheehy Skeffington
wrote that the League regarded war as the negation of the feminist
movement and in particular of the militant suffrage movement
which rated human life of higher value than property. War, she
declared, on the contrary destroyed human life in the pursuit of
property. Of the seven Irish delegates proposed, only Louie Bennett was granted a travel permit, but in the event was prevented
from travelling due to an embargo by the Admiralty. A public
protest meeting was called in Dublin on 11 May by the IWFL, to
protest against the government's action. James Connolly and
Thomas MacDonagh were among the speakers. In a letter of support, Patrick Pearse declared that the incident was another example
of British policy excluding Ireland from international debate, add-
ing that much good would be done if the incident encouraged more
women to support the national forces. In response, Margaret Con-
nery of the IWFL asked why it would not encourage more of the
national forces to support the women.

Two issues of crucial importance to the women's movement in
Ireland emerged at the Dublin protest meeting against government

action vis-à-vis the Hague, i.e. the role of women in the nationalist movement, and the issue of justifiable militarist action for nationalist objectives. The formation of Cumann na mBan in 1914, as a female auxiliary of the Irish Volunteers, had engendered widespread criticism from suffragists. Those who argued that the national struggle should take precedence over the women's campaign were opposed by those who demanded suffrage first – before all else.

Thomas MacDonagh's address to the IWFL meeting laid bare the thorny dilemma with which Irish suffragists would have to grapple within the year. Declaring openly that, as one of the founders of the Irish Volunteers, he had taught men to kill other men, and had helped to arm thousands of Irishmen, he nonetheless described himself an advocate of peace 'because everyone was being exploited by the dominant militarism'. Acknowledging his anomalous position, his one apology for helping create a different kind of militarism in Ireland was his belief that 'it would never be used against fellow countrymen'.[22] Louie Bennett voiced her concern at the tone of this meeting in the *The Irish Citizen*:

> Militarism in the most subtly dangerous form has its hold upon Ireland. Those women who take up the crusade against militarism must not tolerate the 'fight for freedom' and 'defence of rights' excuses for militarism. To use barbarous methods for attainment even of such an ideal as freedom is but to impose a different form of bondage upon a nation.[23]

Writing privately to Hanna Sheehy Skeffington, Louie noted that the tone of the meeting was far more anti-English than anti-militarist, and that while the present war was reckoned barbarous and immoral, it would appear that a war for Ireland would be considered justified. To Bennett this was a thoroughly superficial form of pacifism.[24] The debate was widened by the publication of an *Open Letter* to Thomas MacDonagh by Frank Sheehy Skeffington, in which he enunciated clearly the views of pacifist feminism towards militarism and in particular towards Irish militarism. Describing MacDonagh's speech as remarkable and impressive, Skeffington noted:

> You spoke vehemently and with unmistakable sincerity in advocacy of peace. You traced war, with perfect accuracy, to its roots in exploitation. You commended every effort made by the women to combat militarism and establish a permanent peace. And in the same speech you boasted of being one of the creators of a new militarism in Ireland ... High ideals undoubtedly animate you. But has not nearly every militarist system started with the same high ideals?

Skeffington considered it highly significant that women were excluded from the Irish Volunteers, indicating a reactionary element in the movement. While agreeing with the fundamental objectives of the organisation, and acknowledging its merits, Skeffington commented:

> As your infant movement grows, towards the stature of a full-grown militarism, its essence – preparation to kill – grows more repellent to me ... European militarism has drenched Europe in blood; Irish militarism may only crimson the fields of Ireland. For us that would be disaster enough.[25]

Shortly before the Easter Rising, Louie Bennett and Frank Sheehy Skeffington took part in a public debate with Constance Markievicz on the motion 'Do We Want Peace Now?'. Out of an audience of five or six hundred, only a handful supported Skeffington. Bennett was appalled that Markievicz and her supporters preferred to see the war continue, if it meant defeat for England and subsequent freedom for Ireland. She intervened, strongly disagreeing with what she saw as cowardice. Connolly spoke after Bennett, favouring the idea that now was the time to strike against England. Bennett later wrote how this meeting had depressed her, describing its spirit as 'bad, sinister, lacking in any idealism to redeem its bitterness'.[26] Some months earlier, Connolly had interrupted a Dublin meeting of the Union of Democratic Control addressed by Helena Swanwick, pouring scorn on her argument that Britain stood for the rights of small nationalities.[27] While admiring Connolly intellectually and praising him as a feminist, Bennett found it dificult to work with him in the labour movement because of his commitment to military action. When approached to work with the Irish Women Workers' Union, Bennett declined, explaining to Helena Moloney that 'As a pacifist I would not support any organisation threatening force.'[28]

While fully committed to the internationalist ideal, Bennett was, however, convinced of the need for separate Irish representation at international feminist gatherings. She had first raised this issue in the spring of 1915 with the IWSF.[29] The Hague Peace Congress of that year saw the formation of an International Committee of Women for Permanent Peace (ICWPP). Subsequently a series of national committees were formed in Europe and the U.S. Initially Ireland was part of the British branch, Bennett being the Irish representative on its executive. From the beginning, however, the Irish branch sought separate representation. A formal resolution to the ICWPP in October 1915 asked for independent representation for any nation feeling itself a distinct entity and enjoying or aspiring to enjoy self-government.[30] Expressing the discontent of Irish members, Bennett demanded that the principle of nationality should be clearly established in the consititution of the ICWPP, pointing out that 'The peace movement in Ireland must be indigenous and independent to be in any sense successful.'[31] In January 1916, the Irish branch took matters into their own hands, renaming their branch the Irishwomen's International League (IIL). Prolonged and often bureaucratic correspondence with Head Office in Amsterdam on the issue continued through 1916. The status of small and subject nations was discussed in depth by the ICWPP, and raised by Bennett at every international executive meeting. Strong support was given by the British branch – named the Women's International League (WIL) – which late in 1916 stated:

> Unrest in Ireland we believe to be the result of tyranny and wrong, and the only way to peace is that of freedom and justice. So long as we deny these to Ireland we cannot expect that the rest of Europe will have much confidence in our desire to safeguard the rights of 'small nationalities' ... We are proud to know that the Irishwomen's International League is standing bravely for *all* the ideals for which we are banded together – feminism, nationalism and inter-nationalism, peace and freedom.[32]

Confident that full national status would soon be granted, the IIL pointed out in *The Irish Citizen* of October 1916 that their persistence would promote nationalism in general and Irish nationalism in particular, and declared that the duty of a nation placed as Ireland was, was to contribute to the cause of permanent international peace through a clear and uncompromising advocacy of the principle of nationality. Finally, in December 1916, the IIL was formally accepted as an independent national organisation.[33]

During the early months of 1916, the IIL continued its work in line with its stated objectives, to:

> – work for the complete enfranchisement of women;
> – work for a just and reasonable settlement of the Irish question by helping to promote goodwill and a better understanding between different sections of people in Ireland and by steadfastly opposing the use of destructive force by any section;
> – co-operate with women of other countries in working for permanent international peace.

Regular meetings were held to discuss the Hague resolutions and other topical issues arising from the war. Conscription was condemned; the rights of small nationalities to independence was stressed; and support was given to the establishment of a conference of neutral nations to facilitate a mediated settlement to the war.[34]

The Easter Rising of 1916 – and the murder of Frank Sheehy Skeffington – placed immense strain on women's groups generally, and on pacifist groups in particular. Bennett – who took over Skeffington's mantle as *The Irish Citizen* editor and pacifist voice – notified ICWPP Headquarters that Irish members now had to concentrate on encouraging a more conciliatory spirit among the various sections of Irish life. Her personal view on independence for Ireland was stated quite clearly when she asked: 'How far is it immoral, even criminal, to postpone practical recognition of the "sacred right of freedom" to this particular small nation of Ireland?'[35]

The abandonment of an active suffrage campaign in Britain in favour of various war-works prompted Bennett to describe English suffragists as 'a servile sex'. Noting that Irishwomen were more independent, she urged caution 'for our political women hang on blindly to their particular political half-good fetishes, whether Sinn Féin or Redmondites'. Documenting various committees with little representation of women, Bennett wrote to Hanna Sheehy Skeffington in despair – 'There is no getting away from it, women in general are a poor crowd, willing to be under the thumb of men.'[36] The IIL wrote to Lloyd George, John Redmond and other Irish politicians, uging that women's voice be heard in any Irish settlement and arguing that safe and constructive government must rest on right rather than might, on reason rather than on physical force. Censorship fears prevented the publication of this letter in *International*, the newsletter of the ICWPP.[37] Following their first A.G.M. in January 1917, the IIL informed the head office in Amsterdam: 'We trust that when the re-organisation of Europe is effected, the right of our own country to full and free development on the basis of nationality will be fully acknowledged.'[38]

Despite the turbulent events of 1916, this was the only oblique reference to political developments in Ireland in this first anniversary message. During 1918, the IIL's letter-heading was changed to Gaelic, the English title in smaller print underneath.[39] Writing to headquarters in November of that year, Bennett outlined the continuing concerns of the group: working for peace in Ireland, campaigning against enforced military service, and a desire for self-determination for Ireland. Irish and English branches of ICWPP worked very closely during this period, particularly on the treatment of Irish political prisoners and opposition to conscription in Ireland. During an English speaking tour organised by the British WIL late in 1918, Bennett obtained an interview with Lloyd George in order to seek the release of Irish prisoners. Following her tour, British WIL called for the withdrawal of the military occupation of Ireland.[40]

During 1918, a number of war-related issues led to a temporary unity of purpose among women's groups in Ireland. Chief among these was the campaign against the proposed implementation of the Conscription Act to Ireland. Among the many protest meetings and conferences organised against the introduction of conscription was a mass meeting of women at Dublin's Mansion House, at which all present pledged to resist conscription. A national women's day was held, during which women throughout the country pledged not to take jobs vacated by men being conscripted. In Dublin, representatives of various women's societies marched in procession to the City Hall to sign this pledge.[41]

In May 1919, the ICWPP held its second Congress in Zurich. Plans to hold this post-war Congress side by side with the official Peace Congress at Versailles had to be abandoned as delegates from the defeated powers were refused permission to enter France. The number of participating countries had risen since 1915 from 12 to 16, the largest delegations coming from Germany, Britain and the U.S.A. Among the smaller countries represented for the first time was Ireland, with Louie Bennett and Hanna Sheehy Skeffington among its delegates.[42] At this Congress, the ICWPP was renamed the Women's International League for Peace and Freedom (WILPF), and its headquarters moved to Geneva.[43] An 'Appeal on Behalf of Ireland' issued to the Congress by the Irish branch sought support for Ireland 'in her legitimate struggle for rights of self-determination'. The document urged delegates:

> Help us to regain our birthright, the right to meet and work with other Nations on an equal plane. We want, all of us, to regain it by honourable means. We can say of Dáil Eireann that it is on fire for justice, that it bears ill will to none, if only the alien government which crushes and oppresses the people could be ousted.[44]

A post-Congress document addressed 'To the Smaller Nations', signed by Louie Bennett, called on all smaller nations to make common cause with Ireland in an alliance of non-imperialistic peoples – a true League of Nations:

> We declare our belief that the fate of many other nations is involved in the fate of Ireland: her continued subjection will inevitably encourage further violations of fundamental principles of international morality; but her liberation would make a definite advance towards such a World Commonwealth as alone can promise equal security for all peoples. Therefore the liberation of Ireland is the concern of all who seek peace and freedom.[45]

Despite often radically differing political loyalties, women's groups had joined together on a number of controversial issues. A further remarkable example of such joint action occurred in 1919 with an 'Appeal on Behalf of the Principal Women's Associations of Ireland' to their sisters in other countries to demand the establishment of an International Committee of Inquiry into the conditions of Irish political prisoners. That there were some initial differences among signatories is not surprising when one notes that they included Constance Markievicz, Hanna Sheehy Skeffington, Louie Bennett and Maud Gonne MacBride. With differences sorted out, the petition argued that should England refuse to allow what France, Germany, Austria and Italy had willingly accepted, she would stand self-condemned. Outlining the loss of free speech and press under English military rule, it concluded with an appeal to the civilised world to 'break down the wall of silence with which England seeks to surround Ireland'.[46]

In the autumn of 1920, the Manchester branch of the WIL organised a fact-finding trip to Ireland to investigate conditions. A report of their findings was published and a series of public meetings held throughout England. Audiences were shown 'magic-lantern' slides of photographs taken during the trip, showing ruined homes, wrecked shops and buildings.[47] At all of these meetings resolutions were passed and forwarded to the government, demanding the liberation of prisoners and a truce during which Irish people might determine their own form of government. In the U.S., Jane Addams and Emily Balch were among those who responded. A lobby of Congress and a Commission of Inquiry into Irish affairs was established. In January 1921, Bennett and a colleague travelled to Washington as IIL delegates. From a somewhat different perspective, Mary and Muriel MacSwiney also gave evidence to the Washington Commission. Cognisant of the importance of women's role, Cumann na mBan instructed MacSwiney in her subsequent tour of the U.S. to assure Americans that 'the women of Ireland are standing with the soldiers and that "no surrender" is the watchword.' MacSwiney's biographer notes that 'the organisation did not want women represented as a pacifist group urging the men to lay down their arms'.[48] A broadsheet published about this time, entitled *Irishwomen and the Irish Republican Army*, emphasised that Irishwomen were as proud of their national army as were women of other countries of theirs, ranking them with the world's bravest. The document concluded:

> The women of Ireland consider it a crime for any young Irishman of military age not to carry arms in the defence of his country, and that it is an even greater crime for any person of Irish blood to refuse to harbour and assist our brave soldiers.[49]

The IIL stance in Washington concentrated on the spirit and purpose motivating the Irish people and the constructive activities of

Dáil Eireann, rather than on a chronicle of atrocities. Writing privately to Emily Balch, Bennett commented, 'I urged any groups of women I met in America to make this question of Ireland a moral rather than a political issue, so that it may be in some sense released from the intanglement of the anti-British movement in the States.'[50]

Acceptance of the Treaty by Dáil Eireann and the ensuing civil war had a profound effect both on the IIL organisation and on individual members attempting to ally pacifist convictions with political commitment. Slightly naïvely, the WILPF head office believed that acceptance of the Treaty meant that Ireland could put the nightmare of violence and outrage behind it.[51] Explaining that in fact the Treaty was not popular, but was accepted with bent head and a significant degree of grief and shame, Bennett asked:

> Can you be surprised? We are asked to accept Common Citizenship with an Empire whose deeds we loathe ... There are men and women who could not take the oath of allegiance without sacrificing every instinct of honour in their nature.[52]

She hoped that de Valera would be strong enough to lead his followers away from politics and concentrate on education and economic reconstruction, but she was unsure, noting that: 'The women here are a dangerous element – fierce, vindictive, without any constructive ability but with immense ability for obstruction and destructive tactics.'

When simmering post-Treaty tensions finally escalated into civil war in June 1922, a group of concerned women met in Dublin's Mansion House to co-ordinate peace efforts. Two delegations were picked to present peace proposals to leaders on both sides. (Bennett was the only one included in both delegations.) The government side informed them there could be no truce until anti-government forces surrendered their arms. The republican side refused to negotiate on any terms.[53] The IIL was experiencing its own civil war at this time. Louie informed Geneva of its impending disolution, explaining that its existence over the past two years had been precarious and unsatisfactory to those who tried to be consistently pacifist: 'The civil strife in Ireland in the last few months has driven the larger majority of people into one or other political camp: both sides have raised objections to the attitude of the I.I.L.'[54]

The success of the IIL in raising public awareness in England and the U.S. on the issue of Irish political affairs may in fact have contributed to this crisis. Women like Hanna Sheehy Skeffington and Rosamund Jacob – long associated with the League – had become increasingly republican in attitude. Lucy Kingston noted that the 1920 A.G.M. of the League showed 'great attendance of S.F.s including Gonne McBride, Capt. W. Mrs. S.S. etc.'.[55] As a result

of political differences over the Treaty, the Mansion House Peace
Conference of Women had collapsed. Bennett informed Geneva:

> The Republican section of this conference drifted into party
> propaganda, especially in regard to the prisoners ... the Free State
> element in the I.I.L. have, almost to a woman, resigned on account
> of our association with the Mansion House Conference.[56]

Bennett still thought that they were right to have tried. She also felt,
however, that the time had come for radical changes within the IIL.
She suggested that a new Irish section of WILPF be started under
new influence, commenting, 'Miss Jacob is too Republican, I am too
actively connected with Labour, to be anything but a danger to the
sort of organisation that is needed.' Arguing the necessity of maintaining an all-Ireland organisation 'to maintain social links and to
obliterate the ugly antagonism now existing', she disagreed with
Geneva's proposal for a separate northern section, stating this
would make the process of reconciliation even more difficult.
Reflecting the turmoil and crises of conscience experienced by
pacifists througout Europe in recent years, Louie confessed:

> All that has happened and is still happening here drives one to
> review very seriously one's attitude to pacifism. I am driven to
> think that some forms of anarchy can only be dealt with by the
> use of force ... When accepted moral standards break down, what
> is to be done to secure innocent people from cruelty and loss of
> life and property?[57]

Within a few days of this letter, a committee meeting of the IIL
decided to keep the group going for the moment with Rosamund
Jacob taking over as Secretary pro-tem from Louie Bennett. Two
weeks later at its A.G.M. Bennett formally resigned as Secretary,
warning the group against allowing on its committee ' women who
take prominent place in contemporary politics'.[58] However, the
new committee for 1922-3 included many high-profile political
women. Charlotte Despard was its Chair, at the same time as being
Chair of the Women's Prisoners Defence Association (formed in
1922 with Maud Gonne MacBride). Rosamund Jacob, Hanna
Sheehy Skeffington and Maud Gonne MacBride were also much
involved. Not surprisingly, such a volatile committee led to numerous incidents of disagreement and caused much heart-searching
within the group. One such incident occurred in January 1923,
when Rosamund Jacob was arrested and imprisoned for allowing
Republicans the use of Hanna Sheehy Skeffington's house. Lucy
Kingston commented tartly that while no doubt Hanna would have
agreed with Jacob's action, it was somewhat rash of Jacob, considering her role within the IIL, noting, 'we are not benefitted in any
way by having our Secretary in prison.'[59] Kingston's diary also

reveals that the issue of Despard's resignation was raised more than once, each time Despard declaring herself a pacifist and neutral regarding government. Kingston was relieved that Mrs Dix was joint Secretary – 'she is sane and thoroughly pacifist and does not stink in the eyes of government like Mrs D(espard) and Mme G.McB..' Early in 1923, a special meeting was called to consider a resolution by Louie Bennett: 'That membership of the Irish Section is open to all who hold that in resisting tyranny or striving for freedom only such methods may be used as will not involve the taking of life.'[60]

In a country in the midst of civil war, this resolution stripped the *raison d'être* of a group such as the IIL to its core. After heated discussion the resolution was lost by just one vote. The issue of the legitimate use of force remained a thorny one and would continue to dog the IIL during its remaining years. For the moment, however, the League survived, noting in its annual report: 'Taking into account the terrible crisis through which the country is passing, we have not done too badly.'[61] Over the next two years Bennett disappears from IIL and WILPF records, although indications are that she remained a member. Lucy Kingston and Rosamund Jacob represented Ireland at the 3rd International Congress in Vienna in June 1921, while Marie Johnson filled that role in Washington in 1924. Johnson was happy to tell the Congress that Ireland now had full adult suffrage.

In 1925, the IIL invited the international executive of WILPF to hold its 5th International Congress in Dublin the following year. The invitation was enthusiastically accepted and was viewed by by Jane Addams and her executive as an 'extended peace mission'. Its official history notes that: 'The choice owed something to the courageous stand for non-violence of Louie Bennett and her co-workers, as well as to the tragic situation of Ireland itself.'[62]

Bennett had always been highly regarded by the WILPF executive, and from early 1926 she features regularly in correspondence regarding the forthcoming Congress. In the work of organisation she was assisted by a committee of eleven, with Rosamund Jacob, Lucy Kingston and Helen Chenevix playing key roles.[63] And it was quite a mammoth task for a small national section to undertake. Interesting details emerge from correspondence between Dublin and Geneva over these months, the Irish section advising on sensitive political issues, protocol and customs.[64] The problem of location was solved when the organising committee managed to get the use of National University buildings in Dublin. Lucy Kingston informed Geneva that the government had at last realised the importance of bringing so many visitors to Dublin, although she cautioned: 'We are careful ... not to put our Branch too greatly under the Government "wing"... This would incriminate our League with a certain section of the public.'[65] Bennett further warned Geneva to exercise caution, pointing out that the university president alone had authority to allow the use of college buildings, emphasising: *The Government have nothing whatever to do with it ...* see to it that in all public notices ... he is given credit for lending it, and that no whisper of Government aid is made. This is very important.'[66]

The Congress which took place from 8 to 15 July 1926 was attended by 150 delegates representing 20 countries. This was the first gathering of an international organisation to be held in the Irish Free State following its recognition by Britain in 1921. A reception to mark its opening was attended by both Eamon de Valera and W.T. Cosgrave. This first public function attended by both leaders since the civil war attracted much comment.

The Congress was a great success, not least with the Dublin press, which assiduously covered its many social functions. Among these was a garden party given by the Governor-General at the Vice-Regal Lodge, whose guest list spanned a broad range of Irish political, literary and social life. But the work of the Congress was very serious. Within an overall theme of 'Next Steps towards Peace', plenary sessions included speakers and discussion on Colonial and Economic Imperialism, Women and World Peace, Relation of Majorities and Minorities, Conciliation, Arbitration and Disarmament. Addressing the Congress, R.J. Mortished, Assistant Secretary of the Irish Labour Party, admitted that Ireland could scarcely claim to have either an international or pacifist outlook, commenting that: 'The W.I.L. has come to us with a magnificent defiance of the destructive power of hate and a magnificent faith in the power of love informed by intelligence.'[67] At a public meeting held in the Mansion House on the theme 'Next Steps towards World Peace', Jane Addams spoke of the Irish pacifist known the world over – Frank Sheehy Skeffington.[68] In reply, his widow Hanna, representing the Republican group, thanked Addams for her tribute and urged WILPF to continue its stress on peace and freedom, quoting Pearse: 'Ireland unfree can never be at peace.' Her speech aroused great enthusiasm, and it was reported, 'One could sense the emotional pull between the pacifist and militant Republicans, who were still unreconciled to peaceful methods.'[69] One of the British speakers at the Congress – Helena Swanwick – related how dissident members of Irish WILPF ('The Black women') remained outside the conference because they had taken part in the civil war and were still involved with revolutionary republicans: 'Some of our foreign delegations were much puzzled to choose between these rebels and the members of the Irish section, who pursued the same aims, but by other methods.'[70] And there was criticism from some quarters for such action. *International Woman Suffrage News*, complimenting the Irish committee on a successful Congress, noted:

> The only regrettable feature was the use made of the Congress as a platform for intense nationalist propaganda ... We feel [this is] ... a misuse of what should be purely international and pacifist.[71]

Neither the official WILPF Report of the Congress nor its Journal – *Pax International* – mentions these issues, but praise the Irish section for its efficiency and hospitality, and its tact in getting all parties together. But it is clear, from correspondence between Geneva headquarters and Louie Bennett, that there was unease at such incidents. In the lead-up to the 1929 Congress planned for Prague, Mary Sheepshanks confessed to Bennett:

> The prospect of having those Republicans at Prague fills me with dismay. They did their best to spoil the Dublin Congress and did succeed in doing a certain amount of mischief ... I thought they were so bitter and unscrupulous and unfair in their statements, and of course, many of the Germans and Americans were entirely taken in by them. I do hope you can do something to keep them off Prague.[72]

From this correspondence it can be deduced that there were some lively meetings of the IIL in the months before Prague. Ultimately it was decided that the Irish delegates would be Louie Bennett, Hanna Sheehy Skeffington and Rosamund Jacob. At the last minute Bennett could not travel (her mother was seriously ill), but she forwarded a copy of a paper she had been asked to present, on 'The Machinery of Internal Peace'. A copy of this paper came to the attention of Sinn Féin, whose publication of extracts and hostile editorial comments plunged the IIL once more into fierce controversy. Sinn Féin wrote to WILPF in Geneva, taking issue with Bennett's 'misleading and prejudicial comments regarding the state of goverment in Ireland'.[73] Bennett had described Sinn Féin as attracting young people of an adventurous spirit as well as cranks, vagabonds and villains, commenting, 'an irregular minority of this sort inspires fear in Government and constitutional circles.' Outlining a resulting vicious circle of arrests, victimisation, terrorism and reprisals, Bennett also accused Sinn Féin of not being in sympathy with the ideals of Labour, commenting:

> In Ireland, as elsewhere, the Communist is endeavouring to
> exploit nationalism (in its Republican cloak) for his own eco-
> nomic ends ... It is unlikely that Communism will ever gain any
> real economic hold on Ireland; but it can add zest and money to
> the Republican forces.[74]

Immediately the Irish section was thrown into turmoil. At its next
committee meeting, Lucy Kingston noted: 'L.B. is attacked for her
paper by (1) S. Féin (2) Fianna Fáil (3) Republ. members of our
Committee. Find myself on her side for once, and certainly Mrs.
S.S. and the rest shew no mercy ... An implacable crew where "The
Rock of the Republic" is concerned.'[75] Bennett informed Geneva
that Hanna Sheehy Skeffington was particularly enraged:

> All through the past year there has been considerable dissatisfac-
> tion amongst the really pacifist group, owing to the presence on
> the Committee of people who openly state that they consider the
> use of force essential to achieve a social revolution, or to achieve
> national freedom. They lay emphasis on the W.I.L. object of
> freedom rather than peace ... Things have now reached a climax
> ... and I think a split is inevitable.[76]

The situation outlined by Bennett had been complicated further by
the recent election of Maud Gonne MacBride to the IIL committee.
Its then Secretary – Una M'Clintock Dix – had explained to Geneva:
'Realising that a peace committee with Mme MacBride on it was
farce, I wrote to her privately asking her to resign. She refused, after
consulting Mrs Sheehy Skeffington, saying it would not be fair to
those who elected her.'[77]

A series of stormy committee meetings ensued, debate centering
on acceptance of the Washington Object. (This excluded from
membership those who justified defensive warfare and armed
revolution.) A majority decision in favour of the Object was subsequently amended by a smaller gathering. Bennett and Chenevix
were among those who then resigned from the committee. Kingston noted this was 'the saddest W.I.L. Cte. I ever attended'.[78]
Although Dix disliked this show of sharp practice, she acknowledged that it provided a way out of their dilemma and enabled the
group to remain in existence – however precariously. Another
significant factor in the impasse noted by Dix was the clash between the strong personalities of Bennett and Sheehy Skeffington.[79]
WILPF's Geneva office viewed the matter most seriously, placing
it on its executive agenda and pointing out that any serious dissension within a national branch was a source of concern for the whole
League. By spring 1930, the group appeared to have weathered the
storm. Its A.G.M. voted a return to the Washington Object, and
many former members rejoined, including Bennett. Within a few

months, however, a further controversy would prove fatal. From October 1930, IIL members had been collecting signatures for a Disarmament Declaration initiated by WILPF. In the spring of 1931, the IIL, in association with the League of Nations Society, organised a public meeting to debate the issue. It was decided to invite as guest speaker Patrick McGilligan, Minister for External Affairs in the Free State government. The choice of speaker caused uproar among a section of the committee and members, who on losing a subsequent vote to rescind the invitation, announced their intention of disrupting the meeting. The meeting was cancelled, both the President and Secretary resigning in protest. Rosamund Jacob wrote to Geneva, desperately trying to retain some WILPF presence in Ireland, asking if there was a precedent for two groups to operate within one Section where controversial matters arose. Explaining the precise incident, she informed Geneva that some had disagreed with the choice of speaker because of his political association, while others felt that his personal record rendered him quite unsuitable to stand on a platform for peace and freedom:

> The upshot of the affair is that the cleavage which has always existed in our Section has become so definite that we are in danger of a break-up, unless some new method of organisation can be devised. I think the clearest way to describe the cleavage is to say that some of us would put peace before freedom, and others would put freedom before peace.[80]

Despite her efforts, the group disintegrated at this point. Many former members had become active in the Disarmament Movement and were not anxious – and, one gathers, had not the heart and energy – to continue reeling from one controversial split to another. Involvement in the Disarmanent Campaign provided many women with a means to remain involved in the peace process without divisive political arguments. Louie Bennett was among a group who remained involved with WILPF on a personal basis. In response to an attempt by WILPF in Geneva to revive the Irish Section at its 1932 Congress in Grenoble, Lucy Kingston wrote:

> Much as I should like to accept, I do no think there is any chance of restarting the Irish Section at present. We as a 'Disarmament' Committee are doing very similar work to the W.I.L. programme. By keeping to the simple title of Disarmament, we are able to avoid the bringing in of political side-issues which, I must confess, were the pitfall that our Section suffered from. Some of our members considered that the word 'Freedom' in our title gave the excuse for agitation on nationalistic lines in matters which had nothing to do with Peace.[81]

Kingston concluded that perhaps at some future Congress WILPF could be re-organised in Ireland – 'if things change greatly in this country'. It would be almost 60 years before WILPF was re-established in Ireland.[82]

What interpretation can we put from this distance on the foundering of WILPF in Ireland? Can it be seen as a casualty of Irish militarism? That there was debate and concern from 1915 among Irishwomen on the issue of militarism is beyond question. Increasingly such concern focused on militarism within Ireland. Strong political allegiances, allied to radically differing criteria of pacifism, ultimately proved too strong for such a group to continue. Outside the organisation, attitudes to a pacifist stance regarding the Irish question were hostile. The action of Cumann na mBan in the U.S. in 1921 suggested that there was a recognition by nationalists that the views of a pacifist group with strong international connections could be damaging. The issue of justifiable warfare was divisive in many national sections of WILPF – up to and after the Second World War. Ireland in the 1920s was a country recently emerged from insurrection and civil war, and in which many women believed that the struggle for national independence was not yet complete. While condemning militarism in its imperialistic mode, some women accepted the need for further military action to attain national objectives. Such views 'the really pacifist group' in Irish WILPF could not accept. It is a sad irony that the group should founder on differing emphasis between the words 'peace' and 'freedom' in its title.

The Woman Writer as Historical Witness: *Northern Ireland, 1968–1994.* *An Interdisciplinary Perspective* *Catherine B. Shannon*

Introduction

During the past two decades considerable progress has been made in breaking the long historiographical silence surrounding the role of women in the shaping of modern Ireland. Indeed, Margaret MacCurtain has contributed significantly to this process by encouraging the application of the interdisciplinary methodologies and class and gender analyses associated with women's history on the international stage to the Irish historical experience. Gendered reconsiderations of traditional Irish archive materials and exploration of hitherto neglected primary materials from literary, folklore, oral, family and religious sources are reflected in the new perspectives on Irish women's historical experience contained in this volume.

In the Republic of Ireland, there is a growing awareness of the central role of Irish women in major historical events and developments of the modern era. Enrolments in women's history courses are rising, and articles and books on the historical experience of Mná na hÉireann are attracting general readers as well as academe. Even more encouraging are signs of a heightened concern to integrate or 'mainstream' the new research on Irish women in one recently published survey on modern Ireland.[1] Progress has been much slower in uncovering the history of women in Northern Ireland.

Searching for sources

While the origins and nature of the Northern Irish conflict have been researched exhaustively since the 1970s, scholarly analysis on the roles of northern Irish women in the 'Troubles' and the impact of protracted sectarian and political strife on their daily lives was virtually non-existent until the late 1980s. The reasons for this lacuna derived from the same subtle, often unconscious, patriarchal attitudes that influenced most historical and social science methodology until the late 1970s. This silence was compounded by the very traditional roles ascribed to women by the region's Churches and schools and by an economic structure that afforded northern women little time or resources to have their concerns, needs or experience as women studied.

Thus 'women' as a category were largely left out of research which primarily documented the discrimination experienced by northern Catholics and analysed the attitudes of Catholics and Protestants regarding the controversial political issue of the constitutional link with Britain.[2]

An interesting example of this tendency is that, while published statistics on conflict-related deaths have focused on victims' religious affiliation, civilian or security force status, para-military involvement, and location of residence, there are no summary statistics on deaths categorised by gender. Yet women represent between 7 and 8% of the total casualties. Over 251 women ranging in age from infancy to old age, and from every class and walk of life, have been killed. Politically active women have been exposed to great risks, as the assassinations in the late 1970s of republican activists Maire Drumm and Miriam Daly and of Sinn Féin councillor Sheena Campbell in October 1992 have shown. Ten women serving in the Royal Ulster Constabulary and the Ulster Defence Regiment have lost their lives. Women victims have constituted a large proportion of the casualties in the most deadly bombing incidents such as occurred at the Abercorn Restaurant in Belfast city centre on 4 March 1972, in Dublin city centre on 17 May 1974, at the La Mon House Restaurant on 17 February 1978, at Enniskillen on 8 November 1987 and on the Shankill Road on 23 October 1993.[3]

Women married to politicians or men associated with the judicial and law enforcement system lived with the daily reality that their husband's political convictions or occupation could result in a sudden and premature widowhood.

Women in mixed religious marriages have faced similar risks and have often been subject to severe intimidation and even assassination when their very presence in some areas was perceived as a threat to the dominance of the rival political and/or religious tradition.

As mothers, sisters, daughters and wives, northern women have been left literally to pick up the pieces of families and communities fragmented and fractured by 3,226 killings, 39,872 serious injuries, 35,324 shootings, and 14,967 explosions. Especially in the working-class areas of Belfast and Derry where approximately 80% of the violence has occurred, women have had their lives constricted and constrained by grinding poverty, debilitating unemployment, para-military violence and repressive government surveillance.[4] Eavan Boland's plea that women's experience of the 'wrath and grief' of Irish history must move beyond trivial clichés of 'Cathleen Ní Houlihan' and 'Mother Ireland' on the one hand, or 'Orange Lil' on the other, has particular resonance for northern women.[5] For up to 1985, the few works relating to women's experience of the conflict focused principally upon republican women activists in the nationalist community, and provided few insights into the experience of women in Protestant loyalist areas.[6] The files of the major Irish newspapers reveal rare and mostly episodic rather than analytical coverage of the impact of the conflict on northern women's lives. Moreover, the tendency of the British tabloid press to portray northern women as passive victims of para-military mobsters or bomb-throwing viragoes and godmothers of hate ignored the labyrinthine complexities that governed the lives of women living amidst a conflict described as the most intense, protracted and pervasive in Irish history or indeed, with the exception of Bosnia, in any European country since World War II.[7] Efforts to correct these omissions and distortions have been ongoing since the late 1980s. The publication of a number of articles since 1989 on the economic and social status of northern women provides the necessary contextual framework within which historical analysis of the roles and responses of particular women and groups of women to the conflict can proceed.[8]

Yet difficulties remain regarding the availability of primary sources since the letters, diaries and memoirs that northern women may have written during the Troubles are not yet available. Indeed, it is problematic whether women living in the disturbed areas of the north had the time or inclination to record their experiences. Undoubtedly a desire to preserve anonymity regarding their personal political views and experience of the conflict was for many women, but certainly not for all, intimately linked to personal and family security from sectarian intimidation and/or intrusive surveillance by the Royal Ulster Constabulary and British army. The Provisional I.R.A. and Combined Loyalist Military Command ceasefires of autumn 1994 have brought a change of atmosphere which may encourage the eventual publication of revealing personal accounts that can further our historical understanding of women's role in and responses to the conflict.

Using Oral Sources

Meanwhile, since the mid-1980s the techniques of oral history have
been employed with some success to reveal how northern women
attempted to preserve some semblance of normality in their families and communities. A useful pioneering work of this genre was
Only the Rivers Run Free.[9] Compiled immediately after the emotive
1981 Provisional I.R.A. hunger strikes, the focus was primarily on
republican women who had been imprisoned and women supporters from West Belfast and Derry who perceived the Provisional
I.R.A. as freedom fighters and defenders of their communities. The
material captures the burning sense of grievance among nationalist
women that was spawned by the discriminatory policies of the
Stormont regime and subsequently nurtured by internment without trial in 1971, Bloody Sunday in January 1972, the heavy surveillance placed on Catholic nationalist areas by the Royal Ulster
Constabulary and British Army from 1972, and finally by the 1981
hunger strikes. The views and experience of Protestant women
living in loyalist areas of Belfast who felt besieged by the Provisional I.R.A. and abandoned by Britain are portrayed in *The Crack:
a Belfast Year* by Sally Belfrage. This account was especially effective
in drawing attention to women from both nationalist and loyalist
areas, for whom poverty and social deprivation were more pressing concerns than party politics and religious divisions. Fionnuala
O'Connor's recent *In Search of a State*, based on interviews with a
range of northern Catholics, records a considerable heterogeneity
in the political views of contemporary northern Catholic women
and shows how educational advancement and social mobility have
contributed to shifting patterns of political support and diminishing communal cohesiveness in the Catholic community as a
whole.[10] This volume fills an important void in earlier works in the
attention given to women associated with the Social Democratic
and Labour Party, which commands the support of the majority of
northern nationalists.

My own interviews with a wide variety of northern women
demonstrate that factors of class, educational attainment, geo-
graphic location, age and personal temperament and experience
are increasingly more important influences on northern women's
political and party allegiances than the entrenched nationalist or
unionist views of their menfolk or community. Many profess varied hierarchies of personal identity, at odds with the rigid Irish,
British or Ulster categories employed by the identity demogra-
phers and male leaders of Ulster's polarised political ideologies.
The oral sources in general have underscored the crucial roles that

women played during the early civil rights campaigns, in community development initiatives to combat poverty, unemployment, poor housing and health conditions, as well as in reconciliation work and voluntary support services for prisoners, children and those bereaved by the conflict.[11]

The Writer as Historical Witness

Ricoeurian literary theory, which emphasises the mimetic linkages between a writer's time and location with the perceptions of reality contained in imagined literary artefacts, suggests that creative literature by and about northern women who have lived through the conflict constitutes another potentially rich body of material worthy of examination. The benefits of careful and sensitive study of literature as historical evidence which reveals an author's particular concerns and interpretation of historical events are discussed in the proceedings of the 1985 Conference of Irish Historians, *The Writer as Witness: Literature as Historical Evidence.* According to the Irish historians Oliver MacDonagh and Tom Dunne, provided a writer's bias and motivations are understood and taken into account, fictional works have the capacity to vivify, personalise and render concrete the atmosphere and *mentalité* of specific historical moments.[12] It is striking how a number of recent novels, short stories and plays by northern women writers do provide insights on the experiences, attitudes and circumstances of northern women over the past quarter-century. Moreover, these works often reify the complex dynamics of intra-communal ideological tensions over class, gender roles and political allegiances that often are not explored easily through oral interviews. It is from this perspective that I will examine the writing of Anne Devlin, and some work of the Craigavon Women Writers, as examples of literary sources that can provide useful perspectives on the experiences of particular women or groups of women at specified stages of the conflict.

Anne Devlin's Fictional Perspective on 1968-74

In her short story collection *The Way-paver* and especially in her play *Ourselves Alone*, Anne Devlin explores various barriers that northern Catholic women have faced when they challenged the political and religious orthodoxy and traditions of their community and church in pursuit of personal liberation. Indeed, the quest for personal fulfilment is a consistent theme in all Devlin's writing. Her fictional and dramatic voice draws on her own experience of the early years of the conflict as well as her family background as the daughter of Paddy Devlin, a Belfast Catholic trade union activist who, as a founding member of the Northern Ireland Civil Rignts Association in 1968, played a prominent role in civil rights marches.[13]

Two stories in *The Way-paver* collection recreate the major events and atmosphere surrounding political disintegration in Northern Ireland between 1968 and 1974 from the perspective of two young women facing traumatic times and difficult dilemmas. In *Passages*, Devlin conveys through her central character, Laura, the initial hopes the civil rights campaign in 1968 held for the typical Catholic female university student, newly exposed to then-trendy Marxist interpretations of history. This approach challenged both the ex-clusionist official British history as taught in the Protestant state schools, and the irredentist assumptions of Irish history contained in the curricula of many northern Catholic secondary schools. As Laura explains:

> It was the beginning of the civil rights movement, when educated Catholics had awakened to political consciousness. Coming from Portstewart, I never had any sense of discrimination that Catho-lics in the city seemed to feel. It never occurred to me that there were official and unofficial histories. Or that Protestants could go through school never having heard of Parnell or the Land League. I always thought that history was simply a matter of scholarship. In the seminars during my first year at the university the students were fighting and hacking and forging out of the whole mess of historical detail a theory which made it seem right for them to march through the streets of Belfast to demand equal rights for Catholics.[14]

Laura's rejection of her parents' deferential attitudes to the Protes-tant regime by her participation in a march to Derry is a fictional replication of the famous People's Democracy march to the Maiden City in January 1969, which first propelled Bernadette Devlin, then a Queen's University student, to fame. The anxieties of many parents of Catholic students, that they were risking hard-won academic opportunities and inviting a violent unionist backlash, is reflected in her father's response to the student protests that had begun the previous autumn. 'The fools and trouble-makers, that's what they are, a fine peaceful little country here. What do they want to go making trouble for?' When Laura publicly criticised her father for exhibiting petty bourgeois self-interest, after he said he could not afford a political viewpoint regarding the controversies of Northern Ireland politics, and for defending the Ulster unionist Prime Minister Terence O'Neill as a decent fellow, he responded in anger:

> That's the stuff! You young ones with your education will tell them boys at Stormont where to get off! ... If that's all the good a

university education has done for you I rue the day you ever went to that place ... Your mother and I broke our backs scraping and saving to give you a chance. If this is how you repay us you can take yourself out of here back to your friends in Belfast with their clever remarks and smart ways; but don't ever come here again, shaming me in front of my friends.[15]

His attitude reflected the anxieties of those middle-class Catholics who wanted to give O'Neill time to implement the modest electoral and housing reforms he promised the previous November. In addition there were fears, even among some civil rights activists, that the provocative marching tactics advocated by the student-led People's Democracy would fuel hard-line unionist resistance to reform, as well as endanger the modest gains Catholics had made since World War II.[16]

Anne Devlin's fictional representation of severe unionist backlash and serious communal discord in this story resonates with the actual historical reality. Her father, who actually endorsed the Derry march, helped in successful efforts to protect the students from loyalist attacks in the early stages of the People's Democracy march. However, at Burntollet Bridge, a few miles from Derry, and before the eyes of the mainly Protestant auxiliary police force, known as the B-Specials, the students were viciously attacked by cudgel-swinging Protestant mobs whose ire had been whipped up by the fiery Presbyterian preacher Ian Paisley and Major Ronald Bunting. Anne Devlin, then a student at Coleraine, was among those injured when she was knocked unconscious into the river and subsequently was hospitalised for a concussion.[17] Over the next six months, the civil rights agenda was overwhelmed by sectarian rioting in Newry, Lurgan, and especially Belfast, substantiating the fears of many moderate Catholics such as were represented by the fictional father.[18] In the story, Laura's decision, immediately following these brutal attacks at Burntollet Bridge and later in Derry, to jettison her strict Catholic training by sleeping with her Marxist boyfriend, suggests growing pessimism regarding the efficacy of the civil rights approach in the face of deep sectarian division. The author's own conviction, and indeed her father's, that Northern Ireland began a steady descent into madness in 1969, precisely when civil rights and socialism were swamped by rising unionist paranoia and the recrudescence of irredentist Irish republicanism, is symbolised by the mental breakdown Laura suffered shortly after she lost both her sexual and intellectual innocence. Devlin does not address here the important issue of the British government's culpability for the deepening crisis, given its ongoing failure to protect the Catholic minority by timely intervention, an action that would have been legally justifiable under the Government of Ireland Act, 1920. Devlin deals with the consequences of belated and ultimately bungled British intervention in another story.

The short story *Naming the Names* is set against the background of a deteriorating political situation beginning with the arrival of British troops in Belfast in August 1969 through to 1974 when the level of violence was at its peak.[19] Sent ostensibly to protect the nationalist population from attacks by enraged loyalists, the British army's role was quickly transformed into one of counter-insurgency against an expanding and increasingly effective Provisional I.R.A.

Devlin explains with some sympathy how a typical teenage Catholic girl, whom she calls Finn McQuillen, might have been drawn into active support for the republican para-militaries during this period. Since her parents' home was too crowded, Finn lived with her crippled Granny, who, by telling Finn stories of having once met Eamon de Valera and Countess Markievicz, two heroes of the 1916 Easter Rising, exposed her granddaughter to republican folklore which, in actual fact, was preserved only in a small segment of West Belfast families with links to the old I.R.A. Finn's romantic republican sympathies became more militant after her grandmother narrowly escaped death on 14 August 1969, when Protestant mobs from the nearby Shankill torched her Conway Street home and other streets and factories on the lower Falls Road, while local police stood idly by. With her grandmother hospitalised and herself homeless, Finn never returned to school. Two years later, after taking a job in a second-hand bookshop on the bomb-scarred Falls Road, Finn met the man, apparently with Provisional I.R.A. connections, who had rescued her grandmother while dodging a hail of bottles and stones thrown by a Protestant mob. Immediately after the introduction of internment in August 1971, Finn offered her services to the movement she now considered her protector. Her first duties were to use the shop as a cover from which to pay weekly allotments to the wives of republican internees. Through her job, she met and became friendly with a young historian researching an Oxford thesis on Gladstone and Home Rule. When their casual discussions about Irish history and his grandfather's service in Ulster Volunteers of 1912-14 revealed his links to the Ulster Protestant establishment, Finn faced a real dilemma over where her loyalties lay. This was particularly so after she witnessed an army patrol shoot a young Provisional I.R.A. man trying to escape arrest. He was a childhood friend and his father had rescued her grandmother. When she finally realised she had fallen in love with her historian friend, it was too late. Finn had already reported to the movement that he was the son of a judge. Although she realised 'he was my last link with life ...' and that she would forever carry her guilt, she did not refuse the Provisional I.R.A. request to set up the young man for assassination, nor did she reveal to the police after her arrest the names of any republicans involved in the murder. Instead, she simply repeated a litany of the names of tiny West Belfast streets recently obliterated by a combination of bombings and urban redevelopment: 'Abyssinia, Alma, Balaclava, Balkan, Belgrade, Bosnia'.

Devlin's rendering in a Joycean manner of the deteriorating political situation, depressing physical details and ghettoised atmosphere that characterised the war-torn Lower Falls during the early 1970s draws upon her intimate knowledge of this area and these events. Her father, grandparents and great-grandparents had once been residents of Conway Street. Paddy Devlin personally witnessed the failure of the Royal Ulster Constabulary to interfere when loyalists forced the Conway residents, many of them elderly former neighbours, from their homes prior to torching the houses on 14 August 1969.[20] Subsequently he was involved in securing accommodation and financial help from Stormont officials as well as the Dublin government for these victims. Interruption of schooling owing to the turmoil of 1969-72 was a common experience of a number of republican women whom I have interviewed. Distribution of funds to families of internees from money collected from republican sympathisers in the Republic of Ireland and the United States did take place in the early stages of internment. Even more powerful is the author's imagined understanding of how the confluent pressures of political allegiance, communal loyalty and personal indebtedness for past protection during these traumatic years might drive a young woman to actively support the Provisional I.R.A. by providing intelligence and other services, irrespective of the consequences for her own personal happiness. On a symbolic level, Finn's story is a personification of the principal factors which enabled the Provisional I.R.A. to gain greater support among young people in nationalist West Belfast by the mid-1970s.

Anne Devlin's Dramatic Perspective on 1981-84

Devlin's 1984 stage play *Ourselves Alone* has a heavy ideological content, yet it still provides telling insights regarding the conditions and atmosphere in staunchly republican areas of West Belfast in the early 1980s.[21] Although then residing in England, an extended stay in Belfast in 1983 enabled Devlin to frame her strong critique of Irish republicanism in scenes, dialogue and plot that replicate closely the conditions after the 1981 hunger strikes which triggered a dramatic rise in popular and eventually electoral support for the republican political wing, Provisional Sinn Féin.[22] There were still hundreds of Provisional I.R.A. men in jail, leaving their wives and girlfriends to cope with increased family obligations and often social isolation. This period also featured bitter discord between the Provisional I.R.A. and Official I.R.A. and their respective political wings, Provisional Sinn Féin and the Workers' Party, the latter having rejected para-military violence for a constitutional approach to secure social and economic reform beneficial to both Catholic and Protestant workers. Women's rights were just beginning to enter public debate in the north, in response to vigorous lobbying efforts by feminist activists as well as to the bitter abortion debate then raging prior to the 1984 referendum which made abortion unconstitutional in the Republic of Ireland. Indeed, by 1983 Provisional Sinn Féin, in deference to the rising feminist consciousness of its younger female members, a number of whom had served in prison, set up a Women's Department, allocated a quarter of its thirty-two executive council seats to women and proclaimed as party policy its opposition to all forms of oppression against women.[23] This era also witnessed among Irish constitutional nationalists a questioning of the traditional interpretations of Easter 1916 and the War of Independence that glorified the fallen dead and the irredentist goals of Irish nationalism.[24]

Against this historical background, Anne Devlin portrays her perception of a republican movement flawed by patriarchy and an indifference to the damaging impact of its sacrificial traditions on the nationalist community, and especially the women, whom it was supposed to be liberating. The play's title provides an ironic twist since Sinn Féin, the Gaelic name of the Provisional I.R.A. political wing, translates literally to 'Ourselves Alone'. In relating the stories of three Belfast women in their late twenties, Devlin maintains that even women deeply committed to the republican cause, or simply to the men in it, were often used and abused by insecure and egotistical men in the name of national liberation. Josie McCoy symbolises the first type while Donna, her common-law sister-in-law, represents the latter. As the common-law wife of Liam McCoy, Donna is a pathetic figure who, upon becoming pregnant in her teens, was forced into a loveless marriage to save her family's reputation. She had to give up her son when she left the child's father to live with Liam, who was jailed shortly later for para-military offences. Marooned in her house, Donna spends her days awaiting Liam's return, popping tranquillisers, and providing hospitality and hiding for any volunteer whom Liam's father, Malachy, a local republican boss, brings into her home. Significantly, Donna is never consulted about the use of her home for para-military planning sessions or as a hide-out for arms and men, despite the fact that a previous army search left her house and nerves in shambles.

Josie, Liam's sister and Malachy's daughter, drifts into active republican service basically from family tradition. She becomes more militant in response to repressive surveillance policies and the religious and political discrimination that keeps her unemployed despite her university degree. Josie's competent service as a courier catches the attention of a local republican commander, Cathal O'Donnell. Fascinated by his power and status, Josie becomes his lover even though he never leaves his wife and children.

Frieda McCoy, Josie's younger sister, feels little obligation to sacrifice her personal ambitions and dreams for the republican cause and thereby represents the authorial voice of Anne Devlin. Something of a free spirit, she plans to give up her job as a hairdresser once her talents as a singer and songwriter are discovered. Frieda prefers rock and roll, but her patrons in the local republican drinking club usually press her for patriotic songs that blend well with the wall decorations, portraits of the ten dead hunger-strikers. In fact, the opening scene in which Frieda sings 'The men behind the wire' reflects the actual atmosphere, appearance and entertainment that then prevailed in local republican clubs such as the Felon's Club in West Belfast.[25]

Space does not permit an extensive elaboration of the plot, but a few instances that illustrate the pressures confronting women in republican areas in the early 1980s are noteworthy. Oral material as well as official studies have shown that women in heavily-armed areas of the north were more vulnerable to sexual harassment, exploitation and domestic violence, owing to the easy availability of guns. Many were reluctant to seek police help for fear of retaliation for bringing the police into the area, or because this might endanger a republican or indeed a loyalist activist whose political position they otherwise supported.[26] Such conditions are hinted at in the play, when Frieda reports having felt extremely intimidated when a rehearsal left her the only woman among a group of men in the club and when her father strikes her because she was consorting with a 'Stickie', John McDermott. Her father is especially enraged because McDermott, a Protestant, was soliciting support for the Workers' Party campaign against the referendum calling for a constitutional ban on abortion in the south.[27] Having had her ideological loyalty as well as her virtue questioned by her father, she leaves west Belfast to take up residence near Queen's University with McDermott.

The abortion referendum alluded to here succeeded and brought a constitutional ban on abortion in the republic in 1984. The Sinn Féin leadership was reluctant to oppose vigorously this constitutional ban, maintaining instead that it was unnecessary since abortion was already illegal under Irish law. Malachy's reaction to McDermott partially reflects the attitudes of the more conservative Catholics within the republican community. Although two years later a pro-choice resolution was passed by a narrow two votes at the Sinn Féin party convention, this was reversed the following year. Again the Sinn Féin leadership feared that a pro-choice policy would alienate its more conservative Catholic supporters. What is perhaps more significant is that all eight women on the party executive voted to reverse the new policy in 1986. Despite the incorporation of feminist planks into the Sinn Féin party platform in the early 1980s, knowledgeable observers, including the late Cathy Harkin of Derry, continued to see a huge gap between the stated policy on women's equality and its acceptance by the male rank and file in daily life.[28] On the other hand, republican women were not as cowering as the play suggests, for in early 1984 republican women activists were included among the 500 working-class nationalist women who participated in a 'Women Reclaim the Night' march immediately following two sexual assaults in west Belfast.[29]

The fear of invasive police searches, and the anxiety felt by women in republican families when their men were on a mission, are illustrated by a scene in which Donna and Josie hear rattling bin lids in the background, the signal frequently used in republican areas to warn of an impending raid. An obviously nervous Donna says:

> I'm glad Liam's in prison – God forgive me – it means I don't have
> to lie awake waiting for them to come for him. Listening to every
> sound. I wouldn't go through that again for anything. I hope they
> are not going to raid us. I only got the carpets down at Christmas.
> I'll never get the doors to close. That happened the last time they
> came. They pulled up the carpets and half the floorboards. That
> was after your brother got arrested and I'd no one to help me put
> them back.[30]

Donna's dependence on tranquillisers to cope with her loneliness and her anxieties reflects the contemporary statistics showing an annual tranquilliser consumption rate for Northern Ireland of 35 million by the early 1980s, with women having twice the prescription rate of men.[31] Moreover, Donna's fear of another raid has an historical authenticity given the relatively high rates of searches that still prevailed in republican neighbourhoods through to 1982.[32]

During the 1970s, the republican movement actively encouraged young female recruits to emulate women like Countess Markievicz or Mary MacSwiney, whose contributions to the struggle for independence between 1916 and 1921 were legendary. Articles on heroines in the republican pantheon, on female internees as well as interviews with mothers of serving republican prisoners and those on hunger strike, frequently appeared in *An Phoblacht* or *Republican News*. During the H-Block campaign, the same paper occasionally reported public demonstrations and protests which featured remarks by old women with personal and family links to republicanism of the 1916-to-1922 era. Until a few years ago, a mural depicting an Irish mother holding her dead Provisional I.R.A. son in a Pieta-like portrait was carefully maintained on a west Belfast gable wall, providing a visual reminder of the centrality of the sacrificial motif within the republican tradition.

Similar appeals to this sacrificial Mother Ireland tradition are illustrated and then condemned in the play through Devlin's authorial voice, when Frieda proclaims that, unlike her sister Josie, she will not be a compliant messenger only to end up like their Aunt Cora. During the failed republican campaign of the 1950s, Cora had lost both her hands and her eyesight while moving hidden ammunition for her brother Malachy. Even though the current leadership 'stick her [Cora] out at the front of the parades every so often to show the women of Ireland what their patriotic duty should be', Frieda is not stirred by such appeals. She refuses to consider the hunger-strikers unblemished heroes and repeats to her father the widely-circulated rumour that Bobby Sands beat his wife. She tells him 'We are the dying. Why are we mourning them?'[33] Indeed, she rejects the whole republican enterprise by declaring her total indifference to the goal of Irish unity, and insists that British withdrawal will do nothing to liberate Josie and Donna from a life of service and sacrifice for their men.[34]

The sexual relationships depicted in the play mirror a gradual loosening of strict observance of Catholic moral codes and an increase in premarital co-habitation of young people from the most deprived areas of west Belfast. On the other hand, the obsessive jealousy of the play's male characters towards their wives and girlfriends highlights the contemporary pressures put upon partners of imprisoned republicans to remain 'faithful'.[35] Yet Josie's service to the republican cause and her faithfulness to O'Donnell came to nothing, for he refused to leave his wife and ten children. Josie subsequently falls in love with a recently-arrived republican activist, Joe Conran, whom she had interrogated for her superiors. Her subsequent pregnancy by Conran prompts an admission of war-weariness and a poignant longing for a normal life.

> I'm tired. Tired of this endless night watch. I've been manning the barricades since 'sixty-nine. I'd like to stop for a while, look around me, plant a garden, listen for other sounds; the breathing of a child somewhere outside Andersonstown.[36]

However, Conran proves to be a British agent whose intelligence eventually secures the arrest of O'Donnell and other republicans. Josie and Malachy are forced to leave Belfast, fearing retaliation by the leadership for her failure to discover Conran's true identity during her interrogation. Certainly, the Provisional I.R.A. is known to have executed members suspected of betraying the organisation, but we do not know the disciplinary actions which might have followed failures like Josie's, or even if a female volunteer would have conducted the kind of interrogation depicted in the play.[37]

Frieda discovers that living with McDermott in the allegedly neutral university district is hardly an improvement over west Belfast. She feels watched every time she leaves the house and worries that his connections to the Workers' Party will invite hostility from their neighbours. Ultimately, Frieda decides to leave for England, after a brick comes flying through the window with a note proclaiming 'This is a Protestant street.' In reality, while intimidation had fallen significantly since the early 70s, it had not disappeared entirely, and the area near the university known as the Holy Land experienced such instances in the early 1980s. Indeed, Devlin recalled in her short story *Five Notes After a Visit*, and in a 1986 interview, her own anxiety regarding her personal safety as a Catholic living in a Protestant area.[38]

In the play, Frieda is the only one who defies the constraints imposed by patriarchy and the republican tradition in order to secure her own liberation. In bidding good-bye to Donna, she proclaims: 'I'd rather be lonely than suffocate ... It is Ireland I am leaving' – a peroration which echoes James Joyce, as well as the author's view that happiness and fulfilment will only come to those women who refuse to serve the republican cause and to be constrained by the patriarchal influences within northern culture and society.

Evaluating this play as historical evidence requires that it be read on two levels – first for its specific sociological and historical detail, and second as a literary example of the contemporary debates regarding the relationship of republicanism to feminism, as well as the content of republican ideology and its acceptance of violence to achieve a united Ireland. On the first level, as noted above, the play effectively conveys how unemployment, poverty, and well-founded fears for their own security kept republican women activists and men physically and socially isolated in their own neighbourhoods, living in what one authority has termed 'a prison culture'.[39] These conditions, along with the rigidity of Margaret Thatcher's northern policy, increased republican resolve and made much questioning of the appropriateness of republican tactics by rank and file men like Malachy, Liam and O'Donnell less likely. Indeed, there was a good deal of optimism within the republican ranks at this juncture, owing to the international sympathy and attention generated by the hunger strikes and Sinn Féin's success in winning over 100,000 votes and the west Belfast seat in the 1983 Westminster election. By her actions and especially in her dialogue with Josie, Frieda acts as a foil to Josie's republican orthodoxy and unwavering commitment. She symbolises and articulates the views of those who did not accept the legitimacy of the republican analysis of the cause of the conflict, or the use of violence for political ends. By echoing aspects of the contemporary and bitter debates then being waged between the constitutional nationalists and republicans, between revisionist and anti-revisionist historians, and between republican women activists and their feminist critics, the play does indeed personalise and render concrete the atmosphere of the time.

Yet the intensity of Devlin's hostility to contemporary republicanism inevitably obscures the existence of large groups of women in republican areas whose responses were not as stereotypical as Josie's and Donna's. As I have observed elsewhere, many working-class west Belfast women, including Sinn Féin supporters, campaigned actively for improved housing, health services and a women's centre on the Falls Road where women experiencing the difficulties represented by Donna could seek help and advice. The female characters do not convey the struggle of younger women within Sinn Féin in the early 1980s to ensure that a progressive policy on women was reflected in the party platform, nor that they saw no contradiction between fighting for the liberation of their country and the liberation of women. For them patriarchy and imperialism were two sides of the same coin and the fight to devalue both had to be waged simultaneously.[40] Rita O'Hare articulated this position in her 1980 Ard Fheis speech and these views were echoed by other activists at this time. Nonetheless, the play does reflect the contentions of some feminists that the stated party policy on women's equality had not yet made an impact upon the views and actions of the male party rank and file.[41]

It is important to stress that, unlike the fictional Frieda, most west Belfast women who might have agreed with aspects of Devlin's critique of republicanism did not have the option of exile. As recent research examining political attitudes by gender suggests, there was probably no marked difference between male and female electoral choices in the hotly contested 1983 west Belfast parliamentary election.[42] Thus it is reasonable to conclude that many west Belfast women registered their reservations about the republican analysis and tactics by casting votes for Joe Hendron, the S.D.L.P. candidate, and Gerry Fitt, the independent incumbent. Together these two candidates received 47.8% of the votes cast, compared to the 36.9% which went to Sinn Féin's Gerry Adams. Some of the most dedicated party workers for the S.D.L.P. are women, and the party's central office is run by Gerry Cosgrove, who lives in the lower Falls area of west Belfast.[43]

Anne Devlin certainly was not unique in her view that the ideology, structure and tactics of contemporary republicanism were inimical to the best interests of women. Similar indictments were made by other northern women such as the late Cathy Harkin of Derry, who believed issues of domestic violence, easier access to contraception, divorce, and equitable employment conditions were greater priorities.[44]

It is important to note that the theoretical doubts that Anne Devlin held about republicanism's compatibility with feminism, as well as about the legitimacy of nationalism, were undoubtedly exacerbated by the difficulties her family experienced as a result of the political positions advocated by her father during this era. Paddy Devlin's public criticism of Provisional I.R.A. violence and also of the hunger strikes provoked an orchestrated campaign of harassment and intimidation against him by republican extremists. His Andersonstown home was besieged for a month following the 5 May 1981 death of Bobby Sands, the hunger striker who had been elected M.P. for Fermanagh-Tyrone in a Westminster by-election in April. Devlin's sons were assaulted at school and neighbours who tried to assist the family were also intimidated, ultimately forcing the family to leave Andersonstown for a north Belfast residence. Devlin's electoral popularity suffered a severe reversal in the polarised atmosphere that surrounded Belfast City Council elections on 20 May. He received only 1,343 first preference votes compared to the 7,000 he polled in 1977.[45] Two years later, in the bitterly contested 1983 Westminster elections, Sinn Féin won 13.4% of the total poll and over 40% of the nationalist vote. Gerry Fitt, a former S.D.L.P. colleague of Paddy Devlin who also opposed the hunger strikes, lost the west Belfast seat he had held since 1966 to Gerry Adams by 5,000 votes. Obviously, these were very disturbing results to Anne Devlin on both ideological and personal grounds.

Thus the intensity of the critique of republicanism in *Ourselves Alone* does not rest solely on opposition to patriarchy, but undoubtedly emanates also from the author's intention to deliver as strong a condemnation of the republican movement and the sectarian politics of Northern Ireland as possible. Her success in doing so was reflected perhaps in the warm reception *Ourselves Alone* received from London critics and audiences as well as by the awards the play received.[46] Devlin's play is a telling example of how a talented dramatist can entertain her audience and simultaneously engage in 'politics by other means'. On the eve of her August 1986 Royal Court opening, Devlin acknowledged that in writing *Ourselves Alone*, she was attempting to work out her political and personal views. She had lost faith in abstract theoretical solutions promising a better future and increasingly judged political options and processes by what they offered an individual now. Political allegiances could not be divorced from personal morality. Devlin concisely summarised the political message she intended in the following comment:

> If you are required to die for a cause, it has to offer something better than what you have got. Let's look at our relationships, look at what you've got. If you butcher and murder and kill to get somewhere, it won't stop when you get there.[47]

Thus Devlin's entertaining and successful play qualifies as historical evidence which provides useful insights regarding a specific period of the conflict, but which, like all forms of historical evidence, must be carefully evaluated so that its bias, motivation and limitations are acknowledged and understood.

Recent Writing By and About Northern Women

In the decade since Anne Devlin wrote her play, a feminist consciousness has developed among an increasing number of northern women. There is greater recognition that they have suffered common wrongs and that their subordination is societally determined. Northern women display an increasing willingness, despite differ-

ences in political allegiances and religious backgrounds, to act
co-operatively to remedy these wrongs and to provide an alternative vision of society conducive to autonomy and self-determination for both women and men. Significant steps to alleviate
communal isolation, to facilitate cross-community contacts and to
deal with generic gender problems have been taken by the
Women's Information Group and more recently the Women's
Support Network, an umbrella organisation of 192 women's
groups, which co-ordinates information on services available to
women. In 1990, Protestant women from the Shankill joined with
Catholic women in protests which eventually overturned the decision of the unionist-dominated Belfast City Council to cut funding
for the Falls Road Women's Centre. The mutual trust and good-will
flowing from these efforts eventually led to the Belfast visit in
February 1992 of President Mary Robinson, during which she met
women from all sections of the community. This was the first time
an Irish president had crossed the border, and was followed by
other presidential visits conducive to better cross-border relations.
The benefits of such cross-community co-operation in pursuit of
common goals has not gone unnoticed by men from the deprived
working-class areas of Belfast and Derry. At a public session in
Boston in late October 1994, representatives of the Combined Loyalist Military Command acknowledged the influence of the women
in their communities in convincing them to replicate the Provisional I.R.A. ceasefire. The Reaching Common Ground conference,
held in Boston two weeks later, provided considerable evidence
that northern women, while acknowledging their differences, are
determined to support the ongoing peace process.[48]

This growing confidence and political awareness and co-operation of northern women is evident in the process that produced two
anthologies of writing by the Craigavon Women Writers.[49] The
group, called the Dolly Mixtures, is religiously and politically
mixed and consists mostly of women from working-class backgrounds who live in or near Craigavon's Brownlow estate. Initially
intended as a model estate with easy access to employment in a
local tire factory, living conditions in Brownlow deteriorated
sharply in the 1970s and 1980s owing to economic recession, government neglect and the impact of the conflict. The Dolly Mixtures
meet weekly to discuss their poems, short stories, essays and even
plays, all of which reflect aspects of women's experience of the
'Troubles'. Much of the writing is therapeutic, helping women who
have lost husbands, parents, children and friends in the conflict to
deal with their grief and pain. The volumes convey a strong sense

of the emotional and psychological impact that poverty, unemployment, and sectarian conflict have had on these Craigavon women and their families. Some contributions reflect a growing anger over the arrogance of both republican and loyalist para-militaries taking life for 'their cause', while others reflect frustration with the British government's slow response in answering charges of human rights abuses by security forces.

The anthologies were conceived by Philomena Gallagher, a mother of three, who returned to school in her mid-thirties to gain secondary school credentials. Her contributions are noteworthy as remembrances of innocent individuals who have been killed. Her writing and that of Madge Steele reflect the growing efforts of northern women to promote tolerance, compassion and understanding in their divided community. Overall the message that emerges from these volumes is the women's determination to make peace an everyday reality. One poem in particular, by Madge Steele, reflects the success of the Craigavon women in finding their common humanity.

> Weave the threads of real friendship
> With the colours of life
> Use the pattern of Peace
> And leave out the strife
> Thread the friends that are young
> Along with the old
> And you'll find on your loom
> A fabric of gold.[50]

Conclusion

The anthologies of the Dolly Mixtures are literary artefacts that exemplify the continuous efforts of many northern Irish women, especially those in the working class, to overcome the bitterness and hatreds rooted in the north's turbulent history by openly expressing their past hurts, current fears as well as hopes and aspirations for the future. In doing so, these women are discovering much shared common ground and they are helping to plant seeds of tolerance and trust upon which a just and lasting peace ultimately depends.

Significantly, a heightened political awareness and a desire to build upon previous cross-community co-operative initiatives of women became apparent in the wake of the 1994 ceasefires and the publication in February 1995 of the Joint Framework Documents[51] by the British and Irish governments. Within two weeks of their publication, various local women's groups convened meetings to examine the implications of the framework proposals for women and began to insist on a role for women in the shaping of any new structures to emerge from the proposed multi-party peace talks. In late spring 1995, a committee of twenty-five women representing the voluntary, trade union, academic, religious, and local community sectors organised the conference 'Women, Politics and Ways Forward', which was attended by 160 women at the Rural College in Draperstown on 24 June 1995. Various tactics and strategies designed to increase women's participation in public bodies, in political parties, and especially in the peace process, were proposed. This was an historic occasion, as it was the first time that women from all political spectrums gathered to discuss the serious political issues regarding northern women's exclusion from decision-making bodies and the political process.[52] Four months later, over 400 women from all walks of life convened in Belfast's Europa Hotel, on 4 November 1995, for the 'Women Shaping the Future Conference'. In addition to highlighting the past contributions of women in sustaining the social infrastructure of Northern Ireland during a quarter-century of conflict, recommendations were made to increase the influence of women in northern politics through networking, information sharing and finally by establishing cross-party political groupings.[53]

In addressing women's political participation as a human rights issue and in stressing the potential contribution which women's unique skills and experience could make in negotiating a permanent political settlement, the Draperstown and Belfast conferences, in conjuction with consistent lobbying between 1992 and 1996 by the Northern Ireland European Women's Platform, helped to lay the groundwork for the establishment of the Northern Ireland Women's Coalition (N.I.W.C.) in April 1996. The coalition had seventy women candidates in the special 30 May 1996 elections which were held to determine the level of political party representation at the official peace negotiations in June. The election also selected delegates to the Northern Ireland Forum, a consultative body, modelled on the Republic of Ireland's Forum for Peace and Reconciliation, and designed to promote consensus through dialogue. The N.I.W.C. campaigned on a manifesto that stressed policies of political inclusiveness, equity and respect for human rights. While acknowledging that their candidates often had conflicting political perspectives on the constitutional question, the coalition maintained that there was consensus on the need for a bill of rights as well as on an array of social and economic issues affecting women, families and local communities. While strong political convictions on the constitutional issue led many northern women to vote for the existing political parties, the coalition polled 7,731 votes, enough to secure two seats for N.I.W.C. at the negotiation table and in the Northern Ireland Forum.[54] The two delegates elected reflect the cross-community principles of the coalition. Monica McWilliams, a university lecturer with extensive experience in lobbying and campaigning for civil and women's rights, is a Catholic from a nationalist and rural background, while Pearl Sagar is a Protestant from east Belfast with extensive experience in community politics and development. Although it is too early to determine the long-range political future of the coalition, it was a significant historical breakthrough to have two women participating as elected representatives in ongoing negotiations designed to shape democratic, political and constitutional structures for the people of Northern Ireland.

The obstacles which the region's entrenched political, religious and economic divisions pose for feminist politics and unity, and indeed for a permanent peace, are still immense.[55] There is, however, a dawning recognition that significant progress in building a just society in Northern Ireland will be enhanced by drawing on and institutionalising the energies and commitment of the large numbers of women who are experienced in community politics, but who have been excluded heretofore from the formal political and economic power structures.

The works examined in this essay as well as those of other northern writers provide many insights into the huge costs that protracted political conflict have meant for northern women and their families.[56] Yet all these works have additional historical significance to the extent that they frame important theoretical debates about feminism's relationship to republicanism and loyalism, and about the role of women in northern society in general. They pose for their readers questions that challenge both green and orange nationalism to purge their respective traditions of patriarchal, arrogant and exclusivist elements. Only time and future historians can tell whether the rising feminist consciousness documented in these works will eventually succeed in bringing real and substantial improvement to the everyday lives of women, as well as to the entire Northern Irish community.

Towards a New Ireland:
Women, Feminism & the Peace Process
Mary Cullen

As a feminist, I have been particularly interested in two features of
the peace process over the past few years: the claims for women's
participation in the public negotiations and the grassroots arena
where community groups and women's groups have developed
their own politics. I was privileged to be present at the first Clar na
mBan conference in March 1994 where nationalist and republican
women expressed openly their concern at the exclusively male and
secretive nature of the negotiations then in progress and their
insistence that any agreed new Ireland must take on board a much
broader range of discriminations and conflicting interests than
simply those of the nationalist-unionist nexus. Since then, I have
taken part in many debates about the relationship between women
and the peace process, and have watched with interest and sympathy the emergence of the Northern Ireland Women's Coalition
which crossed the conventional political divides and won itself a
place at the negotiating table.

It has become increasingly clear that the peace process, as presently structured, has no space for serious discussion of a new
Ireland in any holistic sense. Its remit is to deal with nationalist/un-
ionist conflict within a narrow green versus orange model of Irish
politics. I also believe that it is feminism rather than women *per se*
that has the potential to make a radical contribution to debate about
a new Ireland. Putting these two together, it appears to me that the
best way feminists can try to ensure that this potential is realised, and,
paradoxically, the best way we can support the women actively
participating in the peace process, is by working outside the process
to develop a serious internal debate about feminism itself and between feminists and other groups interested in radical change in
society. In this paper I try to explain and justify this conclusion.

When we talk about women and the peace process, we need to
be clear whether we mean the right to take part in the negotiations,

or the contribution women might make to them, or both of these. One claim that women should participate equally with men in the process is based on the argument that women are as fully citizens as men are, and that the dearth of women among the negotiators is due to discrimination based on sex. This does not necessarily imply that women would act differently than men as negotiators, but neither does it exclude the possibility that they might. Another claim to participation includes an explicit or implicit argument that women's contribution is different to men's but equally valuable.

If we think women have a different contribution to make, we need to ask in what way it is different. We might think women in general are more capable of resolving conflict by negotiation and compromise than men in general, and less inclined to use force of any kind to impose a solution. Or our view might be that women are in general more inclined towards peace at any price, even if that includes leaving an issue of perceived injustice unresolved. On the contrary, we might believe women are *more* interested than men in a just solution that seeks to provide for the legitimate needs of all parties, where men tend to opt for a winner and loser situation.

If we believe any of these things, we have to ask on what grounds we do so. One explanation would be that women and men are in some way biologically programmed to think and act differently. Another is that the different social experience of being a female or a male teaches the sexes different values and/or strategies. Yet another would argue that the sex-role stereotypes to which we are socialised to conform condone, foster or encourage different ways of thinking and acting for each sex.

The whole question of male and female 'human nature' is fraught with uncertainties and unresolved questions. Whatever 'biological' differences may exist between the sexes in ways of perceiving and interpreting the environment, and acting to change it, over the centuries these have been so interwoven with social and political interventions that disentangling them is no easy task. Observed differences in general patterns of behaviour between the sexes, in particular with regard to male 'dominance' and female 'subordination', have yet to be explained. Explanations indeed abound but all have the standing of hypotheses, and none has established itself beyond challenge.

Nor is the evidence of history decisive. More physical violence has been and is perpetrated by men than by women, and this cannot be fully explained by saying that in general men are physically stronger, and so more often in a position where they can exercise physical violence at little risk to themselves. This might apply to violence by men against women, but not to violence between men or to violence against children. The role of masculine stereotypes which include aggression and the use of physical force need evaluation. To what extent do these stereotypes reflect the real 'nature' of males or are they are essentially socially-constructed models to which males are pressurised to conform? On the other hand, it is difficult to maintain that women are inherently more committed to peace than men. Women are obviously capable of aggressive behaviour and the use of verbal and physical force. It could be argued that the lesser use of force by women is the result of both lesser opportunity *and* the power of social stereotypes of appropriate female behaviour. Nor does history show a consistent pattern of women as a group actively opposing war. It shows instead that the majority of women, like the majority of men, have supported their own group or country and helped in its war effort. While men have for the most part been the front-line combatants, women have played active and essential roles in war.

When we turn to the longer-term project of building political, social and economic structures that might create conditions favourable to lasting justice and peace, there are few grounds for believing that all women will share the same view as to what sort of structures would be most likely to create a just society. The historical evidence does not show women consistently supporting different political policies than men. In Ireland today, women involved in politics, like men involved in politics, are members of parties and movements which have very different views as to the political structures and social and economic policies that would best serve the community at large.

I believe a stronger case can be made for feminism having an identifiable contribution to make. This starts with definitions of feminism. The roots of feminism lie in the roles and behaviours societies prescribe for women and men. Women are not a separate homogeneous group in society, but comprise half of every race and nation, half of every colour and creed, of every ethnic group and every age group and so on. Women, like men, have been oppressors as well as oppressed, slave owners as well as slaves, colonisers as well as colonised. Yet, within such categories as the rich and the powerful, men are over-represented and women under-represented. And, within all groups and categories, women and men seldom share the same access to resources, power, and opportunities. The life-style and opportunities of the daughter of a wealthy middle-class family in suburban Dublin in the late nineteenth century and of a married woman rearing a family in a slum in the same city at the same time might seem so different as to have no point of contact. Yet in each case, the life-style and opportunities of the woman were affected by her sex as well as by her class, wealth, education, age and marital status, and were observably different to and more restricted than those of her brother or husband. Throughout recorded history the sex of an individual has always cut across and interacted with all other divisions within society.

Feminist theorists argue that the political, social and economic consequences of one's sex cannot be explained by a simple biological determinism, but by the ways in which societies have constructed political, social and economic roles around biological sex. The theorists have given the name 'gender' to this social construction of sex. Our sex, whether female or male, and the gender roles in our society, together comprise one factor which interacts with many more to locate each of us in our time and place and to define the challenges, opportunities and difficulties that face us in our growth to self-realisation.

While men as well as women have been and are oppressed by the unequal distribution of authority, resources, personal autonomy, and freedom to explore different areas of human activity, the specific oppression of women arises from the interaction of sex with this unequal distribution. While concepts of what it means to be human have differed over time and place and society, it appears that women, in comparison with men in the same family, class, ethnic or national group, religious or political organisation, have seldom shared the same degree of autonomy and choice in their personal lives, or the same access to the arenas of public power and decision-making. Societies identified as patriarchal by feminists have sought to control women's lives and define women's 'nature' or 'role' in terms of a male-centred perspective which served the interests of a dominant élite.

While we need to be historically specific and avoid sliding into reductionism or unsustainable generalisation, and while actual gender roles have differed over place and time, it appears that feminism has always grown from individual women's perception that the roles imposed by their own society conflicted both with their knowledge of themselves and with their development as self-directed adult persons. This was, for example, the analysis of Mary Wollstonecraft, daughter of the Enlightenment and the radical republicanism of the late eighteenth century. She rejected Rousseau's dictum in *Emile* that women's role in society was to serve men and that consequently women should be educated in subordination. She insisted that women were rational beings as men were, with the same right and duty to develop and use reasoned judgement. For the thinkers of her day, including Wollstonecraft herself, reason and virtue were closely linked. 'How grossly do they insult us who thus advise us only to render ourselves gentle, domestic brutes,' she wrote, insisting that 'it is a farce to call any being virtuous whose virtues do not result from the exercise of its own reason.'[1]

The basis, justification and ultimate driving force of feminism is the conviction that sex roles which limit women's control over their own lives, and which subordinate women to men, and women's needs to men's needs, deny women's full humanity, and are based on a model of relationships which is oppressive to women, dehumanising to both sexes and detrimental to society as a whole. From this it follows that the feminist project is to try to understand the oppression of women, what it consists of and how it operates, and to identify the conditions which would eliminate it. This is not an easy task. When women reject existing female stereotypes, the only models to hand of self-determination and personal autonomy derive from the male stereotype. The very language of self-determination and autonomy which we use comes from this male model. To a dawning feminist awareness, it is not always immediately obvious that women can hardly aspire to a stereotype which further feminist reflection reveals to be itself oppressive, and which includes dominance over women. Indeed, a main ingredient of the macho-male stereotype of today is the negative one of not behaving like a woman. Feminist theory and strategy face the challenge of breaking one defective mould without creating another equally unacceptable. This presents difficulties, since creating a space for women to exercise autonomy, and to experiment with new models, requires as an essential first step the assertion of equal rights with men in all areas of society, and this can all too easily be equated with acting as men do.

Feminism seldom arrives in our lives complete with a ready-made new human model or a comprehensive theory of how society should be organised. Most of us move towards feminism as a result of a personal experience of discrimination or oppression which is only gradually recognised as part of a wider phenomenon. I remember my own growing awareness as a very young girl and then as a young woman, that society saw me and my life and activities as being restricted and curtailed in ways that did not apply to boys and men. The message was that males were the doers and the leaders, and the shapers and changers of society, while females were the followers. Departures from the pattern were exceptions which did not disturb the norm. To me, as a child in a middle-class family in my time and place in history, the powerful sanction behind the norm appeared to lie in the combined weight of how history presented the past, the paradigm of male-female relationships in the books I read, the lives of the people around me, the apparent dominance by males of the worlds of art, literature, music, science and politics, and the fact that no one appeared to explicitly challenge any of this. I knew that the female model conflicted both with how I experienced myself and with my aspirations for the future, and I remember my growing feelings of injustice and powerlessness. After years of partial denial and sporadic attempts to conform, as a young adult I finally rejected the model. Even then my first rationalisation was to see myself as an odd one out who did not fit the pattern, and to look for a personal accommodation within my own situation. Only later did I realise that many other girls and women felt as I did, and that the problem was not one of individual maladjustment, but of how sexism was incorporated into the structures of society, and that real change would not come from finding loopholes to allow individuals to slip through the net.

When we face our discovery that the personal is political, and begin to try to understand the politics of sexism, we each start from our own place in a particular niche in a particular society at a specific time. Just as we encounter gender roles first as an unquestioned part of the world, only later to be analysed and resisted, so we encounter as givens the other structures of our society, its economic base, its social hierarchies and its political system. These too some of us later come to question and reject. Feminist theory develops in interaction with other analyses of the dynamics and structures of human societies, and the different proposals of philosophers and political thinkers over the centuries as to the ideal forms of political, economic and social organisation. This interaction gives rise to areas of agreement and disagreement, of challenge and dispute, of partial acceptance and partial rejection. From all these emerge different feminist analyses, none of which has as yet established itself as a definitive orthodoxy.

An understanding of the development of Irish feminism over the past century and a half, its interaction with political and ecclesiastical establishments, as well as with other radical movements, and its thinking about the kind of society that would best accommodate feminist objectives, could be the starting point for today's debate. The writing of the history of Irish feminism is still at a relatively early stage, and in particular has not yet developed a sustained historical analysis of its theoretical base or bases. Nevertheless, it seems useful to attempt an overview, however sketchy, if only to suggest what may emerge from more in-depth research and analysis. For a model, I have used the American political scientist Alison Jaggar's study of feminist theories and the organisation of human society.[2] Jaggar describes four main strands of western feminist theory today, which she calls liberal feminism, traditional Marxism, radical feminism and socialist feminism.[3] Underlying each strand of feminism she identifies an explicit or implicit theory of human nature and its needs, which in turn informs the kind of changes in society each strand seeks to bring about. Both liberal and Marxist feminism developed during the period of organised feminist campaigns in the nineteenth century, while radical and late-twentieth-century socialist feminism emerged during the new wave of activity which began with the women's liberation movement in the 1960s.

Liberal feminism emphasises the similarities between the sexes and minimises the differences. Nineteenth-century liberalism grew from the eighteenth-century Enlightenment emphasis on the rational human nature shared by all human beings. Liberal political theory sees human beings as essentially rational agents, each determining what it wants from life. The State should protect the individual's right to autonomy and self-fulfilment but otherwise interfere as little as possible in the individual's life. All barriers to individuals using their reasoned judgement should be removed, including restrictions based on birth, colour, religion and so on. Liberal feminism calls for the removal of sex-based restrictions and for equal rights and equal opportunities for women to compete in all areas of human society.

Jaggar sees liberal feminism as having achieved a lot for women, but sees limitations in a feminism which, explicitly or implicitly, aims at the full incorporation of women into a society based on competition for success, wealth and status. In emphasising the similar nature and potential of women and men, and minimising the biological differences, it tends to overlook the structural nature of the barriers to women's full participation posed by existing patterns of childbearing and rearing, and by the existing organisation of paid work. The paradoxical result is that liberal feminism has had to increasingly contradict liberal principles by looking for State intervention to create a level playing field in the competitive liberal world in the form of State provision of child care, anti-discrimination laws, affirmative action and so on. Further, she argues, in a competitive system the playing field will not stay level. In each generation some men and some women will rise to top positions and so give their children a head start in the next round. So in each generation, further State intervention is needed to try to restore the equal starting point in the competition for the glittering prizes.

Marxist analysis does not see human nature as static but as changing as it creates itself by meaningful work, or praxis. The key to understanding any given society is its system of production. This determines the productive activity, and the social conditions of different groups of people. These in turn influence the development of physical and personality characteristics. The poor may be smaller in physique than the wealthy because they eat less nourishing food. The rich child may be encouraged to develop artistic and intellectual potential, while the poor child may get little opportunity to do so. Changes in human nature and in forms of social organisation can only come with revolutionary change in the mode of production in a society. Where capitalism makes people see each other as potential rivals or enemies, in a socialist system society as a whole would own the means of production and the goal of social organisation would be the full development of all human potential.

Marxism criticised liberal feminist campaigns as benefiting middle-class women only. However, Jaggar argues that Marxism's own analysis of the position of women was inadequate. It claimed that the oppression of women would disappear with the overthrow of capitalism but remained vague about the details. It saw women's incorporation into the labour force as the way to emancipation, but did not develop a political analysis of reproduction, both childbearing and rearing, and domestic work, thus ignoring a central arena of power relations between the sexes.

Radical feminism emerged in the late 1960s and its analysis differed from both liberal feminism and Marxist feminism. In contrast to liberal feminism, radical feminism saw both biological sex *and* socially-constructed gender as core issues. Sexual relationships were central and their influence more pervasive than had been realised. Sexuality, lovemaking, childbearing and child-rearing, areas of human life which most political analysts had seen as 'natural' and outside political analysis, were in reality a crucial arena for political analysis and transformation.

Jaggar sees radical feminist theory as composed of many strands, all emphasising the centrality of both biological sex *and* the social construction of gender roles. Overall the 'contemporary radical feminism movement is characterised by a general celebration of womanhood, a striking contrast to the devaluation of women that pervades the wider society.'[4] Lesbian feminism forms one powerful strand. Some radical feminists advocate the development of a women's culture, separate from mainstream culture and uncontaminated by its misogyny.

Jaggar sees radical feminism making a major contribution to feminist thinking by stressing the significance of both biology and gender and rejecting any aim of making women 'equal' to men. She sees a potential weakness in a tendency to universalism and a failure to be historically specific in analysis, which can slide into a biological determinism. She also believes that a separate women's culture can never become more than a minority movement and so cannot transform the lives of all or the majority of women.

Finally, Jaggar describes socialist feminism as it has developed in the late twentieth century, which she sees as a synthesis of insights drawn from Marxism and radical feminism. The new socialist feminists agree with radical feminists that both gender and biology are political issues of central importance. They agree with Marxists on the value of historical materialism in understanding human nature and human society. Applying the historical materialist method of analysis to sexuality, childbearing and childrearing, and the care and maintenance of family members, they argue that the struggle to control productive forces has always included the control of both women's reproductive capacity and domestic work. Of the four types of feminism she identifies, Jaggar sees contemporary socialist feminism as having the greatest potential to achieve feminist objectives.

Analyses like Jaggar's of the potential and limitations of different feminist theories indicate how much can be learned from a historical-analytical approach. Needless to say, few individuals fit neatly and precisely into any ideal category and most combine elements of a number in their thinking. The nineteenth-century Irish women's emancipation campaigns developed within a liberal political ethos. Most of the activists appear to have shared this ethos to a large extent, though they do not exactly fit the classic liberal model. They claimed women's right to full citizenship on the basis of both similarities *and* differences between the sexes. They argued the Enlightenment case that women and men shared the same rational human nature and the same right to develop and use it. They also accepted that women and men had different roles and contributions, and saw these differences as a strength. Women's experience as mothers and household managers gave them qualities of sympathy, empathy and budgeting skills that few men shared. Yet another claim was based on the moral superiority of women. The Victorian definition of women, unlike previous definitions such as those of Aristotle or the early Church fathers, lauded them as morally superior to men and gave them responsibility for the moral behaviour of family and society. Opponents of women's emancipation argued that this superiority was so fragile that it would disintegrate if women were exposed to the corruption of political life and the 'public sphere'. Feminists, however, used it in support of their contention that women's contribution to the organisation of society's affairs was urgently needed, and that to make it women needed full equality with men.

Emancipationists challenged laws, regulations and customs which severely limited the areas of human activity open to women. During the second half of the nineteenth century they co-operated with British women to win married women's control of their own property, and the repeal of the Contagious Diseases Acts which regulated prostitution on a basis of sexual double standards. Separate Irish campaigns achieved improved standards in girls' secondary education and opened university education to women. They instituted a long struggle for entry to political life, which by the end of the century had gained access to local government both as voters and elected representatives, though it had not yet won the parliamentary vote.

The methods they used were for the most part rational argument and the education of public opinion. They lobbied politicians and governments, wrote letters to the newspapers, organised meetings and petitions. The women who participated in the early campaigns were mostly middle-class, Protestant in religion and in politics supporters of the union. Among the leading figures were the Quaker Anna Haslam[5] in Dublin, and the Presbyterian Isabella Tod[6] in Belfast. They tended to be relatively comfortably well-off and economically independent, either as widows or spinsters who could use their time and money as they wished, or married women whose husbands supported their political activism. Many came to feminism through middle-class philanthropic activity. Most women philanthropists, like most of their male colleagues, believed that the 'educated' classes had a duty to the less well-off, and aimed to improve the lot of the poor within the existing political and economic structures. Only a minority moved on to tackle discrimination against women. Of those who did, many accepted that political and other rights for women would in most cases be of immediate benefit to middle-class women, who would have the responsibility of using their new powers for the benefit of poorer women.

With hindsight these feminists are often seen as conservative in their demands. From a class point of view this is correct, and they did not seek radical change in the political and economic organisation of society. The language they used, of 'women's rights' and the 'advancement' and 'emancipation' of women, might imply an objective of achieving equality with men within the existing structures. Yet they did not see equality as simply an end in itself. They believed that it would be a force for change to a more moral and caring society. Also, to assert the equality of women with men as human beings, to insist on the importance of women's work in the home, and to organise political campaigns to achieve equal participation in education, politics and the professions, was hardly conservative from a gender perspective. This is a separate issue to any judgment as to whether or not their campaigns could have achieved emancipation for all women. There is a danger of being anachronistic and ahistorical if the demands and campaigns are not seen in the context of their own time and place.

Nor is it accurate to see the campaigns as motivated solely by selfish middle-class interests. While most of today's feminists would challenge the maternalistic attitude of nineteenth-century middle-class feminists to poorer women, within its terms they were right in thinking they had to free themselves before they could effectively carry out their duty to help less advantaged women. In addition, they saw gains such as married women's control of their own property as being of real and immediate benefit to working-class women whose earnings were legally at the disposal of their husbands.

During the nineteenth century in Ireland, no vigorous Marxist or socialist feminist analysis emerged to challenge the middle-class women's movement on ideological or strategic grounds. The example of Anna Wheeler shows that the potential existed. Wheeler, an Irish woman, became a respected member of the Saint-Simonian co-operative movement in France and the Owenite co-operative movement in England. In 1825, she co-authored with William Thompson from west Cork a sustained exposition of an ideal society based on mutual co-operation and the elimination of sexism.[7] However, in Ireland itself a strong and sizeable socialist movement within which socialist women could argue and develop their case did not develop. The socialist parties which emerged in Ireland at the end of the nineteenth century and the early years of the twentieth were small in membership.

By the turn of the century, more nationalist and Catholic women were joining the suffrage campaign, now the central focus of feminist action.[8] Among the new organisations was the Irish Women's Franchise League (IWFL), founded in 1908, which was nationalist in sympathy but not prepared to put women's demands on hold pending the achievement of independence. Irish feminism and Irish socialism both became entwined in the complexities of the growing nationalist-unionist conflict and in the divergence between Home Rule and separatist nationalists. Despite their other political sympathies, or in some cases affiliations, the suffrage organisations aimed to combine their efforts to achieve the vote. This became increasingly difficult. For nationalist feminists, the question of whether national independence or women's suffrage took priority came to the fore. Those who put the freedom of the nation first included members of Cumann na mBan, founded in 1914 as a women's auxiliary to the Irish Volunteers, while the IWFL insisted that women's citizenship could not be relegated to second place. To date there is little published information on the interaction between feminism and unionism. The Ulster Unionist Women's Council (UUWC), founded in 1911 to support the male Ulster Unionist Council in opposing Home Rule, attracted many thousands of members. While the UUWC explicitly gave maintaining the union precedence over any other objectives, it did have feminist members and it appears that in the long run their politicisation in unionist politics contributed positively to the suffrage movement.[9] The outbreak of the First World War in August 1914 inevitably made it difficult for all suffrage organisations to maintain previous levels of activity, although some, notably the IWFL, tried to continue.

Some feminists supported the British war effort, others fought in the 1916 rising, and there was also a strong pacifist strand in Irish feminism. In 1915, the International Committee of Women for Permanent Peace, renamed in 1919 as the Women's International League for Peace and Freedom (WILPF), was founded directly from the International Woman Suffrage Alliance. The Irish Women's Reform League (IWRL), founded by the feminist, pacifist and trade-unionist Louie Bennett, and the IWFL with its associated suffrage newspaper, *The Irish Citizen* (1912-20), were to the fore among Irish feminist pacifists and an Irish branch of WILPF was established.

At the same time co-operation and dialogue was developing between the labour movement led by James Larkin and James Connolly and feminists with socialist and nationalist sympathies. The Irish Women Workers' Union (IWWU) was founded in 1911 with the participation of both. Louie Bennett's IWRL explicitly worked for the social and economic interests of working-class women as well as for the vote, and Bennett took over the general-secretaryship of the IWWU in 1916. Many feminists gave active support to the ITGWU during the 1913 lockout, and the labour connection forced the question of class, and specifically whether the vote was for 'women' or for 'ladies', higher on the feminist agenda.[11] Some leading nationalist feminists, including Constance Marckievicz and Hanna Sheehy Skeffington, one of the founders of the IWFL, were socialists, and *The Irish Citizen* carried articles and discussion on socialist issues.

The combined efforts of the feminists of the IWFL, many of whom were nationalists, and the nationalists of Cumann na mBan, many of whom were feminists, extracted from the separatist-nationalist leadership a feminist as well as a socialist commitment in the 1916 proclamation of the Irish republic. However, after the execution of the proclamation signatories and the emergence of a new leadership, between 1916 and 1922 much of the energy of republican feminists was spent on keeping up the pressure on the men to accept women as equal colleagues, and to deliver on the 1916 commitment to women's full citizenship in the coming independent Ireland. In the last issue of *The Irish Citizen* in late 1920 Hanna Sheehy Skeffington commented sadly on how the struggle for national independence had overshadowed and sidelined feminist debate.

In 1918, influenced both by women's contribution to the war effort and by fear of the resurgence of suffrage campaigning, the United Kingdom parliament passed a limited measure of women's franchise, confined to women over thirty. In 1922 Article 3 of the constitution of the Irish Free State explicitly endorsed the full and equal citizenship of all women and men over twenty-one: 'Every person, without distinction of sex ... shall enjoy the privileges and be subject to the obligations of such citizenship.' Women in Northern Ireland had to wait until 1928 for full adult suffrage. However, as other contributors to this volume have shown, during the 1920s and 1930s the politicians who took office in the new southern state, both those who had supported and those who had opposed the Treaty, sought to withdraw various aspects of women's citizenship. During the 1920s women were exempted from jury service and excluded from competition for higher posts in the civil service, while the 1930s saw the introduction of a ban on married women as teachers in national schools and in the civil service as well as a government power to limit the numbers of women in a given industry or exclude them completely. This trend culminated in the 1937 Constitution. Feminist protests succeeded in removing or modifying a number of clauses which either infringed or had the potential to infringe full equality of citizenship, but did not succeed in changing the wording of Article 41.2.1: 'by her life within the home, woman gives to the state a support without which the common good cannot be achieved.' The use of the singular and inclusive 'woman' rather than 'many women', and of 'life' rather than 'work', changed this from a welcome recognition of the value of the work of the majority of women to an insistence on a division between 'public' and 'private' spheres which confined women strictly to the latter.

The feminist organisations which publicly contested the anti-women policies of Cumann na nGaedheal and Fianna Fáil governments during the inter-war years generally campaigned for women's rights to full citizenship within the existing system.[12] They included the Irish Women's Citizens Association, first founded by Anna Haslam as the Dublin Women's Suffrage Association in 1876, and the women graduates' associations of both the National University and Trinity College. The minority of feminists who were socialists tended for the most part to be republicans who opted out of participation in the political structures of the new state. Some found themselves torn between a number of often conflicting loyalties, including feminism, republicanism, pacifism and socialism. The dissident republicans were committed to undermining the authority of the new state and establishing a republic based on the second Dáil of 1921. They were themselves, both men and women, divided as to whether that republic should be socialist. Pacifist feminists also experienced divisive tension on the question of whether pacifism could or could not include a war of defence against aggression. The Irish labour movement was now essentially conservative and the male membership at best ambivalent and at worst hostile to such claims as equal employment opportunities and equal pay for women. The female membership itself, both leaders and rank and file, faced problems in reconciling demands for full equality in employment with the social realities of Irish working-class life. Equal pay might be attractive to a single woman, but if she married, a 'family wage' for her husband might take priority.[13] The ethos of the Free State was increasingly Catholic and specifically anti-communist and anti-socialist. In these circumstances, it is hardly surprising that no systematic debate about feminist objectives and what organisation of Irish society was most likely to satisfy them appears to have developed. However, historians have only very recently begun to examine Irish feminism in the inter-war years and in the 1940s and 1950s. Information on feminism in Northern Ireland during this period is particularly scarce. When the full history comes to be written, we are likely to find that there exists a more multi-faceted legacy of Irish feminist thinking than we now realise.

In Ireland, as elsewhere, the demographic, economic and social conditions of the 1960s opened the way to a new upsurgence of feminist activism. In the southern state the existing organisations, led by the Irish Housewives' Association (1942) and the Business and Professional Women's Federation (1965), achieved a break-through with the appointment of the government commission on the status of women in 1970.[14] With the acceptance and publication of its report, the government committed itself publicly to the prin-ciple, if not necessarily the practice, of formal equality. At the same time the Irish Women's Liberation Movement (IWLM) emerged, inspired by the women's liberation movement in the United States.[15] With hindsight it had become clear that self-determination for women and full equality of citizenship between the sexes required more than simply the removal of legal barriers to women's full participation in all aspects of society. Barriers of 'tradition' and custom, as well as deeply entrenched stereotypes, could be as strong as or stronger than legal prohibitions and in some cases could outlast the latter.

Where the longer-established women's organisations worked through committees and lobbying, the IWLM aimed at sweeping change by way of a mass non-hierarchical movement which sought both to raise and politicise women's consciousness of their own oppression and to jolt public opinion in general into awareness of that oppression. The movement sparked off a nationwide re-sponse, and consciousness-raising and action groups sprang up all around the country. Both socialist and republican activists, as well as liberal feminists, were involved in the central IWLM group which gradually broke up due to internal differences. It was succeeded in 1975 by Irishwomen United (IU) whose membership was strongly left-wing. It too disintegrated after a year or so, and with it attempts to establish a mass movement around a central core group.

The movement has developed in a wide variety of directions and forms. Joining forces with the longer-established groups, both the IWLM and IU helped to push through a range of laws improving the position of women. New organisations providing services by women for women sprang up, to support rape victims and single parents, to offer legal advice, to set up refuges from domestic violence, to offer women-centred health care, providing contracep-tion and non-directive pregnancy counselling, including information on abortion. A strong radical feminist strand emerged with links to lesbian feminism. Feminist publishing houses made available a wealth of writing by and about women. Women's caucuses appeared in political movements and parties along with a new drive to bring women into political life and office. Later developments have included the wide-spread emergence of women's community-based groups, combining action on both local and women's concerns, the growth and expansion of Women's Studies, a specifically Christian feminism with nuns to the fore, and a flourishing of creative art.

In Northern Ireland,[16] the new wave of feminism emerged against the background of the civil rights movement of the 1960s, and developed during the years of conflict which followed. Many women came to feminist awareness through participation in housing allocation campaigns and then in the civil rights movement. In contrast to the sudden emergence of a highly visible central group in the south, a range of individual groups emerged. Community-based groups, combining local and women's concerns, have been a strong feature from the early years. Reproductive issues, including the extension to Northern Ireland of British legislation on abortion, have been to the fore. Women's Aid, providing support and refuges for victims of domestic violence, has also been particularly vigorous. The Northern Ireland Women's Rights Movement was set up in 1975 to ensure that United Kingdom anti-sex-discrimination legislation was extended to Northern Ireland. It developed into an umbrella organisation aiming to co-ordinate the efforts of a wide range of groups. Socialist feminist and lesbian feminist groups also emerged during the 1970s.

The context in which the new feminism in the north developed had elements of the all-Ireland situation in the early decades of the century. Feminists were again torn between conflicting allegiances to orange or green. The pressure not to rock the boat, and to give unionism or nationalism priority over feminism, was strong. Among nationalist women there was debate and disagreement on issues such as the feminist response to the strip-searching of republican women prisoners, and to an extent nationalist/feminist debate was so prominent that it inhibited some unionist women from becoming active feminists.

The 1980s witnessed the emergence of more groups and increasing efforts to achieve unity and understanding across political and religious divides. In the 1990s this developed into a concerted campaign to put gender inequality and women's demands on the agenda at all discussions of solutions to the problems of Northern

Ireland, and continued efforts to build a feminist movement that crossed political, religious and class divides.[17] Both Clar na mBan and the Northern Ireland Women's Coalition emerged from these imperatives. The 1994 ceasefires also gave a new impetus to the efforts which have been repeated throughout the 1970s, 1980s and 1990s to build an all-Ireland feminist movement.

Today, it seems fair to say that feminism is an important aspect of the lives of more women in Ireland north and south than ever before. It has also become a household word which everybody recognises and thinks they understand. Yet, to judge from media coverage, the general public's perception is that feminism is solely a liberal feminist demand for equal rights and equal opportunities for women within existing political, economic and social structures. Those of us who believe that feminism has something more radical, and more subversive, to offer to building a new Ireland face a major challenge in getting the potential of feminist thinking onto the agenda of public debate. In the early stages of the current phase of feminism in the 1970s, there was vigorous debate both north and south about the meaning and objectives of different feminist theories and the changes in society needed to implement them. Today's strategy could be to first revive and cultivate a broad and inclusive internal debate around these issues, and then to initiate constructive dialogue with other movements working for change.

The historical perspective provides a good starting point. It shows us that Irish feminism has never been the preserve of any group or section. It has crossed religious and political boundaries, and challenged religious and political establishments. Feminists have been unionists and nationalists, Protestants and Catholics, capitalists and socialists, soldiers and pacifists. They have dealt with the problem of conflicting loyalties in different ways. Some have brought their feminist thinking into dialogue with their other political beliefs. Some have at times put their feminist convictions on hold. Feminists and feminism do not exist in a vacuum. Both are what they are as a result of the interaction of individuals with the societies of which they are part. This does not mean that all actions and analyses in the past were of equal value or equal validity. It means that we can begin to see how Irish feminists in the past saw the options open to them and why they chose as they did. It helps us to understand how we ourselves have come to hold our particular brand of feminism and presses us to analyse both its potential and its limitations.

Analysis of the changes in society that could deliver our various feminist objectives could be the starting point for both internal feminist debate and engagement with other movements. One example of this would be that middle-class feminists like myself would seriously engage with the thinking of women in community groups in working-class areas in Dublin and other cities, particularly in areas of high male and female unemployment and in those where there is a high traffic in drugs. We would consider our response as feminists to their analysis and the steps they propose to begin a process of change. Their views of what they see as the current middle-class feminist agenda would be another useful debating point. Another debate could concern the role of State-provided child care. Do we see this as the ultimate solution to women's problems in combining family with work outside the home or as a temporary expedient to provide equality of opportunity for women pending a radical overhaul of the organisation of paid employment so that it is no longer based on hours and timetables suited to a man who has a wife to look after home and family? Do we want to rethink family roles to allow more active parenting by fathers as well as mothers? If there is a value for most children in the early experience of good pre-school education, how does this fit in? Such questions in turn lead to another debate: whether feminist objectives can be achieved within a global economy and politics based on free-market competition, or only within one based in some way on socialist principles.

With regard to dialogue with other movements working for change in Irish society, the challenge is to develop a forum for meaningful engagement. As noted already, the peace process in its present form does not provide space for a holistic approach to discussion of a new Ireland, and is unlikely to move in that direction without serious pressure. One possible way to apply this pressure would be the development of a parallel debate about a new Ireland. This would challenge the parties and the two governments to broaden and deepen their analysis of the issues involved and their perception of the interests that should be represented at the talks. It would give the women and men involved, both within the negotiating rooms and within the political parties, a source of support, terms of reference and a pool of ideas on which they could draw and with which they could engage. Irrespective of the outcome of the current peace process, a constructive response to its limitations in the form of a wide-ranging, multi-faceted and inclusive debate about a new Ireland could build towards the future.

Bibliography of Writings of
Margaret MacCurtain
Compiled by Monica Cullinan

1958

Dominic O'Daly 1595-1662: A Study of Irish-European Relationships in the Seventeenth Century. M.A. Thesis, University College Dublin, 1958.

1963

An Agent of the Irish Counter-Reformation: Dominic O'Daly. Ph.D. Thesis, University College Dublin.

Irish Material in Fondo Santa Sede, Madrid. *Archivium Hibernicum,* xxvi, pp 40-49.

St. Mary's University College (Dublin). *University Review,* iii, pp 33-47.

1964

Dominic O'Daly and the Counter-Reformation. *Irish Committee of Historical Sciences, Bulletin,* no. 99, pp 1-2.

The Geraldine War: Rebellion or Crusade? *Proceedings of the Irish Catholic Historical Committee,* pp 11-20.

Review of F.X. Martin, O.S.A., *Friar Nugent: A Study of Francis Lavalin Nugent (1569-1635): Agent of the Counter-Reformation* (Rome and London, 1962). *Studia Hibernica,* no. 4, pp 249-251.

Thoughts on Sunday. *The Furrow,* xv, no. 2, pp 114-120.

1965

Dominic O'Daly: An Irish Diplomat. *Studia Hibernica,* no. 5, pp 98-112.

The Geraldine War – Rebellion or Crusade? *Irish Ecclesiastical Record,* 5th series, ciii, pp 148-157.

Review of B. Millett, O.F.M. '*The Irish Franciscans, 1651-1665.*' *Irish Historical Studies,* xiv, 373-374.

1967

Daniel O'Daly. *New Catholic Encyclopedia,* vol. 10, pp 641-642.

An Irish Agent of the Counter-Reformation, Dominic O'Daly. *Irish Historical Studies,* xv, pp 391-406.

The Teaching of History in Irish Schools, by a Study Group. Ed. J. McKenna. *Administration,* xv, pp 268-285.

William Walsh. *New Catholic Encyclopedia,* vol. 14, p. 784.

1968

From Renaissance to Bourbaki. *Irish Mathematics Teachers' Association Newsletter,* no. 10, pp. 5-8.

1969

The Birth of Modern Ireland; M. MacCurtain and M. Tierney, p. 245. Dublin: Gill and MacMillan.

Review of M. Roberts, *The Early Vasas: A History of Sweden 1523-1611* (Cambridge, London, 1968). *Irish Historical Studies,* xvi, 519-522.

1970

Youth And Dissent. *Doctrine and Life,* xx, no. 2, pp 74-80.

1972

The Gill History of Ireland. General editors, J. Lydon and M. MacCurtain. 11 Vols. Dublin: Gill and Macmillan, 1972-1975.

Review of J. de Broucker, *The Suenens Dossier: The Case for Collegiality* (Dublin, 1970). *The Furrow,* xxiii, no. 3, pp 192-193.

Tudor and Stuart Ireland, pp 211. Dublin: Gill and Macmillan.

1973

Education: A Church-State Problem in Twentieth-Century Ireland. *The Furrow,* xxiv, no. 1, pp 3-12.

1974

Pre-Famine Peasantry in Ireland: Definition and Theme. *Irish University Review,* iv, pp 188-198.

Review of B. Bradshaw, *The Dissolution of the Religious Orders in Ireland Under Henry VIII* (London, 1974). *The Tablet,* ccxxviii, no. 7011, p. 1106.

Review of H. Fenning, *The Undoing of the Friars of Ireland: A Study of the Novitiate Question in the Eighteenth Century* (Louvain, 1972). *The Tablet,* ccxxviii, no. 6975, p. 227.

Women – Irish Style. Doctrine and Life, xxiv, no. 4, pp 182-197.

1975

The Fall of the House of Desmond. *Journal of the Kerry Archaeological and Historical Society,* no. 8, pp 28-44.

Review of S. Lynam, *Humanity Dick* (London, 1975). *The Tablet,* ccxxix, no. 7054, pp 866-867.

Review of M. Perceval-Maxwell, *The Scottish Migration to Ulster in the Reign of James I* (London, 1973). *History: The Journal of the Historical Association,* lx, pp 453-454.

1978

Women in Irish Society: The Historical Dimension; ed. M. MacCurtain and D. Ó Corráin, p. 125. Dublin: Arlen House, The Women's Press. Preface by M. MacCurtain.

Women, the Vote and Revolution. *Women in Irish Society: The Historical Dimension;* ed. M. MacCurtain and D. Ó Corráin. Dublin: Arlen House, The Women's Press, pp 46-57.

1979

Preface, *Margaret Anna Cusack: One Woman's Campaign for Women's Rights,* by I. ffrench Eagar. Dublin: Arlen House, The Women's Press, pp vii-xii.

Rural Society in Post-Cromwellian Ireland. *Studies in Irish History: Presented to R. Dudley Edwards;* ed. A. Cosgrove and D. McCartney. Dublin: University College Dublin, pp 118-136.

1980

Review of N. Canny, *The Elizabethan Conquest of Ireland: A Pattern Established, 1565-1576* (Hassocks, 1976). *History: The Journal of the Historical Association,* lxv, 302-303.

Review of *A New History of Ireland, Vol. III: Early Modern Ireland 1534-1691;* ed. T.W. Moody, F.X. Martin and F.J. Byrne (Oxford, 1976). *History: The Journal of the Historical Association,* lxv, pp 301-302.

Towards an Appraisal of the Religious Image of Women. *Crane Bag,* iv, pp 26-30.

1982

The Roots of Irish Nationalism. *The Celtic Consciousness;* ed. R. O'Driscoll. Portlaoise: Dolmen Press, pp 371-382. Originally published: Canada: McClelland and Stewart, 1981.

Women of Eccles Street. *The Lanthorn: Year Book of the Dominican College, Eccles Street, Dublin. Centenary Year 1982;* ed. E. Kane. Dublin: Dominican College.

1983

Preface; *Missing Pieces: Women in Irish History. 1: Since the Famine,* Dublin: Irish Feminist Information Publications Ltd. with Women's Community Press. p. 3.

1985

The Historical Image. *Irish Women: Image and Achievement;* ed. E. Ní Chuilleanáin. Dublin: Arlen House, pp 37-50.

Marriage in Tudor Ireland. *Marriage in Ireland*; ed. A. Cosgrove. Dublin: College Press, pp 51-66.

Women: The Historical Image. *Books Ireland*, no. 90, pp 10-11.

Review of J. Casway, *Owen Roe O'Neill and the Struggle for Catholic Ireland* (Philadelphia, 1984). *Irish Literary Supplement*, iv, no. 2, p. 171.

Sisters and Brothers; by M. MacCurtain and N. Kinsella. *Freedom to Hope? A Festschrift for Austin Flannery, O.P.*; ed. A. Falconer, E. McDonagh and S. Mac Réamoinn. Dublin: Columba Press, pp 39-55.

Sisters. Freedom to Hope: the Catholic Church in Ireland Twenty Years after Vatican II; ed. A. Falconer, E. MacDonagh and S. Mac Réamoinn. Dublin: Columba Press, pp 39-46.

1986

The Flight of the Earls. *Milestones in Irish History*; ed. L. de Paor. Dublin: Mercier Press in association with Ráidio Telefís Éireann, pp 52-61.

Women: Part of the Laity? *Pobal: The Laity in Ireland*; ed. S. Mac Réamoinn. Dublin: Columba Press, pp 54-63.

1987

Moving Statues and Irish Women. *Studies*, lxxvi, pp 139-147.

1988

A Lost Landscape: the Geraldine Castles and Tower Houses of the Shannon Estuary. *Settlement and Society in Medieval Ireland: Studies presented to F.X. Martin, O.S.A.*; ed. J. Bradley. Kilkenny: Boethius Press, pp 429-444.

Reconciliation of Histories. *Reconciling Memories*; ed. A. D. Falconer. Dublin: Columba Press, pp 30-36.

Review of B. Fitzpatrick, *Seventeenth-Century Ireland: The War of Religions* (Dublin, 1988). *The New Nation*, no. 2, pp 22-23.

Review of J. A. Gaughan, *Alfred O'Rahilly: Academic* (Dublin, 1986). *Irish Literary Supplement*, vii, no. 1, p. 47.

1989

Breaking the Mould. *The Tablet*, ccxliii, no. 7757, pp 312-313.

Fullness of Life: Defining Female Spirituality in Twentieth-Century Ireland. *Women Surviving: Studies in Irish Women's History in the Nineteenth and Twentieth Centuries*; ed. M. Luddy and C. Murphy. Dublin: Poolbeg Press, pp 233-263.

1990

Du XIIe Au Début Du XXe Siècle: Une Longue Période Coloniale. *L'Europe Aujourd'hui: Les Hommes, Leur Pays, Leur Culture. L'Irlande*;

ed. A. d'Haenens and N. O'Sullivan. Brussels: Editions Artis-Historia, pp 53-75.

Mary Robinson: Metaphor for Change. *The Furrow*, xli, no. 12, pp 673-676.

Misogynist. Programme Note for M. Harding, *Misogynist*. (World Première October 10.) Dublin: Abbey Theatre.

Review of C. Clear. *Nuns in Nineteenth-Century Ireland* (Washington, D.C. and Dublin, 1988), A. Haverty, *Constance Markievicz: An Independent Life* (London, 1988), C. Murphy, *The Women's Suffrage and Irish Society in the Early Twentieth Century* (New York and London, 1989). *Gender and History*, ii, pp 365-368.

1991

The 'Ordinary' Heroine: Women into History. *Ten Dublin Women*; ed. Women's Commemoration and Celebration Committee. Dublin: Women's Commemoration and Celebration Committee, pp 5-14.

Women, Education and Learning in Early Modern Ireland. *Women in Early Modern Ireland*; ed. M. MacCurtain and M. O'Dowd. Dublin: Wolfhound Press; Edinburgh: Edinburgh University Press, pp. 160-170.

Women in Early Modern Ireland; ed. with an Introduction by M. MacCurtain and M. O'Dowd, pp 340. Dublin: Wolfhound Press; Edinburgh: Edinburgh University Press.

1992

An Agenda for Women's History in Ireland, 1500-1990. Part 1: 1500-1800. M. MacCurtain and M. O'Dowd. *Irish Historical Studies*, xxviii, pp 1-19.

Review of *Field Day Anthology of Irish Writing*, volume 1; ed. S. Deane. (Derry, 1991). *Irish Literary Supplement*, xi, no. 2, 4.

Review of J. McL. Côté, *Fanny and Anna Parnell: Ireland's Patriot Sisters* (London, 1991). *Irish Literary Supplement*, xi, no. 2, pp 34-35.

Review of R. Loeber, *The Geography and Practice of English Colonization in Ireland from 1534 to 1609* (Dublin, 1991). *Irish Economic and Social History*, xix, pp 110-111.

1993

The Real Molly Macree. *Visualizing Ireland: National Identity and the Pictorial Tradition*; ed. A.M. Dalsimer. Boston, London: Faber and Faber, pp 9-21.

Review of *U.C.G. Women's Studies Centre Review*, Volume One, 1992, ed. A. Byrne, J. Conroy and S. Ryder. (Galway, 1992). *Journal of the Galway Archaeological and Historical Society*, xlv, pp 184-186.

The Role of Religion in Ireland: The Historical Dimension. *Social Compass*, xl, pp 7-13.

1994

Boy Meets Girl in Papal World: The Catechism of the Catholic Church. *Irish Independent, Weekender*, 4 June, p. 2.

Ennistymon. *Irish Country Towns*; ed. A. Simms and J. H. Andrews. Cork: Mercier Press published in association with Ráidio Telefís Éireann, pp 108-119.

From Dublin to New Orleans: Nora and Alice's Journey to America 1889; ed. S. Hoy and M. MacCurtain, pp 143. Dublin: Attic Press.

Review of *Irish University Review Special Issue – Eavan Boland*, Vol. 23 (1), 1993; ed. A. Roche and J. Allen-Randolph (Dublin, 1993). *Irish Literary Supplement*, xiii, no. 2, pp 21-22.

Review of R. M. Rhodes, *Women and the Family in Post-Famine Ireland: Status and Opportunity in a Patriarchal Society*. (New York and London, 1992). *Irish Literary Supplement*, xiii, no. 1, pp 27-28.

Review of *Towards the 1994 Synod: The Views of Religious*; ed. A. Flannery (Dublin, 1993). *The Tablet*, ccxlviii, 704.

Sister Act. Interview by Thomas O'Loughlin. *History Ireland*, ii, pp 52-54.

1995

Late in the Field: Catholic Sisters in Twentieth-Century Ireland and the New Religious History. *Chattel, Servant or Citizen. Women's Status in Church, State and Society; Historical Studies, xix*; eds. M. O'Dowd and S. Wichert. Belfast: The Institute of Irish Studies, The Queen's University of Belfast, pp 34-44. Also published in: *Journal of Women's History*, vi, no. 4/vii, no. 1, pp 49-63; *Irish Women's Voices: Past and Present*; ed. J. Hoff and M. Coulter. Bloomington, Ind.: Indiana University Press.

1996

Reflections on Walter Osborne's Study from Nature. *America's Eye: Irish Paintings from the Collection of Brian P. Burns*; eds. A.M. Dalsimer and V. Kreilkamp. Chestnutt Hill, Mass.: Boston College Museum of Art, pp 29-32.

Review of C. Falls, *Elizabeth's Irish Wars* (London, 1995). *Irish Times, Weekend*, 23 March, p. 7.

Review of M. Luddy, *Women in Ireland, 1800-1918: A Documentary History* (Cork, 1995). The Irish Reporter, no. 22, p. 80.

Review of A. Thurston, *Because of Her Testimony: The Word in Female Experience* (Dublin, 1995). *The Furrow*, xlvii, pp 121-122.

Contributors

Caitriona Beaumont is a lecturer in history at the University of Glasgow. She was awarded a Ph.D. by the University of Warwick in 1997. She is currently researching the history of voluntary organisations for women in Ireland and England throughout the period 1920-1960. She hopes to publish her doctoral thesis, 'Women and citizenship: A study of non-feminist women's societies and the women's movement in England, 1928-1950', in the near future.

Caitriona Clear is a lecturer in history in University College, Galway. She is author of *Nuns in Nineteenth-Century Ireland* (Dublin, 1987) and has published on the topic of women's household work in twentieth-century Ireland and on homelessness in nineteenth-century Ireland.

Monica Cullinan is an Assistant Librarian in Humanities in the Library of University College, Dublin. She was a founding member of the University College Dublin Women's Studies Forum and has completed a Master's Degree in Women's Studies in University College Dublin.

Mary Cullen is a former senior lecturer in modern history and, at present, an academic associate at St Patrick's College, Maynooth. She was a founding member and first president of the Irish Association for Research in Women's History. She has published and lectured widely on Irish women's history. She is a member of the executive committee of the Women's Studies Centre at Trinity College, Dublin where she teaches a course on the history of Irish feminism in the M.Phil. programme.

Rosemary Cullen Owens is author of *Smashing Times: A History of the Irish Suffrage Movement 1889-1922* (Dublin, 1984, 1995). She is currently completing a study of Louie Bennett and the pacifist movement in Ireland. She teaches women's history for the MA and Certificate in Women's Studies at the Women's Education Research and Resource Centre, University College, Dublin.

Mary E. Daly is Associate Professor of History at University College, Dublin. Her publications include *Social and Economic History of Ireland Since 1800* (Dublin, 1981); *Dublin: the Deposed Capital – A Social and Economic History, 1860-1914* (Cork, 1984); *The Famine in Ireland* (Dundalk, 1986); *Industrial Development and National Identity, 1922-1939* (Dublin, 1992) and *Women and Work* (Dundalk, 1997). She is currently president of the Irish Economic and Social History Society.

Maryann Gialanella Valiulis is a specialist in modern Irish History. She is the author of *Almost a Rebellion: The Irish Army Mutiny of 1924* and the award-winning *Portrait of a Revolutionary: General Richard Mulcahy and the Founding of the Irish Free State.* She is currently completing a study of the re-construction of the gender ideology in the Irish Free State. Dr Valiulis is a lecturer in Women's Studies and Academic Coordinator of the Centre for Women's Studies at Trinity College, Dublin.

Joan Hoff is Professor of History at the Contemporary History Institute at Ohio University. She was co-founder and co-editor of the *Journal of Women's History* from 1988-1996. A specialist in U.S. foreign policy and politics, and women's legal history, her books include *Law, Gender and Injustice: a Legal History of U.S. Women* (New York, 1991, revised 1994); *Rights of Passage: the Past, Present and Future of the ERA* (Indiana, 1986); *Without Precedent: the Life and Career of Eleanor Roosevelt,* co-edited with Marjorie Lightman (Indiana, 1984); and *For Adult Users Only: the Dilemma of Violent Pornography,* co-edited with Susan Gabar (Indiana, 1989).

Phil Kilroy is the author of *Protestant Dissent and Controversy in Ireland 1660-1714* (Cork, 1994) and of numerous articles on religious dissent in seventeenth-century Ireland. Her most recent publication is a study of Quaker women in Ireland, 1660-1740, to be published in *The Irish Journal of Feminist Studies.* She is currently writing a scholarly biography of Madeleine Sophie Barat, 1779-1865. She is currently joint treasurer of the Irish Association for Research in Women's History.

Maria Luddy is senior lecturer in history at the Institute of Education, University of Warwick. She is the author of *Women and Philanthropy in Nineteenth-Century Ireland* (Cambridge, 1995), and *Hanna Sheehy Skeffington* (Dublin, 1995), and editor of *Women in Ireland, 1800-1918: A Documentary History* (Cork, 1995). She is also an editor of the *Field Day Anthology of Irish Writing,* vol. iv (forthcoming). She is a member of the Executive Committee of the Irish Association for Research in Women's History.

Cliona Murphy is Professor of Modern European History at California State University Bakersfield. She is author of *The Women's Suffrage Movement and Irish Society in the Early Twentieth Century* (Hemel Hempstead, 1989) and co-editor (with Maria Luddy) of *Women Surviving: Studies in Irish Women's History in the 19th and 20th Centuries* (Dublin, 1990). She is presently working on Anglican evangelism in pre-Famine Ireland.

Maureen Murphy is Professor of Curriculum and Teaching at Hofstra Univesity. She is the editor of *A Guide to Irish Studies in the United States* (New York, 1979, 1982, 1989, 1994), Máire MacNeill's *Máire Rua, Lady of Leamaneh* (Whitegate, 1990), Sara Hyland's *I Call to the Eye of the Mind: A Memoir* (Dublin, 1996) and Asenath Nicholson's *Annals of the Famine in Ireland* (Dublin, 1997). She is the co-editor with James MacKillop of *Irish Literature: a Reader* (Syracuse, 1987) and with Diane Ben Merre of *James Joyce and his Contemporaries* (New York, 1989). Her current project is a study of Irish domestic servants in the United States to be called *Hope from the Ocean.* She has served as president of the American Conference for Irish Studies and as chair of the International Association for the Study of Anglo-Irish Literature.

Mary O'Dowd is senior lecturer in history at Queen's University Belfast. She is author of *Power, Politics and Land: Sligo 1568-1688* (Belfast, 1985); and editor (with Margaret MacCurtain) of *Women in Early Modern Ireland* (Edinburgh, 1991) and (with Sabine Wichert) of *Chattel, Servant or Citizen: Women's Status in Church, State and Society* (Belfast, 1995). She is editor of the section on politics in the forthcoming *Field Day Anthology of Irish Writing*, volume iv. She is currently president of the Irish Association for Research in Women's History.

Rosemary Raughter completed her MA thesis on eighteenth-century female philanthropy at University College, Dublin. She lectures in women's history for the Women's Education Research and Resource Centre, University College, Dublin and for the People's College, and is joint editor of a forthcoming collection of essays on prostitution in Ireland from the eighteenth century to the present day. She is currently joint treasurer of the Irish Association for Research in Women's History.

Elizabeth Steiner-Scott is a lecturer in the Department of History, University College, Cork, and is also Co-ordinator of the MA in Women's Studies. She is currently co-editor of the *Irish Journal of Feminist Studies,* and edited *Personally Speaking: Women's Thoughts on Women's Issues* (Dublin, 1985). She is a member of the Executive Committee of the Irish Association for Research in Women's History.

Catherine B. Shannon is Professor of History at Westfield State College and the University of Massachusetts, Amherst. She studied at University College, Dublin and has held a senior fellowship at the Institute of Irish Studies at Queen's University Belfast. She is author of *Arthur J. Balfour and Ireland, 1874-1922* (Washington, 1988).

Notes

Introduction

1. Margaret MacCurtain and Donncha Ó Corráin (eds), *Women in Irish Society: the Historical Dimension* (Dublin, 1978), preface.

2. *History Ireland*, vol 2, no 1 (Spring 1994), p. 54.

3. For a list of MacCurtain's publications see pp 278–83 above.

4. Margaret MacCurtain also received a Higher Diploma in Education from University College, Cork and a Diploma in Theology from Pont Institute Regina Mundi.

5. In 1984 Margaret MacCurtain was forced to initiate legal proceedings at the college in order to maintain her position in UCD. She won the case. In almost thirty years of service, Margaret was never advanced beyond the grade of college lecturer.

6. Christina Murphy, 'The Saturday Interview' in *The Irish Times*, 17 May 1975.

7. See p. 124 above.

8. See p. 70 above.

9. See p. 90 above.

10. See p. 88 above.

11. See p. 188 above.

12. Cited by Steiner-Scott, see p. 143 above.

13. See p. 260 above.

Joan Hoff:
The Impact & Implications of Women's History

1. For the reasons why liberal, socialist, and even radical feminists have not dealt to any great degree with theories of citizenship as they relate to the state, see Mary G. Dietz, 'Context is all: feminism and theories of citizenship' in *Daedalus*, 116 (Fall 1987), pp 1-18. Female political scientists have studied the question of citizenship slightly more than female historians, but usually not from any particular feminist perspective. U.S. historians of women who have addressed the subject include Linda Kerber, Joan R. Gunderson, Hilda Smith, and Ruth H. Bloch.

2. Courts in the United States continue to define the ideal worker's wage as his [sic] sole property, despite the fact that it is produced by the joint efforts of the ideal-worker husband and the marginalised-caregiver wife, thus creating a clash between the ideal-worker norm and the norm of parental caregiving. In fact, most fathers perform as ideal workers (to the extent that their class, race, and personality allow them to do so), whereas most mothers do not, because they must provide daily domestic services required by their husbands. This work/family conflict has led to the impoverishment of divorced women and their children which cannot be resolved by alimony or other current rules of family law. Instead, a new system of family entitlements must be introduced which treats the reproductive family as a single economic unit with women's domestic contributions recognised as deserving economic entitlements. While we like to talk about both parents working in the United States, in fact, only 40 percent of married women work full-time. (See Joan Williams, 'Married women and property' in *Virginia Journal of Social Policy and Law*, 383 (1994), pp 383-408.)

3. Hilary Charlesworth, Christine Chinkin and Shelley Wright, 'Feminist approaches to international law', unpublished paper delivered to the American Society of International Law, October 1991.

4. Joan Hoff, 'Liberation hurts: Polish women after communism' in *The Warsaw Voice*, 5 July 1992, p. 10.

5. Mary Condren, 'Sacrifice and political legitimation: the production of a gendered social order' in Joan Hoff and Maureen Coulter (eds), *Irish Women's Voices: Past and Present* (Bloomington, Indiana, 1995), pp 160-179; Margaret MacCurtain in 'Women, the vote and revolution' in Margaret MacCurtain and Donncha Ó Corráin (eds), *Women in Irish Society: the Historical Dimension* (Dublin, 1978), pp 46-57; Maryann Gialanella Valiulis, 'Power, gender, and identity in the Irish Free State' in *Journal of Women's History*, 6-7 (Winter/spring, 1995), pp 99-136; Ailbhe Smyth, 'Paying our disrespects to the bloody states we're in: women, violence, culture, and the state' in *ibid*, pp 190-215; Joan Hoff, 'Comparative analysis of abortion in Ireland, Poland and the United States' in Mary O'Dowd and Sabine Wichert (eds), *Chattel, Servant or Citizen: Women's Status in Church, State and Society* (Belfast, 1995), pp 254-267; Elizabeth Meehan, 'Women and citizenship in the European Union' in *idem*, pp 268-277.

6. Linda Kerber, 'A constitutional right to be treated like American ladies: women and the obligations of citizenship' in Linda Kerber, Alice Kessler-Harris, Kathryn Kish Sklar (eds), *U.S. History as Women's History* (Chapel Hill, South Carolina and London, 1995), p. 18.

7. *Ibid.*

8. For more details see Joan Hoff, 'Comparative analysis of abortion in Ireland, Poland and the United States' in *Women's Studies International Forum*, 7, no 6 (Winter 1995), pp 621-646.

9. I admit that when I talk about citizenship I am ethnocentrically referring to what are fairly clearly defined and agreed principles of democracy among western industrialised nations. Ireland exists in that international frame of reference. We all know what democracy means. Most of the definition is not a secret, but there are two secret or unstated parts to it, as I note below. I am using an American definition here because the United States represents the longest functioning system of democracy which the world has ever known. For better or for worse, other nations, especially those in the recently liberated countries of eastern Europe and Russia, at least pay lip-service to the American version of democracy. So what is it?

Ideally, American democracy consists of four basic principles. First, there is the supposition that no other country in the world has trusted its past and future for so long to so many free elections and the peaceful transition of power. The corollary to this is that democratic government in the United States was (and is) owned and operated by informed voting citizens. Thirdly, it is usually assumed that our unique system of checks and balances, along with our two-party system, makes us impervious to the plutocratic, oligarchic, or autocratic pitfalls which have plagued other democracies because these ensure the enactment of just laws and policies which have been vigorously debated by an informed and involved citizenry. Finally, judicial interpretations of our written Constitution have produced for Americans the greatest amount of civil liberties and freedoms – freedom of expression, freedom of religion, freedom of association, freedom to vote, freedom to travel – ever granted by any government to its people. The unstated or secret aspect of American democracy is that it has always been based on a strong middle-class, educated base which many nations of the world do not enjoy. We do not tell poor developing nations with large illiterate populations this for obvious reasons, but it has always been a very important secret ingredient of the success of American democracy. The other secret component of democracy in the United States and in every western industrialised nation that calls itself democratic is that women have never been granted the same reproductive and sexual rights as men.

Few would quarrel with this description of American democracy – in theory. In practice, however, democratic citizenship even in the United States falls far short of this idealisation for many reasons, but the one I want to stress is the fact that women remain second-class citizens of the United States, despite the advances which they have made in the areas of education, political power, and work opportunities in the last twenty-five years. These advances have also occurred in Ireland since 1980, according to a poll reported in the *Irish Independent* in an article unfortunately entitled 'You've come a long way, baby!' (2 February 1992). Irish women may have come a long way, but the headline writer for that newspaper had not.

10. For details see Joan Hoff, *Law, Gender and Injustice* (Bloomington, Indiana, 1994), pp xi-xiv, 346-49.

11. Clar na Mban, 'Charter of women's rights' submitted to the Forum for Peace and Reconciliation, 30 December 1994.

12. The terms 'resurrection', 'contribution', 'compensatory' and 'her-story' have all been used to describe what this essay refers to as remedial history. See Mari Jo Buhle, Ann G. Gordon and Nancy Schrom, 'Women in American society: an historical contribution' in *Radical America*, 5, no 4 (1971), pp 3-66; Bernice A. Carroll (ed.), *Liberating Women's History: Theoretical and Critical Essays* (Urbana, 1976), pp 75-92; Linda Gordon et al, 'Historical phallacies: sexism in American historical writing' in *ibid.*, pp 55-74; and Joan Wallach Scott, 'Women in history: the modern period' in *Past and Present*, 101 (1983), pp 141-157 (Virginia Woolf quotation at p. 141). In this essay Scott uses the term 'conventional history' to refer to patriarchical history. For a discussion of the economic, cultural and political significance of the doctrine of separate spheres, see Barbara Welter, 'The cult of true womanhood: 1820-1860' in *American Quarterly*, 18 (1966), pp 151-74; Linda K. Kerber and Jane de Hart Mathews (eds), *Women's America: Refocusing the Past* (New York, 1982), pp 3-22; Anne Firor Scott, 'On seeing and not seeing: a case of historical invisibility' in *Journal of American History*, 71 (1984), pp 7-21; and Linda Kerber, 'Separate spheres, female worlds, woman's place: the rhetoric of women's history' in *Journal of American History*, 75 (1988), pp 9-39.

13. For more details on all these stages in the writing of women's history see Joan Hoff, 'Introduction: an overview of women's history in the United States' in *Journal of Women's History Guide to Periodical Literature* (Bloomington, Indiana, 1992), pp 9-37.

14. For example, in her collection of essays *Making the Invisible Woman Visible* (Urbana, Illinois, 1984), Anne Firor Scott recounts the transition which she made from pre-feminist to feminist historical writing. The essays and lectures in her book contribute not only to our understanding of one woman's personal and professional odyssey but also to the general field of white women's history during a time when the new social history collided so productively with the study of the 'other half' of the American population. In particular, Anne Scott has demonstrated in her own life and work that 'the historian who calls attention to something hitherto overlooked ... teaches others to have a broader vision of the past.' Her unending (and highly successful) campaign to make white southern women not only visible but also integrated and important components of U.S. history laid solid groundwork for others who would follow. She did not, however, account for race or class differences among southern women, as she herself admitted in 1984 (see Anne Scott, 'On seeing and not seeing', p. 7). Scott has extended her research to include African American women (see 'Most invisible of all: black women's voluntary associations' in *Journal of Southern History*, 56 (1990), pp 3-22).

Even more impressive is the first volume of Gerda Lerner's work: *Women and History: the Creation of Patriarchy* (New York, 1986), because she does not ignore class or race. Picking up where Simone de Beauvoir left off, this is an ambitious, theoretical and multi-disciplinary effort in which Lerner argues that male dominance over women is the product of historical development and, therefore, is not 'natural' or immutable. Just as particular historical processes created patriarchy, so too particular historical events can end it. Lerner also argues that the first forms of slavery were based on gender, not class. Lerner has not only transcended the limitations of the second-stage, pre-feminist historians, but has also overcome the limitations of Marxist theory which influenced her early work. Writing in her second volume, *The Creation of Feminist Consciousness* (New York, 1993) about a 'holistic history' of women and men that would illuminate 'how the patriarchal system organises and secures the co-operation of women without which it cannot exist', Lerner is attempting to re-conceptualise history through understanding of the 'interrelated aspects of the system of patriarchal dominance' rather than continuing 'to regard class, race and gender dominance as separate, though intersecting and overlapping systems' (see Lerner, 'Placing women in history: a theoretical framework', unpublished 1988 paper; and *Creation of Feminist Consciousness*, pp 3-20).

15. Arina Angerman, et al (eds), *Current Issues in Women's History* (London, 1989), pp 1-20.

16. Nancy F. Cott and Elizabeth H. Pleck, *A Heritage of Her Own: Toward a New Social History of American History* (New York, 1979), p. 17.

17. Carroll Smith-Rosenberg, 'The female world of love and ritual: relations between women in nineteenth-century America' in *Signs*, 1 (1975), pp 1-29. With this article Smith-Rosenberg set in motion a debate over women's erotic lives with each other that is still in progress, despite all recent attempts by post-structuralists to downplay the importance of women's socially-constructed and distinctive culture within what remains the reality of a private female sphere (see Linda Kerber, 'Separate spheres, female worlds, women's place: the rhetoric of women's history' in *Journal of Women's History*, 75 (1988), pp 14-17, 37-39).

18. Susan Moller Okin, *Women in Western Political Thought* (New Jersey, 1979), pp 10-11; Judith A. Baer, *The Chains of Protection: the Judicial Response to Women's Labor Legislation* (Westport, Connecticut, 1978), pp 168-169, 180-181, 216-217; Jo Freeman, 'Women and public policy: an overview' in Ellen Boneparth (ed.), *Women, Power and Policy* (New York, 1982), pp 49, 62-65.

19. Hilda L. Smith, 'Female bonds and the family: recent directions in women's history' in Paula Treichler, Cheris Kramarae and Beth Stafford (eds), *For Alma Mater: Theory and Practice in Feminist Scholarship* (Urbana, 1985), pp 272-291; 'Female bonds and the family: continuing doubts', unpublished paper, portions of which appeared in the Organization of American Historians, *Newsletter*, February 1987, pp 13-14 (quotations are on p. 13). Joan W. Scott also noted a similar trend in 'Women in history: the modern period', pp 151-3.

20. Lisa Vogel, 'Telling tales: historians of our own lives' in *Journal of Women's History*, 2, no. 3 (1991), pp 89-101. Vogel denies the 'triumphalist' interpretation of the post-structural historians of women who insist that the feminist stage of women's history in the 1970s suffered from terminal 'methodological and theoretical errors'. Instead, she describes this early women's history as grounded in the politics of the second women's movement and, therefore, concludes that its practitioners 'did not essentialise women and ignore difference. They did not produce a feminism that exalted women's sphere and culture. And they did not operate within a stolidly simpleminded epistemology' (p. 92). Clare Dalton, 'Where we stand: observations on the situation of feminist legal thought' in *Berkeley Women's Law Journal*, 3 (1987-1988), p. 9.

21. Joan Scott, *Gender and the Politics of History* (New York, 1988), pp 2, 11.

22. Somer Brodribb, *Nothing Mat(t)ers: A Feminist Critique of Postmodernism* (Melbourne, 1992), pp 7-8, 20.

23. Margaret MacCurtain and Mary O'Dowd, 'An agenda for women's history in Ireland, part I: 1500-1800' in *Irish Historical Studies* (May 1992), p. 2.

24. Jeffrey Weeks, 'Questions of identity' in Pat Caplan (ed.), *The Cultural Construction of Sexuality* (London, 1987), p. 31. See also Kathleen Barry, 'Deconstructing deconstruction (or, whatever happened to *Feminist Studies?*)' in *Ms.: the World of Women* (January/February 1991), pp 83-85. Barry notes that the politics of differences almost always result in the exclusion rather than inclusion of marginal groups by making them the 'other'.

25. Simone de Beauvoir, *The Second Sex* (New York, 1961), p. xviii. For standard rational-isations about the harshness and hopelessness of de Beauvoir's assumptions, see Mary Daly, *Pure Lust: Elemental Feminist Philosophy* (Boston, 1984), pp 137-138.

26. See various versions of my article 'Gender as a category of paralysis' in *Women's History Review*, 3, no. 2 (1994), pp 149-68; in *Women's Studies International Forum* 17, no. 4 (Summer 1994), pp 443-47; in Diane Bell and Renate Klein (eds), *Radically Speaking: Feminism Reclaimed* (Melbourne, 1995), pp 393-412 and 'The pernicious effects of post-structuralism on women's history' in *The Chronicle of Higher Education*, 20 October 1993, pp B1-B2.

27. Gordon, 'What's new in women's history' in Teresa de Lauretis (ed.), *Feminist Studies/Critical Studies* (Bloomington, Indiana, 1986), pp 21-22, 25; Vicki L. Ruiz and Ellen Carol Du Bois, *Unequal Sisters*.

28. Zillah R. Eisenstein, *The Female Body and the Law* (Berkeley, California, 1988), pp 3, 39-40.

29. Joan Wallach Scott, 'Gender: a useful category of historical analysis' in *American Historical Review*, 91, no. 5 (1986), pp 1053-1075; 'Deconstructing equality – versus – difference' 36 (first quotation); 'Rewriting history' in Margaret Randolph Higonnet et al (eds), *Behind the Lines: Gender and the Two World Wars* (New Haven, Connecticut, 1987), p. 22 (second quotation); Lois Banner, 'A reply to 'culture et pouvoir' from the perspective of United States women's history' in *Journal of Women's History*, no. 1 (1989), p. 104 (third and fifth quotations); Myra Dinnerstein, 'Questions for the nineties' in *Women's Review of Books*, February 1989, p. 13; and Dalton, 'Where we stand: observations on the situation of feminist legal thought', p. 11 (fourth and sixth quotations).

30. Linda Kerber, Alice Kessler-Harris and Kathryn Kish Sklar (eds), *U.S. History as Women's History* (Chapel Hill, South Carolina, 1995).

31. See 'Theories about the end of everything', introduction to the *Journal of Women's History*, 1:3 (1990) for reference to the end-of-history theory proclaimed by Francis Fukuyama, U.S. State Department policy planner, on the eve of the collapse of communism in Central and Eastern Europe. For other predictions about the end of women's history, see the summary of a session of the Eighth Berkshire Conference on the History of Women, where a handful of historians expressed concern about the future of women's history in the *Chronicle of Higher Education*, July 5, 1990. This point of view was strongly challenged in a subsequent letter to the editor from Gerda Lerner and Kathryn Kish Sklar.

32. 'The second sex in the third world' in *The New York Times*, 10 September 1995, p. 1 of 'Week in Review' section.

Mary O'Dowd:

From Morgan to MacCurtain:

Women Historians in Ireland from the 1790s to the 1990s

1. I am very grateful to the many people who provided advice, guidance, photocopies and suggestions while I was researching this article. I would particularly like to thank the following: Toby Barnard, Ciaran Brady, Nicholas Canny, Margaret Crawford, Louis Cullen, Mary Daly, Marie Therese Flanagan, Edith Mary Johnston, Maria Luddy, Jim Lydon,

Margaret MacCurtain, Donal MacCartney, R.B. McDowell, the principal and clerk of the archives of Newnham College, Cambridge, Susan Parkes, Nini Rodgers, Sabine Wichert.

2. Natalie Zemon Davis, 'Women's history in transition: the European case' in *Feminist Studies,* 3 (1976), pp 83-103; 'Gender and genre: women as historical writers, 1400-1820' in Patricia Labalme (ed.), *Beyond their Sex: Learned Women of the European Past* (New York, 1980), pp 153-182; Kathryn Kish Sklar, 'American female historians in context, 1770-1930' in *Feminist Studies*, 3 (1976), pp 171-184; Bonnie G. Smith, 'The contribution of women to modern historiography in Great Britain, France, and the United States, 1750-1940' in *American Historical Review*, 89 (1984), pp 709-732; Joan Wallach Scott, *Gender and the Politics of History* (New York, 1988), pp 178-98; Billie Melman, 'Gender, history and memory: the invention of women's past in the nineteenth and early twentieth centuries' in *History and Memory*, 5 (1993), pp 5-40; Maxine Berg, 'The first women economic historians' in *Economic History Review*, xlv, 2 (1992), pp 308-329; 'A woman in history: Eileen Power and the early years of social history and women's history' in Mary O'Dowd and Sabine Wichert (eds), *Chattel, Servant or Citizen: Women's Status in Church, State and Society* (Belfast, 1995), pp 12-21; Joan Thirsk, 'The history women' in *ibid.*, pp 1-11; Ann-Louise Shapiro (ed.), *Feminists Revision History* (Rutgers University Press, 1994); Bridget Hill, *The Republican Virago. The Life and Times of Catharine Macaulay, Historian* (Oxford, 1992); Maria Grever, *Strijd Tegen de Stilte. Johanna Naber (1859-1941) en de Vrouwenstem in Geschiedenis* (Hilversum, 1994).

3. Mary O'Dowd, 'Women and politics, 1500-1800' in *Field Day Anthology of Irish Writing,* vol. iv (forthcoming, New York, 1998); 'Women historians' in *ibid.*

4. Laetitia Pilkington, *Memoirs of Mrs Letitia Pilkington, Written by Herself ,* ... (Dublin, 1749); Mary Lyons (ed.), *The Memoirs of Mrs Leeson, Madam, 1727-1797* (Dublin, 1995); Dorothea Herbert, *Retrospections of Dorothea Herbert 1770-1806* (2nd edition, Dublin, 1988). See also Carolyn Steedman, *'La Théorie qui n'en est pas une;* or, why Clio doesn't care' in Ann Louise Shapiro (ed.), *Feminists Revision History,* p. 87. Letitia Pilkington referred to herself as the 'cream of historians' and to her memoirs as 'my true history' (Janet Todd, *The Sign of Angelica* (London, 1989), p.6).

5. See for example the papers of Lady Elizabeth Hastings, Countess of Moira (1731-1804) (P.R.O.N.I., M/1/1; M/3/5; M/3/14/1-34; M3/6/1-49). Mrs Vesey, associated with the Blue Stocking movement, reorganised her family's papers (National Archives, Dublin).

6. Charlotte Brooke, *Reliques of Irish Poetry* (Dublin, 1789). See also Clare O'Halloran, 'Irish re-creations of the Gaelic past: the challenge of MacPherson's Ossian' in *Past and Present*, 124 (1989), pp 86-89.

7. Maria Edgeworth, *Castle Rackrent* (Oxford University Press Edition, 1995). See also Tom Dunne, *Maria Edgeworth and the Colonial Mind* (Cork, 1984); Marilyn Butler, *Maria Edgeworth, a Literary Biography* (Oxford, 1972), p. 365; W.J. McCormack, 'Maria Edgeworth (1768-1849)' in Seamus Deane (ed.), *Field Day Anthology of Irish Writing* (3 vols, Derry, 1991), i, pp 1011-13.

8. Claire O'Halloran, 'Irish re-creations of the Gaelic past: the challenge of MacPherson's Ossian', pp 91-92.

9. Mary O'Dowd, 'Women and politics, 1500-1800'.

10. Elizabeth Owens Blackburne, *Illustrious Irishwomen, Being Memoirs on Some of the Most Noted Irishwomen* (2 vols, London, 1877), ii, pp 27-51.

11. For comparison with women elsewhere see the literature cited in note 1 above and especially Kathryn Kish Sklar, 'American female historians in context, 1770-1930'.

12. *Woman and her Master* (2 vols, London, 1840).

13. Natalie Zemon Davis, 'Women's history in transition: the European case'; Kathryn Kish Sklar, 'American female historians in context, 1770-1930'; Bonnie G. Smith, 'The contribu-

tion of women to modern historiography in Great Britain, France, and the United States, 1750-1940'.

14. See extract printed in Mary O'Dowd (ed.), 'Women historians' in *Field Day Anthology of Irish Writing*, vol. iv (forthcoming, New York, 1998). See also Riana O'Dwyer, 'Woman and her master: Lady Morgan and feminism' in *University College Galway, Women's Studies Centre Review*, vol. 3 (1994), pp 117-127.

15. *Ibid.*, pp 121-122.

16. *Woman and her Master*, i, pp 59-63.

17. *Ibid.*, pp 176-80, 193.

18. Anna Brownell Jameson, *Memoirs of Celebrated Female Sovereigns* (2 vols, London, 1831); *Beauties of the Court of King Charles the Second* (London, 1833). See *D.N.B.* for her Irish origins. Julia Kavanagh, *Women in France during the Eighteenth Century* (2 vols, London, 1850); *Women of Christianity* (London, 1852); *French Women of Letters: Biographical Sketches* (London, 1862); *English Women of Letters: Biographical Sketches* (London, 1862). For Kavanagh's Irish background see Noreen Higgins, 'Julia Kavanagh (1824-1877) – a novelist from Thurles' in *Tipperary Historical Journal* (1992), pp 81-83. See also C. J. Hamilton, *Notable Irishwomen* (Dublin, 1904), p 190-202.

19. Elizabeth Owens Blackburne, *Illustrious Irishwomen, Being Memoirs of Some of the Most Noted Irishwomen from the Earliest Ages to the Present Century* (2 vols, London, 1877).

20. *Ibid.*, i, p. vii. For biographical details of Blackburne see D.J. O'Donoghue, *The Poets of Ireland: A Biographical and Bibliographical Dictionary of Irish Writers of English Origin* (Dublin and London, 1912); *The New Ireland Review*, xxvii (1907), p. 369.

21. *Illustrious Irishwomen*, vol. ii, p. 345.

22. See, for example, Frances Gerard, *Some Celebrated Irish Beauties of the Last Century* (London, 1895); *Some Fair Hibernians* (London, 1897); L.M. McCraith, *The Romance of Irish Heroines* (London, 1913); C.J. Hamilton, *Notable Irishwomen* (Dublin, 1904).

23. Helena Concannon, *Women of '98* (Dublin, 1919); R. M. Fox, *Rebel Irishwomen* (Dublin, 1935); James F. Cassidy, *The Women of the Gael* (Boston, Mass., 1922).

24. Sister of Mercy, *The Life of Reverend Mother Catherine McAuley* (Dublin, 1864); Member of the Order of Mercy, *The Life of Catherine McAuley* (New York, 1866); Sarah Atkinson, *Mary Aikenhead: Her Life, her Work and her Friends* (Dublin, 1882); Katharine Tynan, *A Nun, her Friends and her Order, Being a Life of Mother Xaviera Fallon* (London, 1892); K.M. Barry, *Catherine McAuley and the Sisters of Mercy* (Dublin, 1894); P.M. MacSweeney (ed.), *Letters of Mary Aikenhead* (Dublin, 1914).

25. Among Concannon's publications are *Women of '98* (Dublin, 1919); *Daughters of Banba* (Dublin, 1922); *The Poor Clares in Ireland* (Dublin, 1929); *Irish Nuns in Penal Times* (London, 1931); *The Queen of Ireland: A Historical Account of Ireland's Devotion to the Blessed Virgin* (Dublin, 1938); *The Irish Sisters of Mercy in the Crimean War* (Dublin, 1950); *A Garden of Girls or Famous School Girls of Former Times* (Dublin, [1921]; revised edition, New York, 1928). Concannon also wrote a school textbook: *Irish History for Junior Grade Classes: The Defence of our Gaelic Civilisation 1460-1660* (Dublin, 1921).

26. Mary M. Macken, 'Musings and memories. Helena Concannon, M.A., D. Litt.' in *Studies*, 42 (1953), p. 96. See also obituary in *Irish Press*, 28 Feb. 1952; *Irish Independent*, 28 Feb. 1952; Maryann Valiulis, 'Neither feminist nor flapper: the ecclesiastical construction of the ideal Irish woman' in Mary O'Dowd and Sabine Wichert (eds), *Chattel, Servant or Citizen: Women's Status in Church, State and Society* (Belfast, 1995), pp 168-178.

27. The biographical approach to Irish women's history continues to be popular. See, for example, the numerous biographies of Constance Markievicz and Maud Gonne, praised for their nationalism and only belatedly, for their feminism (Seán O'Faoláin, *Constance Markievicz or the Average Revolutionary* (London, 1934); Jacqueline Van Voris, *Constance*

de Markievicz:In the Cause of Ireland (Amherst, Massachusett, 1967); Nancy Cardozo, *Maud Gonne: Lucky Eyes and a High Heart* (New York, 1978); Margaret Ward, *Maud Gonne: Ireland's Joan of Arc* (London, 1990)). The most recent collection of women's lives is Mary Cullen and Maria Luddy (eds), *Women, Power and Consciousness in Nineteenth-Century Ireland: Eight Biographical Studies* (Dublin, 1995).

28. R. W. Dudley Edwards and Mary O'Dowd, *Sources for Early Modern Ireland, 1534-1641* (Cambridge, 1985), pp 185-201.

29. *An Illustrated History of Ireland, 400-1800* (Kenmare, 1868; new edition, 1995) . See also note 32 below.

30. For example, she described the rebellion of the earl of Kildare in 1534 as a 'wild career of lawless violence with but few followers and without any influential companions'. She was also anxious to distance herself from the rebellion of 1798, declaring that she would 'neither palliate nor excuse' the violence in Wexford in 1798. She condemned Wolfe Tone for being 'tinctured with republican sentiments' and claimed that 'Catholics were only prevented from adopting similar opinions by their inherent belief in the divine right of kings' (*An Illustrated History of Ireland*, pp 391, 614-5, 619-621).

31. For Cusack's turbulent relationship with the Catholic Church see Irene Ffrench Eagar, *Margaret Anna Cusack: A Biography* (Dublin, 1970, revised edition, 1979).

32. Cusack wrote several versions of her history. *An Illustrated History of Ireland* was the earliest version and was written for a popular market. *The History of the Irish Nation, Ecclesiastical, Social, Biographical, Antiquarian and Industrial* (London, 1876) was an extended edition which included more extensive quotations from secondary sources and had more illustrations. It was also presented in an elaborated casing and was clearly intended for a more select (and wealthier) readership. *The Student's Manual of Irish History* (London, 1870) was an abbreviated version intended for use in schools. The preface suggests that it was particularly directed at schools in England.

33. *An Illustrated History of Ireland*, preface.

34. Joan Thirsk, 'The history women', pp 2-7; Bonnie Smith, 'The contribution of women to modern historiography in Great Britain, France, and the United States, 1750-1940', pp 723-4. It is worth noting in this context that the only woman invited to contribute to Thomas Davis's Irish Library was Annie Hutton, who was commissioned to edit the correspondence of Cardinal Rinuccini (see *The Embassy in Ireland of Monsignor G.B. Rinuccini, Archbishop of Fermo, in the Years 1645-1649*, edited and translated by Annie Hutton (Dublin, 1873)). See also below.

35. T.C. Barnard, '1641: a bibliographical essay' in Brian Mac Cuarta (ed.), *Ulster 1641: Aspects of the Rising* (Belfast, 1993), pp 183-186.

36. Like other women with similar interests in document-based research, Hickson began her studies at local and family level before progressing to examining archives further afield (Mary Agnes Hickson, *Selections from Old Kerry Records* (1st series, London, 1872; 2nd series, London, 1874)). See also Bonnie G. Smith, 'The contribution of women to modern historiography', p. 720; Mary Frances Cusack, *A History of the Kingdom of Kerry* (London, 1871); *A History of the City and County of Cork* (Kenmare, 1875); *Transactions of the Kilkenny Archaeological Society*, i (1849-1851), pp 7, 125, 127, 282, 286 (for female membership of one of the first local history societies in Ireland).

37. Mary Hickson, *Ireland in the Seventeenth Century or the Irish Massacres of 1641-2, Their Causes and Results* (2 vols, London, 1884), i, pp 1-166.

38. Mary Agnes Hickson, 'The depositions of 1641' in *English Historical Review*, ii (1887), pp 133-137, 527. See also Lecky's correspondence in Trinity College, Dublin for Hickson's interest in editing documents.

39. A notable exception is T.C. Barnard, '1641: a bibliographical essay'.

40. T. More Madden, *The Memoirs (Chiefly Autobiographical) from 1798 to 1896 of Richard Robert Madden* (London, 1891), pp 61, 122-3; Leon Ó Broin, *An Maidíneach. Staraí na nÉireannach Aontaithe* (Dublin, 1971), pp 155-6, 173, 190; R. R. Madden, *The United Irishmen, their Lives and Times* (revised edition, 4 vols, London, 1857-60), i, preface. Harriet Madden also wrote for some time the weekly column which appeared under her husband's name in the *Morning Chronicle* (Ó Broin, *An Maidíneach*, pp 205, 207-8). See also Bonnie Smith, 'Historiography, objectivity, and the abusive widow' in Ann-Loise Shapiro (ed.), *Feminists Revision History* (Rutgers, 1994), p. 26 on the familial nature of many research projects in the nineteenth century.

41. Rosa Mulholland Gilbert (ed.), *Calendar of Ancient Records of Dublin*, vols viii-xvii (Dublin, 1901-1916). Lady Gilbert also arranged for the Corporation of Dublin to purchase her husband's library (Douglas Hyde and D.J. O'Donoghue (eds), *Catalogue of the Books and Manuscripts Comprising the Library of the Late Sir John T. Gilbert* (Dublin, 1918), p. iv).

42. Elisabeth Lecky, *A Memoir of the Right Honourable William Edward Hartpole Lecky* (London, 1909); W.E. H. Lecky, *Historical and Political Essays* (London, 1908) with preface by Elisabeth Lecky; Donal McCartney, *W.E.H. Lecky. Historian and Politician, 1838-1903* (Dublin, 1994), p. 185. See also the catalogue to the Lecky papers in Trinity College, Dublin.

43. Lady Gilbert, *Sir John T. Gilbert, Irish Historian and Archivist* (Dublin, 1905); Mary Ferguson, *Sir Samuel Ferguson in the Ireland of his Day* (2 vols, London, 1896). Mary Ferguson also wrote a synthesis of Irish history before 1169 which made use of her husband's literary work as well as the unpublished papers of Eugene O'Curry in the Royal Irish Academy (Mary Ferguson, *The Story of the Irish Before the Conquest* (3 editions, Dublin, 1868, 1890, 1903)). Richard Bagwell's wife, Harriet, also compiled a memoir of her husband (unpublished, in possession of Bagwell's granddaughter, Mary). Mulholland also financially subsidised her husband's historical writing.

44. *Memoirs of Richard Lovell Edgeworth, Esq, Begun by Himself and Concluded by his Daughter, Maria Edgeworth* (2 vols, London, 1820); William T. W. Tone, *The Life of Theobald Wolfe Tone* (2 vols, Washington, 1826); Marianne Elliott, *Wolfe Tone, Prophet of Irish Independence* (New Haven and London, 1989), pp 309, 407, 411-413; *Irish Times*, 6 February 1996, p. 9.

45. *Ibid.*, p. 407.

46. 'The women of Young Ireland' (National Library of Ireland, MS 10906, p 29); Mrs Morgan John O'Connell, *The Last Colonel of the Irish Brigade* (2 vols, Dublin, 1892); A.I. O'Neill Daunt (ed.), *A Life Spent for Ireland: Being Selections from the Journals of the Late W.J. O'Neill Daunt*. Mary Frances Cusack edited O'Connell's speeches in *The Speeches and Public Letters of the Liberator* (2 vols, Dublin, 1875).

47. R.R. Madden,*The United Irishmen, their Lives and Times* (3 series, 7 vols, London, 1842-45) . Madden's papers in Trinity College, Dublin include many of the papers and correspondence which he received from women relatives of members of the United Irishmen. Anne McCabe, a graduate student in Queen's University, Belfast, is currently compling a list of them.

48. For a general account of the Gaelic literary revival see Seamus Deane, *A Short History of Irish Literature* (London, 1986), pp 141-209.

49. Eibhlin Breathnach, 'Charting new waters: women's experience in higher education, 1879-1908' in Mary Cullen (ed.), *Girls Don't Do Honours: Irish Women in Education in the Nineteenth and Twentieth Centuries* (Dublin, 1987), pp 55-76.

50. John Kenyon, *The History Men* (Pittsburgh, 1984), p. 163; entries for J.R. Green and Alice Stopford Green in *D.N.B.* Stopford Green carefully preserved the memory and scholarly reputation of her husband. Her correspondence in the National Library of Ireland includes many references to the posthumous revising and updating which she did on her

husband's books. She also acknowledged that 'Everything I live on, house, money, books, training come to me from that great and hard struggle of Mr Green.' (Alice Stopford Green to Oliver Wendell Holmes, 22 Dec. 1919, Alice Stopford Green Papers (National Library of Ireland, MS 11487(2)).) See also her speech at a commemoration ceremony for her husband in Oxford (*loc. cit.*, MS 8714(1)).

51. *Henry II* (London, 1888); *Town Life in the Fifteenth Century* (2 vols, London, 1894).

52. Alice Stopford Green to Oliver Wendell Holmes, 22 Dec. 1919, Alice Stopford Green Papers (National Library of Ireland, MS 11487(2)); Alice Stopford Green's speech at commemoration ceremony for her husband in Oxford (*loc. cit.*, MS 8714(1)).

53. Alice Stopford Green, *The Old Irish World* (Dublin, 1912), pp 168-197 was a response to a critical review of *The Making of Ireland and its Undoing, 1200-1600* (London, 1908) by the historian Robert Dunlop. See also *The Irish Nation*, 26 Dec. 1908-Jan. 1909 (copy in Alice Stopford Green papers in National Library of Ireland); Roy Foster, 'History and the Irish question' in *Transactions of the Royal Historical Society*, 5th series (1988), reprinted in Ciaran Brady (ed.), *Interpreting Irish History* (Dublin, 1994), pp 137-9.

54. See Steven Ellis, 'Nationalist historiography and the English and Gaelic worlds in the late middle ages' in *I.H.S.*, xxv (1986-7), reprinted in Brady, *Interpreting Irish History*, p. 162, note 4 and p. 173, note 47 for an example of the way in which Stopford Green's work is criticised for its nationalist bias while still being considered a reliable source for its contribution to the economic and social history of late medieval Ireland.

55. J.J. Lee, 'Some aspects of modern Irish historiography' in Ernst Schulin (ed.), *Gedenkschrift Martin Gohring. Studien zur Europaischen geschichte* (Wiesbaden, 1968), p. 435.

56. *The Historical Association, 1906-1956* (published by the Historical Association, London, 1955), p. 22; Mrs J.R. Green, 'Irish national tradition' in *History*, new series, ii (1917-1918), pp 67-86.

57. See Alice Stopford Green Papers, National Library of Ireland, MS 10428 for the text of a lecture on how to teach history to girls which she delivered at Notting Hill High School, 18 Nov. 1895. See *loc. cit.*, MS 15126(2) for Green's correspondence with Bonaparte Wyse, Minister for Education in Northern Ireland, on the proposed use of her books in schools in Northern Ireland.

58. See, for example, *The Old Irish World* (Dublin, 1912), pp v-vii. Stopford Green's papers in the National Library of Ireland indicate that she corresponded with a wide range of historians and literary scholars in Ireland and in England.

59. See Alice Stopford Green to Strachan, 8 June 1904 (Alice Stopford Green Papers, National Library of Ireland, MS 15122); Alice Stopford Green to Douglas Hyde, 7 Feb. [1909] (*loc. cit.*, MS 17771)); same to Mrs Douglas Hyde, 20 Feb. 1909 (*loc. cit.*); same to Douglas Hyde, 1 May 1909 (*loc. cit.*); same to same, 19 Dec. 1914 (*loc. cit.*); R.B. McDowell, *Alice Stopford Green: A Passionate Historian* (Dublin, 1967), pp 79-81.

60. Alice Stopford Green Papers, National Library of Ireland, MS 17771.

61. Alice Stopford Green to Douglas Hyde, 18 Jan. 1909 (Alice Stopford Green Papers, National Library of Ireland, MS 17771).

62. Alice Stopford Green to Mrs Douglas Hyde, 20 Feb. 1909 (*loc. cit.*).

63. Alice Stopford Green to the National Academy Committee, March 1922 (*loc. cit.*, MS 18471). Over ten years before the establishment of the Institute of Historical Research in London, Stopford Green also envisaged extending the School of Irish Studies to include a centre for the study of history and offered to sponsor a series of publications relating to the history of the Ordnance Survey, a proposal which was to be taken up almost seventy years later by the Institute of Irish Studies at Queen's University Belfast (same to Richard Best, no date (Alice Stopford Green Papers, National Library of Ireland, MS 15114(2)); same to same,

16 Jan. no year (*loc. cit.*, MS 15114 (7)); Angelique Day and Patrick McWilliams (eds), *Ordnance Survey Memoirs of Ireland*, vol 1-32 (Belfast, 1990-1995)).

64. *Pagan Ireland (Epochs of Irish History - 1)* (Dublin, 1904); *A Textbook of Irish Literature*, parts i, ii (Dublin, 1906, 1908); *Cuchulainn, the Hound of Ulster* (London, 1909).

65. See Robin Flower's tribute to Hull in *The Times*, 16 January 1935; obituary in *The Irish Times*, 15 January 1935; obituary by R.R. Marett in *Folklore*, vol. xlvi (1935), pp 76-77; 36th Annual Report of the Irish Texts Society, 1934, p. 3. A Hull memorial volume was published by the Society in 1939 (see Douglas Hyde (ed.), *Sgéalta Thomáis Uí Chathasaigh* (Dublin, 1939)).

66. Eleanor Knott (ed.), *The Bardic Poems of Tadhg Dall Ó Huiginn* (two vols, Irish Texts Society, Dublin, 1922); Agnes O'Farrelly was also commissioned to edit a text on the flight of the earls (7th Annual Report of the Irish Texts Society, 1905, p. 4).; Sophie Bryant was nominated to the council of the society by Hull (8th Annual Report of the Irish Texts Society, 1906, p. 8).

67. These include Maud Joynt (see obituary by Eleanor Knott in *Éigse*, vol. ii (1940), pp 226-229 (I am grateful to Briana Nic Dhiarmada for supplying me with a copy of this reference); Eleanor Knott the first woman member of the Royal Irish Academy (see obituary by Daniel A. Binchy in *Ériu*, vol. xxvi (Dublin, 1975), pp 182-1850; Kathleen Mulchrone, Professor of Celtic Studies in University College, Galway (see *The Catholic Bulletin* (1938), pp 615-17); Cecile O'Rahilly, Nessa Ní Shéaghdha (see obituary in *The Irish Times*, 9 June 1993) and many others.

68. See Maxine Berg, 'The first women economic historians' in *Economic History Review*, xlv, 2 (1992), pp 308-329.

69. Eleanor Hull, *A History of Ireland and her People*, i, pp 20, 21, 25, 27-29, 86, 322-3, 336, 344-6, 434-6. *Epochs of Irish History – I: Pagan Ireland*, pp 112-125; *A Textbook of Irish Literature*, part i, pp 77-8; *Folklore of the British Isles* (London, 1928), pp 48-54, 58-60.

70. Sophie Bryant, *Liberty Order and Law under Native Irish Rule: A Study in the Book of the Ancient Laws of Ireland* (London, 1923), pp 320-330; Sophie Bryant, D.Sc., Litt.D. Memorial volume, 1850-1922 (privately printed, North London Collegiate School, London, 1922, copy in N.L.I.), pp 31-37.

71. Mary O'Dowd, 'Women historians' in *Field Day Anthology of Irish Writing*, vol iv includes extracts from the writings of Hull, Stopford Green and others outlining this view.

72. Mary M. Macken, 'In memoriam: Mary T. Hayden' in *Studies*, vol. 31 (1942), pp 369-371.

73. Obituary by G.A. Hayes-McCoy in *Analecta Hibernica*, no 26 (1970), pp xii-xiv.

74. Obituary in *The Irish Times*, 8 February 1952 and by F.S.L. Lyons in *Trinity*, no 14 (Michaelmas, 1962), p. 35. See also R.B. McDowell and D.A. Webb, *Trinity College, Dublin, 1592-1952* (Cambridge, 1982), p. 352.

75. Brian Walker and Alf McCreary, *Degrees of Excellence. The Story of Queen's Belfast 1845-1995* (Belfast, 1994), p. 77.

76. Obituary by Gearóid Ó Tauthaigh in *The Irish Times*, June 1980.

77. At twenty-nine O'Sullivan was considered too young for the prestigious chair in philosophy (see obituary by Mary F. Macken in *Studies*, xxxvii (1948(, pp 1-6). For the activities of other women graduates at this time see pp 176-7 below.

78. For contemporary women historians in England see Maxine Berg, 'The first women economic historians' in *Economic History Review*, xlv, 2 (1992), pp 308-329; Joan Thirsk, 'The history women' in Mary O'Dowd and Sabine Wichert, *Chattel, Servant or Citizen: Women's Status in Church, State and Society* (Belfast, 1995), pp 8-11.

79. *Old Galway: the History of a Norman Colony in Ireland* (Cambridge, 1942); *Italian Merchant Bankers in Ireland in the Thirteenth Century* (Dublin, 1962).

80. Mary Clancy, "... It was our joy to keep the flag flying': a study of the women's suffrage campaign in County Galway' in *University College Galway Women's Studies Centre Review*, vol. iii (1994), pp 98-101; 'On the "western outpost": local government and women's suffrage in County Galway, 1898-1918' in Gerard Moran (ed.), *Galway: History and Society* (Dublin, 1996), pp 557-87; 'The wives of Ulick, 1st earl of Clanricarde' in *Journal of the Galway Archaeological and Historical Society*, vol. xxi (1945), pp 174-183; 'The use of leisure in Old Galway' in *ibid.*, vol. xviii (1939), pp 99-120.

81. Christopher Townley, 'The Galway Archaeological and Historical Society' in *Galway Archaeological and Historical Society*, vol. xxxv (1976), p. 9.

82. *Ibid.*; Minute book of the Galway Archaeological and Historical Society, 1900-1960 (Hardiman Library, University College, Galway). I am grateful to the librarian of the Hardiman Library for permission to use this source.

83. Obituary in *The Irish Times*, 8 Feb. 1952. See also obituary by F.S.L. Lyons in *Trinity*, no 14 (Michaelmas, 1962), p. 35.

84. Maxwell was a close friend of Dame Myra Curtis, Principal of Newnham College, 1942-54 (*Newnham College Roll Letter* (1972), pp 53-57), and she was also friendly with the historian, Dorothy George, whose *English Social Life in the Eighteenth Century, Illustrated from Contemporary Sources* (London, 1923) was similar in format and purpose to Maxwell's *Irish History from Contemporary Sources, 1509-1610* (Dublin, 1923). See also Maxine Berg, 'The first economic women historians'. I am grateful to Dr R.B. McDowell for providing me with personal details about Maxwell's circle of friends in London.

85. Constantia Maxwell, *A Brief Bibliography of Irish History* (Historical Association, Dublin, 1911; revised editions, 1911, 1921); *A School History of Ireland* (Dublin, 1914); *A Short History of Ireland* (Dublin, 1914); Constantia Maxwell, 'The colonisation of Ulster' in *History*, new series, i (1916-1917), pp 86-96, 147-58; *The Foundation of Modern Ireland*. Part I. The civil policy of Henry VIII, and the reformation (London, 1921); *Irish History from Contemporary Sources*; David Fitzpatrick, 'The futility of history: a failed experiment in Irish education' in Ciaran Brady (ed.), *Ideology and the Historians* (Dublin, 1991), pp 178, 179, 180, 181.

86. 'Mary Hayden' in *Ten Dublin Women* (Dublin, 1991), pp 47-53.

87. 'Women in the middle ages' in *The Irish Review*, Sept. 1913, pp 344-358; 'Charity children in 18th-century Dublin' in *Dublin Historical Record*, vol. v (1942-3), pp 92-107; *A Short History of the Irish People* (Dublin, 1921).

88. It is also worth noting that Maxwell and O'Sullivan are remembered by former students as enthusiastic and stimulating teachers while Hayden was noted as an outstanding public speaker (personal communications from Professor James Lydon and Dr R.B. McDowell; Mary M. Macken, 'In memoriam: Mary T. Hayden' in *Studies*, vol. 31 (1942), p. 370).

89. G.A. Hayes McCoy and James Lydon were two of O'Sullivan's most successful students. For others see lists of 'Research in Irish universities' in *Irish Historical Studies*, vol. i (1938-1957). For Hayden's support of Dudley Edwards see Edith Mary Johnson 'Managing an inheritance: Colonel J.C. Wedgwood, the *history of parliament* and the lost history of the Irish parliament' in *Proceedings of the Royal Irish Academy*, vol. 89, section C, no 7 (1989), p. 179. Hayden also wrote the preface to R.W. Dudley Edwards, *Church and State in Tudor Ireland* (Dublin, 1935), pp vii-x. I am grateful to Dr R.B. McDowell for information on Maxwell's appreciation of Moody's activities.

90. Preface to *Irish Historical Studies*, i (1938-9), reprinted in C. Brady (ed.), *Interpreting Irish History: The Debate on Historical Revisionism* (Dublin, 1994), p. 36.

91. See, for example, *Irish Historical Studies.*, vol. v (1946-7), pp 260-261; vol. xi (1958-9), pp 248-249. A more favourable review of the revised edition of *Dublin Under the Georges* (London, 1956) appeared in *ibid.*, vol. xi (1958-9), p. 24.

92. See, for example, *I.H.S.*, vol. i (1938-9), p. 87.

93. *Ibid.*, vol. iv (1944-5), pp 361-367. *Italian Merchant Bankers in Ireland in the Thirteenth Century* (Dublin, 1962) was treated more fairly by J.A. Otway Ruthven in *I.H.S.*, vol. xiv (1964-5), pp 265-7.

94. Preface to *Irish Historical Studies*, i (1938-9), reprinted in C. Brady (ed.), *Interpreting Irish History*, p 36. I am grateful to Dr Brady for suggesting this point to me. The following comments have benefited from discussion with him.

95. Ciaran Brady (ed.), *Interpreting Irish History: The Debate on Historical Revisionism* (Dublin, 1995), pp 23-4, 140-1.

96. The obituary was probably written by Dudley Edwards (*I.H.S.*, vol iii (1942-3), pp 401-2).

97. *Calendar of University College Galway for 1968-1969* (Dublin, 1968), p 94; personal communications from Dr Ciaran Brady and Dr Nini Rodgers.

98. See, for example, *Calendars of University College Cork, 1948-55* (Cork, 1949-1956); Department of Education, *Notes for Teachers – History* (Dublin, 1933, 1955, 1962).

99. The tradition continued into the second half of the twentieth century. Among the women historians who have been involved in the writing of school textbooks are M.E. Collins, *Conquest and Colonisation* (Dublin, 1969); *Ireland, 1868-1966* (Dublin, 1993); Mary E. Daly, *Social and Economic History of Ireland since 1800* (Dublin, 1991); and Margaret MacCurtain, who edited the series *A History of Ireland* (3 vols., Dublin, 1969). Maureen Wall was one of the founders of the Dublin Historical Association and wrote the first pamphlet of the Association, *The Penal Laws*, which was primarily intended for a student/teacher readership. In 1966 Margaret MacCurtain was one of two historians who served on the Study Group on the Teaching of History in Irish Schools ('The Teaching of History in Irish Schools' in *Administration*, 15 (1967), pp 168-285).

100. *I.H.S.*, ix (1954-55), pp 83-85; xiv (1964-5) pp 61-64.

101. I am grateful to Professor Donal McCartney for pointing this out to me.

102. *Dublin University Calendar 1938-39* (Dublin, 1939), p. 28; *Dublin University Calendar 1951-2* (Dublin, 1951), pp 26-27; *Calendar of the Queen's University of Belfast, 1956-57* (Belfast, 1956), p. 38.

103. Síle Ní Chinnéide was appointed an associate professor in University College, Galway in 1966.

104. John A. Murphy, *The College, A History of Queen's/University College, Cork, 1845-1995* (Cork, 1995) pp 127-31, 286, 346.

105. I am grateful to Professor Donal McCartney for this information.

106. National University of Ireland, *Calendar for the Year 1969* (Dublin, 1969), p. 379. In the same year Ruth Dudley Edwards was awarded a prize on the basis of her travelling studentship exams. In 1925 Sheila Kennedy (Síle Ní Chinnéide) entered for the studentship and was awarded a prize (*The National University of Ireland Calendar for the Year 1951* (Dublin, 1951), p. 661).

107. Margaret Griffith studied at Oxford and Jocelyn Otway Ruthven completed a Ph.D. in Cambridge.

108. Ada K. Longfeld served as treasurer of the Irish Historical Society in 1940, but her service was temporary and may not have been unrelated to the fact that in the same year she was obliged to retire from her position in the National Museum due to marriage. In 1947 Mary O'Friel became a committee member of the Ulster Society for Irish Historical Studies, and in the 1950s Maureen Wall was for a short time a member of the committee for the Irish Historical Society. *I.H.S.* ii (1940-1), pp 127, 353; v (1946-7), p. 273; xviii (1972-3), pp 141-2; xix (1974-5), p. 342; obituary of Ada K. Longfeld by Mairead Dunlevy in *Journal of the Royal Society for Antiquarians in Ireland*, vol. 118 (1968), pp 169-70.

109. See Ciaran Brady, 'Constructive and instrumental: the dilemma of Ireland's first new historians' in Brady, *Interpreting Irish History*, pp 3-6, for an account of the institutionalisation of Irish history.

110. Emily Lawless to W.E.H. Lecky, 5 July 1889, 30 December 1890 (Trinity College, Dublin, Lecky Correspondence, nos 550, 639); see Seamus Deane (ed.), *Field Day Anthology of Irish Writing* (3 vols, Derry, 1991), ii, p. 1216 for a short biography and list of Lawless's writings.

111. Bonnie Smith, 'Historiography, objectivity, and the abusive widow' in Ann-Louise Shapiro (ed.), *Feminists Revision History* (Rutgers, 1994), p. 26. See also Natalie Zemon Davies, 'Women and the world of the Amales' in *History Workshop Journal*, 33 (1992), pp 121-37.

112. Carolyn Steedman, *Past Tenses: Essays on Writing, Autobiography and History* (London, 1992), pp 57-8, 179, 188.

Phil Kilroy:
The Use of Continental Sources of Women's Religious Congregations & the Writing of Religious Biography:
Madeleine Sophie Barat, 1779-1865

1. Madeleine Sophie Barat was born in Joigny, France in 1779. She was educated by her brother, Louis Barat, both in Joigny and later in Paris. In 1800, with a number of other women, she began educating young women in Amiens. From this small beginning communities of women grew, not only in France but also in Europe and the Americas. Until her death in 1865, Madeleine Sophie Barat was the acknowledged leader of the Society of the Sacred Heart, known in the nineteenth century as Les dames du Sacré Coeur.

2. For a discussion on the canonisation process see Catherine M. Mooney, *Philippine Duchesne: A Woman with the Poor* (Paulist Press, 1990), pp 1-31.

3. In November 1865 there was an extensive report sent to the Vatican, indicating the state of the Society of the Sacred Heart on the death of Madeleine Sophie Barat (Society of the Sacred Heart, General Archives, Rome, H-I., 5; Extrait des Archives de la Congrégation des Religieux et Religieuses, appendice iv, Etat de la Société du Sacré Coeur en 1865, année de la mort de sa vénérable fondatrice).

4. Austin Gough, *Paris and Rome: The Gallican Church and the Ultramontane Campaign 1848-1853* (Oxford, 1986), pp 22-33.

5. The General Archives, held in the Istituto del Sacro Cuore, Via S. Francesco di Sales, 18, 00165 Rome are open to researchers.

6. Charles Molette, *Guide des Sources de l'Histoire des Congrégations Féminines Françaises de Vie Active* (Paris, 1974).

7. Jeanne de Charry, *Correspondance Sainte Madeleine Sophie Barat, Sainte Philippine Duchesne. Texte des Manuscrits Originaux Présenté avec une Introduction, des Notes et un Index Analytique, 1804-1815* (Rome, 1988); *1818-1821* (Rome, 1989); *1821-1826* (Rome, 1992); *1826-1829* (Rome (forthcoming)). Jeanne de Charry has also edited the letters of Joseph Varin to Madeleine Sophie Barat (*Lettres à Sainte Madeleine Sophie Barat (1801-1849). Texte Intégral, d'après les Manuscrits Originaux, Présenté, avec une Introduction, des Notes et un Index Analytique* (Rome, 1982). Jeanne de Charry is the author of a major study of the Society of the Sacred Heart (*Histoire des Constitutions de la Société du Sacré Coeur, 1ère Partie: La Formation de l'Institut* (2 vols, Rome, 1975; 2de éd 1981); *2me partie: Les Constitutions définitives et leur approbation par le Saint-Siège* (3 vols, Rome, 1979). These have been translated into English as *History of the Constitutions of the Society of the Sacred Heart. Part 1: the Formation of the Institute* (2 vols, Rome, 1st ed. 1975; 2nd ed.

1981); *Part 2: The Definitive Constitutions and their Approbation by the Holy See* (3 vols, Rome, 1979).

8. In 1826 the General Council decided to write the history of the congregation. To this purpose several members were asked to write parts of the history (General Archives, Rome, A-II., a-1, Box 1. Early histories of the Society). In addition, Josephine de Coriolis wrote a history of the congregation. (Histoire de la Société du Sacré Coeur, General Archives, Rome. A-II., b-2.)

9. The conferences of Madeleine Sophie Barat were printed in two volumes in 1900 (London). Her formal circular letters were also printed in two volumes (London, 1904; 1917).

10. General Archives, Rome, C-I., 1-f Box L. (Listings). Adèle Cahier (1804-1885) prepared the bulk of the material necessary to begin the process for beatification/canonisation.

11. General Archives, Rome, C-I., A-a, Official documents: Canonisation, 8 vols (1872-1876); 17 vols (1882-1897); 19 vols (1877-1908); 8 vols (1881-1910).

12. Archives Françaises de la Société du Sacré Coeur, 7 rue des Feuillants, 86000 Poitiers. These archives are open to researchers.

13. For a discussion on the material held for this period in the National Archives of France see Brigitte Waché, *Initiation aux Sources Archivistiques de l'Histoire du Catholicisme Français* (Lyon,1992), pp 31-44.

14. Archives du ministre des affaires étrangères à Paris, Correspondance politique. Volumes 967-988: Dispatches of the French Ambassador in Rome and the minutes of the department of foreign affairs 1832-1848.

15. Archives Nationales, Archives Privées, 101, de Gramont. Eugénie de Gramont (1788-1846) entered the Society of the Sacred Heart in 1806 and from 1814 until her death in 1846 she took part in the governing of the Society. She was headmistress of the Rue de Varenne in Paris almost from its foundation in 1820 until her death. The de Gramont family were forced to flee France during the Revolution. At the restoration in 1815 the family were rewarded for their loyalty to the Bourbons.

16. Archivio Segreto Vaticano, Rome: Fondo Segretaria di Stato; Fondo Nunziatura di Parigi.

17. Archives de l'Ambassade de France près le Saint-Siège, volumes 7-18: Dispatches of the Minister of Foreign Affairs in Paris and the minutes of the French Ambassador, 1830-1848.

18. Both archives are held separately from the General Archives, Rome and may be consulted by researchers.

19. Adèle Cahier, *Vie de la Vénérable Mère Madeleine-Sophie Barat, Fondatrice et Première Supérieure Générale de la Société du Sacré Coeur* (2 vols, Paris, 1884).

20. Louis Baunard, *Histoire de Madame Barat, Fondatrice de la Société du Sacré Coeur* (2 vols, Paris, 1876). This work had run to its sixth edition by 1892. An illustrated edition was published in 1900 for the centenary of the Society of the Sacred Heart and a second edition printed for the canonisation of Madeleine Sophie Barat in 1925.

21. General Archives, Rome, C-I., E, Box 1, Cahier.

22. General Archives, Rome, C-I., A, 1-e, Box 1. Many scholarly women have endured the same experience. See Natalie Zemon Davis, 'Women and the world of the Annales' in *History Workshop Journal*, 33 (1992), pp 121-137.

23. The biography of Madeleine Sophie Barat 1779-1865 by Phil Kilroy will be published by Cork University Press in the spring of the year 2000.

24. Adèle Cahier to Matilde Garabis, 31 December 1871, finished 2 January 1872 (General Archives, Rome, C-I., E, Box 1, Cahier).

Rosemary Raughter:
A Natural Tenderness:
The Reality & the Ideal of Eighteenth-Century Female Philanthropy

1. *A Letter to his Excellency Earl Camden, President .... and the Rest of the Members of the Association for Discountenancing Vice and Promoting the Practice of Virtue and Religion, by a Member of that Association* (Dublin, 1795), pp 18-19. The Magdalen Asylum (1766) was founded by Lady Arbella Denny; the Female Orphan House (1791) was founded by Mrs Edward Tighe and Mrs Margaret Este and managed 1791-1842 by Mrs Elizabeth Latouche; the Bethesda Lock Penitentiary (1794) was superintended by a ladies' committee.

2. Edward Wakefield, *An Account of Ireland* (London, 1812), vol. ii, p. 801.

3. R.F. Foster, *Modern Ireland 1600-1972* (London, 1988), p. 217.

4. This issue is discussed in Joseph O'Carroll, 'Contemporary attitudes towards the homeless poor, 1725-1775' in David Dickson (ed.) *The Gorgeous Mask: Dublin 1700-1850* (Dublin, 1987), pp 64-85.

5. John Watson, *Gentleman and Citizen's Almanack* (Dublin, 1765), p. 74; J. T. Gilbert, *History of Dublin*, vol. 1 (Dublin, 1854), pp 77-79.

6. Deirdre Lindsay, 'The sick and indigent roomkeepers' society' in *The Gorgeous Mask*, pp 133-156, p. 145.

7. R. Lee Cole, *History of Methodism in Dublin* (Dublin, 1932), p. 84; *The Strangers' Friend Society in Dublin* (Dublin, n.d.), pp 5, 8.

8. For an account of Denny's career see Beatrice Bayley Butler, 'Lady Arbella Denny, 1707-1792' in *Dublin Historical Record*, vol. ix, 1 (1946-1947), pp 1-20.

9. Registers of the Magdalen Asylum, Leeson Street, 1766-1798 (Representative Church Body Library, Dublin).

10. Elizabeth Hamilton, *Letters on the Elementary Principles of Education*, quoted in Jane Rendall, *The Origins of Modern Feminism* (Chicago, 1985), p. 77.

11. Sarah Trimmer, *The Oeconomy of Charity, or an Address to Ladies* (Dublin, 1787), p. 19; *Reports of the Society for Promoting the Comforts of the Poor*, vol. 1 (Dublin, 1800), pp 69-70.

12. An address to the charitable of St Michan's parish (1766) (Presentation Convent, George's Hill, Dublin).

13. *A Letter to the Public on an Important Subject* (Dublin, 1767), p. 11.

14. Subscription list 1766-1772 in Respect of the School for Poor Girls at Mary's Lane (Presentation Convent, George's Hill, Dublin); List of donors and subscribers to the Female Orphan House, Dublin, 1791-1804 (National Library of Ireland, MS 1554); *Annual Report, House of Refuge, 7 Upper Baggot Street* (n.d., ?1803), p. 3

15. A.C.H. Seymour, *The Life and Times of Selina, Countess of Huntingdon*, vol. ii (London, 1839), p. 198.

16. This monument is described in Ian Campbell Ross, *Public Virtue, Public Love: the Early Years of the Dublin Lying-in Hospital* (Dublin, 1986), p. 30.

17. *Oeconomy of Charity*, p. 19; Melantius, *Letters Addressed to Mrs Peter Latouche* (Dublin, 1792), p. 26.

18. Mrs Martha McTier to Dr William Drennan, Belfast, ?March 1796 in D.A. Chart (ed.), *The Drennan Letters* (Belfast, 1931), p. 234.

19. Rules observed in the schools for poor girls which began in 1766 in Mary's Lane (Presentation Convent, George's Hill, Dublin).

20. John Macauley, *A Monody on the Death of the Late Lady Arbella Denny* (Dublin, 1792).

21. *A letter to his excellency Earl Camden*, p. 19.

22. Nemo, *A Brief Record of the Female Orphan House* (Dublin, 1893), pp 32-33.

23. F.K. Prochaska, 'Women in English philanthropy, 1790-1830' in *International Review of Social History*, 19 (1974), pp 426-45, p. 441; Maria Luddy, *Women and Philanthropy in Nineteenth-Century Ireland* (Cambridge, 1995), pp 209-13.

24. *Oeconomy of Charity*, p. 23.

25. Richard Ryan, *Biographia Hibernica*, vol. ii (London, 1822), pp 74-75.

26. Beatrice Bayley Butler, 'Lady Arbella Denny', pp 8, 14, 15.

27. Reminiscences of Teresa Mulally (Presentation Convent, George's Hill, Dublin); Annals of the Presentation Convent, George's Hill (*loc. cit.*); Roland Burke Savage, *A Valiant Dublin Woman* (Dublin, 1940), pp 117, 146-149.

28. Cited in Rendall, *The Origins of Modern Feminism*, p. 77.

29. *Seventh Report of the Society for Promoting the Comforts of the Poor* (Dublin, 1805), p.

20; *Reports of the Society for Promoting the Comforts of the Poor* (Dublin, 1800), pp 69-70.

30. *Seventh Report of the Society for Promoting the Comforts of the Poor,(op. cit.)*, p. 20.

31. 'Essay on charity' in *A Female Hand*, vol. 1 (Dublin, 1782), pp 220-34, p. 222.

32. Eubante, *Hints for a System of Education for a Female Orphan House* (Dublin, 1793), pp 14-15.

33. Prochaska, 'Women in English philanthropy', p. 441.

34. Rev Beaver H. Blacker, *Brief Sketches of the Parishes of Booterstown and Donnybrook* (Dublin, 1874), p. 233.

35. Dr Coppinger, *The Life of Miss Nano Nagle* (Cork, 1794), pp 7, 8.

36. Nano Nagle to Miss Fitzsimons, Cork, 17 July 1769, in T.J. Walsh, *Nano Nagle and the Presentation Sisters* (Dublin, 1959), pp 345, 346.

37. *Ibid.*, p. 346.

38. *Ibid.*, p. 347.

39. Biographical notes on Mary Tighe, Theodosia Blachford and William Blachford (National Library of Ireland, Wicklow Papers, MS 4810).

40. *Ibid.*; C.H. Crookshank, *Memorable Women of Irish Methodism* (London, 1882), p. 142.

41. Richard Tighe, *A Short Account of the Life and Writings of the Late Rev William Law* (London, 1813), pp 9-10; Theodosia Blachford to Mrs Sarah Tighe, n.d. (National Library of Ireland, Wicklow Papers, MS 4814).

42. Mother Clare Callaghan to Bishop Coppinger, n.d. and Nagle to Fitzsimons, 17 July 1769, in Walsh, *Nano Nagle and the Presentation Sisters*, pp 381-2, 345; Biographical notes on Mary Tighe (National Library of Ireland, Wicklow Papers, MS 4810).

43. Coppinger, *The Life of Miss Nano Nagle*, p. 4; Biographical notes on Mary Tighe (National Library of Ireland, Wicklow Papers, Ms 4810).

44. David Hempton and Myrtle Hill, 'Women and Protestant minorities in eighteenth-century Ireland' in Margaret MacCurtain and Mary O'Dowd (eds), *Women in Early Modern Ireland* (Dublin, 1991), pp 197-211; Rendall, *The Origins of Modern Feminism*, p. 74.

45. This process is discussed in Caitriona Clear, 'The limits of female autonomy: nuns in nineteenth-century Ireland' in Maria Luddy and Cliona Murphy (eds), *Women Surviving* (Dublin, 1989), pp 15-50.

46. *The Orphan House: Being a Brief History of that Institution* (Dublin, 1792), p. 5; *Report of the Female Orphan House* (Dublin, 1851), p. 3; Nemo, *A Brief Record of the Female Orphan House*, pp 32-33.

47. An address to the charitable of St Michan's parish (1766) (Presentation Convent, George's Hill, Dublin).

48. *Sketch of a Sermon, to Which is Prefixed a Dedication to the Governors and Governesses of the Female Orphan House* (Dublin, 1796), pp 9-10.

49. *Reports of the Society for Promoting the Comforts of the Poor (op. cit.)*, pp 42, 44. The school was founded in 1789 by Lady Lifford and Mrs Stewart.

50. Nagle to Fitzsimons, 17 July 1769, in Walsh, *Nano Nagle and the Presentation Sisters*, p. 346.

51. An address to the charitable of St Michan's parish (1766) (Presentation Convent, George's Hill, Dublin).

52. *Annual Report, House of Refuge*, p. 1; *Sixth Report of the Society for Promoting the Comforts of the Poor* (Dublin, 1804), p. 166.

53. Registers of the Magdalen Asylum, Leeson Street, 1766-1798 (R.C.B. Library, Dublin).

54. Teresa Mulally to Archbishop Troy, n.d. (Presentation Convent, George's Hill, Dublin).

55. Joseph Robins, *The Lost Children* (Dublin, 1980), p. 12.

56. Sarah Scott, *A Description of Millenium Hall* (first published 1762; reprinted London, 1986), pp 64, 67-68.

57. Nagle to Fitzsimons, 17 July 1769, in Walsh, *Nano Nagle and the Presentation Sisters*, p. 346; Crookshank, *Memorable Women*, p. 147.

Maria Luddy:
Women & Politics in Nineteenth-Century Ireland

1. See the comments by Mary E. Daly, 'Women and labour: margins to mainstream?' in *Saothar*, 19 (1994), p. 70.

2. Some women had the municipal franchise in the townships of Blackrock and Dun Laoghaire, as a result of special charters. Women in Belfast acquired the municipal franchise in 1887. (See E. Garvey, *The Position of Women in Local Administration* (London, 1896)).

3. For some recent writings on the concept of 'separate spheres' see Linda Kerber, 'Separate spheres, female worlds, women's place: the rhetoric of women's history' in *Journal of American History*, 75, 1 (1986), pp 9-39; Amanda Vickery, 'Golden age to separate spheres? A review of the categories and chronology of English women's history' in *Historical Journal*, 36, 2 (1993), pp 384-414; Leonore Davidoff, 'Regarding some old "husbands' tales": public and private in feminist history' in *idem, Worlds Between: Historical Perspectives on Gender and Class* (Oxford, 1995), pp 227-76.

4. On the suffrage issue see Rosemary Cullen Owens, *Smashing Times: a History of the Irish Women's Suffrage Movement 1889-1922* (Dublin, 1984); Cliona Murphy, *The Women's Suffrage Movement and Irish Society in the Early Twentieth Century* (Brighton, 1989). For the Ladies' Land League see Jane McL. Côté, *Fanny and Anna Parnell: Ireland's Patriot Sisters* (Dublin, 1991); Anna Parnell, *Tale of a Great Sham*, edited by Dana Hearne (Dublin, 1986). For women and nationalism see Margaret Ward, *Unmanageable Revolutionaries: Women and Irish Nationalism* (London, 1983); Rebecca O'Conner, *Jenny Mitchel, Young Irelander, a Biography* (Dublin, 1988); Brigitte Anton, 'Northern voices: Ulsterwomen in the Young Ireland movement' in Janice Holmes and Diane Urquhart (eds), *Coming into the Light: the Work, Politics and Religion of Women in Ulster 1840-1940* (Belfast, 1994), pp 60-92.

5. For accounts of women's involvement in parliamentary politics through canvassing and petitions see Mary O'Dowd, 'Women and politics, c. 1500-1850' in *Field Day Anthology of Irish Writing*, vol 4 (forthcoming). For the political influence of aristocratic women in England see Peter Jupp, 'The roles of royal and aristocratic women in British politics, c.1782-1832' in Mary O'Dowd and Sabine Wichert (eds), *Chattel, Servant or Citizen: Women's Status in Church, State and Society* (Belfast, 1995), pp 103-113.

6. Maurice Bric, 'Priests, parsons and politics: the Rightboy protest in County Cork, 1785-88' in *Past and Present*, 100 (1983), pp 100-123; 'The Whiteboy movement, 1760-80' in W.J. Nolan (ed.), *Tipperary: History and Society* (Dublin, 1995).

7. A.G.L. Shaw, *Convicts and the Colonies* (London, 1966), p. 183.

8. Public Record Office, London, Colonial Office Papers, Ribbonism 1842-1867, CO 904/9, f. 306 (4 Dec. 1843). See also the *Clare Journal*, 28 April 1831 for a report of a woman arrested with a group of Terry Alts.

9. See reports of the case in *The Constitution or Cork Advertiser*, 28 March, 24 August 1833.

10. See the following articles by James Donnelly Jr: 'The Rightboy movement 1785-8' in *Studia Hibernica*, 17/18 (1977-8), pp 120-202; 'The Whiteboy movement 1761-5' in *Irish Historical Studies*, xxi (1978), pp 20-54; 'Pastorini and Captain Rock: millenarianism and sectarianism in the Rockite movement of 1821-4' in S. Clark and J.S. Donnelly Jr (eds), *Irish Peasants, Violence and Political Unrest 1780-1914* (Manchester, 1983), pp 102-39.

11. K. Theodore Hoppen, *Elections, Politics and Society in Ireland 1832-1885* (Oxford, 1984), pp 406-8.

12. Galway county election petition, H.C. 1872 (241-1), xlviii, 539, cited in Hoppen, *Elections*, p. 406.

13. *Waterford Mail*, 18 September 1868; *Report from the Select Committee on the Newry Borough Election Petition*, H.C. 1833 (76), x, 612, cited in Hoppen, *Elections*, p. 406.

14. *Report from the Select Committee on the Londonderry Election Petition with the Minutes of the Proceedings and Evidence*, H.C. 1833 (180), x. For another example see *Report from the Select Committee on the Newry Borough Election Petition*, H.C. 1833 (76).

15. *Galway County Election Petition*, H.C. 1872 (241-1), xlviii, 539.

16. Draft of letter from Lord Eglington to J.H. Walpole, undated, c. March-April 1852 (Mayo Papers (National Library of Ireland, MS 11031)).

17. Hoppen, *Elections*, p. 407.

18. *Tipperary Advocate*, 15 July 1865, cited in Hoppen, *Elections*, p. 407.

19. Letter addressed to Lord Lieutenant from magistrates at Stranorlar petty sessions, 16 August 1852 (Outrage Papers, 1852, 7/1-7/434 (National Archives of Ireland)).

20. Letter from Theo Kane to John Wynne, 15 July 1852 (Outrage Papers, 1852, 17/291 (National Archives of Ireland)).

21. *The Banner of Ulster*, 24 August 1869.

22. James S. Donnelly Jr., *Landlord and Tenant in Nineteenth-Century Ireland* (London, 1973), p. 89.

23. *Cork Constitution*, 11 May 1847. For other examples of food riots see *Cork Examiner*, 24 August, 4, 23, 25, 30 September, 2 October 1846; *Roscommon and Leitrim Gazette*, 2, 9 January, 24 April, 22, 24 May 1847; *Northern Whig*, 15 April, 13 May 1847.

24. Donnelly, *Land and People*, p. 91.

25. *The Connaught Telegraph*, 17 January 1880.

26. Cited in Eugene Broderick, 'The famine in Waterford as reported in the local newspapers' in Des Cowman and Donald Brady (eds), *Teacht na bPratai Dubha: the Famine in Waterford* (Dublin, 1995), p. 187.

27. Anonymous typescript, 'Women of Young Ireland' (National Library of Ireland, MS 10906). See also Anton, 'Northern voices', pp 60-92.

28. Report of a lecture by James Reidy on 'The influence of the Irish woman' in *The Gaelic American*, 24 March 1906.

29. *The Irishman*, 28 October 1865.

30. Jane McL. Côté, *Fanny and Anna Parnell: Ireland's Patriot Sisters* (Dublin, 1991), pp 130-219.

31. *Select Committee on Irish Jury Laws*, H.C. 1881 (117) viii, 107. For peasant women's involvement in the Land War see Janet K. TeBrake, 'Irish peasant women in revolt: the Land League years' in *Irish Historical Studies*, 28, 109 (1992), pp 63-80.

32. *Freeman's Journal*, 12 March 1881.

33. *Belfast Newsletter*, 18 March 1881, cited in Margaret Ward, *Unmanageable Revolutionaries: Women and Irish Nationalism* (Dingle, 1983), p. 23.

34. Maria Luddy, *Women and Philanthropy in Nineteenth-Century Ireland* (Cambridge, 1995).

35. For more information on these societies see *ibid.*, pp 64-6. For earlier references to women's anti-slavery activitiy in Ireland see, for example, letter from John Campbell to Miss H. Kiernan, 16 May 1828 (Public Record Office of Northern Ireland, D1728/2/6).

36. For information on these societies see Report of the Hibernian Ladies' Negroes' Friend Society, 1833; Catherine Elizabeth Alma, *An Appeal from the Dublin Ladies' Association* (Dublin, 1837); Annual Reports of the Dublin Ladies' Anti-Slavery Society, 1859-61; Annual Reports of the Cork Ladies' Anti-Slavery Society, 1845-7.

37. Annual Report, Dublin Ladies' Anti-Slavery Society, 1860, p. 5.

38. Richard S. Harrison, 'Irish Quaker perspectives on the anti-slavery movement' in *The Journal of the Friends' Historical Society*, 56, 2 (1991), p. 115.

39. Alma, *Appeal*.

40. Kathleen E. McCrone, 'The National Association for the Promotion of Social Science and the advancement of women' in *Atlantis*, 8, 1 (1982), pp 44-66.

41. *Englishwoman's Review*, 15 January 1897, pp 58-63.

42. For more information on Tod see Maria Luddy, 'Isabella M.S. Tod, 1836-1896' in Mary Cullen and Maria Luddy (eds), *Women, Power and Consciousness in Nineteenth-Century Ireland: Eight Biographical Studies* (Dublin, 1995), pp 197-230.

43. Jellicoe's topic was 'On the conditions and prospects of young women employed in the manufactories in Dublin', while Atkinson gave a paper on 'St Joseph's Industrial Institute' in *Transactions of the National Asssociation for the Promotion of Social Science* (London, 1861).

44. Cuttings on 'Social Science' in Larcom Papers (National Library of Ireland, MS 7779).

45. David Hempton and Myrtle Hill, *Evangelical Protestantism in Ulster Society, 1740-1890* (London, 1992), Chapter 7.

46. 'Womanhood and its mission. Part ii' in *Dublin University Magazine*, 317, 53 (May 1859), p. 696.

47. See, for example, Rev. John Gregg, *Women: a Lecture Delivered in Trinity Church* (Dublin, 1856). Much prescriptive literature outlining women's role was available in nineteenth-century Ireland. For some examples see Maria Luddy (ed.), *Women in Ireland, 1800-1918: a Documentary History* (Cork, 1995), pp 12-19.

48. Linda K. Kerber, *Women of the Republic: Intellect and Ideology in Revolutionary America* (Chapel Hill, North Carolina, 1980).

49. Mary E.L. Butler, *Irishwomen and the Home Language* (Gaelic League pamphlets no. 6, Dublin, c. 1901).

50. *Northern Whig*, 23 July 1887.

51. Maria Luddy, 'Women and the Contagious Diseases Acts in Ireland' in *History Ireland*, 1,1 (1993), pp 32-4.

52. For the best general account of the Contagious Diseases Acts see J.R. Walkowitz, *Prostitution and Victorian Society: Women, Class and the State* (Cambridge, 1980).

53. *To the Members of the Belfast Committee for the Repeal of the Contagious Diseases Acts* (Belfast, 1878), p. 1.

54. Rosemary Cullen Owens, *Smashing Times: Women and the Irish Suffrage Movement 1879-1922* (Dublin, 1984), p. 25.

55. *Northern Whig*, 17 June 1886.

56. Diane Urquhart, '"The female of the species in more deadlier than the male?" The Ulster Women's Unionist Council, 1911-1940' in Janice Holmes and Diane Urquhart (eds), *Coming*

into the Light: the Work, Politics and Religion of Women in Ulster 1840-1940 (Belfast, 1994), pp 93-123.

57. Anon., 'Irish women and home rule' in *The Englishwomen's Review*, 16 October 1893.

58. Luddy, 'Tod', p. 222. See also *Londonderry Sentinel*, 21 March 1893.

59. Cited in Linda Walker, 'Party political women: a comparative study of liberal women and the Primrose League, 1890-1914' in Jane Rendall (ed.), *Equal or Different: Women's Politics 1800-1914* (Oxford, 1987), pp 175-6.

60. Ian d'Alton, 'Keeping faith: an evocation of the Cork protestant character, 1820-1920' in Patrick O'Flanagan and Cornelius Buttimer (eds), *Cork: History and Society* (Dublin, 1993), p. 770.

61. *Ibid.*, pp 165-91.

62. Cited in *The Englishwoman's Review*, 15 April 1880, pp 172-3.

63. Laura Stephens, 'Irish workhouses' in J.P. Smyth (ed.), *Social Service Handbook* (Dublin, 1901), p. 79.

64. *Ibid.*, p. 87.

65. Annual Reports, Dublin Women's Suffrage and Local Government Association, 1896, p. 3; 1897, p. 4; 1899, p. 3, appendix to report, pp 2-3. See Virginia Crossman, *Local Government in Nineteenth-Century Ireland* (Belfast, 1994), pp 91-97.

66. *Hansard*, 4, xxxvii, 1449 (2 March 1896).

67. Women's Association of Poor Law Guardians, Seventeenth Annual Report, 1899, p. 9.

68. Anna Haslam, 'Irishwomen and the Local Government Act' in *The Englishwoman's Review*, 239 (15 October 1898).

69. See *17th Annual Report of the Society for Promoting Women as Poor Law Guardians*, 1899, p. 9.

70. *Ibid.*

71. Mrs Maurice Dockrell, 'Irishwomen in local government' in Lady Aberdeen (ed.), *Women in Politics: the International Congress of Women, 1899* (London, 1900).

72. Jane Lewis, *Women and Social Action in Victorian and Edwardian England* (Aldershot, 1991).

Maureen Murphy:
Asenath Nicholson & the Famine in Ireland

The author acknowledges permission from Lilliput Press to use material in this essay that appears in the introduction to her edition of Asenath Nicholson, *Annals of the Famine in Ireland in 1847, 1848 and 1849* (Dublin, 1997).

1. Asenath Nicholson, *Ireland's Welcome to the Stranger, or, Excursions through Ireland in 1844 and 1845, for the Purposes of Investigating the Condition of the Poor* (London, 1847), p. 2. The introduction to A.T. Sheppard's edition of *Ireland's Welcome to the Stranger, The Bible in Ireland* (New York, 1997) provided valuable biographical landmarks.

2. Nicholson, *Welcome*, p. iii.

3. Centennial Committee, *Centennial Celebration of the Settlement of Chelsea Vermont. September 4 1884* (Keene, 1884), p. 78. Michael Hatch is listed as living in District #2 in 1807 when Asenath was fifteen years old (Chelsea Historical Society, *Chelsea, Vermont, 1784-1984* (Barre, 1984), p. 280). In Chelsea's early years, teachers came from the district itself with women generally hired for the summer terms at a wage of $1.00 per week. Chelsea Historical Society, *Chelsea*, p. 48.

4. Richard H. Shryock, 'Sylvester Graham and the popular health movement, 1830-1870' in *Mississippi Valley Historical Review*, 18 (1931-32), p. 174.

5. A letter from William S. Tyler, tutor at Amherst College in 1833, suggests that Graham boarding houses had a broader social purpose than health reform:

The boarders in this establishment are not only Grahamites but Garrisonites – not only reformers in diet, but radicals in politics. Such a knot of Abolitionists I never before fell in with. Slavery, colonization, constitute the unvarying monotonous theme of their conversation except that gave place to an occasional comment on their peculiar style of living.

(Thomas Le Duc, 'Grahamites and Garrisonians,' in *New York State History*, 20 (1939), p. 190.)

6. Asenath Nicholson, *Nature's Own Book* (New York, 1835), p. 6.

7. Herbert Asbury, *The Gangs of New York* (Garden City, 1928), p. 16.

8. Nicholson, *Welcome*, p. iii.

9. Nicholson received a grant of twelve testaments for distribution in the south and west of Ireland in 1845; in 1846, she received a grant for one Bible and fourteen testaments ('Grants to individuals' in *Hibernian Bible Society Annual Report (1842-1849)*, (Dublin, 1849)).

10. Nicholson, *Welcome*, pp 437-438. Nicholson saw Nangle's article when she visited the Tract Depository on Sackville Street. She published Nangle's attack in *Ireland's Welcome to the Stranger* with the note that the 'respectable person in Birmingham' was the English Quaker philanthropist Joseph Sturge. Sturge had seen the letter of introduction after Nicholson visited Achill. Later, Sturge entrusted Nicholson with funds for Famine relief. (Nicholson, *Welcome*, p. 437). Nicholson would have been recommended to Sturge as a fellow abolitionist. Later, both would be involved with the American peace activist Elihu Burritt. Nangle was always controversial. Nicholson had read the Halls' indictment of Nangle for his lack of charity toward the people among whom he worked. Like Nicholson, they were predisposed to the Achill Colony: 'We consider every conscientious accession to the Protestant faith as a contribution in aid of the well-being of the state.' (Samuel and Anna Hall, *Ireland, its scenery and its characters. III* (London, n.d.), p. 398.) The local attitude toward Nangle is reflected in songs like 'An Púca', a parody of an aisling which describes Nangle as living in the Judas colony west in Slievemore and who fought with Pluto and destroyed hell.

11. Nicholson, *Welcome*, p. 424.

12. Nicholson, *Welcome*, p. 113. In a letter to Dorothy Wellesly that included his short poem 'Parnell' ('Parnell came down the road, he said to a cheering man;/Ireland shall get her freedom and you still break stones.'), W. B. Yeats wrote that the poem was based on an actual saying of Parnell's (Dorothy Wellesly (ed.), *Letters on Poetry from W. B. Yeats to Dorothy Wellesly* (New York, 1940), p. 136)). There is a possibility that Yeats knew Nicholson's *Ireland's Welcome to the Stranger*. He wrote about evangelical Protestantism saying:

...one of its missionaries who travelled Ireland has written her life, has described meeting in peasant cottages where everybody engaged in religious discussion, has said that she was everywhere opposed and slandered by the powerful and wealthy because she was on the side of the poor. I can turn from the pages of her book with sympathy. (*Dramatis Personae*, London, (1936), p. 12.)

13. Nicholson, *Welcome*, p. 257.

14. Nicholson, *Welcome*, pp 321-322.

15. Margaret MacCurtain, 'The Real Molly Machree' in Adele M. Dalsimer (ed.), *Visualizing Ireland: National Identity and the Pictorial Tradition* (Boston, 1993), pp 9-91.

16. Nicholson did not identify the house where she stayed in Kingstown, but she described her bedroom overlooking the burying ground (Asenath Nicholson, *Annals of the Famine in Ireland in 1847, 1848, and 1849* (New York, 1851), p. 40). There was an ancient graveyard at Carrickbrennan in Monkstown, but there was no other burial ground until Deans Grange was established in 1863 (Peter Pearson, *Dun Laoghaire. Kingstown* (Dublin, 1991), p.71).

The subscription list for Samuel Lewis's *A Topographical Dictionary of Ireland* (1837) lists George Pim as living at Carrickbrennan.

17. Helen Hatton mentions a number of accounts of dogs devouring the dead and dying including Nicholson's story of an Achill girl attacked by starving dogs (Helen Hatton, *The Largest Amount of Good: Quaker Relief in Ireland 1654-1921* (Montreal, 1993), p. 136). The horror of a dog cooked for dinner appears in North Longford oral tradition where it is said that St. Patrick cursed the region with barrenness because a pagan chief of Sliabh Chairbre insulted the Saint by serving him a dog for his dinner.

18. Nicholson, *Annals*, p. 40.

19. Nicholson, *Annals*, p. 41.

20. Society of Friends, *Transactions of the Central Relief Committee of the Society of Friends During the Famine in Ireland in 1846 and 1847* (Dublin, 1852), pp 53-54.

21. Mary E. Daly, *The Famine in Ireland* (Dundalk, 1986), p. 88.

22. Nicholson, *Annals*, p. 43.

23. Friends, *Transactions*, pp 376-384. Maria Luddy has noted that there is almost nothing published on Irish Quaker women ('An Agenda for women's history, 1800-1900' in *Irish Historical Studies*, xxviii (1992), p. 24, n. 9).

24. *The Dublin Almanac and General Register of Ireland in the Year of our Lord 1847* (Dublin, 1847) lists two women undertakers, Anne Kenny and Mary Reed, and one coffin maker, Elizabeth Connolly, at numbers 2, 22 and 44 Cook Street.

25. William Bennett, *A Narrative of a Recent Tour of Six Weeks in Ireland in Connection with the Subject of Supplying Small Seed to Some of the Remoter Districts: with Current Observations on the Depressed Circumstances of the People and the Means Presented for the Permanent Improvement of their Social Condition* (London, 1847), p. 96.

26. William Wade Hinshaw, *Encyclopedia of Quaker Genealogy*, III (Richmond, 1940), p. 152.

27. James DeKay, *Chronicles of the Frigate* Macedonian *1809-1922* (New York, 1994), p. 237. An engraving of the *Macedonian* laden with Famine relief supplies and riding at anchor in Cork Harbour appeared in the *Illustrated London News* on 7 August 1847.

28. Augustus Hare, *The Life and Letters of Maria Edgeworth* (London, 1894), ii, p. 238.

29. Hare, *Edgeworth*, p. 323.

30. Nicholson to Central Relief Committee, 7 July 1847 (National Archives, Dublin, Central Relief Committee Papers, Society of Friends).

31. Nicholson does not identify this school. A donation of $1.54 in pennies from the boys of Ward School #3 in New York's Tenth Ward is listed in *The Report of the General Irish Relief Committee* (New York, 1849), p. 47. The Tenth Ward, now the Lower East Side, was a squalid area of tenements crowded with new immigrants.

32. Nicholson, *Annals*, p. 69.

33. Fr. Augustine, O.F.M. Cap., *Footprints of Father Theobald Mathew, O.F.M. Cap., Apostle of Temperance* (Dublin, 1947), p. 380.

34. Nicholson, *Welcome*, p. 236.

35. Caitriona Clear estimated that 81% of all Irish convents in 1840 were dedicated to working with the poor (*Nuns in Nineteenth-Century Ireland* (Dublin, 1987), p. 101).

36. Nicholson, *Annals*, p. 244.

37. Nicholson, *Annals*, p. 72.

38. Funds to the Connacht Industrial School meant that there was an income of 5000 and later 7500 pounds where previously there had been nothing (Friends, *Transactions*, p. 438).

39. Nicholson, *Annals*, p. 70.

40. The Journal of the Society of Friends Relief Committee in the Dublin Quaker Archives records that the Central Relief Committee also gave Susan Hewetson of Rossgarrow, Donegal, funds for local relief: a check was drawn for her on 13 January 1847.

41. Nicholson had her relief supplies routed through the Central Relief Committee. She had, however, trouble getting one of her shipments and Richard Webb had to intervene on her behalf. After that, she apparently did not work through the Committee (Nicholson, *Annals*, pp 69-72).

42. Friends, *Transactions*, p. 208

43. Nicholson, *Annals*, p. 200.

44. Richard Webb wrote of the Ballina workhouse that '... a large proportion of the sufferers only applied for admission in the hope that they should be provided with a coffin when dead, which was more than could be expected if they died outside the workhouse walls.' ('Extracts from the Letters of Richard D. Webb' in Friends, *Transactions*, p. 198.)

45. Professor Diana Ben-Merre has pointed out the similarity between Nicholson's boy who was turned away from the workhouse and the character of Jo in Charles Dickens, *Bleak House* (London, 1853).

46. Elizabeth Malcolm, *Ireland Sober, Ireland Free: Drink and Temperance in Nineteenth-Century Ireland* (Syracuse, 1986), p. 144.

47. Cecil Woodham-Smith, *The Great Hunger, 1845-1849* (New York, 1962), p. 145.

48. Christopher Morash, 'Imagining the Famine: Famine and the literary imagination' (unpublished lecture), Dublin, 1993.

49. Woodham-Smith, *Hunger*, p. 85.

50. Seamus Heaney, 'For the commander of the *Eliza*' in *Poems 1965-1975* (New York, 1980), p. 25.

51. Nicholson, *Annals*, p. 156.

52. Daly, *Famine*, p.84.

53. Nicholson, *Annals*, p. 156.

54. Nicholson, *Annals*, pp 300-301.

55. Nicholson's conclusions in 1848 were the same as those reached by Desmond Bowen in *Souperism: Myth or Reality? A Study of Catholics and Protestants During the Great Famine* (Cork, 1970). Bowen concluded that incidents of souperism were isolated rather than general and that the mythology of souperism had obscured the heroic work of most of the clergy who worked among the poor during the Famine.

56. Nicholson, *Welcome*, p. 174.

Elizabeth Steiner-Scott:
'*To Bounce a Boot Off Her Now & Then ...*':
Domestic Violence in Post-Famine Ireland

1.'To bounce a boot off her now and then...' quoted in Conrad Arensberg and Solon T. Kimball, *Family and Community in Ireland* (Harvard, 1968, 2nd edition), p. 132. Earlier versions of this article were presented at a Women's Studies Seminar at University College Cork, April 1994 and at the Women's Studies Forum, Queen's University Belfast, and at the Women's Studies Colloquium, Colby College, Waterville, Maine, April 1994. The discussions following those presentations were very useful, and I am grateful to the participants for their comments and criticisms.

2. Frances Power Cobbe, 'Wife torture in England' in *The Contemporary Review*, 32 (1878), pp 54-87.

3. Petitions to Lord Lieutenant for mitigation of sentences, National Archives, Dublin, Criminal Index Files, 1853-1920 (hereafter referred to as CIF). It should be noted that there were also 56 appeals by women for abusing their husbands and/or children during the same period.

4. For historical background to the lack of divorce in Ireland, see A.W. Samuels, 'The law of divorce in Ireland' in *Journal of the Statistical and Social Inquiry Society of Ireland*, lxvi (June 1887), pp 186-92; J. Roberts, *Divorce Bills in the Imperial Parliament* (Dublin, 1906); 'Divorce in Ireland' in *The Irish Law Times*, xliv, 26 March 1910, pp 74-75; William Duncan, 'Desertion and cruelty in Irish matrimonial law' in *The Irish Jurist*, 7 (1972), pp 213-40; W.R. Duncan, 'Supporting the institution of marriage in Ireland' in *The Irish Jurist*, 2 (1978), pp 215-32; David Fitzpatrick, 'Divorce and separation in modern Irish history' in *Past and Present*, no. 114 (1987), pp 172-97.

5. Anna Clark, 'Humanity or justice? Wifebeating and the law in the eighteenth and nineteenth centuries' in Carol Smart (ed.), *Regulating Womanhood: Historical Essays on Marriage, Motherhood and Sexuality* (London, 1992); Linda Gordon, *Heroes of their Own Lives: the Politics and History of Family Violence* (London, 1989); J. Lambertz, 'The politics and economics of family violence from the late nineteenth century to 1948' (unpublished M. Phil. thesis, University of Manchester, 1984); Elizabeth Pleck, *Domestic Tyranny: The Making of Social Policy Against Family Violence from Colonial Times to the Present* (Oxford, 1987); Nancy Toames, 'A "torrent of abuse": crimes of violence between working class men and women in London' in *Journal of Social History*, vol.11, no.3 (1978), pp 328-45.

6. 16, Vic, c. 30. An Act for the Better Prevention and Punishment of Aggravated Assaults Upon Women and Children and for Preventing Delay and Expense in the Administration of Certain Parts of the Criminal Law, 1853.

7. Anna Clark, 'Humanity or justice? Wifebeating and the law in the eighteenth and nineteenth centuries', p.200, and J. Lambertz, 'The politics and economics of family violence from the late nineteenth century to 1948'.

8. As quoted in Clark, op.cit., p. 202.

9. F.P. Cobbe, *The Life of Frances Power Cobbe by Herself* (2 vols, London, 1894), ii, p.74.

10. F.P. Cobbe, 'Wife torture in England', p. 60.

11. *Ibid.*

12. Reproduced in Jerome Nadelhaft, 'Wife torture: a known phenomenon in nineteenth century America' in *Journal of American Culture*, 10 (1987), pp 39-59.

13. F.P. Cobbe, 'Wife torture in England,' p. 61.

14. William Duncan, 'Desertion and cruelty in Irish matrimonial law' in *The Irish Jurist*, vol. 7 (1972), p. 216.

15. For a review of the nineteenth-century Matrimonial Causes Acts in England, see Lee Holcombe, *Wives and Property: Reform of the Married Women's Property Law in Nineteenth-Century England* (Oxford, 1983).

16. N. Toames, 'A "torrent of abuse": crimes of violence between working class men and women in London'.

17. A. James Hammerton, *Cruelty and Companionship: Conflict in Nineteenth-Century Married Life* (London, 1992), p. 39.

18. V.A.C. Gatrell, 'The decline of theft and violence in Victorian and Edwardian England' in V.A.C. Gatrell, Bruce Lenman and Geoffrey Parker (eds), *Crime and the Law: The Social History of Crime in Western Europe since 1500* (London, 1980), p. 289.

19. David Lloyd, *Anomalous States: Irish Writing and the Post-Colonial Moment* (Dublin, 1993).

20. See Maria Luddy and Cliona Murphy (eds), *Surviving Women: Studies in Irish Women's History in the Nineteenth and Twentieth Centuries* (Dublin, 1990); Joanna Bourke, *Hus-*

bandry to Housewifery: Women, Economic Change and Housework in Ireland, 1890-1914* (Oxford, 1993).

21. *The Irish Times*, 4 January 1878.

22. *The Irish Times*, 7 February 1878.

23. *The Irish Times*, 11 March 1878.

24. CIF, 1872, S-15.

25. CIF, 1873, M-40.

26. CIF, 1886, McK-98.

27. CIF, 1891, H-67.

28. *The Irish Times*, 11 April 1878.

29. *The Irish Times*, 13 August 1878.

30. Joanna Bourke, *Husbandry to Housewifery*, p. 266. Bourke quotes from Michael J.F. McCarthy, *Priests and People in Ireland*, Dublin, 1903, p. 300; Helen Hawthorn, 'The ideal girl' in *Ireland's Own*, 26 November 1902, p. 8; Mrs. Frank Pentrill, 'Everyday thoughts: the teapot and kettles' in *Irish Monthly*, 1882, p. 526; 'Grania', 'Are mothers the ruin of Ireland?' in *Irish Homestead*, 15 February 1913, p. 130.

31. *The Cork Examiner*, 8 March 1878.

32. *The Cork Examiner*, 3 September 1878.

33. *The Irish Times*, 23 March 1878.

34. CIF, 1897, P-17.

35. CIF, 1908, F-33.

36. Gatrell, 'The decline of theft and violence in Victorian and Edwardian England', p. 296.

37. *Ibid.*, p. 300.

38. Cited in Iris Minor, 'Working class women and matrimonial law reform, 1890-1914' in David E. Martin and David Rubinstein (eds), *Ideology and the Labour Movement* (London, 1979), p. 117.

39. A. James Hammerton, 'Victorian marriage and the law of matrimonial cruelty' in *Victorian Studies* (Winter 1990), p. 277.

40. Catherine MacKinnon, 'Reflections on sex equality under the law' in *The Yale Law Journal*, vol. 100, no. 5 (1991), p. 1281.

41. J. Stephen, *A History of the Criminal Law of England* (London, 1883), quoted in MacKinnon, 'Reflections in sex equality', p.1281.

42. Christine Boyle, 'Violence against wives – the criminal law in retreat?' in *Northern Ireland Law Quarterly*, 31 (Spring 1980), p. 37.

43. Elizabeth Malcolm, *Ireland Sober, Ireland Free: Drink and Temperance in Nineteenth-Century Ireland* (Dublin, 1986), pp 120-21.

44. Colm Kerrigan, *Father Mathew and the Irish Temperance Movement 1838-1849* (Cork, 1992), p. 136.

45. Malcolm, *op. cit.*, p. 176.

46. *Ibid.*, p. 265.

47. *Ibid.*, p. 321.

48. C.L. Innes, *Women and Nation in Irish Literature and Society, 1880-1935* (Georgia, 1993), pp 12-13.

49. David Cairns and Shaun Richards, *Writing Ireland: Colonialism, Nationalism and Culture* (Manchester, 1988), p. 77.

50. Maud Eden, 'Purity or divorce' in *The Irish Citizen*, September 1919.

51. David Fitzpatrick, 'Divorce and separation in modern Irish history' in *Past and Present*, no 114 (1987), pp 195-96.

52. David Fitzpatrick, 'Marriage in Post-Famine Ireland' in Art Cosgrove (ed.), *Marriage in Ireland* (Dublin, 1985), p. 128.

53. William Duncan, 'Supporting the institution of marriage in Ireland' in *The Irish Jurist*, 2 (Winter 1978), p. 219.

54. See for example 'Why women need women lawyers,' signed by 'L. L. B.' in *The Irish Citizen*, 29 June 1912. These views echo those of the Women's Co-operative Guild, which proposed in a report to the Royal Commission on Divorce and Matrimonial Causes in 1912 that women should be introduced into the legal administration as a means to make family law more responsive to the problems of the poor and of women especially (Iris Minor, 'Working class women and matrimonial law reform', p. 110).

55. 'Wives and madmen' in *The Irish Citizen*, 13 June 1914.

56. L.A.M. Priestly-McCracken, 'Wife-beating' in *The Irish Citizen*, September 1919.

57. *Ibid.*

58. Sandra R. Larmour, 'The state and sexuality: Ireland 1929-1937' (unpublished M.A. thesis, University College, Cork, 1992). I am grateful to Sandra Larmour McAvoy for sharing many valuable insights about the relationship between Irishwomen and the Irish Free State in the 1920s and 1930s.

59. Conrad Arensberg and Solon T. Kimball, *Family and Community in Ireland*, p. 132.

60. See Christine Boyle, 'Violence against wives'; Patrick Horgan, 'Legal protection for the victims of marital violence' in *The Irish Jurist*, 2 (Winter 1978), pp 233-53; K. Yllo and M. Bograd (eds), *Feminist Perspectives on Wife Abuse* (London, 1988); J. Pahl, *Private Violence and Public Policy: the Needs of Battered Women and the Response of the Public Services* (London, 1985); J. Hanmer and Stanko, *Stripping Away the Rhetoric of Protection: Violence to Women, Law and the State in Britain and the U.S.A.* (Bradford, 1985); J. Hanmer, Radford and Stanko, *Women, Policing and Male Violence: International Perspectives* (London, 1989); Susan Edwards, *Policing 'Domestic' Violence: Women, the Law and the State* (London, 1989). On domestic violence in Ireland, see Maeve Casey, *Domestic Violence Against Women* (Dublin, 1987); Karina Colgan, *You Have to Scream with your Mouth Shut: Violence in the Home* (Dublin, 1995); Eileen Evason, *Hidden Violence* (Belfast, 1982); Caroline Fennell, 'Criminal law and the criminal justice system: woman as victim' in A. Connelly (ed.), *Gender and the Law in Ireland* (Dublin, 1993); Monica McWilliams and Joan McKiernan, *Bringing it Out in the Open: Domestic Violence in Northern Ireland* (Belfast, 1993); Kate Shanahan, *Crimes Worse than Death* (Dublin, 1993).

61. David Lloyd, *Anomalous States: Irish Writing and the Post-Colonial Moment*, p. 5.

62. J.J. Lee, *Ireland 1912-1985: Politics and Society* (Cambridge, 1989), p. 652.

Cliona Murphy:

A Problematic Relationship:
European Women & Nationalism, 1900-1918

1. Margaret MacCurtain, 'Women, the vote and revolution', in Margaret MacCurtain and Donncha O'Corrain (eds), *Women in Irish Society: the Historical Dimension* (Dublin, 1978), pp 48-51.

2. Beth McKillen, 'Irish feminism and national separatism 1914-1923' in *Éire/Ireland*, 18, 3 (1982), pp 53-67, continued in 18, 4 (1982), pp 72-90.

3. Rosemary Cullen Owens, *Smashing Times: the History of the Irish Suffrage Movement, 1890-1922* (Dublin, 1983).

4. Cliona Murphy, *The Women's Suffrage Movement and Irish Society in the Early Twentieth Century* (Brighton, 1989). See also 'Suffragists and nationalism in early twentieth-century Ireland' in *History of European Ideas*, 16, 4 (1993), pp 1009-15.

5. Margaret Ward, *Unmanageable Revolutionaries: Women in Irish Nationalism* (Dingle, 1983); Mary Cullen, 'How radical was Irish feminism between 1860 and 1920?' in P.J. Corish

(ed.), *Radical, Rebels and Establishments: Historical Studies*, xv (Belfast, 1985), pp 185-201; Dana Hearne, 'The Irish Citizen, 1914-1916: nationalism, feminism, militarism' in *Canadian Journal of Irish Studies*, 18, 1 (July 1992), pp 1-15.

6. Margaret Ward, 'Marginality and militancy: Cumann na mBan, 1914-1936', in Austin Morgan and Bob Purdie, (eds), *Ireland: Divided Nation, Divided Class* (London, 1980), pp 96-110; Margaret Ward, *In their own Voice: Women and Nationalism* (Dublin, 1995); Carol Coulter, *The Hidden Tradition: Feminism, Women and Nationalism in Ireland* (Cork, 1993); C.L. Innes, *Women and Nation in Irish Literature and Society 1880-1935* (London, 1993); Aideen Sheehan, 'Cumann na mBan policies and activities' in David Fitzpatrick (ed.), *Revolution? Ireland 1917-1923* (Dublin, 1990), pp 88-97.

7. See Murphy, *The Women's Suffrage Movement*; Cullen Owens, *Smashing Times*; Margaret Ward, 'Suffrage first above all else! an account of the Irish suffrage movement' in *Feminist Review*, 10 (1982), pp 22-36; Marie O'Neill, 'The struggle of Irish women for the vote' in *Breifne*, 8, 3 (1993), pp 338-53; Mary Cullen, 'How radical was Irish feminism between 1860 and 1920?'.

8. See Murphy, *The Women's Suffrage Movement*, chapter 7.

9. Charlotte Fallon, *Soul of Fire: a Biography of Mary MacSwiney* (Cork, 1986).

10. Frances C. Gardiner, 'Political interest and participation of Irish women 1922-1992: the unfinished revolution' in *Canadian Journal of Irish Studies*, 18, 1 (July 1992), pp 15-40; Maryann Gialanella Valiulis, 'Defining their role in the new state: Irishwomen's protest against the Jury's Act of 1927' in *Canadian Journal of Irish Studies*, 18, 1 (July 1992), pp 43-60; '"Free women in a free nation": feminist nationalist expectations of independence' in Brian Farrell (ed.), *The Creation of the Dáil* (Dublin, 1994), pp 75-90.

11. Elizabeth Badinter, *Mother Love, Myth and Reality: Motherhood in Modern History* (New York, 1981); George L. Mosse, *Nationalism and Sexuality: Respectability and Abnormal Sexuality in Modern Europe* (New York, 1985); Bonnie Smith, *Changing Lives: Women in European History since 1700* (Lexington, 1989); Sian Reynolds (ed.), *Women, State and Revolution: Essays on Power and Gender in Europe since 1789* (Massachusetts, 1987). See *Proceedings of the Conference of the Society for the History of European Ideas*, vols 4-6 (1992). The conference, which was held in Brussels in 1990, had a workshop which focused on nationalism and feminism. See also a number of references given in the notes below.

12. Eric Hobsbawm, *Nations and Nationalism since 1780* (Cambridge, 1990); Ernest Gellner, *Nations and Nationalism* (Cornell, 1983).

13. Helena Blackburn, *Women's Suffrage: a Record of the Women's Suffrage Movement in the British Isles* (London, 1902); Hedwig Dohm, *Women's Nature and Privilege* (London, 1896); Kaethe Schirmacher, *The Modern Women's Rights Movement: a Historical Survey* (New York, 1912).

14. Cliona Murphy, 'The tune of the stars and stripes: the American influence on the Irish suffrage movement' in Maria Luddy and Cliona Murphy (eds), *Women Surviving: Studies in Irish Women's History in the Nineteenth and Twentieth Centuries* (Dublin, 1990), pp 180-205.

15. See Eric Hobsbawm, *Nations and Nationalism*; Eugene Weber, *From Peasants into Frenchmen* (Stanford, 1976) for an elaboration of nationalism being imposed from above.

16. Judith Jeffrey Howard, 'Patriotic mothers in the post-risorgimento: women after the Italian revolution' in C. Berkin et al (eds), *Women, War and Revolution* (New York, 1980), pp 237-58.

17. Roger Chickering, '"Casting their gaze more broadly": women's patriotic activism in imperial Germany' in *Past and Present*, 118 (1988), pp 156-185, 169.

18. *The Irish Citizen*, April 1914.

19. Hanna Sheehy Skeffington, 'Reminiscences of an Irish suffragette' in A.D. Sheehy Skeffington and Rosemary Owens, *Irish Women's Struggle for the Vote* (Dublin, 1975), p. 2.

20. *The Irish Times*, 18 April 1912, p. 8.

21. Lucia C. Birnbaum, *Liberazione della Donna: Feminism in Italy* (Middleton, 1986), p. 20.

22. See Linda Clark, *Social Darwinism in France* (Alabama, 1984); Ann Taylor Allen, 'German radical feminism and eugenics,1900-1918' in *German Studies Review*, 11 (1988), pp 31-56.

23. Karen Offen, 'Depopulation, nationalism and feminism in fin de siècle France' in *American Historical Review*, 89 (1984), pp 648-678, p. 671.

24. Victoria de Garzia, *How Fascism Ruled Italy 1922-1945* (Berkeley, 1992), p. 25.

25. Richard Evans, *The Feminist Movement in Germany* (London, 1976).

26. Linda Clark, *Social Darwinism in France*, p. 56.

27. *Irish Catholic*, 17 Feb. 1912, p. 8.

28. Hanna Sheehy Skeffington, 'Reminiscences', p.18.

29. The Ancient Order of Hibernians were particularly noted for their roughness in their encounters with the Irish suffragists. See Murphy, *The Woman's Suffrage Movement and Irish Society in the Early Twentieth Century*, pp 128-9.

30. There were some, as evident from the few supportive members of the Irish Parliamentary Party and the language used in the Proclamation of 1916.

31. Donald Meyer, *Sex and Power: the Rise of Women in America, Sweden and Italy* (Middleton, Connecticut, 1987), p. 121.

32. Richard Evans, *The Feminists*, p. 94.

33. Karen Offen, 'Depopulation, nationalism and feminism in fin de siècle France', p. 662.

34. Charles Sowerwine's studies on the French left indicate that there was little support for women's suffrage in socialist circles. See in particular *Sisters or Citizens? Women and Socialism in France since 1876* (Cambridge, 1982).

35. *Catholic Bulletin*, Oct. 1912, p. 791.

36. Margaret Cousins, *We Two Together* (Madras, 1950), p. 86.

37. Sheehy Skeffington Papers (National Library of Ireland, MS 22,664).

38. *Votes for Women*, 28 Oct. 1910, p. 55.

39. Cousins, *op. cit.*, p.172

40. Offen, 'Depopulation, nationalism and feminism in fin de siècle France', p. 662

41. *Ibid.*, p. 663.

42. Richard Evans, *The Feminist Movement in Germany*, p.180.

43. Angela V. John, *Our Mother's Land: Chapters in Welsh Women's History, 1830-1939* (Cardiff, 1991).

44. Donald Meyer, *Sex and Power: the Rise of Women in America, Sweden and Italy*, p. 123.

45. Mineke Bosch and Annemarie Kloosterman (eds), *Politics and Friendship: Letters from the International Women's Suffrage Alliance, 1902-1942* (Columbus, 1990); Jo Vellacott Newberry, 'Anti-war suffragists' in *History*, 62 (1977), pp 411-426. See also pp 222-3.

46. Karen Offen, 'Nationalizing feminism – feminizing nationalism: gender and politics in early Third Republic France', paper presented at the Conference of the Society for the History of European Ideas, Brussels, September 1990.

47. R. Chickering, '"Casting their gazes more broadly": women's patriotic activism in imperial Germany' in *Past and Present*, 118 (1988), pp 156-185.

48. Donald Meyer, *Sex and Power: the Rise of Women in America, Sweden and Italy*, p.169.

49. Jo Vellacott Newberry, 'Anti-war suffragists', p. 414. See also de Garzia, *How Fascism Ruled Italy 1922-1945*.

50. It should be noted that not all British suffragists were supportive of the war and many members of the National Union of Women's Suffrage Societies were opposed to it.

Maryann GialanellaValiulis:
Engendering Citizenship:
Women's Relationship to the State in Ireland
& the United States in the Post-Suffrage Period

1. Margaret MacCurtain, 'The historical image' in Eiléan Ní Chuilleanáin (ed.), *Irish Women: Image and Achievement* (Dublin, 1985), p. 49.

2. *Dáil Debates*, 15 February 1927, vol. 18, col. 489.

3. Dissenting report as to jury sevice for women, State of Massachusetts, Senate - no. 41, January 1924, p. 33.

4. See, for example, de Valera's eulogy on the death of Margaret Pearse for a classic statement of Republican Motherhood (see Maryann Valiulis, 'Neither feminist nor flapper: the ecclesiastical construction of the ideal Irish woman' in Mary O'Dowd and Sabine Wichert (eds), *Chattel, Servant or Citizen: Women's Status in Church, State and Society* (Belfast, 1995), p. 169).

5. Linda Kerber, 'The obligation of citizenship' in Linda Kerber, Alice Kessler-Harris and Kathryn Kish Sklar (eds), *U.S. History as Women's History* (Chapel Hill, North Carolina, 1995), p. 34.

6. Table showing the status of women as jurors in the United States in *Women Lawyers' Journal*, vol.19 (August 1932), p. 35.

7. Congress, House, Representative. Blanton speaking on the issue of jury service for women in the District of Columbia (*Congressional Record*, 1st Session of the 69th Congress (1927), vol. lxvii, p. 8245).

8. Congress, House, Representative. Underhill speaking on the issue of jury service for women in the District of Columbia (*Congressional Record*, 1st Session of the 69th Congress (1927), vol. lxvii, p. 8239).

9. Grace Harte, 'Women jurors and the American scene' in *Women Lawyers' Journal*, vol. xxv (January 1939), p.34.

10. Jennie L. Barron, 'Jury service for women' in *League of Women Voters Publications*, December 1924, p. 12.

11. *Ibid.*, p. 8.

12. State of Massachusetts, 'Hearings before the Commission on Jury Service,' 11 September 1923.

13. Quoted in Linda Kerber, 'The obligation of citizenship' in *U.S. History as Women's History*, p. 30.

14. *Seanad Debates*, 30 March 1927, vol. 8, col. 687.

15. *Dáil Debates*, 22 March 1927, vol.19, col. 26.

16. *Congressional Record*, 1st Session of the 69th Congress, vol. lxviii, part 8, p. 8241.

17. *Dáil Debates*, 23 February 1927, vol. 18, col. 755.

18. *Ibid.*

19. *Dáil Debates*, 13 March 1924, vol. 6, col. 2101.

20. Dissenting report as to jury service for women, State of Massachusetts, Senate - no. 41, January 1924, p. 35; *Congressional Record*, 1st Session of the 69th Congress, vol. lxvii, part 8, p. 8240.

21. *The Irish Independent*, 11 February 1927.

22. *The Irish Independent*, 14 February 1927.

23. *Congressional Record*, 1st Session of the 69th Congress, vol. lxvii, part 8, p. 6031.

24. *Congressional Record*, 1st Session of the 69th Congress, vol. lxvii, part 8, p. 8240.

25. Dissenting report as to jury service for women, State of Massachusetts, Senate - no. 41, Jan. 1924, p. 33.

26. *The Irish Times*, 4 March 1927.

27. Anise Troth, 'How we won jury service in Georgia' in *Independent Woman*, February 1954, p. 64.

28. *The Evening Herald*, 11 February 1927.

29. *Seanad Debates*, 8 April 1927, vol. 8, col. 813.

30. State of Massachusetts, 'Hearings before the Commission on Jury Service,' 11 September 1923.

31. Hall v. State, Supreme Court of Florida, 14 March 1939, 187 So. 392, p. 401.

32. *Congressional Record*, 1st Session of the 69th Congress, vol. lxvii, part 8, p. 6029.

33. *Dáil Debates*, 15 February 1927, vol. 18, col. 489.

34. *Seanad Debates*, 30 March 1927, vol.8, col . 687.

35. State of Massachusetts, Hearings before the Commission on Jury Service, 11 September 1923.

36. State of New York, Hearings held before the Judiciary Committee of the Senate and Assembly of the State of New York, 1 March 1927.

37. *The Irish Times*, 22 February 1927.

38. State of New York, Judiciary Committee of the Senate and Assembly of the State of New York, Mrs Ezra Tomkins of the New York League of Women Voters speaking on the issue of jury service for women in the State of New York, 1 March 1927, p. 6.

39. State of New York, Judiciary Committee of the Senate and Assembly of the State of New York, Mrs Wittick, Vice Chairman of the New York State Women's Party, speaking on the issue of jury service for women in the state of New York, 1 March 1927, p. 18.

40. Letter from Burnita Shelton Matthews, Research Secretary, National Women's Party, 13 January 1922 (National Women's Party Papers).

41. Letter to the Editor, *The Irish Independent*, 1 April 1927.

42. Letter to the Editor, *The Irish Times*, 17 February 1927.

43. Jennie L. Barron, 'Jury service for women' in *League of Women Voters Publication*, December 1924, p. 9.

44. Burnita Shelton Matthews, 'The woman juror' in *Women Lawyers' Journal*, vol. xv (January 1927), p. 16.

45. Amber Wallin Anderson, 'Jury service for women' in *Georgia Bai Journal*, 11 (1948), p. 198.

46. Letter to the Editor, *The Irish Times*, 15 February 1927.

47. Jennie L. Barron, 'Jury service for women', p. 7.

48. Letter to the Editor, *The Irish Times*, 15 February 1927.

49. *Ibid.*

50. *The Irish Times*, 17 April 1927.

51. Jennie L. Barron, 'Jury service for women' in *League of Women Voters Publication*, December 1924, p. 6.

52. State of New York, Judiciary Committee of the Senate and Assembly of the State of New York, Mabel Leslie of the Women's Trade Union League speaking on the issue of jury service for women in the state of New York, 1 March 1927, p. 37.

53. Letter to the editor, *The Irish Times*, 15 February 1927.

Caitriona Beaumont:

Women & the Politics of Equality:

The Irish Women's Movement, 1930-1943

I would like to thank the School of Irish Studies Foundation Award and the Michael Postan Award for financial support during the research of this paper.

I would also like to thank Margaret MacCurtain for her interest, her encouragement and her support over the last eight years.

1. In 1918, the Representation of the People Act extended the parliamentary franchise to women over thirty in Britain and Ireland who were householders or the wives of local government electors. Men with the correct property qualifications were entitled to vote when they reached the age of twenty-one.

2. *Irish Times Pictorial*, 6 February 1943.

3. Nora Connolly was an active member of the Irish republican women's organisation Cumann na mBan, quoted in Margaret Ward, *Unmanageable Revolutionaries: Women and Irish Nationalism* (Dingle, 1983), p. 224.

4. See Rosemary Cullen Owens, *Smashing Times: The History of the Irish Suffrage Movement, 1890-1922* (Dublin, 1983), and Margaret Ward, *op. cit.*

5. In Britain, the vote was not granted to women over the age of twenty-one until 1928.

6.'Vote No' Handbill published by the National University Women Graduates' Association (1937) (University College, Dublin, National University Women Graduates' Association Papers, 1/51).

7. *Irish Press*, 26 June 1937.

8. See for example Maryann Valiulis, 'Power, gender, and identity in the Irish Free State' in *Journal of Women's History* (Winter/spring 1995), vol. 6, no. 4; vol. 7, no. 1, pp 117-136; Mary Jones, *These Obstreperous Lassies: a History of the Irish Women Workers' Union* (Dublin, 1988). See also pp 159-172 above.

9. The 1925 Civil Service Regulation (Amendment) Act proposed to exclude women from the higher grades in the civil service on the grounds of sex. Similarly, the 1927 Juries Act attempted to deny women the right to sit on juries, one of the basic duties of citizenship, on the grounds that they had more important work to attend to in the home. See Mary Clancy, 'Aspects of women's contribution to the Oireachtas debate in the Irish Free State, 1922-37' in Maria Luddy and Cliona Murphy (eds), *Women Surviving: Studies in Irish Women's History in the Nineteenth and Twentieth Centuries* (Dublin, 1990), pp 217, 223. See also the contribution of Maryann Gialanella Valiulis to this volume.

10. The 1924 Juries Act gave women leave to apply for an exemption from jury service. By the end of 1924, 3,276 women in County Dublin had successfully applied to have their names removed from the jury roll (see Maryann Valiulis, *op. cit.*, p. 123).

11. *Ibid.*, pp 120-25.

12. *United Irishwomen*, vol 1, no. 4, November 1925.

13. *Ibid.*

14. See Mary Clancy, 'Aspects of women's contribution to the Oireachtas debate in the Irish Free State, 1922-37', pp 206-32.

15. As a result of this legislation, the number of women serving on juries in the Irish Free State was radically reduced.

16. Equal pay, equal opportunities and an equal moral standard were the core demands of feminist organisations in both Britain and Ireland during the inter-war period.

17. The society was formally known as the Irish Women's Suffrage and Local Government Association, founded in 1876 by the suffragist Anna Haslam (see Rosemary Cullen Owens, *op. cit.*, pp 25-32).

18. *United Irishwomen*, vol. 1, no. 4, November 1925.

19. In evidence to the Committee of Vocational Education in 1940, membership for the Irish Women's Citizens' and Local Government Association was recorded as 187 (evidence to the Committee on Vocational Education (National Library of Ireland, Ms 941, no. 200, vol. 20, 1940)).

20. Mary Hayden had been a keen supporter of women's suffrage and had championed the right of women to a university education.

21. As well as protesting against the 1925 Civil Service (Amendment) Bill and the Juries Act, the Association gave its support to progressive legislation including the 1925 School Attendance Bill.

22. *United Irishwomen*, vol. 1, no. 6, January 1926. The arguments in favour of family allowances discussed at this meeting were first put forward by the English feminist, Eleanor Rathbone, in her influential book, *The Disinherited Family* (London, 1924).

23. The National Council of Women of Ireland was affiliated to the International Council of Women and represented the Irish Free State at international conferences on women's rights.

24. The United Irishwomen, renamed the Irish Countrywomen's Association in 1935, was an organisation for rural women set up in 1910 by Sir Horace Plunkett. The Mothers' Union, the largest society for women in the Church of England, was established in Ireland in 1887. The Union's principal object was to uphold the sanctity of marriage.

25. The National University Women Graduates' Association was set up in 1908 as a branch of the Women Graduates and Candidate Graduates Association. This organisation had been founded six years earlier to represent the interests of women in Irish universities and to ensure that female students received all the advantages of university education which were available to men.

26. In 1930, the Dublin branch of the association had only sixty-seven members. The total membership for all three branches of the organisation in 1940 was 300. Evidence to the Commission on Vocational Education (National Library of Ireland, MS 941, no. 200, vol. 20, 1940).

27. See Leah Levenson and Jerry Naderstad, *Hanna Sheehy Skeffington: A Pioneering Irish Feminist* (Syracuse, 1986).

28. Mary Macken was a former member of Inghinidhe na hEireann while Agnes O'Farrelly had been involved in the Gaelic League movement.

29. *National University Women Graduates' Association Annual Report 1929-30* (University College Dublin, National University Women Graduates' Association Papers, 1/16).

30. Amongst those who attended the first meeting of the Joint Committee of Women's Societies and Social Workers were representatives from the Irish Women's Citizens' and Local Government Association, the Mothers' Union, the Irish Save the Children Fund, the Central Association of Irish School Mistresses and the National University Women Graduates' Association. (*Report of the Joint Committee of Women's Societies and Social Workers 1935-42* (University College, Dublin, National University Women Graduates' Association Papers, 1/60).)

31. Mary Clancy, 'Aspects of women's contribution to the Oireachtas debate', p. 213.

32. When the new legislation was enacted, fifteen years was judged the age of consent in cases of indecent assault (*ibid.*, p. 215).

33. *Ibid.*, p. 212.

34. Marie Stopes's *Wise Parenthood* and Margaret Sanger's *Family Limitation* were amongst the books banned under the 1929 Censorship of Publications Act.

35. During this period ninety-three per cent of the Irish population were Catholic (see John Whyte, *Church and State in Modern Ireland 1923-1979* (New Jersey, 1980) and Dermot Keogh, *The Vatican, the Bishops and Irish Politics 1919-1939* (Cambridge, 1986)).

36. *Report of The Lambeth Conference 1930* (1930), p. 43.

37. The Constitution of the Mothers' Union, 1926.

38. Deputy Rowlette, Senator St John Gogarty and Senator Kathleen Clarke raised a number of objections to the ban on birth control in the Dáil and Seanad but were unable to persuade the government to amend the Bill (see Mary Clancy, 'Aspects of women's contribution to the Oireactas debate', pp 214-15).

39. 'Fifty years' work, 1935-85: The Joint Committee of Women's Societies and Social Workers' (unpublished leaflet, courtesy of Mabel Kelly).

40. In 1917, two women were appointed to the Dublin Metropolitan Police Force to 'assist the police in the suppression of immoral conduct, investigating cases of indecency in which women were involved, watching disorderly houses, detecting cases of fortune telling, watching for shop lifters etc.' These women were not attested police officers and had no power of arrest ('Joint Committee of Women's Societies and Social Workers: Memorandum on Women Police.' November 1955 (National Archives of Ireland, Department of An Taoiseach, S/6210)).

41. Loc. cit.

42. Loc. cit.

43. Loc. cit.

44. Loc. cit.

45. The marriage bar also applied to women working in the civil service.

46. The 1936 census revealed that 552,176 women were engaged in home work in comparison with 226,816 women who were in paid employment.

47. The public service marriage bar was not repealed until 1972.

48. See Mary Daly, 'Women in the Irish Free State, 1922-1939: the interaction between economics and ideology' in Journal of Women's History (Winter/spring 1995), vol. 6, no. 4, vol. 7, no. 1, p. 110.

49. Mary Daly has written that Section 16 of the Conditions of Employment Act was never enforced and that employment opportunities for women in industry continued to improve during the second half of the 1930s (ibid.).

50. The Irish Women Workers Union was established in 1917 to represent working-class women employed in industry. The Union had a membership of 6,000 women in 1940 (evidence to the Commission on Vocational Education (National Library of Ireland, Ms 937, no. 108, vol. 20, 1940)). For further details of the Union's campaign against the Conditions of Employment Act see Mary Jones, These Obstreperous Lassies, pp 125-33.

51. Forty-First Annual Report of the Irish Trade Union Congress and Proceedings of the Forty-First Annual Meeting, Guild Hall, Derry, 1935.

52. The Irish Times, 11 May 1937.

53. Ibid.

54. The Irish Press, 11 May 1937.

55. A clause was added to Article 9 which read 'No person may be excluded from Irish nationality and citizenship by reason of the sex of such person.' Article 16 was amended to guarantee voting rights to 'every citizen without distinction of sex' and a clause added stating that no citizen shall be excluded from voting at an election 'on the grounds of sex' (Bunreacht na hEireann (1937)).

56. 'Memorandum on the status of women to the president and members of the executive council from the National University Women Graduates' Association', 23 May 1937 (University College, Dublin, National University Women Graduates' Association Papers, 1/51).

57. Letter to the executive council of the Irish Free State from the Joint Committee of Women's Societies and Social Workers, 24 May 1937 (National Archives of Ireland, Department of An Taoiseach, S/9880).

58. In its amended form, Article 45.4.2. stated that 'the State shall endeavour to ensure that the strength and health of workers, men and women, and the tender age of children shall not be abused and that citizens shall not be forced by economic necessity to enter avocations unsuited to their sex, age or strength' (Bunreacht na hEireann (1937)).

59. Ibid.

60. 'Memorandum on the status of women', 23 May 1937 (University College, Dublin, National University Women Graduates' Association Papers, 1/51).

61. *The Irish Press*, 15 May 1937.

62. *The Irish Press*, 12 May 1937.

63. *The Irish Press*, 15 May 1937.

64. Letter to the president of the executive council from the Irish Women Workers' Union, 24 May 1937 (National Archives of Ireland, Department of An Taoiseach, S/9880).

65. *The Irish Press*, 26 June 1937.

66. *Bunreacht na hEireann* (1937).

67. 'Memorandum on the status of women', 23 May 1937 (University College, Dublin, National University Women Graduates' Association Papers, 1/51).

68. Letter to the executive council of the Irish Free State, 24 May 1937 (National Archives of Ireland, Department of an Taoiseach, S/9880).

69. 'Vote No' Handbill (University College, Dublin, National University Women Graduates' Association Papers, 1/51).

70. *Irish Press*, 23 June 1937.

71. This meeting took place in the Mansion House on 21 June 1937. Speakers including Mary Hayden, Mary Kettle and Hanna Sheehy Skeffington argued that it was difficult to believe promises of equality from a government responsible for Section 16 of the Conditions of Employment Act.

72. See Caitriona Beaumont, 'Women and the politics of equality 1930-43' (unpublished M.A. thesis, University College Dublin, 1989); Mary Clancy, 'Women's contribution to public political debate (with particular reference to women's issues) in the Irish Free State, 1922-37' (unpublished M.A. thesis, University College Galway, 1989); and Mary McGinty, 'A study of the campaign for and against the enactment of the 1937 constitution' (unpublished M.A. thesis, University College Galway, 1987).

73. *Irish Independent*, 25 November 1937.

74. Another reason for the change in name was to ensure that women in the public service could join the League. Public servants were restricted from joining any political organisation (interview with Andrée Sheehy Skeffington, 13 June 1989).

75. In 1940, the Women's Social and Progressive League had some 500 members, the majority of whom were educated middle-class women living in the Dublin area.

76. Formally known as the United Irishwomen (1910), the society was set up 'to organise women of all classes and every rural district in Ireland for social service.' See Pat Bolger, (ed.), *And See her Beauty Shining There: the Story of the Irish Countrywomen* (Dublin, 1986).

77. Evidence to the Commission on Vocational Education (National Library of Ireland, MS 931, no. 45 C, vol. 9, 1940). By 1948, the I.C.A. had set up 218 guilds with a membership of 6,000 women.

78. In 1929, the first I.C.A. summer school was held at Slievenamon. The summer school soon became an annual event providing day-time classes in traditional handicrafts, keep fit, and domestic science as well as social activities involving music, dance and drama.

79. *Annual Report of the Irish Countrywomen's Association 1940-41* (1941).

80. *United Irishwomen*, vol. 1, no. 6, January 1926.

81. Esther Bishop (ed.), *Irish Countrywomen's Association* (Dublin, 1950), p. 24.

82. The Catholic Women's Federation of Secondary School Unions was founded in 1936 'to promote and foster Catholic social principles and action, especially from the women's point of view.' By 1940, the Joint Committee of Women's Societies and Social Workers was one of the largest organisations for women in Ireland, representing over 28,000 women (evidence to the Commission on Vocational Education (National Library of Ireland, Ms 941, no. 200, vol. 20, 1940)).

83. *Loc. cit.*

84. *Loc. cit.*

85. *Loc. cit.*

86. Hilda Tweedy, *A Link in the Chain: The Story of the Irish Housewives' Association 1942-1992* (Dublin, 1992), p. 18. By 1945, seventy-seven women had joined the Irish Housewives' Association.

87. Shortages of food and other essential items during the early 1940s were caused by the disruption of trade routes during the Second World War.

88. In 1944, a scheme for family allowances was introduced in Ireland where all children after the second were paid an allowance of 2s 6d. The allowance was made payable to the head of the household until 1974 when it became payable to the mother.

89. Hanna Sheehy Skeffington, 'Election manifesto to the electors of Dublin South City', (Courtesy of Andrée Sheehy Skeffington).

90. Sheehy Skeffington's campaign was backed by the Women's Social and Progressive League, the I.C.A., the Irish Housewives' Association and the Women Graduates' Association.

91. The three other independent women candidates who also supported welfare reforms were: Margaret Ashe (Galway), Maryann Phillips (Tipperary) and Mary Corbet (Tipperary). Of the four only Margaret Ashe retained her deposit.

92. Hanna Sheehy Skeffington, 'Women in politics' in *The Bell*, vol vii, no 2, November 1943, p. 143.

Caitriona Clear:

No Feminine Mystique:
Popular Advice to Women of the House
in Ireland 1922-1954

1. Cited in the Report of the Commission on Vocational Organization (hereafter CVO report), 1943, R.76/1, p.28ln.

2. Maura Laverty, *Kind Cooking* (Tralee, 1946), p.110.

3. *Catholic Bulletin*, vol xxvii, July-December 1937, p. 558.

4. Mary Hayden, 'Women's role in the modern world' in *Irish Monthly*, vol. 68, August 1940, pp. 392-402; p.398.

5. For Maire McGeehin, see CVO report, 1943, Addendum 111, p.473.

6. On recommendations about crèches, see notes 31 and 43 below. On women's political position in the Free State see Mary Clancy, 'Aspects of women's contribution to Oireachtas debate 1922-37' in Maria Luddy and Cliona Murphy (eds), *Women Surviving: Studies in Irish Women's History in the Nineteenth and Twentieth Centuries* (Dublin, 1990); Yvonne Scannell, 'Changing times for women's rights' in Eiléan Ní Chuilleanáin (ed.), *Irishwomen: Image and Achievement* (Dublin, 1985). See also pp 181-5.

7. Katharine Tynan, 'A trumpet call to Irish women' in *The Voice of Ireland: a Memorial of Freedom's Day by the Foremost Leaders* (New York, 1924), pp 170-74. On domestic reform in early twentieth-century Ireland see *The Irish Homestead*, a periodical edited by George Russell; Pat Bolger (ed.) *And See her Beauty Shining There: the Story of the Irish Countrywomen* (Dublin, 1986); Joanna Bourke, *Husbandry to Housewifery: Women, Economic Change and Housework in Ireland 1890-1914* (Oxford, 1993).

8. Arland Ussher, 'The boundary between the sexes' in John A. O'Brien (ed.), *The Vanishing Irish* (London, 1954), p.163.

9. 'Grandmother envies the housekeeper of today' in *The Irish Press*, 28 December 1936.

10. *23rd Annual Report of the Department of Agriculture and Technical Instruction, 1922-3* (Dublin, 1925), pp 176-82; 28th annual report of the Department of Agriculture and Technical Instruction, 1929-30 (Dublin n.d.), pp 148-54.

11. 'Domestic modern girls' in *The Irish Press*, 8 September 1931.

12. *Cookery Notes* (Dublin, 1944) (price 6d); Josephine Redington, *The Economic Cookery Book: Tried Recipes etc. Suitable for All Households, Schools and Domestic Classes* (9th edition, Dublin, 1927. The 1st edition was published in 1905). The former book was used in the Presentation Secondary, Sexton St., Limerick, in the 1940s by Nancy Clear from Parteen, Co. Clare and the latter by Brighid O'Flaherty from Carraroe in Coolarne Domestic Science college, Athenry, Galway in the 1940s. See also Margaret Roper and Ruth Duffin, *The Bluebird Cookery Book for Working Women* (Dublin, 1939); Maura Laverty, *Flour Economy* (Dublin, 1941). On recommendations about domestic training, see e.g., *Report of Inquiry into the Housing of the Working Classes of the City of Dublin 1939-43* (Dublin, 1940) , pp 141-5; Commission on Emigration and other Population Problems, 1948-54, R.84, pp 172-3, and addendum No.1 by Rev. Thomas Counihan, p.192; *Commission on Youth Unemployment 1951, Classes of the City of Dublin, 1939-43*, pp 141-5; Commission on Emigration and other Population Problems, 1948-54, R.84, pp 172-3.

13. Maura Laverty, *Never No More: the Story of a Lost Village* (London, 1942), p. 15.

14. *Kind Cooking*, introduction, pp 1-10 and passim.

15. This does not mean that they are not to be found in other books not consulted by me. Kathleen Ferguson, *Lessons in Cookery and Housewifery for the Use of Children, Book 1* (Dublin, 1903). This was part of a series of booklets on matters related to housekeeping (*leabhairini na seamróige*) which cost 1d each. On boxty pancakes see Maura Laverty, *Never No More*, p.109.

16. *Never No More*, pp 84-87.

17. Commission on Vocational Organization, Minutes of Evidence, evidence of Irish Countrywomen's Association (National Library of Ireland, MS 930, vol. 9, pp 1833-42). The ICA gave evidence on 21 November 1940.

18. *Kind Cooking*, p. 29.

19. *Ibid.*, p.3.

20. *Catholic Bulletin*, vol.19, August 1929, pp 765-7.

21. *Woman's Life: the Irish Home Weekly* (2d every Thursday), 5 September 1936 (factory worker); 16 January 1937 (wife and mother); 20 Feb 1937 (street-seller); 27 March 1937 (nurse); 17 April 1937 (secretary in trade union); 26 August 1939 (Gaiety girls); 30 September 1939 (radiographer); 7 October 1939 (commercial traveller).

22. *Woman's Life*, 17 April 1937; 25 July 1936 (interview with Miss Annie McGlynn, packer in Brown and Polson).

23. eg. 5 September 1936; 21 January 1937.

24. eg. 2 January 1937; 16 January 1937.

25. eg. 20 February 1937; 17 April 1937.

26. Cynthia White, *Women's Magazines 1693-1968* (London, 1970); Janice Winship, *Inside Women's Magazines* (London, 1987).

27. *Woman's Mirror: the Irish woman's very own weekly* (2d every Friday), 4 June 1932; 18 June 1932.

28. 'The duties of the health visitor' in *Irish Nurses' Union Gazette*, no. 32, January 1930, p. 2.

29. *Report on the Conference Between the Department of Local Government and Public Health and Representatives of Local Public Health and Poor Assistance Authorities at Mansion House Dublin, 8-9 July 1930* (Dublin, 1930). See, for example, p. 20.

30. Annie M.P. Smithson, 'The children of our slums' in *Irish Monthly*, vol liii, October 1925, pp 553-6.

31. *Woman's Life*, 27 March 1937, interview with Miss Digby, nurse and vice-president of St. Andrew's Baby Club, Dublin.

32. *Cookery Notes* (Dublin, 1944), p. x, pp 60-1.

33. Evidence of ICA to CVO (NLI MS 930, vol. 9, pp 18252-4). See also *National Nutrition Survey Report, 1941-44* (Dublin, 1948; compendium, 1953), K.53/1-K.53/5.

34. *Cookery Notes* (Dublin, 1944), pp 60-1.

35. *Economic Cookery Book*, pp 20-21; 'Hygiene and housewifery in rural districts and small towns'; *Cookery Notes* (Dublin, 1924), A/14; on sanitary facilities in 1946, see *Census of Population 1946*, vol iv, Tables 29-59, pp 104-210. See also pp 206-19 above.

36. *Economic Cookery Book*, pp 2-5.

37. James Deeny, 'Poverty as a cause of ill-health', paper read to Statistical Society, Dublin, 31 May 1940, and published, with the accompanying discussion which took place, in the *Journal of the Statistical and Social Inquiry Society of Ireland*, xvi, 93rd series (1939-40), pp 75-89.

38. C. Clancy-Gore, 'Nutritional standards of some working-class families in Dublin 1943' in *Journal of the Statistical and Social Inquiry Society*, xvii, 97th series (1943-44), pp 241-53.

39. Hilda Tweedy, *A Link in the Chain: the Story of the Irish Housewives' Association, 1942-1992* (Dublin, 1992).

40. Louie Bennett, 'The domestic problem' in *The Irish Housewife*, i (1946), pp 29-30.

41. Seth Koven and Sonya Michel, *Mothers of a New World* (London, 1993), p.6.

42. Commission on Vocational Organization, minutes of evidence; evidence given in December 1940 by the Joint Committee of Women's Societies and Social Workers, the National Council of Women in Ireland and the Catholic Federation of Women Secondary School Teachers (NLI MS 930, vol. 9, pp 3065-3080).

43. CVO Report, 1943 and addendum 111 to the report, pp 471-4.

44. 'As I see it' in *Christus Rex: an Irish Quarterly Journal of Sociology*, 11, no. 2, April 1948, p. 75; *ibid.*, 11, no. 2, April 1949, pp 74-5; *ibid.*, 11, no. 3, July 1948, pp 64-5.

45. The term is borrowed from Betty Friedan's classic and influential study of white middle-class American housewives in the late 1950s and early '60s, *The Feminine Mystique* (London, 1983).

46. May Laverty, 'The terrors of washing up' in *The Irish Press*, 7 September 1935; Margot Moffett, 'That ideal home' in *The Irish Housewife*, i, 1946, pp 9-13.

47. Ann Hathaway, *The Homecraft Book* (Dublin, 1944), pp 9-13. I wonder if Ann Hathaway was the nom-de-plume of Mary Frances Keating, who was noted in the introduction to her article in *The Vanishing Irish* ('Marriage-shy Irishmen,' pp 164-76) as having written a book of household advice for Irishwomen, of which I can find no trace. 'Hathaway', like Keating, was a domestic correspondent. It was suggested to me by Kathleen Clear, née Synnott, Limerick, whose mother Katie Synnott, née Larkin (the wife of a cabinet-maker, living in a servantless semi-detached house with 8 'children' under 25 at home at that time), bought the book in 1944, that 'Hathaway' was a pun – hath-a-way – suggesting resourcefulness and ingenuity.

48. Hathaway, *The Homecraft Book*, wellingtons, p. 24; light-bulbs, p. 40; candles, p. 40; eggshells and egg-water, pp 34-5; shoulders, p. 70; neuralgia, p. 80.

49. *Woman's Life*, 9 January 1937.

50. Minutes of ICA evidence to the CVO (NLI MS 930, vol. 9, pp 18337-8); on the dismissive treatment of the ICA see Nell McCafferty's apologetic comment in McCafferty and P. Murphy, *Women in Focus* (Dublin, 1986), p. 37.

51. John D. Sheridan, *While the Humour is on Me* (Dublin, 1954), p. 59.

52. Hilda Tweedy, *A Link in the Chain*, p. 15.

53. *Dublin Opinion*, April 1937; September 1951; January 1951.

Mary E. Daly:

'Turn on the Tap':

The State, Irish Women & Running Water

1. *Commission on Emigration and Other Population Problems* (Dublin, 1954); J. O'Brien (ed.), *The Vanishing Irish* (London, 1954).

2. Damian F. Hannan, *Displacement and Development: Class Kinship and Social Change in Irish Rural Communities* (Dublin, 1979), pp 48-55.

3. James Meenan, *The Irish Economy since 1922* (Liverpool, 1970), p. 190.

4. Unless otherwise stated data on water supplies come from the Population Census 1946-71, volumes on housing.

5. Michael Shiel, *The Quiet Revolution: the Electrification of Rural Ireland, 1946-1976* (Dublin, 1984), p. 152.

6. National Archives of Ireland, Department of the Environment (hereafter D/E), SS3 Box, Report of committee on water and sewerage and other functions of sanitary authorities, 1958.

7. Sue Bowden and Avner Offer, 'Household appliances and the use of time: the United States and Britain since the 1920s' in *Economic History Review*, vol. xlvii, no 4 (Nov. 1994), pp 725-748.

8. National Archives of Ireland, D/E, Housing, 207/13. Reserved housing, general file.

9. National Archives of Ireland, D/E, Sanitary Files. Box 6. 205/12, Rural water supply, general file.

10. Bowden and Offer, *op. cit.*, p. 734; Christine Bose, 'Technology and changes in the division of labour in the American home' in *Women's Studies International Quarterly*, 2 (1979), pp 295-304.

11. Joanna Bourke, *Husbandry to Housewifery: Women, Economic Change, and Housework in Ireland, 1890-1914.* (Oxford, 1993), pp 201-236.

12. Florence Irwin, *The Cookin' Woman* (London, 1949).

13. Mona Hearn, *Below Stairs: Domestic Service Remembered in Dublin and Beyond, 1880-1922* (Dublin, 1993).

14. *Husbandry to Housewifery*, pp 213-4.

15. Bina Agarwal, 'Women and technological change in agriculture: the Asian and African experience' in Ifikhar Ahmed (ed.), *Technology and Rural Women: Conceptual and Empirical Issues* (London, 1985), pp 70-1; Eugenia Date-Bah, 'Technologies for rural women of Ghana: the role of socio-cultural factors' in *ibid.*, pp 227-8.

16. Conrad M. Arensberg and Solon T. Kimball, *Family and Community in Ireland* (Cambridge, Massachusetts, 1968), p. 36.

17. Patrick McNabb, 'Social structure' in Jeremiah Newman (ed.), *Limerick Rural Survey, 1958-64* (Tipperary, 1964), p. 195.

18. A district in south Monaghan surrounding the town of Carrickmacross.

19. *Bealoideas*, vii, (1937), pp 171-2.

20. For photographic images of women collecting water see Myrtle Hill and Vivienne Pollock, *Images and Experience: Photographs of Irishwomen c.1880-1920* (Belfast 1993), pp 27, 148; Shiel, *Quiet Revolution*, pp 107, 197.

21. Mary E. Daly, *Dublin: the Deposed Capital, 1860-1914 – A Social and Economic History* (Cork, 1984), chapter 8.

22. *Report of Local Government Board*, 1874.

23. *Ibid.*, 1874, 1878; Bourke, *Husbandry to Housewifery*, p. 213.

24. Daly, *Dublin*, p. 283.

25. National Archives of Ireland, D/E, Sligo, Box 701.

26. Shiel, *Quiet Revolution*, pp 26-30.

27. National Archives of Ireland, D/E, SS3, Report of committee on water and sewerage and other functions of sanitary authorities, 1958.

28. National Archives of Ireland, N 201/3, Housing standards.

29. *Commission on Emigration and other Population Problems*, para 440.

30. National Archives of Ireland, D/E, S13166 D/63.

31. National Archives of Ireland, D/E, SS3, Report of committee on water and sewerage and other functions of sanitary authorities.

32. Shiel, *Quiet Revolution*, p. 63.

33. *Ibid.*, pp 123-5.

34. *Ibid.*, pp 170, 182.

35. *Ibid.*, pp 198-9.

36. National Archives of Ireland, D/E, 205/12, Rural water supply general file.

37. Shiel, *Quiet Revolution*, p. 44.

38. *Ibid.*, pp 180-192.

39. Cited in Diarmait Ferriter, *Mothers, Maidens and Myths: a History of the ICA* (Dublin, 1995), p. 25.

40. National Archives of Ireland, D/E, Sanitary files, Box 2, SS3.

41. National Archives of Ireland, D/E, Sanitary files, Box 10, 208/10/2. Financing sanitary services works.

42. National Archives of Ireland, D/E, Sanitary files, Box 7, 205/12/3; Ferriter, *Mothers, Maidens and Myths*, pp 41-3.

43. National Archives of Ireland, S13166/C/61.

44. National Archives of Ireland, D/E, Sanitary files, Box 25 259/3, Five Year Programme.

45. I am indebted to my father Seamus Crowley, B. Agr.Sc., for this insight.

46. National Archives of Ireland, S13166D/63.

47. Kevin Boland, *The Rise and Decline of Fianna Fáil* (Dublin, 1982).

48. National Archives of Ireland, S13166D/63.

49. Damian F. Hannan and Louise A. Katsiaouni, *Traditional Families? From culturally prescribed to negotiated roles in farm families* (Dublin, 1977), p. 63.

50. Hannan, *Displacement and Development*, p. 114.

51. Hannan and Katsiaouni, *op. cit.*, p. 185.

Rosemary Cullen Owens:

Women & Pacifism in Ireland, 1915-1932

1. Jill Liddington, *The Long Road to Greenham: Feminism and Anti-militarism in Britain since 1820* (London, 1989), p.5.

2. The later and current title of this organisation is the International Alliance of Women (IAW). Key figures in its formation were Carrie Chapman Catt and Susan B. Anthony (USA), Vida Goldstein (Australia), and Dr Anita Augsburg (Germany). A predecessor of this group was the International Council of Women (ICW), formed in 1888, which had member councils in 16 European countries on the eve of war in 1914. In 1904 the more radical feminists broke away and founded the IWSA, which by 1914 had member societies in 20 different European countries (see R. Evans, *Comrades and Sisters: Feminism, Socialism and Pacifism in Europe 1870-1945* (Sussex, 1987), chapter 5. See also Liddington, *The Long Road to Greenham*).

3. Among those in attendance were Charlotte Despard, Jane Addams, Charlotte Perkins Gilman, Kathleen Courtney, Helena Swanwick, Alice Parks and Mary Sheepshanks.

4. *Jus Suffragii* (monthly journal of the IWSA), 1 December 1914, cited in Liddington, *The Long Road to Greenham*, pp 94-95; see also Anne Wiltsher, *Most Dangerous Women: Feminist Peace Campaigners of the Great War* (London and Boston, 1985), p.57.

5. Carrie Chapman Catt had succeeded the veteran suffragist Susan B. Anthony as President of the American Suffrage Association in 1900. In 1904 she was elected President of the newly formed International Woman Suffrage Alliance. Her ambivalent attitude to the war, culminating in her acceptance of U.S. involvement in 1917, alienated her from many former colleagues. Jane Addams, feminist, pacifist, social reformer, was the founder of the Hull House Settlement at Chicago. Here disadvantaged immigrants and women activists became involved in radical politics and trade union work. She was elected chairman of the Woman's Peace Party in Washington in 1915 and of the subsequent International Committee of Women for Permanent Peace. She served as elected president of its successor, the Women's International League for Peace and Freedom (WILPF) from 1919 to her death in 1935. She was awarded the Nobel Peace Prize in 1931 (Liddington, *The Long Road to Greenham*; Wiltsher, *Most Dangerous Women*; see also Adele Schreiber and Margaret Mathieson, *Journey Towards Freedom* (Denmark, 1955).

6. Other activities engaged in by the IWRL during the war included the opening of a café and recreation centre for women and girls, and the demand for minimum wages for women employees at the new Dublin munition factory. In association with the IWSLGA the League sought to involve women in temperance work and protection of young girls on the street (*IWSF Annual Report*, 1913-14; see also minutes of IWSF executive 15 August 1914, 13 March 1915 (Sheehy Skeffington Papers, National Library of Ireland, MS 21196)).

7. *The Irish Citizen*, 21 November 1914.

8. Sheehy Skeffington Papers, National Library of Ireland, MS 22667 (ii).

9. *The Irish Citizen*, 11 December 1915.

10. *Jus Suffragii*, 1 January 1915; The subtitle *The International Woman Suffrage News* was used from 1920, changing to *The International Women's News* in 1930.

11. *Jus Suffragii*, 1 March 1915.

12. *The Irish Citizen*, 30 January 1915, 6 February 1915, 13 February 1915, 20 February 1915, 27 February 1915.

13. Gertrude Bussey and Margaret Tims, *Pioneers for Peace, Women's International League for Peace and Freedom 1915-1965* (London, 1965), p. 18; see also Liddington, *The Long Road to Greenham*, pp 94-96.

14. Diaries of Lucy O. Kingston, March 1915 (hereafter Kingston Diaries), Diaries in possession of Daisy Lawrenson Swanton. Lucy Kingston (1892-1969) was a life-long campaigner for the rights of women and peace. Her involvement in the suffrage movement, WILPF and CND are documented in Daisy Lawrenson Swanton, *Emerging from the Shadows: the Lives of Sarah Anne Lawrenson and Lucy Olive Kingston* (Dublin, 1994).

15. Wiltshire, *Most Dangerous Women*, pp 89-90; see also Margaret Mulvihill, *Charlotte Despard: a Biography* (London, 1989), p.115.

16. Evans, *Comrades and Sisters*, p.125.

17. Cited in Liddington, *The Long Road to Greenham*, pp 98-100. The book was anonymous, but Liddington identifies two of its authors as Charles Ogden and Mary Sargant.

18. *The Irish Citizen*, 27 February 1915.

19. Evans, *Comrades and Sisters*, pp 127-129. Detailing the lack of support among women's groups throughout Europe for the feminist-pacifist campaign, Evans cites Lida Gustava Heyman's observation that it was only through engaging in social welfare work that many of the branches of the anti-war German Women's Suffrage League were able to keep even 10% of their members. Both the other (and larger) suffrage organisations in Germany supported the war. The umbrella Federation of German Women's Associations numbering 250,000 women in 1914 condemned the peace movement and branded participation in the Hague conference as 'incompatible with the patriotic character and the national duty of the German women's movement.' A similar situation occurred in France, Russia and Britain.

For an Australian perspective see Darryn Kruse and Charles Sowerine, 'Feminism and pacifism: "woman's sphere" in peace and war' in *Australian Women, New Feminist Perspectives* (Melbourne, 1986).

20. Evans, *Comrades and Sisters*, p. 131. Leading figures in the Socialist Women's International in France, Russia and Germany all opposed the war and continued to do so despite the action of male leaders of the Second International in supporting the war effort.

21. *The Irish Citizen*, 24 April 1915. The delegates were Hanna Sheehy Skeffington, Margaret McCoubrey and Mrs Metge from the IWFL, Louie Bennett, Miss Moser and Mrs Isabella Richardson from the recently formed Irish committee, and Helen MacNaghten from the Northern committee of the IWSF. *The Irish Citizen* of 24 April 1915 notes that members of the IWFL had attended Dublin Trade's Council to inform them of their proposed participation in the Hague Congress, pointing out their resolution regarding claims of subject nationalities. A resolution endorsing the action of the Irish women delegates was proposed by William O'Brien, seconded by Thomas McPartlin, and warmly supported by James Connolly.

22. *The Irish Citizen*, 22 May 1915.

23. *Ibid.*

24. Louie Bennett to Hanna Sheehy Skeffington, 12 May 1915 (Sheehy Skeffington Papers, National Library of Ireland, Ms 22674).

25. *The Irish Citizen*, 22 May 1915; published later in 1915 as pamphlet.

26. R.M. Fox, *Louie Bennet: Her Life and Times* (Dublin, 1957), p.48.

27. Described by Jill Liddington as 'a small Liberal intellectual élite', the UDC questioned Britain's involvement in the war, advocated the establishment of an international organisation after the war to prevent other conflicts, and argued that peace terms should not be punitive. Among its founders were H.N. Brailsford, Bertrand Russell and Ramsay MacDonald (who had resigned as chair of the parliamentary Labour Party on the war issue) (Liddington, *The Long Road to Greenham*, pp 81-83).

28. Fox, *Louie Bennett*, p. 49. For details of munitions preparation by women in Liberty Hall from 1915 see Ruth Taillon, *When History was Made: the Women of 1916* (Belfast, 1996), pp 16-18.

29. In *The Irish Citizen*, 20 February 1915, Mrs L.M. Metge states that she had attempted to raise this issue at the 1913 congress of the IWSA. Carrie Chapman Catt informed her that Ireland must first have some form of national government. Catt's final words to her were 'Go home and get Home Rule!'

30. Louie Bennett to Hon. Sec., ICWPP, 19 October 1915, 26 November 1915, 5 and 18 Jamuary 1916, 14 February 1916 (Women's International League for Peace and Freedom (WILPF) Papers, University of Colorado, Boulder, Western Historical Collection (hereafter, WILPF Colorado)); see also Louie Bennett to Hanna Sheehy Skeffington, 19 June 1915 (Sheehy Skeffington papers, National Library of Ireland, Ms.22648(11)). In February 1915 *The Irish Citizen* published articles and editorials advising separate representation. In particular the example of Bohemia was cited. While sending representatives to the Austrian parliament Bohemian women had succeeded in securing recognition as a separate affiliated country within the IWSA despite differing political aspirations.

31. Louie Bennett to Chrystal MacMillan, 29 January 1916 (WILPF Colorado).

32. 1st yearly report of the Women's International League (WIL) October 1915-October 1916 (WILPF papers, British Library of Political and Economic Science (hereafter WILPF BLPES)).

33. Rosa Manus to Louie Bennett, 18 December 1916 (WILPF Colorado).

34. Louie Bennett to Chrystal MacMillan, 18 January and 4 February 1916 (WILPF Colorado).

35. Fox, *Louie Bennett*, p. 57.
36. Sheehy Skeffington Papers, National Library of Ireland, MS 22,279 (vi).
37. Rosa Manus, Secretary, ICWPP to Louie Bennett, 16 October 1916 (WILPF Colorado).
38. IIL to ICWPP, January 1917 (WILPF Colorado).
39. This read: CONNRAD EADAR-NAISIUNTA BAN NA H-EIREANN.
40. *The Irish Citizen*, November 1918; see also WIL – Special Executive Meeting 22 October 1918 (WILPF BLPES).
41. *The Irish Citizen*, May 1918, Report of IIL; see Louie Bennett to A. Jacobs, 7 November 1918 (WILPF Colorado); Bennett stated, 'We hope that the fact that Ireland has remained free from conscription may help in securing freedom from it for all countries'. The other major issue on which women's groups co-operated was the campaign against venereal disease and the related implementation of Regulation 40 D under the Defence of the Realm Act (DORA).
42. A delegation of five women was chosen to attend but Louie Bennett reported subsequently in the *The Irish Citizen* that Hanna Sheehy Skeffington was refused a passport (*The Irish Citizen*, June/July 1919).
43. This is still the current name and headquarters of the organisation. Proximity to the League of Nations offices was among the reasons for this location.
44. WILPF Colorado.
45. *Ibid.*, 30 July 1919.
46. Louie Bennett to Emily Greene Balch, 1 January 1920 (WILPF Colorado).
47. Helena Swanwick, *I Have Been Young* (London, 1935), p. 336. Swanwick noted the great effect of such slides, audiences commenting that devastated areas in Ireland 'look just like Belgium'; see also Minutes of Executive Committee and Report of WIL, October 1920 -January 1922 (WILPF BLPES). A pamphlet published on their mission to Ireland reported under the headings: Ulster, Sinn Fein, religion, terrorism, war, destruction of Irish trade and industry and propaganda.
48. Charlotte H. Fallon, *Soul of Fire: a Biography of Mary MacSwiney* (Cork and Dublin, 1986), p. 68. Fallon notes the MacSwiney/Cumann na mBan correspondence during this trip indicated that at least one member was disenchanted with women's role in the nationalist movement. In a subsequent interview with *The Washington Times*, however, MacSwiney stated: 'A feminist movement is not necessary in our country. The women of Ireland are on full equality with the men and are comrades in everything .... When our Republic was formed, women were given equal rights in all things. The men are not disturbed when women are given high offices. We are the only country in the world with a woman in the cabinet of our government. Some day, no doubt, a woman will be president of our Republic.'
49. National Library of Ireland, ILB 300 p12 (item 94).
50. Louie Bennett to Emily Greene Balch, 21 March 1921 (WILPF Colorado).
51. Emily Greene Balch to Louie Bennett, 25 January 1922 (WILPF Colorado).
52. Louie Bennett to Emily Greene Balch, 30 January 1922 (WILPF Colorado).
53. Sheehy Skeffington Papers, National Library of Ireland, MS 21194, no 45; see also Fox, *Louie Bennett*, pp 76-70; J. A. Gaughan, *Thomas Johnson* (Dublin, 1980), pp 207-8.
54. Louie Bennett to Emily Greene Balch, 12 October 1922 (WILPF Colorado).
55. Kingston Diaries, 1 December 1920.
56. Louie Bennett to Emily Greene Balch, 12 October 1922 (WILPF Colorado). Rosamund Jacob's account of the Mansion House peace conference noted that it was attended by 'great crowds of women, but none of them apparently really keen on peace'. Louie Bennett presided, with Maud Gonne McBride, Charlotte Despard and Lucy Kingston among the speakers. Jacob observed that the audience had presumed all speakers would be republican, and in objection to remarks by Kingston started singing hymns to the Queen of Heaven which Jacob

noted, 'Miss Bennett received awfully well.' (Rosamund Jacob papers, National Library of Ireland, MS 32582).

57. *Loc. cit.*

58. Kingston Diaries, 2 November 1922.

59. *Ibid.*, 3 January 1923.

60. Annual Report of Irish Section, Women's International League 1922-23 (WILPF Colorado).

61. *Ibid.*

62. Bussey and Timms, *Pioneers for Peace*, p.53.

63. Lucy Kingston to Madeleine Doty (International Secretary of WILPF 1925-1927), 26 February 1926; Rosamund Jacob to Madeleine Doty, 23 March 1926 (WILPF Colorado). The members of this committee were: Louie Bennett, Sybil Le Brocquy, Helen Chenevix, Mrs M'Clintock Dix, Marie Johnson, Lucy Kingston, Rosamund Jacob, Miss Molyneux, Miss Mills, Mrs J. Richardson, Miss M. Stephens, Miss G. Webb.

64. Bennett, Kingston and Jacob were the main correspondents in this regard. In addition to advice on the political minefield that was Ireland in 1926, Jacob advised that in circularising travel arrangements, the names Cobh and Dun Laoghaire should be used instead of Queenstown and Kingstown as 'we want to keep the Irish names once we have got them back' (Jacob to Doty (WILPF Colorado)).

65. Lucy Kingston to Madeleine Doty, 1 January 1926 (WILPF Colorado).

66. Louie Bennett to Madeleine Doty, 16 February 1926 (WILPF Colorado).

67. Report of the 5th Congress of WILPF, Dublin, 8-15 July 1926 (WILPF Colorado).

68. *Ibid.* Louie Bennett had advised that 'world' be included in the title for this public session 'in view of our faction fights here'.

69. Swanwick, *I Have Been Young*, pp 450-452. Rosamund Jacob recounted that when Hanna rose to speak 'a roar of applause broke out for all the world as if it was De Valera, and went on and on with cries of Up the Republic!' (Rosamund Jacob Papers, National Library of Ireland, MS 32582).

70. Swanwick, *I Have Been Young*.

71. *The International Woman Suffrage News*, August-September 1926.

72. Mary Sheepshanks (International Secretary of WILPF 1927-30) to Louie Bennett, 20 November 1928 (WILPF Colorado).

73. Sinn Féin to WILPF, 25 October 1929 (WILPF Colorado).

74. *Ibid.*

75. Kingston Diaries, 1 November 1929.

76. Bennett to Mary Sheepshanks, 30 November 1929 (WILPF Colorado).

77. Una M'Clintock Dix to Mary Sheepshanks, 1 February 1930 (WILPF Colorado).

78. Kingston Diaries, 13 December 1929.

79. Una M'Clintock Dix to Mary Sheepshanks, 1 February 1930 (WILPF Colorado).

80. Rosamund Jacob to Camille Drevet (International Secretary of WILPF 1930-1934), 9 April 1931 (WILPF Colorado).

81. Lucy Kingston to Camille Drevet, 23 April 1932 (WILPF Colorado).

82. WILPF Ireland was reformed in 1991 in the wake of the Gulf War.

Catherine Shannon:
The Women Writer as Historical Witness:
Northern Ireland, 1968-1994 – an Interdisciplinary Perspective

1. Margaret MacCurtain, Mary O'Dowd, Maria Luddy, 'An agenda for women's history, 1500-1900' in *I.H.S.*, xxviii, no.109 (May 1992), pp 1-37; Dermot Keogh, *Twentieth Century*

Ireland (Dublin,1994). For an extended discussion of the women-free tone of Irish historiography, see Margaret Ward, *The Missing Sex: Putting Women into Irish History* (Dublin, 1991).

2. Statistics showing the differentials in employment levels between Catholics and Protestants often have included separate figures for women. See Brendan O'Leary and John McGarry, *The Politics of Antagonism* (London, 1993), p. 206.

3. Malcolm Sutton, *An Index of Deaths from the Conflict in Northern Ireland, 1969-1993* (Belfast,1994).

4. Between 1970 and 1974 Belfast and Derry bore the brunt of violence, experiencing 72% of the deaths, 91% of injuries from civil disorder, 55% of the bombings and 33% of the gun battles (Paul Arthur, *Political Realities: Government and Politics in Northern Ireland*, 2nd edition (London, 1984), p. 120; O'Leary and McGarry, *op. cit.*, pp 8-44); R.U.C. statistics to July 1997.

5. Eavan Boland, *A Kind of Scar: the Woman Poet in a National Tradition* (Dublin, 1989).

6. Nell McCafferty, *Armagh Women* (Dublin, 1981); Margaretta D'Arcy, *Tell them Everything,* (London, 1981); M. T. McGivern and Margaret Ward, 'Images of women in Northern Ireland' in *Cranebag*, vol. 4, no. 1 (1980), pp 66-72.

7. *Ibid.*, p. 69. Popular novels set in Northern Ireland often replicate the stereotypical images of northern women found in tabloid papers. See Bill Rolston, 'Mothers, whores and villains: images of women in novels of the Northern Ireland conflict' in *Race and Class*, vol. 31, no. 1 (July-Sept 1989), pp 41-57. See also O'Leary and McGarry, *op. cit.*, pp 13-18.

8. Monica McWilliams, 'Women in Northern Ireland: an overview' in Eamonn Hughes (ed.), *Politics and Culture in Northern Ireland* (London, 1991); Carmel Roulston, 'Women on the margin: the women's movement in Northern Ireland, 1973-1988' in *Science and Society*, vol. 53, no. 2 (1989), pp 219-36; Pamela Montgomery and Celia Davis, 'A woman's place in Northern Ireland' in Peter Stringer and Gillian Robinson (eds), *Social Attitudes in Northern Ireland* (1990-91 edition, Belfast, 1991), pp 74-78; Valerie Morgan and Grace Fraser, 'Women and the Northern Ireland conflict' in Seamus Dunn (ed.), *Facets of the Conflict in Northern Ireland* (New York, 1995), pp 81-96; Eilish Rooney and Margaret Woods, *Women, Community and Politics in Northern Ireland: A Belfast Study* (Belfast, 1995).

9. Eileen Fairweather, Roisin McDonough and Melanie McFadyean, *Only the Rivers Run Free: Northern Ireland, the Women's War* (London, 1984).

10. Fionnuala O'Connor, *In Search of a State: Catholics in Northern Ireland* (Belfast, 1993); Sally Belfrage, *The Crack: a Belfast Year* (London, 1987).

11. Catherine B. Shannon, 'Women in Northern Ireland' in Mary O'Dowd and Sabine Wichert (eds), *Chattel, Servant or Citizen: Women's Status in Church, State and Society: Historical Studies XIX* (Belfast, 1995), pp 238-253.

12. Tom Dunne (ed.), *The Writer as Witness: Literature as Historical Evidence: Historical Studies XVI* (Cork, 1987).

13. Initially in the Northern Ireland Labour Party, Paddy Devlin was a founder of the Social Democratic and Labour Party in August 1970 and subsequently served as S.D.L.P. chief whip in the power-sharing Assembly of 1973-74. He was expelled from the S.D.L.P. in 1977 following his public criticism that the party's original commitment to socialist principles was being undermined by a growing emphasis on the 'Irish dimension', i. e. the unification goal of traditional Irish nationalism (W. D. Flackes and Sidney Elliott, *Northern Ireland: a Political Directory, 1968-1993* (Belfast, 1994), p. 139; see also Paddy Devlin, *Straight Left* (Belfast, 1993), pp 277-83).

14. Anne Devlin, 'Passages' in *The Way-Paver* (London, 1986), p. 14.

15. *Ibid.*, p. 16.

16. Bob Purdie, *Politics in the Streets: the Origins of the Civil Rights Movement in Northern Ireland* (Belfast, 1990), pp 196-7.

17. Paddy Devlin, *Straight Left*, p. 95.

18. Jonathan Bardon, *A History of Ulster* (Belfast, 1992), pp 662-6; Purdie, *Politics in the Street*, p. 221.

19. O'Leary and McGarry, *The Politics of Antagonism*, pp 30-31, 41-42.

20. Paddy Devlin, *Straight Left*, p.106.

21. Anne Devlin, *Ourselves Alone* (London, 1986).

22. O'Leary and McGarry, *The Politics of Antagonism*, p. 213. In the Westminister election of 1983, Sinn Féin polled 13.4% of the total votes, and 42% of the nationalist vote.

23. Catherine B. Shannon, 'Catholic women and the Northern Irish troubles' in Alan O'Day (ed.), *Ireland's Terrorist Trauma* (Hertfordshire, 1989), pp 242-244.

24. Although numerous historians had been critical of the mythic simplicity of popular nationalist views on the origins and nature of the northern conflict since the early 1970s, the proceedings of the New Ireland Forum in 1983-1984 and its report stimulated a growing recognition of the complexity of the northern problem among southern politicians and the general public (see Ciaran Brady (ed.) *Interpreting Irish History* (Dublin, 1994); J. J. Lee, *Ireland, 1912-1985: Politics and Society* (Dublin, 1989), pp 596, 676).

25. Brendan O'Brien, *The Long War: the I.R.A. and Sinn Féin: from armed struggle to peace talks* (Dublin, 1995), pp 34-35; and author's personal observation in June 1983.

26. For contemporary oral evidence of this, see Ellen Fairweather, Roisin McDonough and Melanie McFadyean, *Only the Rivers Run Free*, pp 130-33. In Ardoyne, a Belfast neighbourhood with a strong para-military history, a 1991 survey reported that one out of four women had been victims of domestic violence or sexual abuse. This trend was confirmed in a subsequent regional study (see Ardoyne Women's Research Project, *Unheard Voices: Women's Needs in Ardoyne* (Belfast, 1992); Monica McWilliams and Joan McKiernan, *Bringing it out in the open: a report for the DHSS* (Belfast, 1993)).

27. The Socialist Workers' Party evolved from the 1970 split in the republican movement which produced the Provisional IRA and the Official IRA. In Northern Ireland, the 'Officials' and their political supporters in the Workers' Party were often known as 'Stickies' owing to their custom of sticking paper Easter Lilies on their coat lapels during the annual Easter 1916 Rising commemorations in the early 1970s.

28. See Fairweather, et. al., *op. cit.*, p. 263; Shannon, 'Catholic women and the Northern Irish troubles', p. 244; see also Marie Mulholland, 'Between a rock and a hard place' in *Unfinished Revolution: Essays on the Irish Women's Movement* (Belfast, 1989), p. 35.

29. Eileen Fairweather, et. al., *Only the Rivers Run Free*, p. 130.

30. Anne Devlin, *Ourselves Alone* (London, 1985), p. 20.

31. M. T. McGivern and Margaret Ward, 'Images of women in Northern Ireland' in *Cranebag*, vol. 4, no 1 (1980), p. 67; New Ireland Forum Report, Minutes of evidence, 17 November 1983, p. 17 .

32. From 1969-1983 there were 297,795 house-searches in a community of 400,000 households. The highest number of searches occurred in 1973-74 for a total of 149,470. These had fallen to an average of 4,084 per annum between 1980-1982 (see W. D. Flackes and Sydney Elliott, *Northern Ireland: a Political Directory, 1968-1993* (Belfast, 1994), p. 472).

33. This observation echoes the point frequently made by the S.D.L.P. leader John Hume during this era that rather than being defenders of the Catholic community, the Provisional I.R.A. campaign was not only morally indefensible, but ineffective because it was causing more deaths of Catholic civilians than any other group (John Hume's speeches at Symposia on Northern Ireland, John F. Kennedy Library, March 1982, March 1984). See also Brendan O'Leary and John McGarry, *The Politics of Antagonism*, p. 260.

34. Anne Devlin, *Ourselves Alone*, pp 22, 30, 58.

35. In fact, much of the stigma attached to co-habitation and out-of-wedlock births has disappeared in both the Catholic and Protestant working-classes. In 1991 out-of-wedlock births accounted for 75% of births to mothers under twenty (*Social Trends: Annual Report of Social and Economic Statistics* (Belfast, 1992), Table 24). A more relaxed attitude regarding the social liaisons of partners of men sentenced for long periods has been manifest in recent years (confidential sources).

36. Anne Devlin, *Ourselves Alone*, p. 77.

37. Brendan O'Leary and John McGarry, *The Politics of Antagonism*, p. 39.

38. Anne Devlin, *The Way-Paver*, pp 121-131; *Sunday Times*, 7 December 1986, p. 44.

39. Padraig O'Malley, *The Uncivil Wars: Ireland Today* (Boston, 1983), p. 272.

40. See Shannon, 'Catholic women and the Northern Irish troubles', p. 243; Eileen Fairweather, et. al., *Only the Rivers Run Free*, pp 260-261. For more recent statements endorsing the compatibility of republicanism and feminism see Gerardine Meaney, *Sex and Nation: Women in Irish Culture and Politics* (Dublin, 1991); Claire Hackett, 'Self-determination: the republican feminist agenda' in *Feminist Review*, no. 50 (Summer 1995), pp 111-116.

41. Interviews with I. McCormick, E. Evasion, M. Clark-Glass, July 1986; January 1987. See also Marie Mulholland, 'Between a rock and a hard place', p. 35.

42. Valerie Morgan, 'Bridging the divide' in *Social Attitudes Survey, 1991-92* (Belfast, 1992), p. 37. Indeed, anecdotal evidence from this era suggests that even higher percentages of west Belfast women voted for S.D.L.P. candidate Hendron and the independent incumbent Gerry Fitt than are reflected in the overall election figures.

43. Author's interview with Gerry Cosgrove, 26 June 1986. While in the north during the last week of the 1983 election campaign, I saw many nationalist women expend tremendous energy in support of the S.D.L.P.

44. Eileen Fairweather et al, *Only the Rivers Run Free*, pp 128-32, 258-59. In a stinging critique of the ideological foundations of Irish nationalism, and republicanism in particular, Edna Longley maintained more recently that republican women have bought into a sacrificial male death cult that inevitably undermines feminist goals. Longley believes that republican feminism is pure window dressing and that Northern Ireland's politics are based on archaic orange and green tribal loyalties which are antithetical to individual freedom and liberation for both women and men (*From Cathleen to Anorexia: the Breakdown of Irelands* (Dublin, 1990), pp 15-24).

45. Paddy Devlin, *Straight Left*, pp 284-286; author's interview with Theresa Devlin, 21 July 1992. Some of this decline in electoral support may have been attributable to Devlin's expulsion from the S.D.L.P., and not solely to the hostility from extreme republicans.

46. Devlin won the Susan Smith Blackburn Prize in 1985, and the George Devine Award in 1986 for *Ourselves Alone*. Devlin's play opened in Liverpool in October 1985, moved to London's Royal Court Upstairs in November, and then to the main Royal Court Theatre in August 1986. She was short-listed for two Lawrence Olivier Awards – West End Play of the Year and Most Promising Newcomer – in the same year. Her T.V. play *A Woman Calling* won the Samuel Beckett Award for the best first play for television.

47. Andrew Hislop interview with Anne Devlin, *The Times*, 21 August 1986, p. 13.

48. Public meeting at Boston College, 25 October 1995; *Proceedings of the Reaching Common Ground Conference* (Boston, 1995).

49. Philomena Gallagher (ed.), *The Dolly Mixtures: an Anthology of Craigavon Women Writers* (Craigavon, 1991); *Joy and Troubles: an Anthology of Craigavon Women Writers* (Craigavon, 1992).

50. *Joy and Troubles*, p. 3.

51. These documents suggested the principles upon which negotiations involving all the northern political parties, British officials and Irish officials for a permanent settlement would be framed.

52. Clar na mBan, *A Woman's Agenda for Peace: Conference Report* (Belfast, 1994); Eilish Rooney, 'Excluded voices' in *Fortnight*, no. 332, October, 1994; S.D.L.P. Women's Meeting, 24 March 1995; Elizabeth Porter and Monica McWilliams, Conference Report of 'Women, politics and ways forward' (September 1995). Political parties sending representatives to Draperstown were the Alliance Party, the Communist Party, Democratic Left, the Green Party, the Progressive Unionist Party, the Social Democratic and Labour Party and Sinn Féin. The Ulster Unionist Party and the Democratic Unionist Party were not formally represented, although a number of women from the Unionist tradition attended in an individual capacity. The Northern Ireland Women's European Platform in conjunction with the Republic's Council on the Status of Women have consistently stressed that participatory democracy cannot exist without women's voices being heard and without women's participation in politics (*NIWEP-CSW Submission to the Forum on Peace and Reconciliation, 20 January 1995*; see also *NIWEP Annual Report, 1994-95*).

53. Jane Wilde (ed.), *Women Shaping the Future Conference Report* (Belfast, 1996).

54. Through its call for all voices and viewpoints to be represented at the talks and in future fora, by implication the Northern Ireland Women's Coalition supported the presence of Sinn Féin at the negotiation table without the precondition of arms decommissioning demanded by the British government. The Northern Ireland Women's Coalition did, however, call for the reinstatement and maintenance of the ceasefire which had been broken by the Provisional I.R.A. bombing of Canary Wharf in London on 9 February 1996 (see *N.I.W.C. Election Manifesto*, April 1996).

55. From 7-10 July 1996, subsequent to an initial police order re-routing an Orange parade away from a Catholic neighbourhood in Portadown, there was wide-spread rioting, looting, road closures and intimidation of the Royal Ulster Constabulary by enraged Protestants across the province. The subsequent decision, alleged by the British government to have been solely that of the the Chief Constable Sir Hugh Annesley, to allow the Orange march to proceed through this Catholic neighbourhood sparked three nights of rioting and attacks on the police in nationalist communities.

56. Other writers worthy of examination include Jennifer Johnston, Mary Beckett, and Christina Reid.

Mary Cullen:
Towards a New Ireland:
Women, Feminism & the Peace Process

1. Mary Wollstonecraft, *A Vindication of the Rights of Woman* (London, 1982; first published 1792), pp 23-5.

2. Alison Jaggar, *Feminist Politics and Human Nature* (Totowa, New Jersey, 1983).

3. *Ibid.*, p. 9.

4. *Ibid.*, p. 95.

5. See Mary Cullen, 'Anna Maria Haslam', in Mary Cullen and Maria Luddy (eds), *Women, Power and Consciousness in Nineteenth-Century Ireland: Eight Biographical Studies* (Dublin, 1995), pp 161-96.

6. See Maria Luddy, 'Isabella M.S. Tod' in *ibid.*, pp 197-230.

7. William Thompson, *Appeal of One Half of the Human Race, Women, Against the Pretensions of the Other Half, Men, to Retain Them in Political, and Thence in Civil and Domestic Slavery* (London, 1983). For Wheeler, see Dolores Dooley, 'Anna Doyle Wheeler', in Cullen and Luddy, *Women, Power and Consciousness*, pp 19-53.

8. See Margaret MacCurtain, 'Women, the Vote and Revolution' in M. MacCurtain and Donncha Ó Corráin (eds.), *Women in Irish Society: The Historical Dimension* (Dublin, 1978), pp 46-57; Rosemary Cullen Owens, *Smashing Times: the History of the Irish Women's Suffrage Movement 1876-1922* (Dublin, 1984); Margaret Ward, *Unmanageable Revolutionaries: Women and Irish Nationalism* (London, 1985); Beth McKillen, 'Irish feminism and national separatism' in *Eire/Ireland* xii (1982), 3, pp 52-67; 4, pp 72-90; Mary Cullen, 'How radical was Irish feminism between 1876 and 1922?', in P.J. Corish (ed.), *Radicals, Rebels and Establishments* (Belfast, 1985), pp 185-201; Cliona Murphy, *The Women's Suffrage Movement and Irish Society in the Early Twentieth Century* (Brighton, 1989); Carol Coulter, *The Hidden Tradition: Women, Feminism and Nationalism* (Cork, 1993).

9. Diane Urquhart, '"The female of the species is more deadlier than the male"? The Ulster Women's Unionist Council, 1911-1940' in Janice Holmes and Diane Urquhart (eds), *Coming into the Light: The Work, Politics and Religion of Women in Ulster 1840-1940* (Belfast, 1994), p. 95. See also Diane Urquhart, 'Women and politics in Ulster, 1880-1940' (unpublished Ph.D. thesis, Queen's University Belfast, 1996).

10. See pp 220-238 above.

11. See Rosemary Cullen Owens, '"Votes for women, votes for ladies": organised labour and the suffrage movement' in *Saothar*, ix (1983), pp 32-47.

12. See Maryann Gialanella Valiulis, 'Defining their role in the new state: Irishwomen's protest against the Juries Act of 1927' in *Canadian Journal of Women's Studies*, xviii.1 (July 1992), pp 43-60; 'Power, gender and identity in the Irish Free State' in *Journal of Women's History*, 6. 4 and 7. 1 (Winter/spring 1995), pp 117-36. See also contributions of Maryann Gialanella Valiulis, Caitriona Beaumont and Rosemary Cullen Owens in this volume.

13. For a discussion of some of the issues involved see Mary E. Daly, 'Women and trade-unionism in Ireland' in Margaret MacCurtain and Donncha O Corrain (eds), *Women in Irish Society: the Historical Dimension* (Dublin, 1978), pp 71-81; Ellen Hazelkorn, 'The social and political views of Louie Bennett 1870-1956' in *Saothar*, 13 (1988), pp 32-44; Mary Jones, *These Obstreperous Lassies: the History of the Irish Women Workers' Union* (Dublin, 1988).

14. For the genesis of the commission see Hilda Tweedy, *A Link in the Chain: the History of the Irish Housewives' Association 1942-92* (Dublin, 1992).

15. See June Levine, *Sisters: the Personal Story of an Irish Feminist* (Swords, 1982); June Levine, 'Women and politics, 1970-1980' in *Field Day Anthology of Irish Writing*, vol. iv (forthcoming, New York, 1998); Catherine Rose, *The Female Experience: the Story of the Woman Movement in Ireland* (Galway, 1975); Ailbhe Smyth, 'The women's movement in the republic of Ireland 1970-1990' in Ailbhe Smyth (ed.), *Irish Women's Studies Reader* (Dublin, 1993), pp 245-69; Linda Connolly, 'The women's movement in Ireland: a social movement's analysis' in *Irish Journal of Feminist Studies*, i (March 1996), pp 43-77.

16. See Margaret Ward and Joanna McMinn (eds), *A Difficult, Dangerous Honesty: Ten Years of Feminism in Northern Ireland* (Belfast, 1986); Eileen Evason, *Against the Grain: the Contemporary Women's Movement in Northern Ireland* (Dublin, 1991); Catherine B. Shannon, 'Women in Northern Ireland' in Mary O'Dowd and Sabine Wichert (eds), *Chattel, Servant or Citizen: Women's Status in Church, State and Society* (Belfast, 1995), pp 238-47; Monica McWilliams, 'The church, the state and the women's movement in Northern Ireland' in Smyth, *Irish Women's Studies Reader*, pp 79-100; and 'Struggling for peace and justice: reflections on women's activism in Northern Ireland' in *Journal of Women's History*, vol. 6, no. 4, vol. 7, no. 1 (Winter/spring 1995), pp 13-39; Eilish Rooney, 'Political division, practical alliance: problems for women in conflict' in *ibid.*, pp 40-48; Lynda Walker, *Grandmothers and Mentors: Women, Politics and Education in Northern Ireland* (Belfast, 1996).

17. Monica McWilliams, 'Struggling for peace and justice', pp 29-30.

INDEX

THE IRISH CIVIL WAR
An Illustrated History
Helen Litton

In this concise history Helen Litton uses newspaper reports, speeches, eyewitness accounts and a mass of illustrative material to recount the events leading up to the signing of the Treaty and the outbreak of hostilities.

Praise for *The Irish Civil War:*
An Illustrated History

The illustrations are many and fascinating,
the text...lucid and informative in its own right.'
Irish Times

ISBN 0-86327-480-3

THE CELTS
An Illustrated History
Helen Litton

In the eyes of the world Ireland is a Celtic country — but just how Celtic is Ireland? Do we know whether the Celts arrived at all? What was their real impact on this western island at the edge of the known world?

Helen Litton explores 'Celtic Ireland' — from the 8th c. BC to the coming of Christianity to Ireland, in the 5th c. AD. Illustrations and quotations are used to clarify the differing strands of evidence — from Julius Caesar writing on the Celts to evidence of beautiful Celtic art, ringforts, bog bodies and the cult of the human head.

Praise for Helen Litton's
The Irish Famine: An Illustrated History

'As a short intelligent overview of 1845-50, it will be hard to surpass'
RTE Guide

ISBN 0-86327-577-X

Available from WOLFHOUND PRESS
68 Mountjoy Square
Dublin 1
Tel: (+353 1) 8740354
Fax: (+353 1) 8720207